MODERN JEWISH WORLDMAKING THROUGH YIDDISH CHILDREN'S LITERATURE

Modern Jewish Worldmaking Through Yiddish Children's Literature

MIRIAM UDEL

PRINCETON UNIVERSITY PRESS
PRINCETON & OXFORD

Published by Princeton University Press

41 William Street, Princeton, New Jersey 08540
99 Banbury Road, Oxford OX2 6JX

press.princeton.edu

GPSR Authorized Representative: Easy Access System Europe - Mustamäe tee 50, 10621 Tallinn, Estonia, gpsr.requests@easproject.com

Library of Congress Control Number: 2025932924

ISBN 9780691254371
ISBN (e-book) 9780691254418

British Library Cataloging-in-Publication Data is available

Editorial: Anne Savarese, James Collier, Emma Wagh
Production Editorial: Elizabeth Byrd
Jacket: Karl Spurzem
Production: Erin Suydam
Publicity: William Pagdatoon
Copyeditor: Kelley Blewster

Jacket images: Tree of Children's Self-Management in the Medem Sanatorium. Yisroel Biber, *Vinter in vald*, 1937; Yiddish-Russian alphabet chart. Leyb Kvitko, *Alefbeys*, 1947; Hey and hay, Aleph Katz, illustrated by Joseph Schoor, *Fun alef biz sof*, 1939; Man reading, illustrated by B. Malkhi for *Vaksn mayne kinderlekh* by Ida Maze; Olke with the blue parasolke, illustrated by Tirza for *Yidishe Kinder*, 1945, by Kadia Molodowski, originally published by the Central Committee of the Jewish Folk Schools of the Jewish National Workers Alliance. All illustrations have been defined as orphaned works or exist in the public domain.

Printed in the United States of America

10 9 8 7 6 5 4 3 2

MIX
Paper
FSC FSC® C183721

For each of my parents, with inexpressible gratitude

And for Adam Zachary Newton, with whom I remain in the heart of wonder

ואלין מליא
יהון לרקיעיא
And these words will be for skies. . . .

CONTENTS

ILLUSTRATIONS

PREFACE

ANYONE WHO has cared for children has struggled to offer them *something better* than what we ourselves received. Be it material resources, psychological insight, emotional stability, or intellectual opportunity, we search deeply within ourselves and try to conjure or fashion what they need. An individual can do this; so can a community and a culture. Here is one story of how.

Around the turn of the twentieth century, a group of Jewish educators, authors, and cultural leaders undertook a bold project. Idealistic to a man (and sometimes woman), these creators came up against the limits of their ability to repair the world *immediately*, and so trained their gaze on the future. In words and pictures, they would sketch out a more beautiful new world, *a shenere un besere velt*, for the youth of their community—hoping that as child readers matured into adulthood, they might translate such utopian visions into the mundane world of politics, economics, and lived experience. With astonishing rapidity, these leftist cultural activists created a corpus of about one thousand books and several periodicals, which flourished in conjunction with the secular Yiddish school systems that spanned the globe in the 1920s and 1930s. While their vibrant texts cut across continents and ideologies, they shared in their creators' overarching goal: to write a better world into being in a distinctively Yiddish key. The question of what a "better world" looks like is, of course, inextricably bound up in questions of political vision. The stories, poems, and plays written for children during the early twentieth century furnish a record, little consulted until now, of the movements—geographic and ideological—of the Jewish twentieth century.

Although this body of work may be regarded in hindsight as constituting a unity, it was hardly uniform. A contest over the meaning of Jewishness in the modern world played itself out in the increasingly elegant, well-printed, charmingly illustrated pages of Yiddish children's literature. Regarding these texts critically, we gain a wholly new vantage point on the questions that animated Jewish cultural and political life during the first half of the twentieth century. Once we readers attune ourselves to the right frequency, we begin to hear the anxious question that haunts these orphaned texts: *What shall we tell the children?* By virtue of their very existence, as well as their ever increasing sophistication as readers and interlocutors, young people gave urgency and consequence to problems that adults grappled with in their novels and newspapers, their learned journals and *kaffeeklatschen*, their theaters and lecture halls: questions about the status of Yiddish, the value of Jewish religious heritage in an ever more secular West, the meaning of Jewish minoritarian identity, the persistence of antisemitism, and the sustainability of new, freethinking modes of Jewish living. The eventual loss of the books' readership—to genocide, political violence, and linguistic assimilation—does nothing to blunt the incisiveness of the questions addressed in their now-brittle pages.

Every nation's juvenile literature bears the stamp of its founding moment, and in the case of Yiddish, that meant a corpus marked by the emerging principles of child psychology, class consciousness (and sometimes race consciousness), and a growing interest in the experiences of women and girls. It also meant a global perspective before that idea was commonplace. The interwar years gave rise to a truly transnational Yiddish children's literature whose sites of publication ranged from Warsaw and Vilna to Kharkov and Moscow, from New York, Detroit, and Montreal to Tel Aviv, Buenos Aires, and Havana. I propose to import the capacious concept of *worldmaking* from the realms of political science and the arts into modern Jewish literary and cultural studies. Worldmaking entails the erection of a portable homeland, no matter how flimsy or jury-rigged. The willing of a world into being also speaks to the fragility and resilience of Yiddish itself as a medium of the Jewish in-between. Unlike most other juvenile literatures, Yiddish also bears the imprint of its own near disappearance.

Even for those most invested in the language, it is difficult, historically and presently, to disentangle Yiddish from shame. First there was the shame of *too much* Yiddish, too great a reliance on a hybrid tongue that was easily derogated as a mere *jargón* that mixed Germanic, Hebrew, Slavic, and Romance elements. As the twentieth century dawned on the halcyon days of the hybrid language of Ashkenazi Jewry, Yiddish found itself fighting for its speakers' loyalty, crowded out by more practical or prestigious linguistic alternatives. From its inception, creating a literature for children in that language was a project of cultural divination and reclamation; it was a venture of make-believe that sought to secure the Jewish future by creating a usable past, by *making its speakers believe* in its potential as a vehicle for their dreams. Yiddish had never been, since its belated rise as a literary language in the middle of the nineteenth century, a neutral instrument.[1] From the time it was marshaled as an artistic resource, *mameloshn* or the "mother tongue" had required buttressing and validation: Before you could create *in* Yiddish, you had to create Yiddish. "What is Yiddish good for?" Jewish cultural leaders asked implicitly (and sometimes explicitly) in 1900, 1929, 1947, and 1970. The shifting answers furnished by children's literature constitute a chronicle of modern Jewry's relationship with Yiddish.

This is a complicated affiliation, tinged by loss, frustrated desire, hesitancy, renewed urgency, and fresh hope. In our time, many Jews struggle with the shame of *not* knowing Yiddish, of sensing that something incredibly valuable has been discarded—or laid waste. Yiddish cultural leaders sustained a decades-long search for alternatives to that shame, and that search took the form of a literary corpus for children. The most reflexive opposite of shame would seem to be pride, and there was pride in Yiddish. But the most enduring and the most benign alternative to shame was dignity. I chronicle a thoughtful and passionate effort to secure the dignity of Yiddish and of Jewish children by intertwining them.

A scholarly study visualized through a humane lens, this book explores how ambitious modern movements for social transformation looked on an intimate scale: as intimate as the nursery where a parent reads to a young child, or the dark room where a preteen reads herself to sleep by flashlight. Such humble and easily overlooked spaces offer a fresh perspective on the forces that made Jewry modern. At the same time, many of these texts expose the wellspring of deep Jewishness, *yiddishkeyt*, that burbles under the xeriscaped terrain of secular modernity. Whether with subtlety or bald didacticism, works intended for youthful audiences negotiated the tensions between traditional and emerging forms of Jewish identity in what authors and audiences alike perceived as a dizzyingly new world, transcending the assumed binary between "religious" and "secular" to persuade a new generation of what was worth preserving from the Jewish past and how they might seek to transform the Jewish future.

Careful attention to this literature enriches our study of literary history as well as our understanding of the distinctive narrative poetics of juvenile texts. I draw inspiration from Saidiya Hartman's extension of the archive through "critical fabulation" and her evocative compositional method of "historical poetics"—techniques that facilitate "reading against the grain of prevailing knowledge systems."[2] Yet while this book opens a rich new domain for intellectual historians, I write as a literary scholar and seek to disrupt prevailing knowledge systems in a slightly different way, dictated by the distinctive qualities of children's literature and juvenile reading practices. Children read immersively, disappearing into their most cherished books. In chapter 6, I introduce Shprintse, the eponymous

"Unusual Girl from Brooklyn," whose peculiarity—at once a superpower and a liability—is her utter absorption in(to) her reading. She consumes books as they consume her. For *this* book's readers, I seek to conjure the simultaneity of—or at least the rapid oscillation between—the child's immoderate, immediate dissolution into story and the reflective adult's critical discernment. In the case of Yiddish children's literature, the archive is robust (if neglected), and there is little need to confabulate—but there *is* still a need to animate argument with affect, to inhabit a text from the inside. Akin to "history from below," we might style this mode of analysis "literary studies from within."

I foreground the reading practices of children and their caregivers, figures hitherto marginal to the serious study of literature and culture, while claiming as worthy of critical exegesis a set of texts too long dismissed as slight. This feminist and child-centered intervention joins dynamic recent scholarship that is reshaping the field of Yiddish Studies by directing our attention to previously marginal or interstitial spaces and privileging forms of culture previously dismissed as ephemeral. In its attention to the reading world of Jewish children, this work assumes a place alongside Israeli and European scholarship on Hebrew, Yiddish, and Soviet-Yiddish juvenile literatures. Further afield, the book extends the linkages that scholars of children's literature have been drawing between nation-building and narration in environments ranging from the American Confederacy to Russian-language Soviet children's literature.

In addition to addressing scholars in and between several abutting disciplines, including childhood studies, psychology, American studies, migrant studies, comparative literature, history, education, and cultural anthropology, this book poses a radically subjunctive set of challenges to a contemporary Jewish community trying to understand its heritage and chart a meaningful path forward three generations after both the Holocaust and the founding of the State of Israel. Most of that community understands its relationship with Yiddish to be one of inchoate loss. The fortunes of the language have traced a more devastating, less linear, yet also more inspiriting evolution than the exponents of its children's literature could have imagined. Yiddish has been lost, found, socially mediated, and gamified. It has been nostalgized, idealized, and buried—many times over. This book returns us to a moment when Yiddish speakers gazed at a limitless horizon, feeling the language's vitality and addressing their young on matters that concern us still. These stories, poems, and plays have been speaking to us all along; we are only now beginning to listen.

MODERN JEWISH WORLDMAKING THROUGH YIDDISH CHILDREN'S LITERATURE

Introduction

A GARDEN OF CHILDREN

SIX-YEAR-OLD OLKE is dreadfully busy. In Kadya Molodowsky's 1931 narrative poem "Olke," the eponymous heroine must fetch the water, wash the dishes, rinse the shirts, peel the potatoes, and rock her baby brother—and those tasks form just a part of the *first* round of chores that her parents assign her, hollering loudly enough to rattle the windowpanes of their sparsely furnished hovel in the heavily Jewish slum of Okhote.[1] Poverty is the central fact of Olke's life. She is content, though, to knead the sand outside her family's hovel into the makings of an imaginary tea party for her friends—that is, until her parents shout at her to go inside and attend to her domestic duties.

The poem unfolds as a cycle, one whose escalating tension the reader can feel almost bodily: Olke loses herself in a playful reverie, her parents bellow their admonitions, she rededicates herself to the housework, each new task prompting further distraction. The intrusive, recurrent hollering gives voice to the tightening cords of obedience demanded, the constrictions on the heroine's time and attention even as her headspace remains stubbornly free. Young minds, the poem implicitly argues, are drawn inexorably to imaginative play.

But what the poem celebrates is not youthful imagination in general; notice the distinctive shape of Olke's imaginings. Again and again, Olke's mind is drawn to all that can run or fly. Her successive visions of birds, airplanes, and trains point insistently upward and outward, toward mobility and escape. The cycle of daydreaming and being recalled to work is finally broken when the buttons that Olke is supposed to sew spill themselves out in every direction and mount a rebellion against their mandated fixity, arranging themselves into wagons and bicycles and wheelbarrows. At last, the mostly realistic poem turns decisively toward the fantastical: Olke hitches the button-wheels together into a long train that she rides off into the distance.

Each time she entertains a new fantasy, Olke wields a real-world prop: the blue *parasolke* that chimes with her name in the Yiddish original. She opens her umbrella and instantly creates the soothing haven she needs in the moment, furnishing or herself "a roof and a house" in an image of cozy containment. But the blue curvature of the *parasolke* does more than shelter her: It puts the very heavens within Olke's modest grasp. For a poor Jewish girl living in a Warsaw slum, the sky is not—cannot be—the limit; through the force of her imagination, though, Molodowsky's heroine instead turns her tangible limit, the umbrella that is hers and hers alone, into her sky. She has so little power, as of yet, to wrench the world toward her ideals and desires, but Olke creates a world unto herself, where—at least for short intervals—her aspirations reign supreme.

"Olke mit der bloyer parasolke," Olke with her blue parasol, who dreams of escaping the domestic drudgery for which she seems destined, is surely an eloquent exponent for girls in general in a culture that was just beginning to notice and celebrate their potential. But her character's resonance exceeds the bounds of her age or sex. Impoverished yet imaginative Olke, with her blacksmith father and her mother who boils peas to sell in the market, is a powerful emblem for the cultural leaders of secularist, Yiddish-speaking Jewry who constituted a dynamic force in the early decades of the twentieth century. Her iterative opening and reopening of the parasol—holding it aloft as a firm if delicate shelter against the withering heat of adult expectations—stands for nothing less than a gutsy, insistent act of worldmaking. The term "worldmaking" conjures "political action animated by political hope," according to one theorist of the concept.[2] Olke embodies the personal-as-political—when considered critically, her simplest and most apparently neutral actions are freighted with political significance. Olke's situationally constrained yet emotionally potent act of defining a symbolic world resembles the larger project of literary and cultural worldmaking to which Molodowsky and her contemporaries were devoted. Her opening of the blue *parasolke* replicates, microcosmically, the audacious project of creating a vast, multifarious world in letters for children like Olke—children who spoke Yiddish.

When I was six, I did not speak Yiddish, and my only regular chores were feeding the cat and setting the table before dinner. My real "job" was to do my best in school and—could such pleasure even be considered work?—to read like a maniac. It was a skill I had picked up just a few months earlier, under some degree of stress. My mother and I had moved in January from Massachusetts to Miami, and because reading instruction began only in first grade up north, I arrived midyear at my new school pale and lagging academically behind the suntanned kindergartners of the Sunshine State. I remember clearly the spring day when I had come home from school and read a book to the woman who had been reading to me since I was nine days old. I had struggled all that balmy winter to decipher the black letters, but now I held a book in my hands. It had a green cover, which meant I was finally out of the boring monosyllabic red primers (hardly books at all!) about the rat and the cat sitting on the mat. Was this green one about a (bisyllabic) lion, perhaps? In any case, I'll never forget the dazzle of the late-afternoon Miami sunshine pouring in through the sliding glass door. The warmth of the sun fused with the warmth of my mother's enthusiasm, which in turn melted into my own pride at having cracked the code of the little black letters.

But what was my first *Jewish* memory of reading? That came a couple of years later, in second grade, or so I thought. We went to see an exhibition of illuminated Hebrew manuscripts at Miami's Center for the Fine Arts. What I remember was emerging afterward from the museum gift shop with Marvell Ginsburg's *The Tattooed Torah*. It was an understated picture book introducing a young child to some of the realities of the Holocaust from a safe distance: just right for an American Jewish middle-elementary reader.

The main character is a small Torah scroll from Brno, Czechoslovakia, the one favored by bar mitzvah boys thanks to its lightness. Accustomed to a plush ark and being hugged and passed lovingly from hand to hand, the small scroll is shocked one day when soldiers rush into the synagogue, open the ark, and toss the little Torah and its larger neighbors roughly into a truck. In a dark warehouse, it gets tagged and tattooed with an identifying number and then left to languish on a hard shelf surrounded by countless other Torah scrolls. After what seems like forever, a kindly man picks up the Torah lovingly and declares it perfect for the bar and bat mitzvah children at his synagogue in America. Transplanted to its new home, the tattooed Torah once again became the object of affection and solicitude, and, presumably, a totem for its new community's sense of continuity with a severed past.

But here's the rub: I did *not* get this book in 1983, my second-grade year. For one thing, the Center for the Fine Arts only opened in 1984, and the exhibition I recall only hazily, *A Visual Testimony: Judaica from the Vatican Library*, did not go up until July 1987. I would have been ten that summer, heading into sixth grade. We usually stand to learn more from our mistakes and misperceptions than we do from our little certainties, and I can now draw a couple of illustrative lessons from this episode of my own distorted memory.

By the time I *actually* read *The Tattooed Torah*, I had attended a decade of junior congregation, five years of Sunday school, and two years of Hebrew school. Reading that book was certainly *not* my first Jewish reading experience or even my first education about the Holocaust. I had read or heard countless Bible stories and Jewish holiday tales, learned several prayers in Hebrew, and probably cut my teeth on some Chelm stories and assorted other folktales. In my fifth-grade public school social studies class the previous year, we had prepared a room-spanning timeline of the major events of World War II, from which several major events of the Holocaust had surely not been absent. Yet *The Tattooed Torah*, with its nearly monochromatic goldenrod hues (it has since been reissued with new illustrations in a cooler palette), eclipsed all these reading and learning experiences and lodged in memory as the *first*. I had personally experienced the power of the Holocaust, in its unfathomable enormity, to occlude all that came before. Just as a decade of Jewish reading experiences paled next to those beige and marigold pages, so too a set of Yiddish cultural materials, including—and perhaps *especially*—literature for children, has been largely forgotten in the wake of those terrible events that drain the air and light from every chamber of memory.

On to the second lesson. By the summer that the Vatican Library's Judaica collection came to grace downtown Miami, I had long since caught up with my schoolmates' reading ability. Nevertheless, I was drawn to that elementary-level picture book, with its plain and plangent symbolism. Perhaps part of the reason I remember *The Tattooed Torah* so clearly is that it was purchased thoughtfully as I approached my own marking of ritual maturity, the bat mitzvah, as a sentimental gesture toward an earlier time in my childhood. We didn't need the book to induct me into that solemn rite of passage in American Jewish identity, Holocaust education. But the purchase probably did mark my entry into the more quixotic project of reading children's literature critically—that is, when I was older and perhaps a little wiser than its intended audience.

I am still reading children's literature critically. In writing this book, I attempt to peer around the dark monolith we imagine the Holocaust to be, to the decades that came before, when the possibilities for worldmaking through literature seemed nearly endless. For Jews, the decades between the world wars were a time of very real anxiety spiked with a frisson of wide-open opportunity. It felt as if the old world was careening, tilting, shattering. The most optimistic, enterprising Jews saw in its shards the tiles for a new mosaic, whereby they might try to remake things in the image of their aspirations. They wanted to build a nation, or a nation of the spirit—but even more than that, they sought to make a world.[3] No creative enterprise could be more aspirational, more flecked with hope, than the national Jewish project of creating a literature for children. Yet few endeavors touched so many lives so consequentially, only to have been so forgotten as the stories, poems, and plays written for the children whose lives, whether truncated or miraculously spared, unfolded in Yiddish.

Loss on a grand scale is a familiar theme in contemplating the fate of Yiddish, which has been attending its own funeral, metaphorically, for about 150 years—the whole of its modern existence. The patient was already ailing in the first decades of the twentieth century, before the violent blows dealt it by Hitler and Stalin.[4] Any rational hope of recovery was all but wiped out by linguistic and cultural assimilation in the Americas and the triumph of Hebrew over Yiddish in the nascent State of Israel. Many of my students and readers are wistful about the disappearance of Yiddish from their families and from the Jewish mainstream. The forgetting of this fusion vernacular comes to stand in for modern Jewry's encompassing pain at What Has Been Lost: connections with departed or murdered loved ones, an irrecoverable past. I don't entirely share in this wistfulness, though, because I didn't lose Yiddish; my forebears, finding safe harbor in the United States between the 1880s and the 1910s, had managed to do that generations ago. Like the students who now make their way to campus language classes and intensive summer programs, I had the good fortune to *find* Yiddish. I devote far more time and effort to thinking about how to regain and preserve the language, how to help others make it a vehicle for their creative strivings, than about what cannot be retrieved.

I try to foster a kind of literacy, both in the narrow linguistic sense and in the broader cultural one. And what is literacy, anyway? I remember sitting on a preschool-sized chair at my eldest son's elementary school a childhood ago, where the principal implored us kindergarten parents *not* to try to teach our children to read, at least not obsessively or directly. "Help them to build their phonemic awareness," she pleaded. "Let them notice letters and words in their everyday environment." It turns out the activity I had always thought of as "reading" was more precisely known to early-childhood educators as "decoding," and it constituted only a sliver of a far broader set of competencies that would eventually lie at the core of a hoped-for relationship with books, and with the book that is the world. Really, the principal insisted, literacy was about successfully navigating the world, and decoding printed words on the page was just one technical aspect of this infinite enterprise. Reading in its deepest sense, she urged, is about being able to get places.

Despite the tension between the irrepressible Olke and her beleaguered parents, this is a lesson that both parties intuitively understand. Molodowsky weaves a puzzle into the poem's refrain. The bellowing parents, referred to as the single unit *tate-mame*, assign their daughter a wide array of urgent chores but always conclude their tirade with the charge to "Read a little, write a little / Remember, I'll drive you out of the house!" Are they threatening to kick her out if she doesn't practice reading and writing, or if she doesn't complete her whole litany of chores? How can such menace, such a display of brute force, nestle so intimately with such sage and forward-looking parental counsel? "Don't get distracted," her parents practically beg. "Do what you must today to keep our household running but see to your own future as well." They know that the train that can transport their girl to a better life than the one they can provide is made of books, not buttons. When we read the poem as adults, the text invites us to identify with both the long-suffering heroine and the care-worn parents, who bring all their authority to bear on securing a rudimentary education, and therefore a future, for their daughter.

Writing a Better World into Being—in Yiddish

Like Olke's nameless parents, the writers and publishers who created the corpus of Yiddish children's literature invested their faith and their resources in the idea that children's reading could transport them into richer, more meaningful lives, could equip them, as the adults they would soon become, to create a better world. The idea of "writing a better world into being," through telling stories that are aspirational and redemptive, is characteristic of writing for children across most cultures. However, in the case of Yiddish-speaking Jewry, the very idea of writing specifically for children arose in tandem with the sweeping effort of a society to reinvent itself. Since the late eighteenth century, Jewish intellectual and cultural leaders had been trying to bring about a so-called Jewish Enlightenment (*Haskalah* in Hebrew, *Haskole* in Yiddish), a set of changes to the organization of Jewish society that would prod it into conformity with Christian norms with respect to education, economic activity, gender roles, family life, the relationship to the natural world, and more. The proponents of this enlightenment program, the *maskilim*, sought to mediate between the received language of a venerable tradition and the immediate language of their own experience as modern people. This movement flourished throughout the nineteenth century, shifting eastward with the great demographic bloom of Eastern European Jewry and spurring the classic works of Yiddish literature. The end of the nineteenth century found Enlightenment ideals firmly entrenched in the collective Ashkenazi psyche. While the formal program of Haskole dissipated, its energies did not: They merely eddied into other movements, such as Zionism and leftist politics.

The goal was indeed to write a better world into being, but how? Accounting for variation within a corpus of about a thousand individual books and many more periodicals, here is a quick snapshot of how that better world might look:

- economically just (although the particulars of what economic justice would entail varied among authors)
- equal between people of different races, religions, and nationalities
- equal between men and women
- rational, scientific, educated
- democratic

Perhaps most important, that new world would entail *normalcy* for the Jewish nation, whose deep religious civilization would ground a set of distinctive cultural commitments without imposing the strict constraints of a binding religious system.

We might discern the concentrated essence of Haskalah messaging for children in a midcentury Zionist text, one entry among the story collections written *in Yiddish* by the pioneering and prolific Hebrew children's writer Levin Kipnis. Born in the Pale of Settlement in 1894 into a family of twelve, he emigrated to Palestine in 1913 and made a career as an educator. In 1961, he published *Untern taytlboym* (*Under the Date Palm*), a volume of Yiddish holiday stories with New York children's book publisher Farlag Matones (Gifts Press). The book was indeed conceived as a gift—from one of the foremost children's authors in a renascent Zion to the Yiddish-speaking children of the diaspora, who shared a set of socialist cultural aspirations with their Israeli coevals and might be persuaded, with honey rather than vinegar, to share in their Zionism as well. Over a lifetime that spanned almost the entire twentieth century, Kipnis would contribute about eight hundred stories and six hundred poems to the burgeoning canon of Israeli juvenile literature, securing his place in a fondly remembered founding generation.

One of the Passover tales in the collection, "Children of the Field," is based on a Talmudic elaboration of the Exodus story, which mentions the Israelite infants being placed protectively into the ground rather than drowned in the Nile, as Pharaoh had commanded.[5] Kipnis embroiders on this wisp of interpretive text, imagining an apparatus for nourishing the "illegal" baby boys. To replace the maternal breast, each child received two stones whence sustenance flowed (oil and honey, according to the Talmud; milk and honey, in Kipnis's version). As to the infants' daily care, Kipnis furnishes some details that the midrash does not:

> The apple trees cared for the tiny little boys, the blades of grass kept them hidden, and bright-eyed angels with clear wings flew down from the heavens, an angel for each and every child. They stroked the children's little heads so that their hair grew very long, soft and silky, and covered their whole bodies. . . . They gave every child a pebble in each hand, one a milk-stone and the other, a honey-stone. After that, they dug out holes near the roots of the apple tree, and padded them with grass—as a mother makes a bed for her child; they laid the children in the holes—as a mother lays her child in the cradle; and they sang heartfelt songs—as a mother lulls her child to sleep.[6]

Divine protection, typically associated with the masculine God in the Biblical exodus narrative, is reimagined as maternal care in the rabbinic midrash; Kipnis further tweaks the rabbis' imagery to focus on Mother *Nature,* as it were, furnishing the necessary nurture. Thus is a liminal period of vulnerability and exposure transformed into a state of womb-like safety for the generation of boys whose very survival is at risk: "The tiny little boys slept peacefully in their dark cradles, sucking milk from the milk-stones and honey from the honey-stones; they slept peacefully and dreamt of the bright day to come." Meanwhile, when the designated time of salvation arrives, Kipnis marshals the sun itself to ratify the day's specialness ("shining seven times more beautifully than usual") and ensure the blossoming of the hitherto germinal children: "This made the earth split open, and little heads began to sprout forth like pretty flowers. In the blink of an eye, the entire field was full of little children, like a very large *kinder-gortn,* or garden of children."[7] Thus does Kipnis reliteralize an image that had already been bent into figurative daily use by the mid-twentieth century. By foregrounding the image of the *kinder-gortn*, Kipnis redoubles an emphasis on cultivation, a rich and multivalent term we will return to.

Although the boys grow up like tall grass in both the Talmudic and Yiddish accounts, each version builds to an instructively different narrative climax. In the Talmudic tractate Sotah, it's the epiphanic moment when the newly freed grown-up children recognize the divine author of their liberation: "And when the Holy One, Blessed be He, revealed Himself at the Red Sea, these children recognized Him first, as it is stated: 'This is my God, whom I glorify.'"[8] That is to say, they are able to visually recognize God from the original divine revelation during their infancy and can claim with plausible authority, "This is my God." Meanwhile, in Kipnis's secularizing retelling, the human leader takes center stage, and the story crests with a more humanistic appeal to a generation that has been miraculously spared a disabling servile consciousness despite growing up enslaved:

> So the sun illuminated the field: beams of sunlight flooded it, and the children bathed in light. They got up, found their footing, and began to grow bigger and taller—and just like that, they had become young men, tall and handsome as date palms, strong and brave—a large army of heroes standing at the ready and waiting for their liberator.
>
> And the rescuer came.
>
> It happened at midnight.
>
> Moses the Liberator came and called, "Stand up, free children! You, who were never slaves to Pharaoh, you who never felt his heavy hand, you who never molded any bricks and mortar, stand up and lead the way for the entire people!"[9]

Retrieving the idea of cultivation suggested by the garden of children, Kipnis's text manages to straddle the centuries between the biblical exodus and the modern Haskalah and its aftermath. Reading beyond the story's plain meaning in connection with the Passover liberation tale, "Children of the Field" offers an allegory for the cultivation of new, undeformed, post-Enlightenment Jews.

This particular story, then, presents a concentrated synecdoche for the larger project of Yiddish children's literature that flourished during the first half of the twentieth century. Just as Kipnis's Moses eventually comes to redeem a generation that has grown up bucolically in the fields and never known the overseer's lash, so too did Yiddish authors in the early decades of the twentieth century write for a generation of Jews that wasn't supposed to have ever known the "enslavements" that dogged earlier Jewish life, whether imagined as religious superstition or antisemitic violence. In this allegorical reading, it is the educators and authors of books for Jewish children who serve as the liberators and redeemers of a new society of free men and women. Their vision would subtly reshape young Jews' relationship with the past and their purchase on the future. The sustaining milk, honey, and oil would be the stories themselves, and the situation of the Jewish child suckling on this literature was figured as a kind of protected, womb-like, set-off space—a nourishing refuge from a reality that, by the publication of Kipnis's volume in 1961, had turned as cruel and unyielding as Pharoah's Egypt.

Writing for children necessarily stakes claims on a vision for the future, and texts intended for youthful audiences had no choice but to negotiate the tensions between traditional and emerging forms of Jewish identity at a bewildering moment. The first decades of the twentieth century were a time of bracing ideological ferment, when socialism, Soviet communism, and Zionism all appeared as lively and plausible paths, if not messianic destinies, for Jewish communal expression. Roiling beneath the surface of these politico-cultural movements and the institutions they spawned were the animating phenomena of modernity, including secularization, urbanization, mass migration, and rapid yet uneven economic development. These forces worked both centrifugally and centripetally on the Jewish community, flinging its energies outward while pulling into its very core disruption from the far corners of Europe and beyond.

Nor was Yiddish itself a stable entity, capable of absorbing and metabolizing these rapid transformations. Many of its most ardent devotees were multilingual and felt pulled in several linguistic directions. Whither the Yiddish language? Speaking to a nation without a country, the Yiddish arts reflected anxiety about their own belatedness: arriving tardy to the feast of European culture, showing up at last uninvited and in rags to boot. Would a Yiddish culture be able, its leaders fretted, to mature quickly enough to retain its participants, who were pushed by practical necessity and pulled by the lure of cultural prestige to assimilate to the surrounding languages or embrace new ones? Immigration to the Americas, nationalism in Poland and Central Europe, the communist revolution in Russia, and even Zionism, with its emphasis on Hebrew as the language of the whole Jewish people—all these unfolding trends militated against the continued flourishing of the *mame-loshn*. But perhaps the future could be rewritten after all.

However improbably, a vibrant and variegated literature for Yiddish-speaking youth dawned during those tumultuous early decades of the twentieth century and endures today, albeit in attenuated form. The stories, poems, and plays written for children during the heyday of the 1920s and 1930s and again in the postwar 1950s constitute a forgotten record of the Jewish twentieth century. This book has twin aims, then: to reexamine some of the defining events and phenomena of that unquiet century through the lens of "what to tell the children," and at the same time, to grapple with how this body of literature sought to reshape the world by reshaping the Jews, one child at a time. In studying the enterprise of Yiddish children's literature, however, I don't wish to reinforce the nostalgia that can attach to these artifacts of a largely forgotten, superseded world. Instead I want to examine how this neglected corpus can shed greater light on our understanding of Jewish modernity, the relationship between childhood and adulthood, and the interplay between "normal" and "other" cultural spaces, where "normal" has been figured as adult and majoritarian and "other" has been imagined as juvenile and minoritarian.

Children's books are neither trivial nor neutral. Their political freight can be difficult to discern in real time when our own politics, values, and worldview align too neatly with those imagined in their pages. Decades on, though, it becomes impossible not to see how *Curious George* opens with an allegory of the Middle Passage, and how Babar traffics in colonial stereotypes.[10] While children's literature might seem utopian, it is more accurately characterized as what Michel Foucault called a *heterotopia*, or "other place." Foucault situates this concept as part of a shift, at the beginning of the twentieth century, from a preoccupation with time and its entropic sequences to an engagement with space and its network of simultaneities. "Our epoch," he writes in an essay that formed the basis for his 1967 address to a group of architecture students at MIT, "is one in which space takes for us the form of *relations* among sites." Foucault takes particular interest in external spaces that are "linked with all the others, which however contradict all the other sites," concrete or abstract spaces that are "outside of all places, even though it may be possible to indicate their location in reality."[11] Such "other spaces" teach us something about conventional spaces by reproducing features of the ordinary world at an instructively oblique or altered angle, like a mirror image at once reflecting reality and estranging it. A cemetery, for example, abuts the city of the living and reflects some of its hierarchies and other modes of social organization, but it's home to the dead. Ships, antique gardens, prisons, brothels, and fairs all likewise offer revealing-by-distorting reflections aslant "normal" social spaces.[12] Similarly, literature for children replicates many of the genres and other storytelling conventions of literature for adults—demarcations of literary space, so to speak—but at an oblique angle inflected by the presumptive readers' juvenility. In other words, not only do many specific texts for children furnish us with images of heterotopias, such as the ground under Olke's parasol or the Israelite baby boys' *kinder-gortn*, but the corpus of children's literature as a whole can constitute a heterotopian precinct in relation to a given literary tradition. I propose to consider Yiddish children's literature as just such a heterotopia in relation to Yiddish literature and culture more broadly.

This expansive construction of the idea of the heterotopia might not leap too far beyond the concept's original parameters. As a sort of dress rehearsal, perhaps, for his presentation to the budding architects, Foucault appeared on French radio in 1966 and offered a preliminary anatomy of the heterotopia. The better-known elaborations of the concept usually discuss it as a kind of physical enclosure, but what he described on *France Culture* was more free-form and less bounded. Significantly, he illustrated the concept in part by discussing how children constitute and inhabit heterotopias through their imaginative play: "These counter-spaces . . . are well recognised by children. . . . It's the bottom of the garden; it's the Indian tent erected in the middle of the attic; or still, it's . . . on their parent's bed where they discover the ocean, as they can swim between the covers, and the bed is also the sky, or they can bounce on the springs; it's the forest as they can hide there; or still, it's night as they can become ghosts between the sheets and, finally, it's the fear and delight of their parents coming home."[13]

Foucault's vision links the ordinary spaces of home and garden to the children's inventive reclamation of them as the setting for extraordinary adventures. Children's imaginative play tends to combine slavishly imitative and improbably fanciful elements, and in so doing creates a unique kind of "space" in which their everyday experience nests cheek by jowl with their wildest imaginings. Even defining "space" broadly, how does the term stretch to include "the fear and delight of their parents coming home"? Those quivering feelings might be thought to delimit an emotional "zone" describing children's interim autonomy—as cherished as it is limited—over and against the usual control parents exert when present.

The heterotopian space of childhood is often a space without adults, or one that resists, as Olke eventually does, typical adult instruction and hegemony.

It is the zone of children's empowerment, set always against the context of their singular vulnerability and dependence on adult (or supernatural) caregivers. The power differential between adults and children, including surprising role reversals, means that children's literature is always implicitly about power and how it is used. Yiddish children's literature, as a rule, was exquisitely attuned to children's current and future power. An anthology published in 1920 styles children as *kleyne in der groyser velt*: little ones in the big world.[14] But this phrase was a more accurate descriptor of adult Jewish self-perception than of the relative position of children in Jewish society. After all, one of the Jewish collectivity's enduring names for itself was the biblical "Children of Israel." While the original Hebrew (*bnei yisrael*) might bespeak belonging rather than juvenility, the Yiddish translation, *di* kinder *fun Yisroel*, unambiguously identifies the whole nation with its youth. The rise of Yiddish children's literature was predicated on an appeal by writers and cultural leaders to children as the repository of a great deal of social, cultural, and political capital—an immense reservoir of latent but soon-to-be-realized power.

Children's literature might seem at first blush like a utopian exercise in furnishing ideal reading material for the idealized denizens of what one thinker wistfully styled a "universal republic of childhood."[15] But childhood is no more universal than adulthood, and its denizens, all temporary, are just as fully and messily human as the grown-ups they will someday become. Whereas the utopian view of children's literature and childhood itself might give rise to nostalgia, the heterotopian view instead sparks interrogation. As Foucault reminds us, literary utopias console, while heterotopias, in their uncanny mirroring function, disturb.

The Distinctive Poetics of Children's Literature

The "other space" of children's literature is defined by both how it is written and how it is read. Like books for adults, juvenile books generally fit somewhere on a continuum from didactic to aesthetically pleasurable and even whimsical. Unlike literature for adults, however, at least some degree of didacticism remained acceptable in children's literature even as adult fiction reached an apotheosis of aestheticism that rejected instruction in favor of delight.[16] Moreover, even in texts that seem to stake out a position against or entirely apart from instruction, there is a certain inexorable patina of didacticism that inheres in the function of adults (authors, publishers, teachers, librarians, and book buyers) in relation to children (the ostensible readers).[17] We instruct, we encourage, and we *educe* or draw out the knowledge residing in children. We enjoy greater social and political agency owing to our ostensibly superior cognitive abilities, which in turn calls forth adults' sense of responsibility, protection, and (hopefully benign) empowerment in relation to our young charges.

When adults write for children, no matter how delightful and silly the product, how far from heavy didacticism, they are nevertheless teaching their target readers something of cause and effect, and thus of how to be or how not to be in the world. Nonfiction teaches children how things work, preparing them for a life in which it might be useful to know how a radio operates, or how Inuit people hunt and fish, or how ants organize their society (all topics of early twentieth-century Yiddish children's books). And because children are so deeply educable, it is impossible for any book not to teach them *something*—even if it is only an object lesson in the sort of marketing (supermarket aisle! glittery cover!) that might separate their parents from some of the money in their wallets. Books for children reinforce the habits of literacy itself—a politically freighted enterprise bound up in the transfer of power, for *saber es poder*—and often take as their implicit theme the development of the child reader.

It is impossible, then, to write about children's literature without writing about childhood, which is a dynamic set of socially constructed experiences rather than a static and stable span within a lifetime. The field of children's cultural studies seeks to understand the shades of difference and the deep, often biologically driven similarities in how various societies shape and understand their denizens' younger years. The shift from functional to romantic and sacralizing views of childhood, and then again to a phased developmental view, has given rise to reading materials designed especially for children's consumption even as it has repeatedly revised the desiderata governing such texts.[18] Concomitant with these shifting perceptions have been varying approaches to the education of the young: from scaring children straight to modeling good conduct and exemplary thought. Shifting social values have led children's authors to prioritize, variously, hegemony and subversion, to countenance and indeed valorize a degree of juvenile skepticism toward adult caregivers. Henrik Ibsen famously threw his sympathy with those "most closely in league with the future." Indeed, the children's books that seem to age best are often those more concerned with teaching children to question authority than with propping it up.

A further distinctive property of children's literature is situational rather than textual, and it has to do with the circumstances of reading. Books for the very young are unlike most other texts in that they are read aloud in the habitats of nursery, day care, and preschool, and then often reread. The worst of them become a torment, while the best of them lodge in the psyche of both adult and child as poetry—or prayer.

I have been a mother for as long as I've been a scholar and have seldom researched or written for longer than the duration of a school day; I often work in far shorter bursts of time. Having a safe, salutary, always available way for my children to occupy themselves has allowed me to attend to my work and enjoy the pleasure that is bound up in researching, writing, and teaching. I appreciate potty training and sleeping through the night as much as the next parent, but to me, the real milestone that marks "no longer a baby" is when my children learn to read. Of course some of this enthusiasm is bound up in nurturing their independence, their ability to explore their interests and gain knowledge, their empowerment. Yet my delight in their literacy has also been in some measure selfish. The path to raising independent readers, at least the one we have trodden, leads through a period of literary interdependence: reading aloud together as a shared activity. I try to honor the desire of the preschooler who pleads insistently, "Read it again. Again and again and again. A lot of times, okay?" I spend a great deal of time rereading, performing the books' words in different ways, improvising gestures and vocal flourishes, feeling the books' textual and visual messages seep into our shared consciousness. Expressive reading staves off boredom *and* gets a literature professor thinking.

Meanwhile, my years of parenting young children have overlapped with another foundational but oft-undervalued form of teaching: several semesters of Yiddish language instruction. I was aware of recent translations of *Curious George*, Dr. Seuss classics, and *Winnie the Pooh* into the language of Sholem Aleichem, but I wondered: Had any books for children *originated* in Yiddish? It was this naïve and deeply uninformed question that launched over a decade of research into the body of almost one thousand extant Yiddish children's books, as well as several juvenile periodicals spanning several continents and almost the whole of the twentieth century. I combed through hundreds of stories, poems, and plays, seeking to propose a provisional canon of primary texts on which we might focus a cultural conversation about this neglected literature. A few dozen of them appear in my 2020 anthology *Honey on the Page*. Even as I fine-tuned those translations, I began to think seriously about what this literature means as a body of work, how temporally concentrated and geographically diffuse was its production, and what we might learn from this peculiar intersection of time and space, language and culture. How could Yiddish children's literature help to tell the story of twentieth-century Ashkenaz?

In interrogating the juvenile literature and culture of the civilization that I study, I have found a way to unite the work of the mind with the work of the hands. While my inquiry originated in twinned identities as a language teacher and a mother, it continues under the sign of my commitments as a feminist. Choosing to interrogate Yiddish children's literature was not so much about making my time spent reading on the floor "pay," as about realizing that I have chosen to spend my time in this way because I think it has value. Forming deep relationships with the small people called children, participating in their play, and sharing books in order to see the world through their eyes—these activities have inestimable intellectual worth. If we attune ourselves to children's frequencies, their freshness of thought and speech can pry loose our most tightly held, reflexive assumptions, complicating and decentering our adult habits of mind and received ascriptions of value.

With this project, I seek a kind of attunement, not only as a scholar poised to trace the volutions of intellectual and literary history that the canon of Yiddish children's literature reveals but also as a woman making visible the in-between work of translation. I attempt to mediate between the best that has been thought and said, usually by men, and the essential-for-the-species-but-too-easily-overlooked thought-world of children, a realm traditionally overseen by women. I wrestle not only with the question of whether individual works are thematically subversive or hegemonic, radical or reinforcing of cultural norms—but also with the question of how the study of children's literature itself can act as a radical practice within cultural studies by shifting our sense, as heterotopias will, of which kinds of texts and whose experiences are worthy of critical attention.

Researching this book has led me on a quest whose object has shifted throughout the life of the project. I began by seeking something for my Yiddish students and finding an abundance of material that could help me make sense of my own inextricable experiences as a scholar and a mother. Finally, I ended up wanting something on behalf of the neglected texts themselves: to restore to these stories the readership they've lost and the pride of place they deserve as a cultural artifact worthy of study. I want Yiddish children's stories to regain the chance to become irksome through repetition. I want whimsical

Yiddish poems to resound in the mouths of children and their educators. I don't want Kadya Molodowsky's poetry to be the honored guest who sits primly on the antique sofa in the front parlor but rather to be tumbling with the kids on the stained couch in the family room.

Part of embracing the synchronicity between my own journey as scholar, teacher, and parent with the Jewish sojourn into modernity means grappling with and sharing in the anxieties of the cultural workers who began to create a Yiddish literature for children a century ago. What if Molodowsky and Yankev Pat and Moyshe Kulbak did indeed show up one day, plunk themselves down on the sofa, and ask what's become of their collective legacy? What would I tell the Yiddish children's authors, the culturists, the activists of yesteryear? It has been more terrible than you can imagine, I might confess. Within a generation, the children were hopelessly Americanized. Some families emigrated to Israel, and their generations have created in Hebrew but seldom in the *mame-loshn*. Yiddish is in tatters, lost out long ago to English, French, Spanish, and, however improbably, to *Hebrew*. The mother tongue has become the language of secrets that parents keep from children, pungent curses, and bawdy jokes.

And yet: It is also more wonderful than you can imagine. Every few months, a journalist calls, working on a story about the Yiddish linguistic and cultural revival. You can hear Tevye sing in Yiddish on Broadway, dance to klezmer music throughout the year on nearly every continent, attend summer camp and farm in Yiddish. You can read learned articles about Yiddish culture and pedagogy, transmitted instantaneously on the glowing slabs of wizardry we all keep in our pockets. You can learn the language as a kind of game on something called an "app." Half a million Jews, more or less, still speak Yiddish as their daily vernacular, refreshing its fossilizing vocabulary with infusions of English, Hebrew, and Russian. Children play Yiddish board games and read Yiddish comics. Young adult students return summer after summer to study the language; they feel it is their birthright, and they are snatching it back from oblivion. Like the carters and wagoners of yore, the mild-mannered, taxi-driving sons of central Massachusetts have picked up a few words of Yiddish from the many writers, scholars, musicians, and translators they ferry to a bucolic repository for the Yiddish book. Phalanxes of new Yiddishists are working at the horizon of the possible, finding room for maneuver within the constraints of the time and places into which they were born.

Yiddish Cultural Nationalism and Modern Jewish Worldmaking

Every children's literary tradition is marked by its origins. The fairy tales of the Brothers Grimm were not originally meant for children at all, although they were gradually revised, over four decades and seven editions, to suit juvenile readers. While as collectors and editors, Jakob and Wilhelm Grimm prized the oral tales of the German *Volk* above all else, their project evolved to stress the elements of Christian piety considered salutary for children (such as imbuing heroic characters with religious devotion and sanitizing all references to sex outside of marriage).[19] Their tales both reflected and further reinforced the aesthetic tropes and conceptual ideals of German romantic nationalism.[20] Even in the most recently updated Disney adaptations, it is possible to trace a through line from Herder and Schiller to the large-hearted, wasp-waisted princesses of contemporary American girlhood. Hans Christian Andersen's tales likewise fused pan-Scandinavian identity with Christian piety. Even twentieth-century Anglo-American children's tales bear the stamp of Victorian attitudes, pointing back toward the moment when English juvenile literature truly burgeoned and took flight.[21] Although subject to aesthetic and ideological changes over time, the corpora of children's literature shaped in the twentieth century were just as enduringly marked by their origins. What did this mean in the case of Yiddish? Mutually overlapping forces, including cultural nationalism, secularism, and leftist politics, intersected with transformations in family life owing to the widening dissemination of the principles of child psychology and the attitudes and practices that would eventually blossom into feminism. This era saw a new emphasis on the scientific study of childhood and interest of the state in guiding children's development.[22]

For modern European Jewry, culture making *was* nation building. "Since the Jews had no state and their political influence in Poland was weak," David E. Fishman explains, "their cultural institutions were important sources of pride and self-validation." These institutions, including the emerging arena of children's literature "were considered proof that Jews were a nation, a people deserving of collective dignity and national rights."[23] And increasingly, throughout the first decades of the twentieth century, child-rearing became another, complementary form of nation building. Parents, educators, and culturists who worked on behalf of children collaborated in building the Jewish nation by raising its national subjects, or better yet, citizens. Yet even as their political commitments pushed them toward a collective understanding of their child-rearing task, the voices of child psychology (as it was known in the United States; pedology, or "child science," was the reigning term in the USSR) insisted that they were also raising individuals. At the very same time, the nature and meaning of childhood was evolving, and not necessarily in a linear or unidirectional way. This tension gave rise to a multifarious canon with respect to such decisions as how politically explicit or subtle, how mimetically accurate or imaginatively fanciful, and how subversive or hegemonic children's books ought to be.

Yiddish now trails a kugel-scented vapor of nostalgia that threatens to obscure its fierceness as a medium for revolution, for remaking the world. The Jews who developed secular Yiddish culture between the wars fell out along a wide spectrum of progressive ideologies. They were involved in a variety of nation-building projects, and they conceived of "revolution" in different ways. But it is axiomatic that progressive or revolutionary movements try to speak directly to a society's children. However unfairly, parents are often imagined to be retrograde in their thinking, standing in the way of "progress." Wherever societies were being built or radically rebuilt, whether in pre-State Palestine or the Soviet Union, the adults in the cultural vanguard prioritized their address to children. Even if young minds weren't completely blank slates, there was still plenty of room to write new storylines upon them. Surely this strategy bespoke the power of tapping into children's latent cultural capital. At the same time, though, it represented a concession to constraints on the changemakers' power to effect a full revolution *right now*. In speaking to children, revolutionary leaders made an end run around the defenses of the present toward the goalposts of the future.

Harnessing Yiddish to the cause where possible but granting pride of place to other languages, the Soviet Union and the State of Israel came to be fully realized as nation-building projects, which of course Yiddish never did; there has never (yet) been a Yiddish-speaking state. Since victors write history, it stands to reason that both Soviet and Israeli children's literature have each received thoughtful and bountiful attention from scholars, while the study of Yiddish children's literature is only starting to gain momentum in the twenty-first century. The comparison with Hebrew is especially illuminating, as the founding of the State of Israel makes it possible to interrogate the mechanics of conventional nation-building through children's literature—undertaken at the same historical moment and under a similar set of guiding values and aspirations as Yiddish. Jewish cultural nationalism, whether played out in Yiddish or in Hebrew, was at once a thoroughly secular and a deeply spiritual project.[24] But precisely insofar as Yiddish cultural nationalists could never succeed at building a conventional nation "with an army," they perforce embraced the transcendent project of making a symbolic world.[25] Whether the various cultural leaders of the Yiddish Left understood themselves to be mercifully freed of the burden or vexingly deprived of the privilege of building a proper nation, they poured their copious energies into limning the very heavens on the inside of a parasol.

The Structure of This Book

How to organize a discussion of something as multifarious as an entire literary corpus stretching across decades and continents, political ideologies and literary genres? Of course, no single study can do justice to the sheer variety of Yiddish children's books, but I identify a set of thematic and stylistic nodes where several texts and ideas converge. My analysis moves through time and space in tandem, starting in Eastern Europe and shifting its attention with the geographical migrations of Yiddish cultural activity to New York, the USSR, Latin America, and Israel. While most publishing activity for children took place between the world wars, the long twentieth century is the necessary canvas on which to paint the story of this literature's development, flourishing, and denouement.

The book's first section, "Claiming a Usable Past," focuses on works that pull inward, paying special attention to the holidays, history, and heroes that define the Jewish past, deep and recent. This focus on concentration takes on a distinctively Jewish cast in light of concepts like *zamlung* (collection as a cultural activity, especially of folklore) and *kinus* (ingathering, a potent concept in Zionist discourse). Yiddish writers and educators of the early twentieth century were interested in refashioning the past, or retooling its meaning and legacy, and so articulating a vision for the Jewish future. Indeed, this project unfolds against the backdrop of the fully encompassing ingathering that was taking place in the Land of Israel with the creation of a Hebrew literature for Israeli children. If Israeli Hebrew acted as a magnetic force of concentration on the Jewish geographical and conceptual map, then Yiddish might be imagined as having operated as a force of diffusion.

Writing under the sign of "diaspora," from the Greek "to scatter," many Yiddish writers sought to cast as broadly as possible their strivings for democratic processes, economic justice, and gender equality. Their fictions, poetry, and plays reflect rapidly evolving understandings of how children think, feel, and learn. Taking children to be the engaged citizens and national subjects of the future, authors from a variety of stances on the broad Yiddish Left sought to shape the Jewish polity to come. The book's second section, "Contesting the Jewish Future," analyzes the most universalist, outward-turned tendencies in the corpus, taking stock of the features that still marked these works as distinctively Jewish.

This organically unfolding account of how Jewishness meets modernity was interrupted by a set of events that would uproot and transform Jewish life. The Holocaust is, in a profound sense, not a Jewish story—yet Jewish communities have been forced to call on their own creativity to metabolize its harms. Yiddish children's literature had no choice but to reckon with this violent intrusion into modern Jewish life, turning its attention in the 1950s to the project of recovery, cultural preservation, and consolidation. A focus on what we might style "the Jewish timeless," the holiday cycle and the Jewish alphabet, constituted a powerful form of remembering and self-determination. In the Afterword, I visit briefly the two places where Yiddish children's literature and culture continues to be created today: Sweden, where Yiddish is elevated (and subsidized) as an official language, and the Hasidic communities, where Yiddish children's culture enjoys a flourishing market.

Most of this book was researched in the sober spirit of the subjunctive mood, the sense of what could have been. What would the world look like if Yiddish had . . . ? One of the consolations of scholarship is getting to simply chronicle and analyze what happened as thoroughly and honestly as possible; success or failure isn't predicated on changing the course of history. Occasionally, though, an incandescent burst of the indicative breaks through the softening scrim of that subjunctive and declares, "Look at what *is*!" My five-year-old spent long days homebound during the worst of an epoch-defining pandemic. With patience, love, and determination, his father taught him to read. For a while, in our improvised homeschool pre-K, we urged him to write down his thoughts: usually a sentence each day. In late May of 2021, he wrote, "I wish there were more Labzik stories."

For months, he had seen his mother spend long hours holed up in the basement with seemingly imaginary people whose faces appeared in little rectangles on her computer screen. In the mornings, these people were her students. In the evenings, they were a group of grown-ups and near grown-ups making a puppet show. She spoke frequently with a puppeteer who had a big voice.[26] One evening, she shouted rhythmically into her microphone, "Mir viln zen dem meyor! Mir viln zen dem meyor!" (We want to see the mayor!). She was heard menacing someone unseen in a low growl, threatening to tear them apart like a herring should they raise a hand against one of the children.

Finally, in late spring, the show was ready: a film adaptation of *Labzik*, the proletarian pup at the center of Chaver Paver's collection of twelve short stories first published in New York in 1935, the nadir of the Depression. A sound designer had recorded the actors' voices and layered them into a soundtrack complete with lively klezmer and folk music and loud protest scenes full of chanting and stray crowd noise; the familiar growl now belonged to a dauntless Bronx mother, defending an elementary-aged protest leader and unafraid to face down a thuggish police captain. An ingenious fabricator had constructed almost two hundred puppets, by turns winsome and terrifying, most of them manipulated expertly by a professional puppeteer.[27] The videographer had captured it all and woven it together so seamlessly that it looks animated. There was no red carpet thanks to the pandemic, but the focus group at home chomped through a deep bowl of popcorn, cheering the proletpup and his humans and sneering at the authoritarian school principal and his cruel henchmen.

The five-year-old was entranced. He had dozens of questions about the plot, the characters, the puppetry, the Yiddish. For weeks, he quoted snippets from the script in Yiddish, a language he does not speak. "I wish there were more Labzik stories," he wrote. His wishful subjunctive is my indicative: Look what is *now*! We recycled old culture into new. We broke through the weight of counterhistory suffused with its wistful "might have beens" to create something declarative, exclamatory even, in and with Yiddish. The language itself exerts a heterotopian pull: The world that could have been but never fully was promises to teach us a great deal about the world that is—and the world we might yet make.

PART I

Claiming a Usable Past

1

Reading Beyond Mother's Apron

THE PREHISTORY OF A CULTURAL AMENITY

LEAH'S FATHER died early in her childhood. She was betrothed quite young to the only son of a distinguished rabbinical family—so young, in fact, that Leah and her groom played in the sand of her father-in-law's yard when they weren't running around with the local *kheyder yinglekh* (schoolboys).[1] At fourteen, Leah became pregnant with their first child.[2] By then, the couple lived in an attic room in the rafters of a local synagogue, adjoining the women's section.

Her groom, Moyshe Pinkhas, known as Meyshl, would stay out late, carousing in the vibrant fellowship of the Hasidic prayer house, with its after-hours card games.[3] All this was just before the onset of Meyshl's "night of the soul," as his family would eventually refer to his prolonged struggle with mental illness.[4]

Shut out of male conviviality, Leah's nights at home were as frightening as they were lonesome. Everyone knew that at midnight, the souls of the dead gathered to pray; the women's balcony, just beyond the thin wall of her room, trembled with the energy of the dead women's piety, their muted keening of supplications (*tkhines*) and their unrequited longings.[5] By the light of a penny candle, Leah would spend those nights reading Yiddish storybooks (*mayse-bikhlekh*), written with the schematic simplicity of fairy tales.[6] Her reading was apotropaic, warding off any harm to herself and the gestating child. It was also companionable. The fictional cast of poor yet virtuous maidens, dashing heroes, and wicked villains became her familiars, a lively contrast to the dead souls congregating in the next room. The arrival of a baby boy didn't curtail Meyshl's nocturnal socializing, but the evocative stories in the cheaply printed booklets kept the young mother company through countless feedings and rockings.

Later in life, Leah would recall to her grandson, the renowned memoirist Y. Y. Trunk, how that first baby, her listener's father, was "her only solace" during those nights. But that wasn't quite true. Drunk on the oxytocin of mother love, her attention would oscillate between marveling at the awe-inspiring form that had emerged from her womb and imbibing the storybook plots, "which fell on her young and aching girl's heart as dew falls on arid ground." The widely available books had been written by "modern" writers, importing Western conventions of romance and chivalry into the hearts and hearths of Jewish women. Trunk takes pains to emphasize that at the time of her marriage and even her first son's birth, his grandmother was "scarcely more than a girl," surmising that her adolescent reading "determined the spiritual fate" of later children by smuggling modern skepticism into the intimate domestic sphere.[7]

Were the fairy tales that Leah read at fourteen and fifteen "children's literature"? Was teenage Leah—orphaned, married off, delivered of a baby boy—in any meaningful sense a child? In nineteenth-century Eastern Europe, the line between childhood and adulthood was a thin filament, and for Jews, it usually ran through the marriage canopy that was erected during what we now think of as adolescence. But Leah's reading habits were shaped less by her age than by her gender and the educational opportunities it had afforded—and foreclosed.[8] It would be more accurate to think of her books as "women's literature," although that was a capacious category confined neither to adults nor to women. But regardless of how we categorize Leah's developmental phase, she was an impressionable reader. She became a lifelong devotee of fiction, a taste she passed down to her daughter especially.[9] Her artistically and intellectually gifted grandson would insist that his grandmother's reading had shaped a family legacy that enabled his own creative efflorescence two generations later.

Let us consider another scene of childhood reading, this one involving a younger and more volatile reader. Appreciating this textual encounter requires a bit more historical context. The life-world of premodern Jews was thick with layers of accreted law and custom, both of which varied regionally across a diasporic civilization spanning continents. Custom, being more discretionary than law, was especially vulnerable, given to local variation and susceptible to being forgotten over time. In order to secure this aspect of Jewish practice against slippage, Austro-Hungarian Rabbi Isaac Tyrnau authored a book of customs, or *Sefer minhagim,* around 1400. Preserved initially in manuscript form, the book was first printed in Krakow in 1566. It proved so indispensable that it overleapt language and geographical barriers to appear in about fifty printings over three centuries. In 1590, Simon Günzburg prepared a Yiddish translation published in Venice, and just three years later, the Yiddish text—unlike the original Hebrew—was adorned with a series of woodcut illustrations depicting holiday observances and preparations, life cycle events, and the signs of the zodiac.[10] Pictorially enhanced materials are thought to have been used as an educational resource for children, a view that gathers support from this first-person recollection: "When I was young [*katan*], I saw a children's book [*sefer shel tinokot*] that contained all the customs, and it had various illustrations, such as Pharaoh bathing in the blood of children, and the like. We children took a knife and started to pierce and stab not just the bad parts but also all that was good too, until we had made the entire book like a sieve."[11]

This account of rage-fueled juvenile biblioclasm is arresting, especially given the relative scarcity of printed books in the eighteenth century. Even more shocking, though, is the inciting image of a crowned figure in a tub surveying scattered corpses of cherubic children, with armed adults impaling and decapitating them (see Figure 1). The gory woodcut, rendered yet more disturbing by the impossibility of reading the victims' facial expressions, illustrates a midrash, or expansive rabbinic Biblical interpretation, to the effect that Pharaoh was afflicted with leprosy, which his court magicians sought to cure through twice-daily baths in the blood of Jewish children.[12]

The particular way the child readers defaced the volume corresponded closely to the puncture wounds that the picture represented; rather than tearing, burning, or blotting them with ink, the angry youngsters pierced the pages with the point of a knife. The memoirist characterizes the offending book as a *sefer shel tinokot*, a children's book licensed for his use and apparently entrusted to the care of a group of unsupervised young readers.[13] As with Grandmother's Leah's story books, this memoirist's youthful reading left a lifelong psychic impression. Even if the intensity of his reaction were not entirely singular—after all, he describes attacking the book as part of a "we"—his trauma is of special historical note, for the memoirist stirred to such violence was none other than the eighteenth-century Polish false messiah and eventual apostate Jacob Frank.[14]

In exploring the reading habits of Ashkenazi Jewish children before the establishment of a modern Yiddish children's literature, I highlight these two disparate examples—of Leah and Jacob—for the passion of their juvenile literary encounters and for the proximity of their reading experiences to strong negative emotions that we don't usually think of in connection with the catch-all category of "children's literature." Whether the books offered a consoling escape or a goad to action, the emotional stakes of the act of reading ran high. Yiddish children's literature, when it emerged in the first decades of the twentieth century, would be infilled as an artificial island of tranquility atop a roiling

FIGURE 1. A woodcut shows Pharaoh sitting in a bathtub. Soldiers can be seen taking swords to small children, and the scene is littered with body parts. Prague Haggadah, 1526.

sea of fear, anxiety, and shame. Motifs of potential damage and harm run throughout discussions of children's reading—anxieties about teaching literacy and then manifold further anxieties about what that literacy might engender. Ignorance posed one kind of threat, knowledge another. Instead of exhaustively or even systematically chronicling the prehistory of Yiddish children's literature, I wish to emphasize some of the emotional sticking points that delayed and then accelerated the eventual formation of the island.

Childhood reading in Jewish Eastern Europe formed part of a psychodrama that overlaid young people's intellectual and emotional development onto biological, and especially sexual, maturation.[15] Rather than a sexless or desexualized category unto themselves, children were treated as protowomen and protomen. Gender stratification was a significant force in the world of Ashkenazi letters long before age stratification was, and child readers began their consumption of devotional and belletristic literature in the orbit of women readers.

Jewish print culture reflected a set of dichotomies that arose from the differences between men and women, which were conceived as essential, divinely ordained, and immutable. High culture, the apogee of intellectual maturity, was conducted in the Hebrew and Aramaic Holy Tongue, or *loshn koydesh,* of the Talmud and Jewish legal discourse. This learning activity was nearly all for men, but not for *all* men. Those who, by virtue of economic necessity or temperament, lacked access to these languages were said to be "like women."[16] They enjoyed enough basic Hebrew literacy to participate in, if not to lead, communal prayer, but they were shut out of advanced Torah study, and later they missed out on the most elite literature of the Jewish Enlightenment. The split was reinforced from early life through differential language instruction, with Hebrew reserved for boys until at least the late nineteenth century, while both girls and boys spoke the Yiddish vernacular and perhaps a coterritorial language or two.[17] *Loshn koydesh* was the province of educated men, while Yiddish was for everyone else.

The linguistic binary was further reinforced at the lexical level within Yiddish, with higher status ascribed to some forms of reading activity than to others. A holy book was set apart with the Hebrew-derived term *seyfer*, while all other texts—whether conduct manuals, didactic narratives of piety, adaptations of rabbinical storytelling, or Judaized chivalric romances—were lumped together as Germanically derived *bikher* (singular: *bukh*). The way one read holy books, aloud and often in the social setting of the study house, was called *lernen*, while the sometimes sociable, sometimes silent enjoyment of a *bukh* was known as *leyenen*.[18] Until the 1830s, this gender divide was further reinforced visually, with books for women printed in the rounded typeface known as *vaybertaytsh* (literally, "women's Yiddish"), while the square typeface that later became the universal standard was known as *ivre-taytsh* ("Hebrew-Yiddish").[19]

Of course binaries invite contemplation of the crisscrossed and the in-between. Chava Weissler explores the categories of "women who were like men" and "men who were like women." While the former expression enjoyed little currency beyond the occasional appellation for a woman of unusual educational distinction, the latter came to be a frequently invoked catch-all for non-elite men. Women, as *leyeners* (or, in a more archaic form, *leyzerins*) of *bikher*, were to inculcate habits of literacy in their children and to prepare their male offspring to ascend, under masculine tutelage, to the loftier realms of *lernen* and *sforim* (plural of *seyfer*).[20]

In fact, male children troubled the stark binary because they were charged, as Naomi Seidman points out, with enacting a psychologically fraught transit from the feminine to the masculine realm.[21] They began life under the aegis of their mothers, sharing in women's storytelling and reading experiences simply by virtue of being present in the home.[22] Silent reading emerged as a norm only with the fully modern novel; in earlier stages of modernity, much reading was done aloud, including by women. This remained true even after books became reliable fixtures in private homes, and children took part in these reading experiences as listeners.[23] Leisure time for shared reading was especially abundant on the Sabbath: during long winter nights, long summer afternoons, and—for children too young to attend synagogue and the women and older girls who typically cared for them at home—during morning prayer times as well.[24] Consider this scene of tender intimacy the Hebrew-language educator and publisher Zvi Scharfstein remembered from his Podolian childhood:

> On Sabbath mornings, when the male members of the household had gone off to pray at the beit midrash, I the little one (ani hakatan) stayed at home; sometimes in the afternoon, when my father laid down to rest or paid a visit to the home of one of his friends—my mother would sit down at the table to read the Tseina Ur'eina.[25] Sometimes there would be a neighbor or two who would enter and sit by my mother to hear the contents of the weekly portion. I too joined them, pressing against my mother, listening to her read in a voice which was almost a whisper.[26]

Although Scharfstein does not give his age, we may surmise that if he was too young to uphold the decorum of synagogue, he was probably a preschooler or young elementary student. Sabbath reading was by its nature leisurely and somewhat haphazard.

Mothers were also heavily involved in the more focused home-based education, which could only begin to take place with the widespread dissemination of books and other printed matter in the seventeenth century.[27] The kind of mother-son closeness that Scharfstein describes would eventually be interrupted in dramatic fashion by the start of a boy's schooling. Sometimes kheyder education was initiated so early that families relied on *bahelfers*, teachers' aides who would carry their small charges to school on their backs over muddy or snowy streets. It was the most natural thing in the world, then, for the great Yiddish social scientist Max Weinreich to speak quite literally of the period in a boy's life "before he leaves his mother's domain and gets carried to *kheyder*."[28] A boy's school initiation ritual, whether it was the throwing of dried fruit or candy as if from on high or the smearing of honey on the first page of a primer to sweeten all subsequent learning, marked a decisive break with the domestic sphere of women and entry into the masculine world of education.[29]

Seidman describes the trajectory from feminine to masculine in terms of a boy's movement from Yiddish to *loshn koydesh*: the "sexual-linguistic system" that is thoroughly bound up with the paternal, the masculine.[30] The boy moves "from his mother's presence, as well as her language, her stories, and her texts" to the school world where teachers stood in for the father.[31] The family drama endures long beyond childhood insofar as, in the words of Max Weinreich, "We have here explicitly a long-lasting attachment of Yiddish to the mother and Hebrew to the father."[32] Seidman's account of this transition is particularly gripping: She maps the individual boy's experience onto the historical development of Jewish literature and the pervasive anxiety around the freighted relationship between Hebrew and Yiddish, where "the larger history was repeated in microcosmic form in the life of the individual, heightening the connections between the feminized childhood of the Jewish male and the feminized premodernity of Yiddish literature."[33] A primordial, undifferentiated femininity lurked in the home, ready to reclaim the boy's hard-won textual masculinity both within the full extent of an individual life (as Seidman observes) and at the communal level. If not carefully delimited, the mother-son tenderness that enchanted Scharfstein's youthful Sabbaths might compromise the socialization of boys like him into the intellectual trappings of Jewish manhood. Through many houses other than home—the school house, the prayer house, the house of study, to say nothing of the bathhouse—a boy was inducted into homosociality, distanced from his mother and the call of her stories.

Given the self-evident pleasure of shared reading in a warm familial setting, this stratified social order could only be reinforced informally, through the cultivation of embarrassment at whatever was coded as feminine and thus unserious. The newspaper editor and novelist Abe Cahan recalls in his memoir, "A boy who studied gemore was not supposed to read stories in zhargon [jargon, or Yiddish] and yet yeshiva boys devoured them."[34] Masculinity had to be constructed perpetually from day to day and from book to book by demarcating and devaluing the feminine as such, just as in a subsequent era of age-stratified literary culture, "children's literature" would be marked off and held in slight esteem as compared to "serious" works for grown-ups.[35] Sure, one could consume such works as an adult, but it would entail overstepping a boundary as flagrantly as a man reading "women's literature." This frisson of transgression accounts for the emotionally charged notes of apology and anxiety, exculpation and reassurance, that larded the introductions to various literary works consumed by women and children reading together, as well as by non-elite men. These texts were addressed explicitly to the distaff ("you pious and devout women"), to the other segments of Jewish society who were most like them ("women and the ordinary people who cannot study Torah"), or to the lumpen mass of "youth, maidens and children."[36]

One of the most enduring relics of "the feminized premodernity of Yiddish literature," and perhaps the book most unabashed in its address to a mixed audience, is the compendious *Mayse-bukh*, or Book of Exempla, which was first published in Basel in 1602.[37] Its preface made plain that while "pious women" were the primary addressee, the audience would balloon to include "the rabbis [*sic*], his wife, and everyone else."[38] The *Mayse-bukh* was also, implicitly and explicitly, children's literature, for it was anticipated that youth might use the book to study spelling and basic literacy.[39] But as the collection of 255 stories underwent almost a dozen reprintings over just a century and a half, the claims about who could benefit from its instruction grew more extravagant. The preface to the 1753 Redlheim printing insists, “No scholar need be ashamed to read this storybook.”[40]

It is difficult to overstate the audacity of even the original 1602 preface in striking out against a deeply entrenched, sharply hierarchical literary culture. While uprooting the dividing screen between male and female readers, Jacob ben Avraham’s rhetoric promises simultaneously to blur the gradations between ages, between levels of erudition, and between “Godly and secular.”[41] Not only, the advertorial preface promises, will the “dear ladies” now have unprecedented access to “the *Gemoro* in Yiddish and thus the entire Law,” but men might adopt the book as a shortcut to pass themselves off as more learned than they actually are: “Even a person who knows the *Gemoro* well could take from it *midroshim*, stories, and *agodous*, so that everyone would be astonished and say: ‘I believe that he knows the Torah like the back of his hand. He is so well versed in the *Gemoro* that I think he knows the entire Torah. Who has ever before seen such a person?’ For all situations, it gives the law for whatever has happened.”[42]

Such rhetoric should have been a scandal on more than one account.[43] First, it announced the delivery of a *gemoro*, or oral law, to women in their own mother tongue, a diffusion of rabbinic literature that had long been licensed in practice through the dissemination of such unimpeachable texts as the Tsenerene (“women’s Bible”) but that constituted a theoretical violation of the injunction against teaching women Talmud.[44]

But even for male readers who ought properly to aspire to Talmudic learning, the storybook is proffered as a shortcut at best and an aid to deception at worst. Rabbinic textual culture draws a central distinction between law and narrative; the sales pitch on display here recruits the prestige of legal study to justify an almost wholly narrative collection of tales. But stories can teach conduct. This text, proclaims its editor, will stand as a source of moral edification and discernment, a far more fortifying reading experience than the tepid “vapor” commonly on offer from booksellers: “And do not read the *Ki-bukh*, (Book of Cows) and do not let yourself be entertained by *Ditrikh fun Bern* (Dietrich of Bern), and *Maynster Hildebrant* (Master Hildebrand). These are all quite literally nothing but vapor which does not bring any warmth. In addition, they are not holy texts. You would need to seek God’s forgiveness for it. Our holy books say that it is a sin as big as a house to read such books on the holy sabbath.”[45]

Editor Jacob bar Abraham of Mezritsh aimed for his *Mayse-bukh* to replace “harmful and pernicious” secular story books.[46] If readers were seeking diverting content, it would be better to elevate the material by fitting it into a didactic framework of moral improvement. In promising both diversion and edification, the *Mayse-bukh* mobilized a discourse of *harm reduction* and the *cultivation of taste* that would resurface again and again, in relation to both women and children, as early modernity gave way to the fully modern.

What was Trunk's Grandmother Leah actually reading? Most likely, it was the chapbooks of Isaac Meir Dik (1807–1893), whose confections of fantasy and sentimental romance created a mass market for Yiddish fiction in the middle decades of the nineteenth century.[47] Dik had a clear purchase on the conditions of life that would have brought his chapbooks under the candlelight in Leah's rudimentary nursery: His own first marriage was contracted at the tender age of thirteen or fourteen, and while he pursued the education typical of a modernizing maskil, he remained strictly observant.[48] Dik never wrote for children, but the fiction he first popularized constituted an important inflection point in the dialectic of shame and harm reduction that eventually led to the creation of a distinct children's corpus in Yiddish. He is a critical figure for understanding what it meant for children to be reading in the orbit of women.

Once again, the gender dynamic of the author's relationship with his public is central. In translating the Psalms into Yiddish in 1545, Elya Bokher had addressed his readership as "you pious and devout women."[49] More than three centuries later, Dik dropped the assumption of piety while retaining the cozy second-person address to female readers, "mayn tayere lezerin" ("my dear lady-reader"). He appealed less to an idealized trait located within her, piety, than to her personal-feeling relationship with him, the builder—or importer—of story worlds that would extend her frame of reference to exotic locales and meet her emotional cravings for romance and heroism, "escapism and wish fulfillment."[50] Dik was proud of his large female audience, and he was solicitous of women's welfare within the limits of his own reflexive condescension.

Like other maskilim, Dik was appalled at the prevailing norms in Jewish Eastern Europe whereby women's labor supported men's Torah scholarship. He wanted to see women freed of the burden of supporting their menfolk economically; he believed, along with the founders of highbrow modern Yiddish literature, that the norm toward which Jewish society ought to aspire was bourgeois European patriarchy.[51] The rising tide of knowledge overtaking superstition would certainly lift all boats, yet at the same time, Dik felt that women ought not be too educated or too directive within their homes: in short, the golden mean would be for ladies to be enlightened in the proper measure and in the proper way precisely via *his* chapbooks. We can savor the piquant irony whereby the publishing arrangement that brought Dik's fictions to the masses perpetuated the very norms he strove to eradicate. His commercial breakthrough came when Vilna's Widow Romm and Sons printing house agreed to pay a flat fee of four rubles for each chapbook he wrote. The profits from this agreement would subsidize the printing of the landmark Vilna Shas, an ambitiously modern, information-packed folio edition of the Talmud—still in standard use.[52] The pleasure reading of women, the fruits of their labors within easiest reach (three kopecks to purchase a chapbook, just a single kopeck to borrow one for the length of a Sabbath), would underwrite technological advances in the Talmud study that was available to elite men.[53]

As did other proponents of Enlightenment, Dik regarded Yiddish itself a shameful last resort, yet *somebody* had to meet the craving of the female Jewish masses for books in a way that would, once again, minimize the damage being done to them by their reading. Even Hebrew authors did not receive proper honor during their lifetimes, Dik reflects, and if it constituted an abasement to publish in the Holy Tongue, a fortiori in Yiddish:

> Seeing this, I lowered myself to publish all that my pen had brought forth in the Hebrew language, and although I have sullied the honor of my pen (hishpalti kevod iti) I have told various tales composed in the language now spoken to our shame and disgrace (levoshtenu uleherpatenu) by our people living in this land (Lithuania, Poland, Russia). I wrote such for the benefit of the maidens of my people whose eyes look only into the Taytsh Pentateuch, which is written in the defective language of stammerers and contains expressions not fit to be heard by women and honest maidens. Not so my own stories, written as they are in a fine style full of ethical teaching, clean of all matters erotic (divre agavim) or disreputable (dofi), which will instruct girls in the graceful laws to walk the path of righteousness and to avoid all evil. They are covered in old-fashioned coverings in the manner that is pleasing to my people.[54]

Peril abounded. The Bible itself (translated into Yiddish, of course) is too racy for the fragile flowers of Ashkenazi womanhood as Dik imagines them. How noble, how self-sacrificing of the intrepid author to "sull[y] the honor" of his pen with Yiddish for the sake of their literary sustenance! Dik's female readers are so deeply othered by his romantic vision of their delicacy that it's hardly surprising when he turns around and castigates those same female readers for their fickle desire for eros- and plot-driven narrative. He had once tried his hand at writing a stodgier neo-ethical treatise for women, but it was a commercial flop, as the author complained: "Eleven years ago I published a work about this entitled *Divrey yoysher* [Words of Righteousness] in *jargón*. It was highly praised by many knowledgeable readers. Only our women and daughters do not buy it. All they want is a Bove-mayse, nothing more."[55] The women had spoken with their wallets, and if they wanted to subsist on a diet of fiction, that is what Dik would furnish—albeit taking care to try and supplant "bad" fantasy with "good."[56]

Dik had ushered in an era of fantastic and sentimental romances, harnessed to plot arcs of economic advancement that not only coincided with but helped to accelerate processes of enlightenment and secularization.[57] Once he gave himself over unabashedly to fulfilling his readers' literary cravings, he could (and did) boast of selling a hundred thousand copies—yet there remained a residue of disdain for women's tastes that would intensify a generation later into a full-blown moral panic.[58] The decisive turn in women's reading away from the devotional and toward romance would dictate a new direction for children's reading as well.[59] In a landscape saturated with potentially corrupting texts for tender-aged readers, it would become urgently necessary to offer them more wholesome fare.

By the 1880s, the demographic that had embraced Dik at midcentury was smitten with the modern novels of Nokhem Meir Shaykevitch (1846–1905), known by the acronym Shomer. The female reader whom Dik had addressed so intimately was herself the subject of an 1891 satirical sketch by the classic Yiddish writer Y. L. Peretz. "Di lezerin" or "The Female Reader" opens onto an ordinary Friday night in the hovel of an impoverished water carrier, crowded by "seven souls sleeping within four cubits."[60] The Sabbath evening has offered none of the customary sensory pleasures that ought to set it apart from the workaday week: no meat, no fish, no spirits, no challah. The impecunious husband and his wife, worn out from her subsistence commerce in eggs, pig bristles, and rags, have passed out, exhausted, and lie snoring on the bare, yellow earthen floor. Just one child remains awake, as the last penny candle sputters:

> The eldest daughter.
>
> Her messy hair is red. Her face—yellow: nourished with potatoes too few to fill up on. Yet her eyes burn; her sunken breast heaves, her thin hands tremble. . . .
>
> By the flickering flame, she is reading one of Shomer's novels. Her lips tremble with impatience.
>
> She is disturbed. She's afraid: what if the candle goes out on her and she never finds out what happens to the dragon in the end?![61]

Peretz emphasizes the triviality of an adventure plot, gently mocking the emotional investment of Shomer's devoted readers. The girl still living under her parents' humble roof might be anywhere from elementary aged to a marriageable (old) maid "sitting on the shelf," in the Yiddish parlance. She impatiently consumes fiction that was labeled derisively as *shund*: pulp or even trash. With his playful ending invoking the *pipernoter* ("dragon," but more expansively "nonsense" or "balderdash"), Peretz, unlike his subject, does not seem terribly "disturbed" at the intensity of the girl's literary rapture. He appears more bemused than panicked.

But high-culture novelist and tastemaker Sholem Aleichem, encountering the same mass phenomenon, maintained no such chill ironic distance. With a methodical thoroughness that seems more workmanlike than masterful, he takes the king of *shund* to task in an 1888 novella-length pamphlet that imagines putting Shomer on trial for his literary crimes against the Jewish people.[62] His indictment enumerates a list of prosecutorial demands, including, as number ten, "Under no circumstances should such novels be given to our schoolboys or teenage girls."[63] Peretz's depiction of the hungry girl devouring the dragon tale by candlelight comes just three years later, fleshing out the scandal of giving Shomer's work to young people as material for independent reading.

Yet memoirists who recall Shomer's novels as a feature of their youth paint a very different picture of the mode in which his stories were consumed: Like the multifarious books of Ashkenazi early modernity, they were often read aloud and in the bosom of family.[64] The writer Avrom Reyzn recalls his father reading Shomer's novels on Friday nights to the entire family.[65] As his father read, his mother wept, and the boy memorized "entire chapters." He concludes, "One of the most beloved parts of my youth, its greatest joy, was to read a book. Since reading books is still a pleasure, it is worth reminding ourselves of our first sweet memories of reading, reading the legendary Shomer." So what if the novels were candy instead of spinach? Reyzn implies. Reading is supposed to be sweet. The Reyzn family's shared reading experience constituted a stable, nourishing soil in which the individual writer's love of reading could slowly blossom.

But Dora Schulner (1889–1964) embeds her memories of the ostensibly trashy novels within a far more encompassing psychological drama of a family's transformation before her eyes.[66] Her parents' marriage was fairly typical for that time in Radomishle, a town in the province of Kiev. Her father, Motl, educated traditionally but hungry for Enlightenment, earned a paltry living as a schoolteacher. He attempted to satisfy his hankering for literary immersion as the proprietor of a lending library. The profits, however, were mostly intellectual and spiritual and accrued chiefly to the man of house; his wife, Rivka, who "screamed and cursed" at her meager provider in perpetual frustration, was growing progressively more alienated by her husband's absorption in a failing business—that is, until the day he came home with a volume of Shomer to read to his wife, who was illiterate.[67] Schulner, evidently an emotionally sensitive and perceptive child, recounts, "I was only a little girl at the time, but I could see how my father was always chasing after my mother's affection, and it brought me to tears."[68] She longed to spot a flicker of romance between the parents who had made her.

The shared reading of Shomer marked a turning point in Motl and Rivka's stale marriage, and the wise child took it all in, ruminating on the primal mystery of how she came to be: "I sat in bed, watching my parents. Did they love each other or didn't they? That's what I was asking myself in my childish mind." Schulner reports that her mother, "captivated," awaited her father's arrival home, "and when evening came my parents sat at the table and I sat in bed and my father read." Shomer's prose plucked the heartstrings of mother and daughter alike. "My young heart," writes the adult Schulner, "could hardly stand it. I sobbed out loud. My mother comforted me, and that's how my family began to read Shomer." But this shared emotional intensity doesn't just strengthen the vertical bond between generations; it ignites a domestic romance, completing the story arc the girl has yearned for: "My father became very important to my mother. He had brought something pure and beautiful into my mother's life. She started to think more highly of him because now their life made more sense to her. She begged him, 'Motl, can you read a chapter from *The Strong Woman*?' My father would smile and read her whatever she liked."[69]

In the period leading up to the start of a separate Yiddish literature to nourish curious, sensitive children like Schulner, the entire idea of family—its purpose, its constituents—was undergoing rapid and radical change. Schulner does not indicate in which year her father first brought home a Shomer novel, but it is easy to imagine her as a precocious ten- or eleven-year-old, which would place her recollections at about the turn of the century. In the Ashkenazi cultural sphere, old economic arrangements whereby men headed households religiously and communally but women served as primary wage earners had endured—albeit with rising levels of resentment. The holy bargain of yore, whereby women earned their share of the world to come through supporting a husband's labor at learning Torah, was giving way to a secularized imitation. Schulner describes her mother as a homemaker rather than a wage earner, but her father's devotion to his novels and scientific treatises was as passionate as earlier generations' investment in Talmud study. In many other families with Enlightenment-curious men at the helm, women now bore the burden of earning wages *and* continuing to manage a household with principal responsibility for child-rearing—all while their husbands failed to secure the benefits of either this world or the world to come.

The bed where young Dora Schulner listened to her father reading Shomer furnishes a front-row seat to a social metamorphosis taking place on a massive, global scale: the shift in the ideal of marriage from pragmatic or covenantal to companionate. Documenting this transition in the United States between 1900 and 1930, Steven Mintz and Susan Kellogg describe how under the new dispensation, "The middle-class family was assigned primary responsibilities for fulfilling the emotional and psychological needs of its members. Along with providing economic security and a stable environment for children, family life was now expected to provide romance, sexual fulfillment, companionship, and emotional satisfaction."[70] Schulner's family of origin, as she paints it here, wants for economic security and in no wise belongs to the American middle class, but it fulfills the other terms of this new covenant almost to a tee. Furthermore, we can imagine *some* of the evidence of the transformed marriage being kept out of young Dora's view, surfacing only once the girl was securely asleep for the night. Sholem Aleichem famously wrote that "doctors prescribe laughter." Had they existed in turn-of-the-century Radomishle, marriage counselors might have prescribed Shomer. Family stability, Mintz and Kellogg suggest, came to be based on "affection, compatibility, and mutual interest." Thanks to sharing romance novels, Motl and Rivka could now check each of these boxes.

The commodity that initially threatens to drive a wedge between Schulner's parents, books, becomes the very tool for suturing the breach. As Motl woos Rivka with Shomer, transforming their years-long marriage into a romance midstream, Dora's presence is a barely registered afterthought. The girl, obviously as smitten by literature as is the father whom she adores, registers in real time the chasm that her mother's illiteracy has opened up between her parents. Yet Rivka's dependency on her husband is conceptualized as an opportunity rather than a crisis. Only through the pleasure of shared reading—and reading Shomer—can the conditions of their life together "make more sense" to a mother who is increasingly sympathetic toward her husband, and thus also regarded more sympathetically by her daughter.

How do we make sense of the gap between Peretz's dismissive portrait of the girl reading alone as her parents slumber and Schulner's warm, rich account of the intimate romance kindled in her home by all that was "pure and beautiful" in Shomer's fiction? For one thing, modes of reading make a crucial difference in the reception of what's being read. In the clash between old-fashioned, whole-family reading aloud versus the newfangled silent, independent reading, tradition appears to win out. Any content, it seems, no matter how questionable for young readers, could be safely metabolized by a family reading together. In Schulner's home, at least, nobody died of blushing. What is more, the child was not yet the psychological and conceptual center of the family; she was an incidental listener along for the ride. Nobody thought at that point of shaping the family's reading around *her* frailties, real or presumed.

But a Yiddish high culture was emerging swiftly in tandem with a shift toward centering children—idealized and tenderly imagined—within the family unit. Homespun reading practices had yet to catch up to the demands of a rapidly developing high culture that would assert its moral and aesthetic superiority over mass culture. Yes, Shomer sailed into Schulner's unpretentious childhood home and transformed it utterly, but his work sent Sholem Aleichem into conniptions and amused Peretz, while inciting a critical pile-on by several other Yiddish literary elites.[71] At issue was the status of the hybrid language of Yiddish itself. The culturally dominant voices, like Sholem Aleichem's, were desperate to define Yiddish as classy, not trashy. If a pulp-loving mass culture was already flourishing commercially all around them, then that was all the more reason to write off many of the mature Yiddish readers of their day in favor of cultivating a more discriminating readership in the next generation. This would require protecting the delicacy of children's taste, it was thought, and nourishing them with only the most wholesome literary fare.

The journalist Ruvn Brainin was one of the first cultural leaders to think systematically about the question "What Should Our Children Read?" as he titled a wide-ranging essay.[72] Writing in the Krakow newspaper *Der yud* in June 1900, Brainin ruefully concedes that Yiddish had simply not produced any reading material suitable for children. Like Sholem Aleichem, he calls Shomer out by name and regards the prospect of children reading his books with panic: "I personally would advise our parents not to give their children any books to read in Yiddish [*zhargon*]. First, because there is no children's literature in Yiddish; the Shomer-style [Shomer'she] novels can only spoil the taste and the spirit of our children, and in certain cases, morally poison and confound their healthy notions. The best Yiddish writers have never been called to write for children, for the youth. It is self-evident for our discerning and educated Yiddish writers that we cannot educate our youth on Yiddish literature."[73]

In Brainin's view, children enter the world with a clean literary palate that can be spoiled by poorly chosen reading as surely as their tastebuds can be ruined by a poorly chosen diet. So far, Yiddish culture had produced only Enlightenment kale and junk food. He evinces a complicated admixture of shame and pride at Jewish difference, claiming that Jewish children (he really means boys) are more cerebral than their gentile counterparts and more likely to eventually earn a living by mental work than by manual labor—factors that make them especially susceptible to their reading. The reliance on books is furthered, in Brainin's account, by their alienation from nature, art, movement, and sports, all of which play a salutary role in the development of children in other cultures. Yet so strong are the literary cravings of even the poorest Jewish children that they "save up their breakfast money, their Hanukkah money and the like and buy books with their last groschen."[74]

Adult curation of children's reading experiences is essential, according to Brainin, for shaping the political and spiritual Jewish future, and it should be undertaken with great care. From the existing resources, he cobbles together a reading program that will do *the least harm* to these sensitive and hungry young readers. A literary diet ought to include some fiction, but excessive immersion in storybooks or chapbooks threatens to "imprison them in a fantasy world." From works of science and natural history, which ought to be prioritized, children would inexorably imbibe a certain kind of "poetry." Since no suitable materials existed in Yiddish and few in Hebrew, Brainin recommended that parents embrace European classics in translation, such as the stories of Hans Christian Andersen and Jules Verne. *Robinson Crusoe* offers the additional boon of teaching Jewish boys "self-reliance, which is very much needed among our children, who are afraid to stick their noses out beyond their mothers' aprons or to take one step beyond the town limits." Again and again, Brainin invokes the desideratum of cultivating, sharpening, and protecting the *taste* of young readers:

> The feeling for beauty, for poetry is something toward which we must raise our children and strengthen in them, just as we rear them, or should rear them, physically. As we sharpen their minds, so too should we sharpen their *tastes*, by all means possible, so that they can appreciate what is most beautiful and best in life, in nature and in art—which is possible for the poor as well as for the rich and for the persecuted much more than for the persecutor. And to a certain extent, this can be accomplished by means of good,

> suitable books. If we have no other means, then of course we have to use the book, to which our children are attached, as an educational means to improve the *taste*, feeling, and craving for beauty among our young children. Our children especially require good, *tasty* [*geshmakfole*] books because many generations worked zealously to corrupt our children's natural taste. We must improve and correct the flaws of many generations in exile. This is our obligation, and we must not neglect it.[75]

Like the connection that Seidman draws between the intellectual transit of an individual boy from maternal to paternal realms—and correspondingly from Yiddish to Hebrew—we might link this preoccupation with *taste cultivation* to questions of national import and development.

Brainin's concern about the corruption of taste echoes Sholem Aleichem's rhetoric in *Shomer's Trial*, where he charges the bestselling author with "dulling the taste" of the (adult) literary public, and "corrupting the taste" of the "working men, housewives, and young women," the non-elites "who are not expert enough to know the difference between good and bad literature." It is hard to know just how seriously to take the bespectacled, swashbuckling, side-parted crusader for literary justice when he construes the "fabrication" of pulp fiction as the basest crime imaginable: "Fooling someone, stealing his money, and killing him are, in my opinion, lesser crimes than tricking an entire people, murdering an entire literature, and ruining the literary taste of thousands of readers."[76] Is taste, after all, originally immaculate and susceptible to despoliation, or is it an endowment that can mature and improve over time, as a person—or a nation—grows up?

The critic Shmuel Charney acknowledged the rhetorical excesses of Sholem Aleichem's indictment, but he justified them on account of the "danger to young Yiddish literature" posed by a writer like Shomer, who would "weaken the influence of better Yiddish writers to gradually raise [the tastes of] the Yiddish reading public."[77] Charney imagined Yiddish itself as quite young; enthusiasm for Shomer was a youthful indiscretion of the kind the people would naturally leave behind as their tastes matured. Unsurprisingly, Dora Schulner shares this constructive view of taste as susceptible to maturation. She is obviously aware of Shomer's reputation as *shund*, but she justifies her generation's enjoyment of his novels along Charney's lines, imagining a bridge between the would-be gatekeepers of high Yiddish literature and the humble Jews they would need to recruit as readers: "Shomer led us poor children into the salons of the wealthy. He brought us to Paris. Where didn't he take his readers? He prepared his readers to read Mendele, Y. L. Peretz, Sholem Aleichem, and other great writers. In those years it would have been impossible to tackle the classic writers without first reading Shomer. Shomer was the path toward better literature, because it takes skill to read, just as it does to write."[78]

From candy to sweet potatoes and thence, eventually, to green vegetables: It is only natural that Schulner, who bore thoughtful witness to her family's transformative literary romance, expands a narrative of aesthetic development to national scale. Her assumption that taste can be educated echoes the argument that Sholem Aleichem ascribes to Shomer's fictional defense attorney. Shomer only writes trash, the imagined barrister maintains, because there is a market for it. But markets change over time: "The audience, I repeat, is like a little child. It will grow up, it will get smarter."[79] The two decades between Dik's popularity and Shomer's were sufficient time for a cadre of Yiddish high-culture mandarins to consolidate their authority over the Yiddish cultural scene. During the same span, children were coming to be seen as vulnerable and in need of adult protection and guidance, especially with respect to their *tastes*: the site of both aesthetic and moral formation. For many adults, it was indeed too late to relish the savor of Enlightenment kale. One aspect of the audience getting "smarter," or at least more discriminating, entailed the realization that all sorts of non-elites—water carriers in Berdichev, sweatshop workers in New York—might safely enjoy their trashy novels, published in penny editions or serially in the newspapers, if Yiddish cultural leaders devoted sufficient resources to publishing separate, more nourishing work for children.

The days of haphazard, shared family reading were numbered, at least in secularizing households. Brainin suggested that if parents didn't know what their children ought to read next, they should consult educated people for book recommendations.[80] An age of expertise was dawning, and in order to save Ashkenazi children from the dangers of bad reading, canonical writers and expert educators would be recruited to write for them especially. In just a few years, the Great War would orchestrate a convergence point between two developmental arcs: the maturation of modern Yiddish culture on one hand and Ashkenazi childhood on the other. During and immediately after the war, necessity and opportunity would embrace for long enough to stratify the publishing industry by age and engender a literature created expressly for Yiddish-speaking children.

2

What Children Need

THE EARLY YEARS OF YIDDISH CHILDREN'S LITERATURE

NEVER TRUST the nanny.

Her stories of demons and imps, princes and princesses are bound to turn her young charges into the kind of adults who "believe all kinds of nonsense and are scared of their own shadow." So cautions the very first text to posit the need for a Yiddish children's literature, in 1867.[1] What ought to supplant such harmful fare, according to the polemicist, is the nutritious crunch of realistic, exemplary tales, "stories of pure ethical content and good deeds, stories of things that actually happened to adults and children who were good and pious, and how good children should behave."[2] This first, brief mention of Ashkenazi children's reading material encapsulates many of the essential features and aims of the literature that would develop over the subsequent half century, including the combination of anxiety about the influence of youthful reading and the prescription of exemplary texts. Maskilic concerns, chief among them the stamping out of Jewish "superstition," overlap with a broad shift in pedagogical and child-rearing strategies from frightening children into compliance to modeling desired behaviors and habits of mind.

The wrong literary diet threatened to dull children's aesthetic tastes, and correspondingly their capacity for moral discrimination. While the previous chapter focused on the steady march of harm reduction in (women's and) children's reading materials, we turn now toward efforts near the turn of the twentieth century to delineate an affirmative vision of what Ashkenazi children needed—from life and from literature. Of course outlining such a program reveals what *adults* need, and in the case of these deliberations, the adults in question are overwhelmingly male, elite cultural leaders.[3] In the course of examining those perceived needs, we will also trace the contours of the early history of Yiddish children's literature. Which were the core principles to be emphasized, and what aesthetic forms might best tend toward enshrining them?

Children Need Enlightenment

The anxiety about Jewish children growing into superstitious adults, particularly under the corrosive influence of non-Jewish female caregivers, comports with the Haskalah and its contempt for the backward forces of irrationality and magical thinking.[4] Ruvn Brainin's 1900 essay asking "What Should Our Children Read?" echoes many fixations of a more generalized maskilic worldview.[5] He is concerned about fostering rational and critical thinking and wishes to increase the availability of juvenile texts about natural history and the sciences, asserting that they contain their own kind of "poetry" that obviates the need for a great deal of fantastic or sentimental children's literature. Proponents of Enlightenment sought to cultivate a joyful relationship with nature, or, adopting the negative framing they so often did, to redress Jewish alienation from the natural world.[6] Brainin saw this problem through a specifically Zionist lens, reasoning that the biblical pilgrimage festivals observed in ancient Israel were at core *Naturfeste*, nature festivals, connecting the people to the land; exile had balefully severed this bond. Relatedly, he employs language of health and pathology, ruing the diseased state of a body politic that could be cured, in part, through higher-quality reading for youth.[7]

Just as Dik and Shomer embedded maskilic themes in the plots of their stories aimed at women, would-be children's authors propagated Enlightenment "by other means" when they embedded a rationalist worldview in stories for juvenile readers. If Enlightenment ideas were edifying, then these early pursuers of Yiddish children's literature were trying to perfect the recipe for kale chips: a form of nourishment whose satisfying crunch of plot or light salting of formal innovation might distract children from the bitter undertaste of "improving" reading.

Although elements of fantasy would eventually crop up in mainstream or "canonical" Yiddish children's literature, the earliest discussions presumed that children flourished best by reading realistic works. Brainin warns of an escalating *lebns-kampf*, or life struggle, "against our way of life," presumably a reference to mounting antisemitic violence during an era of intensifying pogroms. One strategic response, he asserts, is "to strengthen and sharpen the minds of our children and guard them against all spiritual illness" by means of salutary reading material.[8] Realistic stories offered both a training regimen for inevitable adversity and, eventually, a way of processing trauma.[9] Only later would fantasy be touted by some pedagogues, theorists, and writers as a valuable means of escape from the harsh realities of Jewish life in the twentieth century.

Children Need Empowerment

Mordkhe Spektor, writing during Shomer's commercial heyday in the 1880s, was also concerned about the ill effects of irrational demon stories on vulnerable young readers: "Our Jewish children have no literature at all, not even a single book(let) that a child can read and understand with his mind—and find useful. A Jewish child who has a desire to read ends up reading demon stories with evil spirits or novels just like grown-up readers. Such books are even more detrimental to young children than to adults."[10] But unlike his contemporaries, he was prepared to take immediate action, publishing a sixty-four-page collection of holiday tales in Warsaw in 1889. Whether or not these stories were originally intended for children, they were certainly marketed as juvenile literature, making them the first Yiddish children's stories.[11]

"Kids" (*Kinder*) is a Purim tale describing how two best friends, Leybitshke, age twelve, and Notke, ten, band together to raise funds for Old Shmerl, a broken-down water carrier who is responsible for supporting his orphaned grandchildren.[12] While rich relatives and other town notables turn them away, the boys succeed better with Khaytshe the Cobbler, who addresses them affectionately as "kids" and advises them to steer clear of the rich. Their errand completed, the boys hurry toward Shmerl's hovel and relieve a scene of dismal penury with the fruits of their collection.

Khaytshe's proletarian critique of the Jewish bourgeoisie obviously lies at the center of the tale's messaging, but equally prominent is the persistent distinction between those who honor children and their potential to do good in the world and those who belittle and underestimate them. The critic Chone Shmeruk is not sure, writing in 1984, that we would still regard Spektor's holiday tales as suitable for children; he characterizes this particular story as a "sentimental-naïve tale, that now astonishes with its primitiveness."[13] The story's force, though, lies in its realistic depiction of children's ability to lead with kindness and to bring about a tangible if modest improvement in Shmerl's granddaughter's life. We might see in the boys' success a small-scale instance of how the joyful *kairos*, or interruptive moment, of Purim can reset the ordinary *kronos* of preindustrial Jewish poverty. Fittingly, the tale ends the day *after* Purim, with the granddaughter Leahtshke's delighted first walk outside in her brand-new shoes. Mordkhe Spektor had gotten Yiddish children's literature off to a respectable start.

Children Need Happy Endings

Spektor did not wish to remain alone in the vanguard, though, as he did for over a decade. In his introduction to the holiday tales, he had called on "our *fine* writers" (*undzere* gute *shrayber*; emphasis in the original) to start writing for children, whereby he assured them they could do far more good than they did by writing for grown-ups.[14] His good friend Sholem Aleichem surely read this appeal, which came just a year after his own 1889 indictment of Shomer and the deleterious effects of his fiction on children. Thus far, Shomer's accuser had himself done nothing to supplant the undesirable reading material with anything better.[15] But Brainin's June 1900 essay in *Der yud* seemed to turn up the pressure on both the journal and one of its flagship contributors. In November of that year, the same organ published Sholem Aleichem's "Di fon" (The Flag), his first story explicitly addressed to children.[16]

With this tale, the author establishes a template to which he will return often.[17] A first-person narrator, in this case (and two others) Kopl Kukuriku—whose speech defect leads his classmates to dub him Topl Tuturitu—recalls traumatic yet survivable youthful episodes from the safety of adulthood. The tale is set in the fictional shtetl locale of Kasrilevke, an elastic topos that shrinks and expands to meet narrative necessity over several decades of Sholem Aleichem's writing career. Kopl's family are "a bunch of paupers," but the boy saves enough change to assemble a prized artifact of juvenile Judaica, a paper flag to carry in the children's processional for Simkhes Toyre, the fall holiday that celebrates the completion and recommencement of the annual Torah reading cycle.[18] Holding the prettiest flag topped by the reddest apple and biggest candle, feeling "like a happy prince, a child of royalty," Kopl conforms perfectly to the "king-for-a-day" motif that David Roskies associates with Sholem Aleichem's children's stories.[19] In fact, the *imagined* prospect of how the holiday will unfold, rehearsed in detail in the theater of the boy's mind, is by far the sweetest part, an idyll the reality can hardly match.

But that idyll is summarily shattered when Kasrilevke's rich boy, who cannot tolerate the possibility of being bested even for a single evening, dispatches a minion to ask for a light from Kopl's candle flame, and with the newly rekindled candle, accidentally-on-purpose sets fire to the poor boy's hard-won flag. The grown-up narrator recalls his utter and primal despair: "Had a stone fallen from the sky and struck my head; had a wild beast attempted to devour me; had a corpse dressed in a tattered shroud made an attempt to choke me, my fright would not have been as great as it was when I saw my naked stick and burnt-out flag." Rejoicing turns to mourning, and the moment of God's festal nearness invites theodicy, as he asks, "Is it fair? O Eternal Lord! Did I deserve this? Why did you do this to me?" That's where the plot ends: Innocence gives way to hard experience, the rapacious rich take advantage of the poor with impunity. So conclude many of Sholem Aleichem's child-centered holiday tales.[20]

But this wasn't just a story *about* children, as the author was used to writing; it was to be a story *for* them. Addressing juvenile readers and listeners meant two things to Sholem Aleichem: employing rhetorical markers that identified his audience as *kinder* and providing a *happy ending*. So if the *plot* ends on a note of devastation, then the *story* must be extended with an epilogue designed to reassure—if only anemically:

> Children, you know that all stories either have sad or happy endings.
>
> For the most part, Jewish stories have sad endings. According to one of our proverbs, a Jew, especially a poor one, is not destined to have pleasure. Much can be said about this. When you grow up, you'll understand. But, meanwhile, I must tell you that the story you just heard did not quite end there. That flag caused me much anguish, and I fell ill, burning with fever.[21]

We certainly don't seem to have reached the happy ending yet. The flaming flag and kindled light metonymically slide into fever dreams of "fiery-tongued dragons and serpents and wild beasts in the shape of men"—all typical fare for a boy in the throes of the dangerous psychosomatic illnesses that often help to resolve the plots of Sholem Aleichem's child-protagonist stories. But the narrator insists on happiness; after all, on the holiday there's a *mitsve*, an obligation, to rejoice:

> But since today is erev Simchat Torah we have to be merry and happy, and so I'd like to end this story on a happy note.
>
> First of all, thank heaven, as you can see, I recovered.
>
> Second of all, for your information, the following year my flag was even nicer, my stick more beautiful, my apple redder. In fact, I sat way up by the eastern wall with all the other rich men's children. The lights burned. My flag sparkled. Jews danced around the shul with the Torahs. Reb Melekh, the cantor, his prayer shawl outspread, led the procession like a field marshal. His

> metallic voice quavered as he sang out: "Hel-per of the poor and weak, sa-a-ve us!" As endless streams of women and girls pressed forward to kiss the Torah and shrill into his face, "Live and be well until next year at this time."
>
> And Melech replied, "The same to you and yours."
>
> Dear children—and the same to you and yours. Gut yontev![22]

"It gets better," he assures young readers—eventually. The "happy ending" Sholem Aleichem can offer is endurance, which, if practiced enough, crystallizes into resilience. Significantly, the epilogue repeats nearly verbatim the description of the scene as Kopl had prospectively and ideally imagined it. This is one of the consolations, the author implies, of living in cyclical time, of experiencing childhood as a spiral of liturgical revisitations. This year's holiday is ruined; next year's will be better. The picture you carry in your head endures. Some of Sholem Aleichem's darkest messages are transmitted in his child stories, whether intended for adult or juvenile audiences.[23] For the most part, he avers, Jewish stories have sad endings, but if you luck out and make it to adulthood, you might gain the consolation of seeing the past more clearly.

Is Sholem Aleichem actually writing for children, or is he ironically poking fun at what it *would* look like if he *were* to write for children? Or is he writing for the "inner" children buried under the sediment of adult cares in his adult readers? To demarcate precisely the space of children's literature is to enter a thorny thicket, but one promising approach to the question of whether a particular work is "for children" is the one taken by Barbara Wall, who listens for the "almost indefinable adjustments in pitch and tone" that adults make when addressing children; such subtleties register even when "overhearing a conversation in the next room."[24] The earlier history of Ashkenazi reading practices, before age-stratified publishing, had been akin to children overhearing adult conversation in the same room but not having conversation directed to them. By Wall's standard, listening in from "the next room," Sholem Aleichem's stories for children seem like the visit of a kindly disposed relative or dignitary, not much accustomed to the company of actual children, try as he might to tell them a story.[25] After penning several such tales, the author confessed that he wasn't sure they were appropriate for juvenile readers.[26] His "child stories" (an umbrella term for the tales with child protagonists, whether aimed at juvenile or adult audiences) seem to address several different ages, and some of them are quite grotesque or depict bracing trauma. But who ever said that childhood ought to be happy? As we assess the appropriateness of dark material for young readers, we might also examine our own culturally conditioned biases, among the most reflexive and enduring of which is the association between youth and joy.

The moment when a Yiddish children's literature was coming into being was, not coincidentally, the moment when the linkage between childhood and happiness diffused into the furthest reaches of Western culture. Seriousness was the province of adults, while whimsy ought to reign where children dwelled. Y. L. Peretz, whom Sholem Aleichem regarded as a literary "father" despite the mere seven years between them, rejoiced at the idea of Yiddish-speaking children having a literature to reinforce the playfulness that ought to define a proper childhood. In a 1912 installment of his column tracking new developments on the literary landscape, he celebrated the start of a new publishing venture in these terms: "The child must be a child! Woe to the man who never got to be a child. Woe to the nation whose children are raised as old folks. Jewish children are too serious, too sensible. And they have too little of the freedom and poetry of childhood."[27]

Reaching back to core motifs of the Haskalah, Peretz revives the charge that traditionally religious Jewish childhood was particularly lachrymose. A careworn youth is but the natural extension of Eastern European Jewish life in general, with its crippling poverty, insularity, backwardness, and the constantly looming threat of antisemitic violence. To these externally imposed factors were added the elected pressures of the Torah's demands on "a nation of priests." For Mendele the Book Peddler, the founding figure of modern Yiddish fiction, Jewish adulthood was synonymous with worry, and children were too swiftly burdened with adult cares, as is the protagonist in his novel, *The Wishing Ring*: "The days of Hershele's childhood did not last long . . . and while he was still a child, he became a little Jew: dejected, pensive, with a worried face and all the mannerisms of a grown-up, mourning Jew, he was only missing a beard. . . . Almost as soon as the child is out of his swaddling clothes . . . they heave the yoke onto him and, giddy-up, giddy-up little Jew!"[28]

A Jewish upbringing was a strict training regimen for bearing "the yoke of the commandments," the very encumbrance being thrust onto hapless Hershele. After all, full (male) participation in the religious life of Ashkenaz required the attainment of linguistic and intellectual competencies, to say nothing of attitudes and habits of mind, that were at odds with an ideal of carefree childhood.

Yet for all these canonical Yiddish writers' keen sense of Jewish difference and the particular burdens weighing down the children in their midst, their discourse participated in a far broader equation of childhood and joy as the nineteenth century gave way to the twentieth. Without conducting a full-scale global review, we can spot-check locations as varied as England, the United States, and Russia and notice an emerging consensus. As theorist of childhood Peter N. Stearns writes, "One of the most pervasive beliefs about emotion, at least in American culture, is the idea that children should be happy and that childhood should be a happy, perhaps unusually happy, stage of life." Stearns dates this belief to the second half of the nineteenth century, allowing that until then, "most people in most agricultural societies" did not regard childhood as an especially happy phase of life.[29] In preindustrial societies, "childhood mortality and the need for children's labor constrained emphasis on happiness"; a "good" child was not a happy child but rather an obedient one.[30] Similar dynamics obtained in Victorian England.[31] The Industrial Revolution pulled many children's labor out of the home and into factories, where they worked at a pace set by steam-driven machines with little regard for their emotional states. Widespread compulsory schooling was one progressive response to the crisis of industrialized child labor, and with schooling came leisure time, literacy, and the opportunity for children's literature to flourish. Stearns emphasizes that it became the task of adults to ensure children's happiness, especially through consumerism, with the nineteenth-century custom of giving birthday gifts providing a cyclical prompt for purchasing increasingly available children's books and toys.[32] Not only a physic that would promote the spiritual and intellectual health of the nation, children's literature was also a commodity for consumption in emerging markets. The rise of such market for adult novels in Yiddish had been bound up with the emergence of "classic" canonical writers in the mid- to late nineteenth century. Not all "happy childhood" discourse was linked to capitalist consumption, of course. One of the Soviet revolution's proudest (and arguably most successful) achievements was to democratize who might even aspire to a "happy childhood," as we shall discuss in chapter 8.

The ideal of happy childhood correlated strongly with the ideal of childhood innocence. Children ought to be happy, the reasoning went, because they don't yet know the things that would eventually make them sad. Their "natural state" of joy follows from ignorance but also constitutes an aspirational condition for adults to recall with fond nostalgia, the more so because it eludes the desire to return. In *Emile* (1762), Jean-Jacques Rousseau poses a rhetorical question to parents and educators who would burden children with taxing moral instruction: "Why do you want to deprive these little innocents of the enjoyment of a time so short which escapes them and of a good so precious which they do not know how to abuse? Why do you want to fill with bitterness and pains these first years which go by so rapidly and can return no more for them than they can for you?"[33] A few decades later, William Wordsworth would encapsulate the Romantic view of childhood in insisting, "Heaven lies about us in our infancy!"[34]

Overeducating youngsters, whether they were little Hersheles or Childe Harolds, threatened to lay waste to their childhood, and in the Ashkenazi cultural sphere, this Romantic critique took the form of bemoaning the traditional curriculum. Writing with mythopoeic hyperbole in 1935, Shmuel Charney linked the drudgery of Jewish childhood to the lack of a developed juvenile literature: "Three decades ago, there was nothing for children to read in Yiddish, and what's worse, there was no one to read it" because the Yiddish-speaking child "had, *nebekh* [alas], to study. To study Bible, Talmud, not get sucked into foolish stories."[35] If the detractors of Yiddish children's literature saw it as a "foolish" pursuit, then Charney saw it as a sacred one, and children as near-holy beings. Charney demands that Jewish children be allowed to be human children first, before getting tugged into the particular practices, concerns, and knowledge that is their estate as Jews. They don't need moralizing or tendentious reading, or even reading that describes the Jewish condition specifically. To be a proper child, by his lights, is to be half an angel, practically airborne:

> The heaviness of an open or concealed moralistic tendency pulls them down to live and strive as adults do; it doesn't allow them to soar in the pure, light air, which surrounds the tender souls of little ones. And for us of course, precisely that pure, light, childlike air is as vital as life itself! So then do we want to turn our children into "tiny little Jews"? So then why are all of the children's publications up to this point, for example, those from the "art publishers," stuffed with pictures and names from *Jewish* history and *Jewish* literature? After all, does the entire world of Jewish children consist only of "Jewishness"? Is their sense of fantasy as limited as that of us "nationalists"? . . . The childlike world and also children's literature, the real stuff [*di ekhte*], not the tendentious and not the "patriotic"—is "international." And I have demonstrated the necessity "to translate into Yiddish all the artistic works for children that are found in world literature."[36]

Childhood happiness and innocence were in turn linked to an ethnically and religiously unmarked internationalism in which young children ought rightfully to be allowed to participate before assuming the yoke of Jewish identity, let alone the strictures of Jewish practice.

"World literature," for Charney, writing in 1935, has transcended cultural particulars and is a neutral good attainable through translation, as Brainin had recommended in 1900.[37] Charney's idealized description of "international" children's literature correlates strongly with Paul Hazard's sentimental notion of the "universal republic of childhood," articulated just three years before.[38] Eventually, more critically distant analysts would puncture such sentimentality, as when Emer O'Sullivan notes that "the concept of universal childhood is a Romantic abstraction which ignores the real conditions of children's communication across borders. There is no 'world republic of childhood' in which the conditions are in any way on a par with one another. . . . 'The child' can't be spoken about as a singular entity."[39] Even within the borders of the imagined terrain we call Yiddishland, with its concentration in Eastern Europe and its satellite colonies in the Americas and far beyond, many features of childhood were at wild variance from place to place and person to person.

The aesthetic forms associated with these differences varied as well. Whimsy and fantasy could be imagined as the artistic correlative of the joy, hope, and carefree spirit that were "supposed" to suffuse children's lives. Yet the Haskalah from which so much early children's literature grows is preoccupied with getting the Jews of Eastern Europe to grapple with reality, which, to many, dictated a preference for realistic fiction. And some cultural leaders came to question the early association of childhood with cheer altogether. By midcentury, writing from New York, Shloyme Kazdan would observe that some English children's literature is tragic and ask of authors, "Is it really true that sentimental and 'sad' books are unsuited to the children here?"[40] Literature, like play, could serve as a means for children to metabolize trauma and distress—and eventually, it would have to do precisely that.

(Ashkenazi Jewish) Children Need Yiddish

At first, Yiddish cultural leaders spilled far more ink in decrying than in redressing the lack of an adequate children's literature. Although some were content to rely on works translated from the languages of Western Europe—the particular geographical locus of a "republic of childhood" imagined to be universal—others insisted that children needed to be able to access works originating in their own cultural milieu and mother tongue. Yiddish had begun reliably producing literature of unquestionable artistic merit for adults, so why not for children? It was logical to recruit canonical writers like Sholem Aleichem and Y. L. Peretz to this project of cultural nationalism—up to a point. Sholem

Aleichem's artistic vision was a fundamentally dark one, centering on the sustained critique of economic inequality and marking the shifting contours of Jewish identity in a rapidly modernizing world. He probed the traits (rapacity, gullibility, etc.) that both resulted from and perpetuated injustice. The laughter he famously prescribed was rueful. Yet if he could contribute to the commonweal of a Yiddish youth culture by tweaking his stories cosmetically, then he was more than willing to do his part.

Sholem Aleichem had written his "first little masterpiece" in 1886, a childhood story that was emphatically not for children.[41] "Dos meserl" (The Penknife) included several of the plot elements that typified his child tales. A sickly father, a long-suffering mother, a sensitive boy driven wild by desire for a forbidden object (the titular knife), a febrile dream sequence—the salt, fat, acid, and heat of his story recipe are all present. As Shmeruk points out, the original version, with its erotic elements and suspicion toward traditional Jewish education, would never have passed muster for children.[42] The author reworked the story and republished it in 1903 as a prominent part of a four-volume collection of fiction for adults but under the heading "a mayse far yidishe kinder" (a story for Jewish children). The second volume of that collection was largely devoted to holiday tales for child readers. Perhaps Sholem Aleichem meant to write more for them eventually; he discussed plans with his son-in-law that never came to fruition.[43] But by 1904, after publishing a total of ten short stories, the classic writer had concluded his foray into writing for children.

The involvement of canonical authors like Sholem Aleichem typifies what we might call the *gestural* phase of Jewish children's literature, wherein the most highly respected authors for general audiences turned their attention to writing occasionally for young readers as a kind of civic-minded gesture on behalf of the nation. It is a notable feature of both early Yiddish and Hebrew children's literature that nearly every high-culture figure tried his hand (the canonical authors at this point were almost all male) at writing *something* for children.[44] When the Jewish National Workers' Alliance (Farband) sent Y. L. Peretz a copy of their 1912 textbook and a five dollar honorarium for the inclusion therein of his story "Din toyre mitn vint" (The Wind on Trial), he was overjoyed, proclaiming in his letter back to them that they had granted him "the most beautiful and happiest" day of his life. He returned the money with instructions to pay it forward: "Use it to buy children's books and give them to poor children." He implores the educators to update him "about the progress of your holy work," and "if possible, read my letter aloud to the children."[45]

In the years between the classic writers' early efforts and World War I, Yiddish children's publishing was characterized by spotty success on a limited, regional scale and by artistic ambition that exceeded writers' and publishers' ability to deliver.[46] Attempts to create institutions that would propagate Yiddish publishing for children were subject to fits and starts for a variety of reasons. These efforts were hobbled by ambivalence about the status of Yiddish, as well as the organizers' proximity to revolutionary activity. A significant breakthrough came in Warsaw in 1911, with the start of the series *Mayselekh* (Little Stories), published by Mordkhe Birnboym, one of the pioneers of modern Yiddish education. Indeed, this was the new development that Y. L. Peretz had hailed so warmly in his column, as a tonic to revive the youthful exuberance of the "too serious" Jewish children. Birnboym's imprint produced nineteen illustrated booklets, cheaply printed, that reflected the material available at the time: mostly translations (of Hans Christian Andersen, Edmondo De Amicis, Alexander Pushkin, Rudyard Kipling) and a few works originating in Yiddish (Y. L. Peretz, Judah Steinberg).[47]

Due to cost constraints, most of the early publishing projects were ephemeral: inexpensive chapbooks and periodicals. The first of these periodicals, appearing in 1912–1913, was a children's supplement to a newspaper for adults, *Di idishe vokh* (The Jewish Week).[48] *Grininke boymelekh* (later, standardized to *beymelekh*; Little Green Saplings) appeared in 1914, taking its name from a Romantic-spirited 1901 poem by Hayim Nakhman Bialik, the "national poet" of the Jewish people, who wrote in both Yiddish and Hebrew. The verse, as Naomi Prawer Kadar points out in her elegant reading, evokes the precocity and fragility of Jewish children, especially little boys, with their "prophetic" eyes and frail bodies.[49] The periodical's cover image, depicting the poem's "little Moyshes and Shloymes" in the sheltering shade of the fragile saplings they are imagined to resemble, reinforces the idea of Jewish childhood as a pastoral idyll unfolding in a forest primeval, set off from the danger and harm that lurked on the eve of the Great War.[50] The stories and poems within the magazine's pages were conceived as a refuge from increasingly dire realities, as Adina Bar-El explains:

> Most of the content was literary, with a small proportion of informative articles and games and riddles. No reference at all is made in the content to current events, for example, the war, in whose wake a large influx of Jewish refugee children arrived in Vilna and were placed in institutional residences set up for them. The texts seem to have been selected with the aim of dis-

> tancing the young readers from the difficult events surrounding them. Themes are most often imaginary, with happy endings, or if realistic, such as stories of contemporary Jewish family life and holidays, they project an atmosphere of serenity. Eretz Yisrael [The Land of Israel] as a topic is conspicuously absent.[51]

Just because the early materials for children were cheaply produced doesn't mean they lacked the imprimatur of high culture. The publisher of *Grininke beymelekh*, as well as several stand-alone books for children, was Vilna's legendary Boris A. Kletskin. The new magazine was edited and managed by distinguished cultural activists and educators, including after WWI by the children's author and distinguished pedagogue Shloyme Bastomski, and it ran continuously throughout the interwar period.[52] The growing interest in producing high-quality children's literature followed organically from the rising status of the Yiddish language in the wake of the 1908 Czernowitz conference, wherein participants declared Yiddish "a national language of the Jewish people" and stepped up a self-conscious effort to seed a high culture as an act of nationalism. In Kiev in 1909, it was natural for Nakhmen Mayzel to fold an ambitious children's publishing program into his aspirations for his Kunst farlag (Art Press), whose heady selectivity he could only capture by reference to the sacred: "'Kunst farlag' must be a kind of holy of holies, which not every person is allowed to enter. Only the most talented . . . only true works of art must be printed there."[53] In 1911 the Society for the Promotion of Jewish Enlightenment (known by its Russian acronym, OPE) produced a pamphlet laying out a publishing program for a "model press" for children's literature, conceived as a kind of public utility. They described their initiative as "a national cultural undertaking" that would surely inspire the illustrators, writers, and poets "to unite their powers to work on behalf of our children."[54]

Throughout this period between the Czernowitz conference and the outbreak of the Great War, publishers were growing a market for juvenile literature. "Not only theoretically," insists Charney, "but practically as well, the interest in the Jewish/Yiddish child [*tsum idishn kind*] and his spiritual nourishment was growing."[55] One hesitates about how precisely to translate "tsum idishn kind" because while Charney is speaking most immediately about the early progress of Yiddish publishing for children, Jewish bilingualism still reigned; in creating culture in both Yiddish and Hebrew, much of the populace of Jewish Eastern Europe still breathed, as S. Y. Abramovitsh had formulated the duality, through both nostrils. Despite significant local differences, Hebrew- and

Yiddish-language schooling experiments were infused by a similar spirit, and so was children's publishing at that early stage. In Yiddish, the prestigious Kletskin house offered children Bible stories retold by Sholem Asch as well as a translation of Rudyard Kipling's *Jungle Book*.[56] Bialik himself had helped to establish Moriah as the preeminent Hebrew publishing house of pre-WWI Europe, seamlessly weaving textbooks and children's leisure reading, original Hebrew books and translations of European classics, into a publishing program that focused on gathering the best of the Jewish past and the world's literary present into the contemporary Hebrew canon.[57] On the eve of the war, the list of figures who had committed to write children's works for Kletskin and Moriah included S. Y. Abramovitsh, H. N. Bialik, Dovid Bergelson, Perets Hirshbeyn, Y. Ch. Ravnitzky, Sholem Asch, and Sholem Aleichem. The gestural phase was poised to elicit some very graceful gestures indeed.

The Great War scuttled many of these plans and delayed or reduced the scale of others. Yet witnessing the failed attempts, dead ends, and modest successes in the very first years of Yiddish children's publishing helps us to appreciate the magnitude of the accomplishment when the floodgates finally opened after the war, and the Yiddish material available for young readers surged from a trickle to a flood. During that swell, canonical authors would continue to write here and there for children, but the literature would henceforth develop in tandem with a blossoming school system. Childhood as a theme would give way to living, breathing children as an audience with their own distinctive literary appetites. As Charney acknowledged, "Among the representatives of the Yiddish prewar literature [before WWI], there were very few who had the ability to connect with children."[58] To forge that connection would require writers closer to the world of children and education, who could develop special expertise in the overlap between pedagogy and cultural creation. Unfortunately, events in Europe were about to afford an opportunity—and level an implacable demand—to grow that expertise and the institutions to support it.

Children Need Adult Caregivers

You can't have "bad luck" without . . . *luck*, quips Shmuel Charney in explaining how the Great War "prepared the soil" for a new era in Jewish education. "Jewish children had the 'luck' of the war. It left many of them without a home, so children's homes had to be founded, along with schools and elementary schools with fresh air, with better supervision; the result was to consolidate the position of the new, more modern Jewish education and to simultaneously strengthen interest in Yiddish children's literature."[59]

Across Europe, World War I resulted in a refugee crisis and specifically an orphanhood crisis of unprecedented dimensions.[60] In Central and Eastern Europe, the war could not be separated from "the abrupt and violent dissolution" of the Austro-Hungarian, Russian, and Ottoman Empires or from pogrom violence—all of which left orphaned or otherwise unsupervised children in numbers that are difficult to compute, let alone to fully absorb.[61] As did many other nations and confessional communities, Jewish groups throughout Central and Eastern Europe acted *in loco parentis,* founding and maintaining institutions to care for children whose parents had died or were otherwise unable to rear them.[62] These included orphanages (known as children's homes), schools, and camps.

When Charney alludes to "fresh air" and "better supervision," he acknowledges that those institutions were often guided by the most modern pedagogical thinking and regulated professionally. As the care of unattached children devolved on the community, many of the wards would not be consigned to traditional *khadorim,* the home-based rabbinical classrooms of yore. Residential collectives would include schooling and, insofar as possible, libraries onsite.[63] The institutionalization of childhood on a large scale helped war-torn societies move from "warfare to welfare," ushering in a "professionalization of welfare" and a market for literature responsive to the material, educational, psychological, and aesthetic needs of a generation whose members would not see their hunger for stories met around their parents' Sabbath tables.[64]

The searing need of the war orphans, and the establishment of children's homes to meet it, represented only the most extreme manifestation of a broader shift that had been nudging children's education and care under the sway of expertise for decades. This transformation was, like the changes to family life discussed earlier, a global one. "In the 1890s," writes Stephen Mintz, "there was a growing sense that modern science offered a fresh and correct approach to childrearing, echoing the Progressive era's preoccupation with expertise in other realms."[65] In the Yiddish-speaking world, this Progressive-style expertise would be refined through the development of pedagogical science, institutions of higher education and research, and scholarly periodicals. The laboratory for all those endeavors, as they unfolded in interwar Europe, the United States, and elsewhere in the Jewish world, would be the secular schools. Whether they operated in Yiddish, as did the Central Yiddish School Organization (known as TSYSHO or CYSHO), or in Hebrew, as did the Tarbut network, these schools factored in newly emerging understandings of how children developed, and they sought to broaden traditional Jewish book learning and to integrate mind and body with robust instruction in sports, nature, and, in some places, agriculture.

Children Need Schools

Sholem Aleichem pioneered what has become a staple of schoolchildren's literary encounters today: the author's school visit. When "Di fon" was first published at the end of 1900, a note was affixed to the title: "Read on Khol Hamoyed Sukes this year in the First 'Heder Mesukan' in Kiev." The following year, he paid a similar visit to the girls' school in Bielotserkev.[66] The home-based informal "schools," which had originally just served boys and restricted their curricula to a traditional canon of sacred texts, were coming under the progressive spirit of reform (*mesukan* means "improved"), a generation-long stop on the way to fully modern, secular, coeducation. Political movements gave rise to school networks, which in turn, sponsored publishing houses that produced textbooks and belletristic works as well as periodicals. In saying, then, that children needed schools, the cultural leaders of Yiddishland were also affirming that children needed progressive ideals, solidified through organizations and institutions into ideologies.[67] The Yiddish educational networks in Europe and the Americas generated enough published material to fuel several studies, and their various textbooks certainly invite synthetic scholarly treatment.[68] Although we will occasionally consider a selection culled from a textbook, anthology, or a periodical, the main emphasis of this book is on free-standing works of belles lettres or leisure reading throughout a globally dispersed Yiddishland.

The inextricable institutions of political parties, fraternal organizations, school networks, and publishers all operated under the banner of Yiddish nationalism, which looked somewhat different from that of nations with borders and armies, but which can nevertheless be productively compared and contrasted with other contemporaneous nationalist movements. Children were the future, and improvements in their care were widely understood to advance the interests of the nation. Historian of the Austro-Hungarian Empire Tara Zahra highlights two such innovations, pedagogical reform and child welfare, which arose together at the turn of the twentieth century.[69] The maskilic tendency that fueled the modernization of Yiddish schooling was not entirely different in its aims from the educational priorities embraced by rural ethnic Germans in the Austro-Hungarian Empire before the Great War, which included such novelties as "art education, physical education, and child-centered pedagogy."[70] Yiddish cultural leaders were not insensible to the wave of progressive pedagogies "gaining popularity across Europe and America through the writings of educators such as Ellen Key (Sweden), Maria Montessori (Italy), Celestin Freinet (France), Anton Makarenko (Soviet Union), and John Dewey (United States)."[71] Out of vogue were rote memorization (how the Pentateuch had always been studied, and much Talmud as well) and authoritarian discipline (like the *melamed*'s storied raps on knuckles and backsides), to be replaced with "a pedagogy that would cultivate active bodies, minds, and ultimately, active citizens."[72]

Similar principles informed the founding of the TSYSHO in Warsaw in 1921 as a shared enterprise of Bundist and Zionist socialists, following Polish constitutional reform. The theory underlying such schools had already been laid out before the war, in such works as Esther (Malke) Frumkin's 1910 monograph *Tsu der frage vegen der yudisher folks-shul* (On the Question of the Yiddish Folk School), which outlined the role of "a folk school in the mother tongue" in nationalist political organizing.[73] Participation in TSYSHO schools peaked in the late 1920s, with over two hundred schools enrolling twenty-four thousand students from kindergarten through high school and including an advanced pedagogical institute. In tsarist Russia, Yiddish-language schools were prohibited until 1914, when they began to blossom. The revolution was initially quite friendly to Yiddish education and cultural endeavors, and Yiddish school enrollments increased throughout the 1920s.

Yiddish education gained a foothold in New York City before World War I, with the founding of after-schools by secularists who did not wish to enroll their children in the congregationally based Hebrew schools or Talmud Torahs that had served the needs of American Jews during the nineteenth century.[74] By 1926, four distinct school networks were operating in New York, separated into ideological bands that ranged from politically unaffiliated Yiddishism, to Labor Zionism, to Bundist socialism, to communism.[75] In the curriculum, some of their fault lines were reflected in questions like when or whether to introduce Hebrew instruction into the courses, how to balance Jewish and universalist themes, how to teach about Jewish holidays, and how to mark the bar mitzvah.

The start of the Great War in 1914, with its interruption of the flow of Yiddish printed matter from Europe to the Americas, would mark a decisive moment of cleavage between the two loci of secular Yiddish schooling and cultural advancement, Eastern Europe and New York. It was already clear that American Yiddish-speaking children had a hard time relating to the visual iconography of the youth periodicals being published in Vilna, but there were also thematic differences touching on the treatment of religion and basic ways of life, as well as language differences with respect to the inclusion of Americanisms and the questionable intelligibility of Hebrew-derived words for New York schoolchildren.[76] In 1948, Khayim Shloyme Kazdan (1883–1979) identified the "shprakh-problem": American youth spoke a more lexically impoverished Yiddish than their European counterparts and were therefore less fun to write for. An author, he observes somewhat acerbically, is not a basic language instructor.[77] Another subtle but significant rhetorical gap had to do with the assumption of insularity versus openness toward the surrounding non-Jewish society.[78] In the *goldene medine*, the "golden land" of America, non-Jews were generally warranted to be friendly, so friendly as to threaten Jewish identity by holding out the promise of radical assimilation; it was not so in Poland. The American child, even one belonging to the working class, also grew into a more discerning consumer. "The whole appearance of the books from Europe no longer satisfied him: the paper, the printing, the orthography, and above all the local color and language." These regional differences in taste were another reason, according to Kazdan, to favor periodicals over expensive-to-produce books, since they could more easily meet the demand of smaller segments of a global market.[79]

In the United States, the largest book publishers were the Bund-aligned Arbeter Ring (Workmen's Circle), the Matones imprint of the Sholem Aleichem Folk Institute, and the communist-aligned International Workers Order. But many smaller publishers emerged as well over the course of the 1920s and 1930s, and one-sixth of Yiddish children's literature was published outside of New York by the time Kazdan wrote his comprehensive 1948 survey. The factors stacked against the continued thriving of Yiddish children's literature—genocide in Europe, cultural genocide in the Soviet Union, linguistic assimilation in the United States—would have proven too great to resist in any event. But from Kazdan's immediately postwar perspective, the ideological fragmentation of the market had already played a discernible role in the decline of Yiddish publishing for children. He complained that Yiddish children's literature was answerable to "seven nannies," was stratified "according to the spirit and taste" of each different school network and allied fraternal organization, and distributed each "with its own isolated apparatus."[80] There was no effort at joint publishing or marketing. He speaks in the subjunctive, acknowledging that publishers could have extended the reach of these books with greater cooperation by, for example, appealing to Orthodox schools to adopt the stories would have been suitable for inclusion in their curricula.

Children Need Cultural Authenticity

Kazdan was a Jewish educator, pedagogical theorist, and critic of Yiddish children's literature who was deeply suspicious of . . . children's literature—at least of stories written *specially* for young readers. His position is a complicated and illuminating one. Like many of his cohorts, Kazdan prized literary realism and rejected fantasy and parochialism alike. He wanted older juvenile readers, "youth," to have access to the classic writers who defined the Yiddish canon. Artificially "kiddified" work, he maintained, was harmful to children and ultimately to the Yiddish nation. The schools included works by Peretz and other classic writers in their chrestomathies, but nobody was publishing stand-alone works by the greats for children's leisure reading. This lack of access, maintained Kazdan, "lowers the level of our children's literature, it alienates the youth from the national treasures [*natsyonale oytsres*] and national way of life [*natsyonalen lebnshteyger*]. It alters the character of the book for the young generation. With contrived [*gekinstlte*], specially written and affected [*gemakhte*] works, we won't maintain the character of a literature for the young generation."[81]

From Kazdan's perspective in 1948 New York, each young reader's individual encounter with literature might have implications for the secular Yiddish collective, even if it was rapidly slipping from national to notional. While conceding that children's authors must be constrained by their audience's "vocabulary level and psychology [*psikhik*]," Kazdan aimed to raise children to adult cognitive and aesthetic levels as quickly as possible.[82] Rather than "meeting kids where they were," he hoped to pull them along (or upward) to where the adults were—and elite, discerning adults at that. Kazdan orders up more Enlightenment kale chips even as he frets that nobody is willing to eat them: "The children's literature here has grown away from the *klasikers* and from serious *belles lettres* and has gone down the path of contrived and 'specialized' children's books. Children's poetry and children's fantastic tales have taken the place of honor."[83] Kazdan's tone is disillusioned and, in the aftermath of the Holocaust, understandably valedictory, but his desire to lift children up to intellectual maturity in a way that will bind them to the concerns of the nation is echoed in the discourse of other beleaguered nations and aspirant nationalisms.[84] Zahra characterizes the aim of the ethnic Germans in the Austro-Hungarian Empire as "pedagogical uplift in the rural Heimat."[85] The young people's literature of the Harlem Renaissance, also subject to contestation about whether children needed their books to afford a refuge from harsh realities or an unflinching representation of them, invoked a parallel kind of racial uplift.[86]

In being lifted up—to adulthood, to aesthetic and ethical discernment, to nationalist striving—Yiddish-speaking youth were being called upon to thrive *as Jews*. The culture being created to promote that flourishing figured itself as an ingathering, a concept captured, as befitted an internally bilingual nation, in both the Hebrew term *kinus* and the Yiddish word *zamlung*. During the early bloom of Yiddish children's literature, whether in Europe or North America, this meant drawing on the deep wellsprings of Jewish cultural specificity for the plots and images that would shape storytelling. Like Y. L. Peretz, the distinguished writer Yankev Dinezon had contributed a tale to the Farband textbook. He too received an author copy and wrote back to the New York educators and their students. His letter spoke to both his aspirations for and his expectations of his young readers: "And you, children, dear beautiful Jewish children, you are our Jewish future. Be Jews and be proud of your Jewishness! Learn Yiddish and Jewishness [*yidish un yidishkeyt*], and you will be convinced that you have something to be proud of."[87] Dinezon sought for the next generation of Jewish youth a pride rooted in knowledge, which would be too continually irrigated with new insights to desiccate and harden into empty chauvinism. Closing his note with "Greetings and kisses from afar from one who loves you," Dinezon takes an affectionate, nearly parental tone.

Praising the acuity of his colleague in the Babylonian Talmud, Rabbi Joshua exclaims that "it is not an orphaned generation so long as Rabbi Elazar ben Azarya dwells in its midst."[88] The cultural leaders that founded Yiddish children's literature worried justly about the specter of an orphaned generation. Bialik's poetic speaker had stood, depleted, before his bookcase seeking spiritual refreshment:

> My eye, exhausted, gropes between the lines,
> searching silently among the crowns of the letters,
> and struggling to catch a glimpse there of the tracks left by my soul
> and to find a path to its first stirrings
> in the place where it was born and began its life. . . .
> Like a necklace of black pearls whose string has snapped
> your lines are to me; our pages have been widowed
> and each and every letter has become an orphan

The poem, "Aron hasefarim" (The Bookcase), dates to 1910, but its potency only grew as orphanhood became a grim lived reality on a mass scale because of the

Great War and its dislocations. Orphaned children and orphaned letters were everywhere.[89] Yiddish culturists, at first canonical authors and then trained educators, intervened *in loco parentis* to gather up the remnants of culture and fashion them into new reading materials to fill the bookshelves. The crisis of orphanhood, literal and metaphorical, became the impetus for gathering, collecting, and marshaling existing cultural resources and creating new ones. It was an audacious act of invention. They would have to *make it up* in the double sense of compensating for something they themselves had lacked in their own childhoods and fabricating the old stories into something new.

3

A Sabbath for Socialists

CHILDREN'S LITERATURE BETWEEN THE SACRED AND THE SECULAR

LIPE THE TAILOR knows that beggars can't be choosers, and a poor man must follow whatever work is available. A simple Jew with a rudimentary education, he can just barely manage to mouth the words in the prayerbook. Dwelling with his family in a nameless shtetl, Lipe wanders through Christian villages all week long plying his trade as a patcher of coats. He takes great care to make it home every Friday before sundown. Come Shabbos, his wife's gefilte fish and slow-cooked stew offset the bleak drudgery of Lipe's workaday existence. The day of rest orients the tailor in time, space, and purpose: "He believed that it was thanks to his keeping Shabbos that the Eternal One provided his bread for the week. Lipe really made a point of observing the Sabbath, for truth be told, how better could such a simple Jew, a village tailor who hardly knew the prayers, serve God?"

One winter's Friday, a storm is brewing. Dismissing the fears of the local gentile peasants, Lipe sets a course homeward, steadfast in his belief in his "great God" to get him home safely. As the blizzard gathers strength, though, the familiar forest flattens into a blinding, white wasteland. Sunset finds Lipe in the middle of the woods, bewildered, having lost the path. Will he violate the laws against carrying and traveling on the Sabbath and continue to grope his way homeward, or will he risk his life to stop at sundown and observe the mandated day of rest? With a potent combination of trepidation and resolve, Lipe sets down his pack and walking stick and prepares to succumb to the cold.

We might imagine Lipe's creator to be a pious *melamed*, or schoolteacher, fashioning a tale to convey the sentimental magic of Sabbath observance to his young charges. Yet this tale's actual author, Yankev Fichman, was a well-known socialist educational leader.[1] On the other side of the coin, we might expect secular Yiddish culture during and immediately after the triumph of bolshevism to produce stories and poems that would demonstrate, once and for all, the suppleness of the Ashkenazi fusion language as an instrument for a universal humanism unmarked by the legacy of the Jewish religion. Yet in the early years of Yiddish children's literature, we find a fascination with specifically Jewish folk materials and motifs even among dedicated secularists. Although Fichman wrote more for children in Hebrew than in Yiddish, significant prestige attached to what he did write in *mame-loshn*. This 1924 story, "A Sabbath in the Forest," was published in Warsaw by Kultur-lige, a press with high artistic-literary aspirations and a principled aestheticist bent whose three pillars were "Yiddish popular education, Yiddish literature, and Jewish art."[2] Far from an isolated exception, this tale forms part of a subgenre that celebrates traditional Sabbath observance under circumstances of extreme duress, penned by avowedly secular leftists. The Jewishness of these tales doesn't end with a sentimentalized shtetl setting or incidents loosely pegged to the liturgical calendar—the trappings of Jewish culture; instead, they foreground the robustly *religious* imagery of traditional Sabbath observance. These sabbatarian tales highlight the complicated relationship between sacred and secular as well as the cultural work in which folklore was enlisted during the early decades of the twentieth century.

Today, we tend to think of Jewish observance as a spectrum, with both denominations and individuals falling along a continuum of practices and beliefs. In early twentieth-century Ashkenaz, more binary terms prevailed: People identified and were spoken of as being either pious (*frum*) or not. The "not" might be further described as *fray* (*frei* in German; literally, free, as in freethinking), or *veltlekh* (worldly), or even, in maximally Western terms, as *sekulér*. While the vocabulary for secularism was varied and nuanced, the underlying reality it described was stark.[3] The early decades of the twentieth century were a time of vertiginous Jewish secularization, acculturation, and linguistic assimilation. Within a single generation, enough writers to fill the Great Synagogue in any large city in Eastern Europe had shaved off their beards, doffed their yarmulkes, and donned the short jackets fashionable in Berlin or the loose peasant blouses favored by progressive youth in Moscow. But how far could these freedoms extend before the point of deracination, an end to anything recognizably Jewish? Yiddish (and Hebrew) schooling attempted to point the way toward a robustly and distinctively Jewish, albeit not *religious*, cultural identity for the masses.[4] But what should that kind of cultural Jewishness look like? How would it distinguish itself from traditional religious imperatives, like Sabbath observance, on one hand, and from total assimilation on the other? And could established Jewish practices and concepts be harnessed convincingly to modern programs of social reform?

One strategy for separating Jewishness from Judaism was to recruit folklore, or to be more exacting, the "folkloric." The microgenre of the Yiddish Sabbath tale furnishes an ideal case study for the role of both authentic folklore and more recently invented "fauxklore" in articulating a modern, secular Jewish identity.[5] In the hands of Fichman and similarly inclined authors, even the most traditional Sabbath activities and associations could be invested with new meanings.

Take prayer, for example. We left Lipe freezing in the whited-out forest, his chattering lips reciting the afternoon prayer and his eyes peering through skeletal, leafless branches at a setting winter sun. To the formal liturgy, Lipe adds a spontaneous petition, begging, "Dear, faithful God! Please do something so that my Sabbath won't be spoiled. I, Lipe the Tailor, surely don't need to tell *you* how!" The tailor makes out a little fire through the trees and hesitantly approaches, sensing "that it was not a simple matter." The next thing he knows, a marble palace looms up before him, "a real palace, the likes of which he had never before seen." Reassuringly familiar Sabbath candles burn in all the windows, beckoning him to enter. Inside, Lipe moves among six chambers of escalating luxury, mirroring the six days of the work week. Though each is stocked with all the accoutrements of a Friday night meal, he remains alone until reaching the sixth chamber, where he is welcomed by a congregation of elders (*skeynim*).

God's nearness becomes fully palpable to Lipe only in this congregational setting, through communal singing, a shared meal, and friendly conversation. The story might have privileged the individual's transformative encounter with the divine, but instead it reinforces the presence of God in and through the presence of other human beings. After a Sabbath spent in harmony and comfort with the angelic yet welcoming elders, Lipe witnesses the brief havdalah ceremony, whereupon the palace suddenly disappears, the blizzard abates, and the tailor finds himself back on the forest path just steps from his own shtetl. The resplendent interlude in the forest ends up reinforcing the divinity of Lipe's ordinary gefilte-scented Sabbaths at home. Thereafter, whenever his wife serves her first course, saying

> "Time for the fish, Lipe—it has the taste of paradise!" Lipe the Tailor would smile to himself and reply, "Yes, yes, my Nechama! I've known for a long time that your Shabbos cooking has the true taste of paradise. . . ."
>
> And nobody else in their household knew quite what he meant by those words.[6]

Lipe's extraordinary-ordinary Sabbath might have been observed virtually anywhere in a mythopoeic Ashkenaz unmarked by specific geographical markers. This haziness bestows a folkloric, stylized quality that was typical of secular sabbatarian fiction.

A slim textual thread connects Fichman to the author of another sabbatarian tale, "The Magic Lion," by educator and school system administrator Yankev Pat (1890–1966). In 1912, Fichman edited a chrestomathy, an anthology designed to follow a particular sequence of exemplary texts for an educational purpose, called *Far shul un folk* (For School and Nation), published by the Warsaw house of A. Gitlin. Appearing in a section headed "Belles-lettres and Poetry," the book's third selection is labeled a *folks-mayse* (folk tale) and titled "Der rov un der leyb" (The Rabbi and the Lion). Nearly a decade later, in 1921, Pat released *Der vunderlekher leyb* (The Magic Lion) as a stand-alone storybook with the same publisher. Through the development of this tale, we can trace something of the process whereby an artistically inclined educator laid claim to unattributed folk materials.

Unlike Fichman's humble tailor, Pat's protagonist is "a great rabbi," but his story begins with a similar emphasis on his ordinary Sabbaths at home:

> On Fridays, as Shabbos approached, the great rabbi would don his special clothes and beaver-fur hat, and with his white beard, he looked just like a real angel. Then he would say to his family, "Come, let us welcome the Sabbath Queen!"
>
> Then his face would light up, and his eyes would shine with a pious glow just like that of the holy Shabbos candles that illuminated his household.[7]

Like Lipe, he is accustomed to praying "in his own synagogue" and sharing songful meals "at his own table, full of guests." This homeostasis is disturbed when the rabbi must undertake a twelve-day journey through the desert wilderness for an otherwise unspecified "matter of life and death." Before setting out with an armed caravan, he contracts with one of the party's members to rest with him over the Sabbath and then, together, to make up the lost time and rejoin the group. When that man abandons the plan, the rabbi faces a choice similar to Lipe's: "Different ideas about what to do battled within the rabbi. To go? Then he would violate the Sabbath, which he had never done in his life. Stay in the desert alone? Wild animals might tear him to pieces and devour him, or robbers might attack him." Once the rabbi decides to dismount and observe the day of rest, "an extraordinary holiness shone forth" from his face.

He takes comfort in the familiar rituals of donning festive clothing and reciting the familiar prayers: "He prayed out loud with his whole heart, and the louder he prayed, the calmer and safer he felt, secure in the knowledge that nothing bad would happen to him in the wilderness." After praying, he recites blessings over two loaves of challah bread, punctuating his humble repast with the usual mealtime songs—sung with such gusto that he fails to register the approach of a desert lion, "a real, terrifying lion, the king of the jungle." Noticing the beast, the rabbi takes his impending death philosophically, for "when one's appointed time came, one must die."[8] Instead of attacking, however, the beast lies down and casts the rabbi a reassuring glance. Over the course of the Sabbath, they befriend each other, sharing rituals and meals alike.

Mortal Enemies or Root and Branch?

Pat paints the day of rest as an opportunity for contemplation of and communion with the natural world, whereas Fichman imagines the Sabbath as a day for family togetherness—even if Lipe's absence from home means this value is honored in the breach. By recasting the Sabbath as a temporal and experiential treasure of the Jewish folk, both stories valorize the cessation from labor: a consummately socialist message. With their cross-hatching of halachic observance and humane values, these stories enact a mutual accommodation between traditional Jewish legal ideals and more broadly universalist ones, prodding us to reconsider and complicate our understanding of the relationship between religious and secular. Writing with the benefit of hindsight in 1981, Israel Knox explains the ideology that thrust Jews into modernity at the turn of the twentieth century:

> What, then, is Jewish secularism? It affirms that Jewish reality is pluralistic, within religion and within the community, and hence cannot be equated solely with formal religion and its institutionalized expression which is in the synagogue. It draws a sharp distinction between *Judaism*, as the religion of Jews, and *Jewishness*, as comprising the totality of our historic experience—social and economic, ethical and cultural. Jewish secularism extracts from Judaism its national content and holds that its theological components are a matter of private choice, the prerogative of the individual to accept or reject, but, in either case, as no longer an indispensable condition for Jewishness.[9]

A worldview that came to be regarded as a coherent whole was due, as Gabriella Safran reminds us, to the accretion of countless unitary "cultural practices in public and private—reading, speaking, performing, and imagining themselves in ways unconnected to older religious norms."[10] In the case of the Sabbath tale, however, the practice of reading is not so much *unconnected* to older religious norms as unconstrained by them.

At mid-century (1948), Yudl Mark, an author (for adults and children), grammarian, and pedagogical theorist, published a polemical disquisition troubling the binary between "religious" and "secular" and teasing apart the gradations among "assimilated," "secular," and "worldly." He excoriates the anti-Jewishness of some would-be secularists and argues for the transmission, through the secular Yiddish schools, of a rich corpus of Jewish cultural materials that unabashedly draw their color and shine from traditional religious observance. He even utilizes sabbatarian imagery to make his point, maintaining that while secularism does not bear *sole* responsibility for the regnant assimilation, the ideology has made it tacitly acceptable for Jewish homes to forego holidays and "any hint of Shabbos." This lack of orientation in traditional Jewish time in turn leaves the weekdays "so utterly empty, so workaday-gray." The "finest and deepest qualities" of the idealistic, modern, progressive Jew of the twentieth century were nourished, Mark insists, "with the juices of generations-old yidishkeyt," and contemporary Yiddish educators must bring forth new fruit that retains "a Jewish flavor" from a four-thousand-year-old tree. After all, "How can a branch disown its trunk [*shtam*] and spit on its roots?"[11]

More recently, David Biale observed of "secular" and "religious," "These two mortal enemies are very much defined by and through the other. And not only does it appear that religion and secularism in modernity are deeply implicated in each other, but it may well be that their contemporary entanglement owes something to the way the secular emerged out of the religious, not so much its polar negation as its dialectical product."[12] With respect to the Sabbath tale, adopting Biale's dialectical view allows us to notice not only the surprising degree of Jewish legal punctilio in these tales but also the accent on nonlegalistic values that dovetail more obviously with the concerns of modernizing reformers. Shabbos is indeed kept, but with subtly different emphases than in traditional *aggadot* (rabbinic lore) or Hasidic tales.

Why the Sabbath?

Why should hopes for national regeneration of an active, energetic polity be rooted in a weekly mandated period of rest? Fichman's story literalizes the image of "a palace in time," Abraham Joshua Heschel's signature designation for the Sabbath. Heschel claims that "the meaning of the Sabbath is to celebrate time rather than space."[13] For members of a deterritorialized nation, there is a certain allure to investing in a temporal edifice from which none might banish or exclude them. As a particularist practice, Sabbath observance valorizes the minority and subaltern status of European Jews. Sabbatarian tales dramatize their protagonists' concern to uphold the strictures of the day against the rhythms of a majority non-Jewish world. But demarcated as a palace in time, the Sabbath also represents a subversion of the capitalist ethos wherein time is money. In Pat's story, the Sabbath is an occasion for the leisurely contemplation of nature, whereas in Fichman's it is a day to privilege family above getting and spending or even just working to subsist. The worker's empowered relationship to time and prerogative to cease labor are the linchpins of a socialist critique of capitalism.

The weekly cessation of work is transformed from a religious obligation to a period of discretionary time that the worker might lavish on family and personal pursuits. Readers didn't need to actually *believe* in a supernatural divinity to understand that if God could be said to own that weekly span of time, then the boss did not. In wistfully evoking a secular claim on the Sabbath that never fully materialized in fact, Knox traces socialist sabbatarianism to Chaim Zhitlovsky, one of the original theorists of intentional Jewish secularism. Zhitlovsky saw Shabbos as "the sacred *social* holiday in which there was realized for the first time, to a certain degree, the *right to rest* for the slave and the worker."[14]

Not only did the Sabbath tale speak to these politically and philosophically immediate concerns, but it also laid compelling claim to a usable Jewish past, even as it consigned Jewish religious heritage safely *to* the past. The stylized protagonists of these stories are distinctly retrograde.[15] Pat's characterization of his hero is telling in this regard: "A long time ago, there lived a great rabbi who always kept the Sabbath faithfully and never forgot to act as it is written in the Torah and the Holy Books."[16] This characterization presents a fairly distant if sanguine view of Jewish religious observance, as if "the Torah," broadly understood, were absolute and monolithic. It reads like a description from without. An observer at closer range would likely have recognized that a halachic lifestyle tends to be conceived of in more multifarious terms by its practitioners and is therefore not easily given to such breezy summation. Although the authors embed a great deal of information about the laws and rituals of the Sabbath, instructing their readers was not a primary goal. As David Fishman observes of another 1912 chrestomathy, the seminal *Dos yidishe vort* (The Yiddish/Jewish Word), "the book did not teach children to perform the

Sabbath or holiday rituals per se or intend for them to return to the lifestyle of the nineteenth century shtetl. It attempted to implant in them favorable images of the rituals, figures, and objects of the old way of life as part of their Jewish national consciousness."[17] Pat and Fichman contributed to the rearing not of a generation of Sabbath observers but rather of a generation of future Sabbath nostalgists, who would feel a sense of connection and belonging to this quintessentially Jewish island in time but would likely not choose to dwell upon it every seven days. The lines between secular and religious were altogether fuzzier than they might first appear. While conventional wisdom dictated, according to Fishman, that "Yiddishists were archsecularists" who "rejected traditional Judaism in its entirety," this depiction is "more a caricature than a portrait."[18] Staunchly secularist schools incorporated much traditional Jewish content recast as folk literature.[19] The bridge between traditional religiosity and the secular Jewish present was made of folklore.

Folkloric Jewishness

Under the rubric of folklore, secularizing culturists allowed themselves to cherish the Sabbath as a national patrimony, a behavioral and emotional technology meant to engineer rest, refreshment, and resistance. Beginning in the final decade of the nineteenth century, but accelerating after 1905, gathering authentic folkloric materials was a widespread grassroots prerogative; some of the topics for collection and scrutiny had to do with children and their experiences, and these resources were used in turn in Yiddish schools.[20] The folkloric was also considered a wellspring of inspiration at the loftiest reaches of high culture. We might trace an entire literary genealogy of modernist heirs to the protomodernist Rabbi Nakhmen, with his folklorizing, neoromantic tales of rivers and deserts, princesses, kings, beggars, and enchantment. Maskilic writer I. M. Dik embedded "a veritable encyclopedia of Eastern European Jewish folklore" in his fiction.[21] The classic Yiddish writers all wrote in folkloric modes, each inflected with its own distinctive sensibility. Eliezer Shteynbarg animated his verse fables with imagery and situations from the demotic shtetl, and the lyric poet Itsik Manger reimagined the biblical past as a folk source and transposed it onto Jewish Eastern Europe.

Two figures stand out, however, for composing forerunners of the Sabbath tales under consideration here: Y. L. Peretz and S. An-sky (1863–1920). Both artists mounted ethnographic expeditions (though on differing scales) to collect authentic Jewish folk materials. Peretz used to pay neighborhood domestics half a ruble to a ruble for each song they brought him.[22] Not only were they both personally enamored of the stories, songs, sayings, and practices that they accumulated, but both men also utilized them as the "raw materials" for their own refined, high-literary production.[23] For both Peretz and An-sky, folklore offered the armature of a new religion.[24] In his neo-Hasidic tales, Y. L. Peretz found a way to channel religious populism, foregrounding interpersonal kindness and acts of ethical supererogation and displacing scholarly erudition and other trappings of rabbinic elitism.[25] An-sky enacted a similar transformation of Talmudic and Hasidic folk materials, coming to regard folklore as a new Oral Torah that promised not only to consolidate the Jewish past and secure the Jewish future but also to secure revolution by other means.[26] "To educate our children in a national Jewish spirit," insisted An-sky at a conference devoted to showcasing his ethnographic expedition, "we must give them folktales, folk songs, in short what forms the basis of children's education for other peoples."[27] By his reckoning, ethnographers and folklorists, as well as the belletristic authors who utilized folk materials, were the people's new secular sages.

David Roskies has characterized the ethnographic surveys of the shtetl for the purpose of collecting folklore and folksongs undertaken by young cultural workers as "slumming," a bracing descriptor. When these naïve materials were brought back to the cities and made over by priestly authors into stylish *folkloric* literature to promote the cohesion of national identity, the artists might similarly be said to be "slumming" in a conjured past: "The neoromantic writers in Yiddish and Hebrew could appropriate folklore, fantasy, and storytelling only as something bracketed in time, something removed from the industrial present by virtue of its style, simplicity, marvelous occurrences, dualistic schemes, and heroic struggles." If writing fauxklore for adults could be characterized as carrying out "an act of noblesse oblige," then writing for children in a similar vein could justify what might otherwise be imagined as a debasement of an author's artistic aspirations.[28]

"Secular writers," notes Biale, "sometimes claimed that the historical culture of the folk, as opposed to that of the rabbis, could inspire a nonreligious renaissance of Jewish culture in the modern period."[29] Ironically, the "historical culture of the folk" often took rabbis and other figures of piety as its subject. Hasidic culture, well established for over two centuries, had already introduced a robust strain of populism into discourse about rabbis and religious devotion. Yet the Sabbath wonder tales under discussion here do not entirely conform to the convention; they celebrate punctilious observance of the Sabbath rituals, not only the marking of the day through positive ritual performances but also abhorrence at the idea of violating the day's prohibitions.[30] Whereas the humanistic Peretz always underscores righteousness *bein adam le-havero* (the interpersonal), these stories remove almost all human actors besides their protagonists. Nevertheless, the sabbatarian tales affirm the value of community in the breach ("A Sabbath in the Forest") and friendship, however unconventional ("The Magic Lion").

Sources and Antecedents: From Folklore to Fauxklore

Neither Pat nor Fichman was telling a wholly original tale. The collection of tales first published in Basel as the *Mayse-bukh* includes several selections wherein the protagonists are rewarded for honoring the Sabbath, but one of them appears to be a direct antecedent of Pat's story.[31] Though three Jews are traveling together in this earlier tale, only the protagonist decides to pause and rest at the advent of the Sabbath. He is kept company by a friendly bear, who devours the pious man's two feckless companions after the day's conclusion. Of course, the wild beast in Pat's and other more recent retellings is a lion rather than a bear. In medieval Jewish folklore, the lion motif was associated with themes of repayment and the sequence of potency-impotency-restored potency.[32] For example, *the Mayse-bukh* itself also includes the story of Rabbi Shmuel He-hasid, who rescues a lion from a pursuing leopard and then is invited to mount the beast, which transports him to his destination.[33] It is hardly surprising that the motif of the beastly Sabbath companion was eventually combined with that of the lion. In 1802, Eliezer Paver rewrote several of the stories and homilies included in *the Mayse-bukh* and published them under the title *Sefer hapleyes* oder *gerimte geshikhte* (Book of Wonders, or the Famous History), which was reprinted more than twenty times through the nineteenth and twentieth centuries. The story takes on new life as a Hasidic tale that dates back in written form at least to an 1896 work published in Krakow and possibly all the way back to Moshe ben Menahem Mendl Raysher's 1867 collection, *Sha'arei Yerushalayim*.[34] The sort of collection in which this story originally appeared in print was part of a publishing spurt in the last decade of the nineteenth century, a veritable craze for *mayses peyles/ploim*, or wonder tales. In addition to the volume of wonder tales [*Mayses noraim ve-niflaim*] that appeared in Krakow in 1896, publications with similar titles sprang up in Munkacz, Krakow, and Lemberg within a few years.

Then, of course, there is the more immediate antecedent in Fichman's 1912 chrestomathy intended for use in both daytime and evening schools. Not only does Fichman's 1912 folk tale already have in place the plot of the rabbi and lion spending the Sabbath together mutually unharmed, but in fact the narrative frame is significantly more detailed in the earlier story. Instead of transpiring in a vague desert locale, the folk tale explains that the Jews of Jerusalem (Sephardim, it specifies, efficiently accounting for all the "exotic" elements present in the story) needed to send an emissary to the Jewish community of Egypt in order to solicit funds for the support of indigents and scholars. Thus, the rabbi of the tale is given a specific mission—charitable collection—that involves a specific itinerary through what must be the Sinai Desert. In Pat's retelling, the protagonist undertakes a task of life-and-death importance (*pikuah nefesh*), but its nature is left unspecified. The caravan of other travelers is made up of Arabs (*Araber*), not generic gentiles, and the leader of the party is identified as a sheikh (*shakh*). The rabbi's original arrangement—the one that must fall through in order to create the conflict—is slightly different as well. In Pat's version, he contracts with one individual member of the caravan to spend the Sabbath with him, whereas the earlier folk tale has him paying the sheikh to hold the entire caravan for him. When Friday afternoon arrives, however, the sheikh laughs at him and tells him he cannot hold up the entire caravan for one man. As he considers whether to travel on with the group or to rest alone for Shabbos, the emissary in the folk tale couches his reasoning in more legalistic terms than Pat's rabbi: His coming to harm in the desert is a matter of doubt [*safek*], whereas violating the Sabbath laws would mean certain renunciation of his heavenly portion (*oylem habe*). Certainty overrules doubt in Jewish legal discourse. The folk tale also places more emphasis on the emissary's interaction with other members of the caravan, who are divided between those who scoff at him as a madman and those who shake their heads in pity at his self-endangerment.

Pat's version emphasizes the companionship that develops between rabbi and lion. In the unattributed folk tale, the emissary eats and drinks all his provisions himself, and the lion presents himself only after the traveler has finished his dinner. Pat has the rabbi share his bread, and the author also slips in the didactic and relatively minute halachic detail that in the absence of wine, one might bless the Sabbath over the bread. In Pat's story, the two figures "pray" together: the rabbi by reciting the Shabbos liturgy and the lion by roaring. Pat's lion is altogether more anthropomorphic, eating the Sabbath meals, bellowing his leonine prayers, and even going for a stroll [*shpatsir*] during the long, idle afternoon. Both versions feature the lion speeding the rabbi all through Saturday night to overtake the caravan, but the folk tale again emphasizes how they are received by the rest of the caravan party, and this detail presents the single most significant difference between the two versions. Not only does the sheikh humble himself and beg forgiveness for leaving the rabbi behind, but the wonderstruck onlookers acknowledge that a holy man is in their midst, and they confer upon him the moniker Ariel, meaning "lion of God." And so, the story tells us in conclusion, "In the city of Hebron, there can be found to this day the Ariel family, which descends from that holy man." The folk tale, at least as it appears in Fichman's chrestomathy, is an etiological tale explaining the surname of the Ariel family and its presence in Hebron (the staging place for the caravan). As such, and given the geographical specificity, this tale might not be a wonder tale at all according to a narrow definition; it might rather be counted as a fable.[35] What is important for our analysis is not to categorize the tale strictly but to observe that Pat drops the narrative frame, ending the tale with the traveler's dismount from his beastly chariot and the lion's swift withdrawal from the scene. Presumably Pat excludes the material about the origins of the Ariel family because his audience is not a Hasidic one, and there is no reason why that etiology would hold any particular resonance or yield a frisson of discovery at the tale's conclusion. To make the tale more general—by stripping it of spatial and identity markers—was to render it more mythopoeic. Ironically, removing some of the traces of the actual folk materials made Pat's tale *seem* more stylized and folkloric than its antecedents. Thus is fauxklore made.

The Rhetorical Grammar of the Sabbath Tale

In his anatomy of the Russian folk tale, the folklorist and early structuralist critic Vladimir Propp discerns a category he calls the wonder tale (*volshebnaia skazka*).[36] Incorporating motifs of magic, enchantment, or the fantastic, although not exclusively defined by them, the wonder tale represents to Propp "the most splendid variety of artistic folk prose . . . full of high ideals and elevated aspirations."[37] In Jewish letters, the wonder tale originated in the aggadic literature of the Talmud, then wended its way through medieval story collections (notably the *Mayse-bukh*, 1602) and thence through the corpus of Hasidic tales—a genre that passed from an original oral form to earnest and faithful redaction in the religious sphere and ultimately to modernist reworking as described above. Passing the spiritual test of deciding to keep the Sabbath despite all environmental obstacles, the hero receives help through supernatural, magical means of unspecified but presumably divine origin. He is rewarded with the restoration of the status quo.

Propp's compositional syntax of motifs and how they function in relation to one another offers a useful springboard as we attempt a similar analysis of the Sabbath tale. The Russian wonder tale opens with spatial indeterminacy, which corresponds to the temporal indeterminacies in Western European folk-tale traditions ("once upon a time").[38] The Sabbath tale similarly unfolds in a fuzzy locale: an unnamed and therefore archetypal shtetl or, more exotically, a *midber* (desert, wilderness). The homeostasis and well-being of the initial situation are emphasized, and the action only begins when misfortune or privation compromises this stability.[39] Often, the rupture is associated with a journey, as is the case with these Sabbath tales. Here, the Shabbos tale begins to diverge from the Russian wonder tale, for in Propp's model the absence of the hero from home is associated with prohibitions, and "the prohibition in folklore is always violated. Otherwise there would be no plot."[40] Part and parcel of the Sabbath tale, by contrast, is the faithful upholding of a set of prohibitions—chiefly against carrying or traveling on the sacred day. Yet other aspects of the tales do run parallel: the presence of two archetypal kingdoms (matching up with Fichman's binary between Jewish and gentile spaces); the presence of donors or gift givers, including animals, who put themselves at the hero's disposal; and the defining plot point of test and reward for the hero.[41] The upholding of the Sabbath corresponds to this function, and the marriage and crowning typical of the Russian wonder tale are replaced by a new appreciation for the ordinary domesticity that the resolution of the conflict restores.

The forest and desert are liminal places of uncertainty and danger in both Jewish folk and high literature, with the arboreal settings that would have been familiar to Eastern European readers taking on particular prominence. The forest figures in Hasidic tales about apostasy, attempted rape, and cannibalism and is frightening enough to require the composition of an amulet specifically against "fear of the forest."[42] For S. Y. Abramovitsh's Mendele, the nighttime forest holds out "the wildest and most frightening notions."[43] Even for Sholem Aleichem's Tevye, the forest is a site of uncertainty, fluid identity, and vulnerability, a stretch to be traversed—as with Fichman's tailor—between opposing certainties. At the same time, the forest features positively in Hasidic literature as a site for seclusion in prayer [*hisboydedes*] and in connection with the recognition of the thirty-six Hidden Righteous, the small cadre of humble, holy individuals in whose merit the world is sustained, according to legend. These more positive associations still rely on the forest's capacity for concealment, though. In Fichman's tale, the space surrounding the forest is starkly binary: On one side lies Lipe's familiar shtetl and on the other, the non-Jewish peasant villages where he works as an itinerant tailor and patcher. The separation between home and away corresponds, in turn, to those between Shabbos and workaday, protected and exposed, inside and outside, and Jewish and gentile.[44]

Fichman's punchline at the conclusion of the story enacts a sort of martial-arts maneuver on the wonder tale itself, using its own weight to overturn its signification. Lipe spends the most materially luxurious, ritually fulfilling Sabbath imaginable, only to realize in its aftermath that the tunes favored by the holy elders in their palace are the same ones he knows from his ordinary *shtibl* (small, informal synagogue), and the lavish, magical meal delights him with the same flavors found in the humble dishes that his wife, Nechama, prepares week after week. Thus is the cumulative weight of the enchanted palace—with all its luxury—commensurate with, if not subordinated to, the homely rituals of Lipe's regular Sabbaths. Who needs a magical palace, Fichman seems to suggest, when the properties of the Sabbath itself are so elevating and divinely magical?

Postures of Simplicity: Folkstimlekhkeyt as an Aesthetic Ideal

"Folklore" and "folkloric" as I use them here are the most straightforward English equivalents for a nuanced Yiddish nomenclature. With his *Folkstimlekhe geshikhtn* (Folkloric Tales), Peretz introduced a term so new to Yiddish literature that the typesetter for the first advertisements of the work mistook it for *folks shtimlekhe* ("in the folk voice").[45] Shoshke Erlich draws the distinction between *folks-mayse* and *folkstimlekhe mayse* (or *geshikhte*) as one between artistic intentionality and spontaneously occurring, "found" discourse. A folk tale is anonymous and pertains to the realm of folklore; a *folkstimlekh* tale is carefully constructed, either on the basis of authentic folk motifs or out of the imagination of an artist who composes in stylized "folktale wording" (*stilizirt . . . folks-maysedikn nusekh*). But the term *folkstimlekh* is not a universally accepted one. Erlich's note is immediately followed by Mordkhe Schaechter's brief history of the term and a critique of its ambiguity and his proposal, as a replacement, of the term *poshut-folkish* (plain folk-ish).[46] Based on the term's appearance in Harkavy's descriptive dictionary of 1893, Schaechter concludes that *folkstimlekh* must have been circulating decades before Peretz's story collection popularized the term, even though he can't point to a specific attestation. After explaining the High German abstract-noun-to-adjective formation *tümlich* (, Schaechter offers a piquant definition: "noent tsum poshetn folk, in gayst un gust funem poshetn folk" (close to the plain folk, in the spirit and taste of the plain folk). The style of narration of these sabbatarian tales lies somewhere between the poles of *folkstimlekhkeyt*, by which I mean the high-art posture of folksiness, and *folkshprakh*, by which I mean the popular vernacular—although they sit closer to the former than the latter.

One marker of high-culture folklore is lyricism about the natural world. In a sketch that S. Y. Abramovitsh ultimately used to introduce his collected works, the author presents his mediating alter ego, Mendele, as a romantic, lovesick for the beauties of nature:

> And as for going to do *tashlikh*, such a serious Jewish ritual, to cast off our sins—for me it becomes a scenic stroll. When I'm supposed to be reciting all those words, I stare at the river and let my mind wander over to the green marsh that extends all the way off into the distance. I see before me a running, babbling brook, geese swimming proudly. A breeze blows gently; tall reeds whisper their secrets; the brook burbles and reflects a weeping willow, its branches bending into the water. . . . The sky is clear, the air fresh, a Godly silence is in the valleys, hills, and groves all around. Something draws my soul, it longs, craves—Oh, Master of the Universe!—I myself don't know what for. . . . I live for these walks. In field and forest, I am not at all what I am in the city: I'm free, slipped from the yoke. What is "wife" to me, or "child," or "Jew," or "worry"? I take pleasure, lose myself in delight at the Almighty's creation; I give myself over with all my senses and get drunk on the beauty of God's world![47]

How similar this seems, at first blush, to the tone Fichman uses to describe the tailor Lipe, as he wraps up the work week of a summer Friday: "From the very moment he set out for home, he could feel all the cares of the week leave him, and his heart would fill with the joy of the holy day. This was especially true in the beautiful summer weather, when the fields were so green and fragrant they seemed to sing, and God himself took pleasure in the little world he had created."[48] However, a dramatic transformation had taken place during the half century between the publication of these two texts. Abramovitsh ironically labels his mouthpiece's weakness for the natural world an "affliction" or "pathology" at odds with his responsibilities as a family man and an upright Jew. By the 1920s, that veil of irony had fallen away, and lyricism about the natural world, in sync with Jewish observance, was celebrated as an earnest ideal. Instead of feeling a tension between religious duty and the seductive delights of nature, as Mendele does, Lipe integrates his anticipation of the Sabbath rest with his appreciation of the natural world through which he passes on his way home. Whereas Abramovitsh presents a conflict between nature and culture, Fichman and his contemporaries reorder Jewish experience to present nature *as* culture.

Indeed, modernizing Jewish culturists employed lyrical descriptions of the natural world, especially the Sabbath and holidays, in order to synchronize Jewish liturgical time with natural time as marked by universally recognized days and seasons.[49] Yankev Pat's desert-bound rabbi presumably mirrors the omniscient narrator's evident satisfaction in the Friday sunset: "As with every dusk, one side of the sky—the western side—glowed a wonderful red, and the sun set in a golden sea and withdrew itself into night, while on the eastern side of the sky, the darkness was heavy with lonesome shadows. From the east blew an evening wind that wafted the night clouds about the sky."[50] Surely it is only because of his unusually exposed situation that the protagonist has leisure and opportunity to notice the dramatic sunset; were he at home, he would likely be inside the synagogue praying with a quorum at dusk.

Not only is this lyricism lavished on the natural world, but the socialist sabbatarians extend it to ritual observance as well, imbuing the day itself with a rosy glow that fuses the natural setting and the ritual performances into an aestheticized unity. When Lipe finally enters the chamber where the elders are singing the psalms that greet the Sabbath, the narrator observes:

> Suddenly he could hear a soft song arising from somewhere, floating from afar and coming closer. And what a song—a tenor so pure it would break your heart, then a moment of silence, falling like soft dewdrops and pouring out like a lively stream amid the grassy steppe. The song arose from the depths and spread itself, like the wings of a mighty bird, over all the chambers of the palace, reaching higher and higher. Lipe didn't move a muscle but let the sweet song pour into every part of him. It lifted him up and carried him around like a light feather. He was amazed that the melody seemed so familiar. Couldn't he have sworn he'd heard it once in his own little synagogue?[51]

In its intricate interweaving of nature imagery (dewdrops, stream, steppe) with prayer imagery, this passage stretches toward the sublime. In doing so, it supports a second, more adult reading of Lipe's journey: Perhaps the Sabbath respite that he finds is his eternal rest. Some children's literature is bisemic, or intended to be interpreted on different levels by children and adults.[52] More sophisticated—or world-weary—readers might hear in this narrative echoes of Hans Christian Andersen's tragic literary fairy tale "The Little Match Girl," with its portrayal of death by exposure to the cold being eased by visions of spiritual warmth.[53]

The Invention of Childhood and Cultural Recapitulation

Although children's texts sometimes encoded adult messages, folklore and fantasy were considered especially well-suited for young readers. As Hans-Heino Ewers observes, "In terms of their poetic and literary competence, 'youth' and 'folk' are on the same level, no matter how different they may be in other respects."[54] This helps to explain why the classic fairy tales collected by the Brothers Grimm and Alexander Afanasyev or authored by Charles Perrault and Hans Christian Andersen were marketed and received as children's literature despite their often-dark subject matter. This linkage of youth and folk, the vestige of a time before the "invention of childhood," is equally chauvinistic toward both children and adults.

Boris Levinson, a Bundist educational theorist who maintained, along with Yudl Mark, that Yiddish language alone was insufficient as a basis for Yiddish cultural flourishing, argued for transposing Jewish rituals to a secular key. Kindergartners, he asserts, naturally live "in their own fantastic, enchanted world." In a traditionally observant Jewish family, the four- to six-year-old's developmentally typical tendency toward magical thinking has fused with the child's experiences of Passover, Yom Kippur, and the weekly Sabbath, after which "the other six days of the week are only a long, dreary tail/aftermath (ek)." Levinson has observed the children of freethinkers pining after the holiday candles in neighboring homes and asks on their behalf, "What can be given to this child instead, if the parents no longer believe in it?"[55] His answer in 1910 was: an entire corpus of children's literature that had yet to come into being. Levinson's embrace of the mysterious, the fantastic, and the heroic for children was colored by the fin de siècle Romantic view of childhood discussed in the previous chapter.

Children's status as national subjects was important, but cultivating their individual personhood was paramount and would ultimately tend toward fuller national flourishing. The whole cultural diet couldn't be cruciferous vegetables. The evidence, according to Kenneth Moss, points away from the idea of the Jewish educator as "proverbial instiller of national patriotism." A child was not generally regarded as a passive vessel waiting to be filled by various nation-building or reformist ideologies, "but a budding individuality deserving access to the full range of human experience."[56] But the idea of varying children's literary diet with fantasy—or with fantasy in the guise of folklore—eventually came to seem as passé as Romanticism itself. Felicity Hughes questions the reflexive designation of fantasy as befitting youth:

> The first and major impediment to useful criticism . . . lies in the acceptance by critics of the idea that fantasy is peculiarly suitable for children, not for adults. In order to interpret this supposed fact in a way that attributes no inferiority to children (a considerable feat) many critics rely on some version of the "culture epoch" theory which states that individual human development recapitulates the development of the race. According to this view children are primitives and are most appropriately served by primitive literature-myths, fables, folk tales and fairy tales.[57]

Hughes lays out the idea of cultural recapitulation: The individual's trajectory mirrors that of the collective, and the impressionable child accepts that which the discerning adult rejects. This ideology received a specifically Jewish elaboration in the Haskalah, when cultural leaders envisioned the maturation of the folk from naiveté to sophistication, corresponding to the passage from childhood to adulthood.[58] Many Yiddishist pedagogues and culture makers implicitly expected that individuals must move from piety to freethinking as part of their developmental maturation. Though their ultimate aspiration might have been toward cosmopolitan universalism, socialists especially chose to foreground the materials of Jewish tradition for children, however secularized or modernized, so they might, first, "know their own." Bundist pedagogue Shloyme Gilinsky, when asked why he taught his charges about Yom Kippur, said that "in order to be able to say no, one must first understand the meaning of yes."[59] This impulse to master the uniquely Jewish, to accept before rejecting, underlay the most common organizational scheme for the school chrestomathies: tracing an arc from the particular to the universal.

In his editor's introduction to the 1912 chrestomathy that included the lion story, Yankev Fichman bemoans the difficulty of bridging the demands of *shul* and *folk*, that is, "regular" and evening schools. He complains that the mandate to satisfy both kinds of reader (schoolchild and working-class adult) has "foreclosed the possibility of holding fast to a certain program, and set a different stamp" on the book, without specifying what he thinks has been lost. The solution he hits upon is aestheticism; he avers an unyielding commitment to gathering only works of high aesthetic merit, for "to educate children on artistic works means to educate them on true works, for only in authentic [*ekht*] art do the deep truths of life, morality, and beauty express themselves."[60] It would have been all too easy, in a moment steeped in folkloric consciousness, to reduce the corpus of Yiddish children's literature to a set of ethnographic data points. The critic and theorist Shmuel Charney explicitly warned against this tendency, asserting that only the "aesthetic" interest in folklore could ultimately nourish and regenerate the Jewish people: "[It is] more than a 'key' [to the psychology of the 'folk']. For us, it is a treasure, something which we wish to enjoy in itself. We seek in it not the soul of the people but an additional soul [*neshome yesera*]. We treasure it according to the artistic pleasure, not the scientific utility, which it brings us."[61]

Here again, now in a theoretical vein, is the dialectical tension between religion and secularity in the quest for an authentic, modern yiddishkeyt. The functionalist, flatly ethnographic interest in Jewish folklore bespoke, to Charney, the workaday, whereas the aesthetic interest was, Sabbath-like, both ornamental and refreshing. As we have seen with Yudl Mark and Boris Levinson, such juicy sabbatarian imagery hydrates the theory of many a socialist pedagogue. They wished to reveal to their charges the additional soul present only on Shabbos, only in Yiddish, a treasure to be valued beyond its instrumental use: Obviously the harbingers of the brave new secular world were not entirely ready to dispense with the Sabbath and all that it represented to them. Call it a cultural lion's paw. Once Shabbos ends, the king of the jungle speeds his new friend, the rabbi, through the desert to catch up with the caravan. The lion then disappears into the wilderness, but the echoing thunder of his footsteps lingers.

4

Room

THE FOUR WALLS OF JEWISH BOYHOOD

THE BOY'S father is an important man of affairs: a banker, perhaps, or a timber contractor to the tsar's army. He might trade commodities futures on the exchange. Or maybe he's preoccupied with a different kind of exchange altogether: the give and take of wending, never-ending Talmudic discussion. Let's say he spends his days and many of his nights in the *beyz-medresh*, the house of study, immersed in a form of intellectual and spiritual labor understood to sustain the entire Jewish people; he has no time for frivolity. He hopes that today marks the beginning of his son's pathway toward the family business.

However mundane or holy the father's work, it will have to wait on this special morning. A paternal obligation beckons.[1] Then again, maybe just a parental duty: Perhaps the lad's mother will be entrusted with the sacred task at hand.[2] She might recruit the assistance of the teacher's aide, whose helpfulness is inscribed in the very name of his position, *bahelfer*. After all, she has watched her son closely, observed his behavioral and mental maturity.[3] She calculates the competing claims on her own time: keeping a stall in the marketplace, say, while managing the younger children underfoot. *She* declares that the time has come.

Whether by father, mother, or *bahelfer*, the boy is wrapped in a woolen prayer shawl and thus secured against so much as a peep from God's own pesky paparazzo, the evil eye. The veil protects in both directions: Safeguarded from view, neither will the boy glimpse any impurity en route to the nearly cultic sacrifice of his childhood leisure.[4] He learned long ago to walk, jump, run—but today the precious young bundle is carried. Yiddish writer Shimen Frug immortalized the memory of his school initiation, which would have occurred in 1867, in a memoir as brief as it is honeyed. The day engenders mixed emotions: Frug's reluctance protrudes from his acquiescence to the inevitable milestone as surely as a sharp elbow or knee pokes out from the enveloping tallis:

> I turned seven, and my mother—may she be well—said, "Well, it's time, time to start *kheyder*, my child! Done, finito, enough frolicking all over the place, flitting about free and easy as a bird, fresh and happy as the wind."
>
> So Avreml the teacher's assistant draped me, wrapped me all up, in an old, yellow prayer shawl and took me off to *kheyder*.
>
> It was a beautiful, brisk, bright morning. Fine and bright, pure and fresh, the sunbeams poured in through the little window in the *kheyder* and sparkled on the rabbi, the prayerbook, the table. And the examination began: "Just tell me, young man, what is this?" "An *aleph*." "Right!" "And this?" "A *heh*." "And this?" "A *tof*."
>
> And with each letter, with each answer, endless honey cake, raisins, candy, nuts, and almonds rained down on me. And the rabbi, Rov Binyumen (may he have a radiant afterlife), said, "You see? Little angels are throwing this to you, my child! You should study Torah eagerly, study Torah and study Wisdom [*khokhme*]. And remember, my child, he who does not wish to learn remains forever blind."[5]

The teacher's "examination" is gentle by design: a pretext to shower the initiate with sweets, as if from on high. Later on, sticks may prevail (or cattails, riding crops, belts, etc.—according to the cumulative historical record), but that very first school morning was a time for carrots.[6] Though some of the particulars vary, Frug's recollections show an extraordinary degree of continuity in this ceremony throughout medieval, early modern, and fully modern Ashkenaz.[7]

The pedagogy of positive reinforcement is woven into the instructions laid out in the *Brantshpigl* (1596) for its largely feminine readership: "When the child first begins to study, he is doted upon."[8] The description in Tsvi Hirsh Koydnover's ethical treatise *Kav-hayashar* (Frankfurt, 1705) dilates on the segment of the ritual enacted in the classroom. The teacher recites the alphabet forward and backward, reading the letters off a chart or tablet and prompting the new student to repeat after him. They progress to reciting Deuteronomy 33:4 ("Moses commanded us the Torah, etc.") and the opening verse of Leviticus. Rather than enjoying sweets thrown from on high, Koydnover describes the child licking honey from the alphabet tablet, and in that way incorporating the sweetness of the learning to come. On this liminal day, the boy is especially susceptible to impurity, so he is carried home with his eyes shielded once again and guarded all afternoon from the approach of any menstruating woman. His parents fast throughout the rest of the day, eating only that evening at a feast they sponsor for the poor and dispensing charity according to their means. "Then," concludes Koydnover, "the father can be confident that the child will be God-fearing."

Most of these ritual intricacies don't survive into the post–World War I era of modernized schooling. Yet the kheyder endured as an important institution in Yiddish fiction and life-writing for adults and children alike, and its pupils often took part in some sort of school initiation designed to link learning with sweetness. "School," of course, would be a generous designation for the one-room, usually home-based primary educational setting where elementary-aged boys were instructed in basic Jewish textual literacy by rabbis who famously ran the gamut from nurturing to casually irascible to downright abusive. The kheyder-as-topos evokes thick layers of lived experience: the feel of a hard, wooden bench beneath thinly upholstered posteriors, the draft creeping into a poorly insulated room, the jockeying of boisterous boys for a prized seat near the wood-burning stove, the sting of rapped knuckles at a wrong answer or wandering attention, and the undercurrents of competition and jocularity flowing through an all-male space.

The "room" of this chapter's title is meant to evoke the tension between the contradictory elements that constituted the kheyder: on one hand, confinement to a single schoolroom dedicated to reproducing a narrowly construed, ideally educated Jewish male. Enrollment, as Frug understood early on, meant relinquishing the freedoms and pleasures of childhood that were enjoyed "outside." Yet on the other hand, entering kheyder meant *having room* to live and grow: Initiates were inducted into the nearly boundless freedom of imagination accorded to Jewish boys within a set of behavioral, intellectual, and legal constraints. This room-cum-school was the site where literacy and thus liberty—the radical freedom of Hebrew textual competency—could be forged.[9] However willingly or reluctantly, boys traded their physical mobility for precious textual freedom.[10]

During Frug's lifetime, the historical kheyder was being reformed and institutionalized into something more closely resembling a modern school.[11] Yet the literary kheyder would long outlast the real thing, remaining undiminished as a touchstone for Jewish authenticity. Witness the inclusion of Frug's brief memoir in a textbook for use in New York's socialist Workmen's Circle Yiddish after-schools. Transcending the divide between shtetl and urban life, the kheyder stood in for Jewish premodernity even as it provided a meaningful point of contrast in the modern, secularizing cityscapes of both Europe and the Americas.[12] Secular Yiddish evocations of the Eastern European kheyder continued to be published into the 1970s, not only by many of its former "inmates," but also by the distinguished poet, short story writer, and teacher Kadya Molodowsky—who designated a suite of nostalgic tales *Kheyder Stories,* despite the fact that as a girl, she would have had no direct access in her youth to what transpired within those four drafty walls.

Kheyder stories were a mainstay of Yiddish children's literature from its inception, taking as their subjects the charged social dynamics and intellectual wrangling that defined Jewish schooling and, however much this view excluded half the population, Jewish childhood. The experience of the individual is often set with precision against a culture sketched only impressionistically. Most of these backward-looking tales are narrated in the first person by participant-observers recalling their experiences of childhood spent in a pious milieu—from the distant shores of both adulthood and a secular or freethinking worldview. In theorizing the figure of the child in modern Jewish literature, Naomi Sokoloff notes, "Nostalgia and reassessments of origins are natural stances for authors who have traveled far from their beginnings."[13] The authors of these narratives had traveled across literal and figurative oceans, and their school tales helped readers to metabolize the ongoing processes of secularization and global migration as they impinged upon the intimate lives of their own transforming families.

In Yiddish children's literature, boys are almost always represented in relation to a group, even if that relationship is usually troubled for the protagonist. A survey of kheyder tales, whether composed in Yiddish or Hebrew, offers up a roll call of the sensitive boys, the mild misfits who, disproportionately, grow up to be writers.[14] Their contemplative narration of their early tribulations unfolds against the backdrop of a less inwardly oriented, more rough-and-tumble sort of boyhood, thus ratifying their singular artistic destinies. Since kheyder culture was overwhelmingly male, though not exclusively so, these are necessarily stories about the construction of Jewish boyhood as a prelude to varieties of Jewish manhood.[15]

Portraits of the Artist as a Young Charity Case

Kheyder stories offer such a vast corpus unto themselves that I focus the discussion on two exemplars, from the early and late phases of Yiddish children's literature: a pair of Hanukkah tales by Sholem Aleichem and Isaac Bashevis Singer, respectively. Hanukkah is the most acquisitive time of year for the Jewish child, and each story describes a boy protagonist's guilt-ridden decision to defy parental expectations in favor of gratifying his own desires. A minor holiday, the festival of lights means a break from regular classes but imposes no need to be in synagogue all morning, so the drama of acquisition can be witnessed and scrutinized in real time each day in the boys' shared social space. The stakes of our protagonists' disobedience are heightened by their families' relative poverty compared to those of their classmates. The Hanukkah setting also means the usual rules are relaxed and schoolboys are permitted unusual frivolity. Taken together, these psychologically penetrating stories about schoolboys on the outs belong to a microgenre we might think of as Portraits of the Artist as a Young Charity Case. At their center is the interplay between the kheyder, the family, and the world beyond—and the long arc of growing up and getting even through becoming a teller of stories.

Wintertime kheyder is more than just the two-dimensional backdrop to various school tales. Like the sites Michel Foucault designates as heterotopias (a concept discussed in the introduction), the kheyder brings together representatives of several families in varying economic circumstances and with differing priorities and worldviews. Just as the cemetery is implicitly linked to all other spaces because "each family has relatives there" (and I would add: Everyone expects to join them one day), so too is the kheyder an institution where just about every family in Jewish Eastern Europe has relatives. Even those priced out of private tuition were educated at the communal expense in similarly structured and staffed schoolrooms.[16] A heterotopian mirror, the kheyder stands as a countersite to the homes and other locales where friendships and family dynamics coalesce.

Spin . . .

We turn first to Sholem Aleichem's Hanukkah tale, "The Dreydl," included in his 1903 collection of eight *Mayses far yidishe kinder* (Stories for Jewish Children). Despite the first-person narration, we learn surprisingly little about the speaker until the second of the tale's eight sections. Instead of introducing himself, the never-named narrator begins with a long peroration on his most cherished friendship: "More than all my friends in cheder and more than anyone in the whole town and more than anyone in the world, I loved my friend, Benny Polkovoi."[17] More precisely, as the Yiddish has this last phrase, "mayn khaver beni meir polkovoys." The genitive claiming Benny as his father's—*Meir* Polkovoy's—is important because the rest of the section goes on to explain that Benny is bigger, stronger, and richer than his classmates, by virtue of his father's meteoric economic rise as a *polkovoy*—that is, a regimental tailor who secures a contract to outfit the tsar's army.

Before the plot is set into motion, the narrator—now an adult with a mature understanding of socioeconomic relations—indulges in a long disquisition about Meir's social status and surname. Understandably, the existing translations skip over this revealing if somewhat tedious and even improbable section of the tale. Improbable because we are being asked to believe that as a child, the narrator was privy to details about his friend's powerful father that he registered at the time with the accuracy of a recording device and recalled well enough, decades later, to insert effortlessly into the recollected events.

The main drama, about a specific boy and his social relations as colored by the community's economic inequality, develops against the backdrop of a more generalized tension between old ways, internal to the Jewish community with its robust self-governance, and new norms being imposed from without. Nothing illustrates these tensions more clearly than the vexed question of legal nomenclature. For centuries, Jews living in what would become the Russian Pale of Settlement had identified themselves by an ad hoc mixture of Hebrew patronymics, Yiddish matronymics, spousal genitives, and monikers highlighting prominent features of an individual's identity. Formal surnames had been imposed upon Russian Jewry relatively late and were regarded as an intrusion by the bureaucratic state.[18]

The denizens of Sholem Aleichem's storied Kasrilevke will never forget that Meir is but a simple tailor, even after twenty successive years of his "mentshlen zikh": pursuing upward mobility, trying to make himself over into a petit bourgeois "mensch," elevated slightly by dint of his occupational surname, or aptronym, "Polkovoy." Even so, his identification document (*pas*)—itself an imposition of the state's administrative apparatus—names him quintuply as Kanievsky (toponym from Kan[i]ev) Meshchanin ([мещанин] = petty bourgeois) Meir (his Hebrew name) Movshovitsh (patronymic for Moses) Teletsi (heifer), an altogether absurd mashup of actual and aspirational identities.[19] Why should an urban tailor be named after an animal, like a farmer? And if an animal it must be, the narrator wonders, why such an effeminate one as a heifer, when the word meaning "bull," Bi(c)k, is a perfectly respectable and customary surname? No matter how wealthy you become, your townsmen keep the score and stand ready to remind all comers, even the schoolchildren of the next generation, of your humble origins. But never mind, urges the narrator; "let's get back to my friend Benny."[20] Let's not, though, and instead file this naming intricacy away for later.

Once Benny and his father have been introduced, the narrator can finally turn to the history of their friendship, which goes back to his very first day in school. He recalls his arrival as clearly as Shimen Frug remembers his kheyder initiation, if far less sweetly:

> I got my first glimpse of the rebbi when my mother brought me to his kheder. The rebbi, a man with thick brows and a pointy skullcap, was studying Genesis with all his pupils. Without the slightest hesitation—there was no need to take an exam or furnish a birth certificate—the rebbi told me: "Move to that bench over there—between those two boys."
>
> I squeezed in between the boys and was immediately accepted. The rebbi and my mother did not spend much time chatting, for everything had already been arranged during the holidays.
>
> "Remember now, study diligently," Mama said, standing by the door. She turned and looked at me with a feeling of mingled joy, love and compassion.[21]

Could anything be more utterly unceremonious? Given all that we know of the initiation ritual, this scene reads as not just jarring but downright devastating. Whatever the boy has gained in apparently seamless acceptance by his peers (he will be cruelly hazed later), he has more than lost in the withholding of any ritual welcome. Our narrator is the school's newcomer, and no effort is made to offer him any sort of a sweet beginning.

Of course there is no need for a birth certificate, a document that would register the boy's existence in the eyes of the administrative state. It's a bitter joke to imagine that the most quintessentially Jewish communal space, the schoolroom designated for the initiation of the young into distinctively Jewish ways of reading, learning, thinking, and speaking, should rely on the trappings of tsarist officialdom to induct its charges. But there absolutely *is* a need, one that goes unmet, for an examination: an indulgent "test" contrived to elicit the boy's correct answers, to shine a light on his promising aptitude, and to initiate him into the romance of learning and the sweetness that rains down on diligent students from on high. It is left to the boy's relatively uneducated mother, in her surfeit of "mingled" feeling, her recognition of the pregnant fullness of her son's liminal moment of entry, to lend the occasion whatever faint bit of gravity and joy her paltry words might convey. It is difficult to overstate the significance of the neglected initiation ritual, yet its absence tracks precisely with Sholem Aleichem's representation of Jewish modernity as a domain stripped of illusions. He is above all the chronicler of modern Jewish disenchantment. The curriculum and disciplinary methods are antiquated; the kheyder is represented as a changeless institution. But in his telling, the romance is gone.

The class is engaged in rote recitation and translation of the first Torah portion of Genesis. Fittingly enough for a story that will focus on trust and deception, the text under study is the snake's seduction of Eve. Naomi Sokoloff observes, "Because of his studies the boy, in a remarkably literal way, is absorbed into adult discourse."[22] Sholem Aleichem dramatizes the bidirectional nature of this encounter. In a faint echo of the fruit proffered in Eden, the boys exchange handfuls of buttons and carobs under the table while parroting their teacher's *khumesh-taytsh*, or fossilized Yiddish translation of the Pentateuch. They absorb the ancient words into their playscape even as the words burrow under their conscious thoughts.

Eventually we learn that the narrator is known as "the widow's son," for his scholarly father has died untimely, leaving his impoverished mother to rear—alone—a son as learned and pious as the departed. Had the father lived, he might occasionally chuck his son under the chin during a lighter moment in synagogue or absent-mindedly run his ritual fringes across his son's earlobe while puzzling out a difficult Talmudic commentary. In other words, there might be fleeting moments of intimate pleasure to compensate for the heavy yoke of parental expectations. As it happens, the boy is left to puzzle out a far more inscrutable enigma than any medieval commentator's question: "May my dear father in the other world forgive me for saying this, but I simply couldn't understand what sort of person he was. According to Mama, he spent all his time either studying or praying. Didn't he ever have a desire, as I did, to step outdoors and see a summer sunrise? When the sun rose on a gloriously divine morning, how could one savor a plain weekday morning service?"[23]

The narrator contemplates his own multisensory enjoyment of the natural world: diving into the mucky local swimming hole, listening to the chorus of bleating lambs and croaking frogs. The father's legendary piety and scholarly devotion ultimately set him apart as a figure impossible to understand, let alone emulate: "I only know that Mama constantly badgered and reminded me that I had had a father, threw up to me a dozen times a day the fact that she was paying kheder tuition for me."[24] His father evokes incomprehension, his mother, guilt. His teacher is an emotionally distant disciplinarian. Whom does the boy actually love?

Benny.

Benny is the object of extravagant affection because he uses his brawn to protect the narrator from the other boys' abusive hazing rituals, earning not only enduring loyalty but also a degree of subservience that veers sharply into self-abnegation. The social dynamics of the kheyder are bound up in uneven power relations. Naturally, the poor boy has special insight into how these reflect class differences. His classmates are constantly scheming to win buttons, bits of carob, and other small treasures from each other, all the while evading their teacher's censure and punishment. Come Hanukkah, they can freely indulge their desire to gamble for small stakes by spinning the dreydl.

Benny, the class ringleader, is the most consistent winner of this game of blind luck; for him and him alone, the dreydl always lands on the winning letter *giml*. His relentless fortune is at once wholly predictable, like a law of nature, and uncanny. *Giml, giml, giml* for Benny—and all the other boys' Hanukkah *gelt* is raked in by his pudgy fingers. What's more surprising is the narrator's irresistible compulsion to gamble. Normally an acute student, he cannot connect stimulus to response, can no more identify an obvious manipulation than he can rein in his need to try again: "Each time I ran to Benny's house, I lost every last kopeck, and I left his house depressed, heartbroken, vexed to the quick, and terribly upset. But not at Benny, God forbid! I had nothing against him! Was it Benny's fault that he was lucky at *dreydl*? Had the *dreydl* landed on G at my turn, then *I* would have been the winner, but since it landed on G for *him, he* was the winner. That's what Benny said, and, alas, he was right!"[25] Which is more dispiriting: the irrational yet unbreakable cycle of loss, or the otherwise insightful boy's blind parroting of Benny's hollow justifications?

After gambling away his *khanike gelt* and other small assets, the Widow's Son goes so far as to pawn a costly prayerbook that his mother had purchased on his father's recent *yortsayt*, or death anniversary, to induce the boy to pray with greater devotion. He sells the precious miniature book for a fraction of its value, loses *that* money forthwith, and succumbs to intense guilt, dreaming that his father, whom he is expected to memorialize by reciting the kaddish prayer, visits him and exposes his ignorance of the correct *yortsayt* date. Like so many child protagonists in Sholem Aleichem's universe, he wakes from his fever dream chastened and ultimately reassured of his mother's love. "Whippings heal," as he says elsewhere in the story, "shame is forgotten."

In stolid middle age, the two school chums meet by chance on the train and reminisce. Even in childhood, Benny had chubby, sticky cheeks. Now the narrator is able to pick him out of the crowd by his piscine pop-eyes. A gold watch chain spans Benny's formidable paunch. "Once he had been a rich man's son; now he was a rich man himself."[26] No residue of the lowly tailor's craft remains. The erstwhile chums trade stories of the good old days until the narrator gently palpates the still-sore spot by asking, "Do you remember, Benny, that Hanukkah, how it went for you playing *dreydl*?" Changing colors, seizing up with uncontrollable laughter, Benny can barely get the words out to satisfy his friend's curiosity about his "luck" so long ago: "It was, ha, ha, ha, a *dreydl* of pure *gimls*, nothing but *gimls*." It's difficult to imagine that no other boy in kheyder would have noticed that the trick dreydl had a *giml* carved on every side, but perhaps the spinning top was weighted to land on the winning letter. Either way, the game was rigged, and such was Benny's "luck."

Although the adult narrator indulges in some lengthy descriptions of little interest to most children, the story displays its liveliest rhetorical flourishes when he taps into the deep recesses of juvenile folklore. When the classmates beat up the narrator on his second day in kheyder, Benny, as Leviant translates, "began to work them over." But he does so in a very culturally specific way, "giving smacks, making a '*pozer*' and a '*shalsheles*,' meaning, boxing the ears of any boy who tried to pick a fight with me."[27] The Yiddish is so densely idiomatic as to discourage translation, but it reveals so much that it's worth our taking a moment to unpack. "A pozer mit a shalsheles" refers to two of the cantillation marks that indicate how a given verse in the Torah is to be chanted in the synagogue reading. They are akin to musical notes, and these two are especially notable notes—both as visual signifiers and as auditory cues. The *pozer* (֡) rises and cascades down over the course of about ten notes, suggesting an arpeggiated flurry of blows. And the *shalsheles* (֓) triples that sound into a rising and falling pattern of about thirty notes that occurs only four times in the Torah. As the kheyder boys approached their bar mitzvahs, probably still a few years away at the time of the story's main events, these cantillation traditions would have formed part of their curriculum, at least informally in synagogue. In the meantime, the boys incorporated them into their own fight slang. The visual and aural elements are mutually reinforcing, at once suggesting the shape that some especially ornate punches might trace through the air, gesturing at the thorough working over that Benny's victims received up and down the length of their bodies, akin to the range of the musical scale and evoking the sound of their moaning. But is the richness of this recollected lore truly pitched at an audience of *kinder*, or is it for adult readers who remember—rather nostalgically, perhaps—their own school days?

"Dos dreydl" is typical of its author's "child stories" in oscillating between the poetics of adult literature and the distinct aesthetics of children's literature. But if the story's poetics tiptoe gingerly into the twentieth century, its themes sit squarely in the Spanish Baroque. The sudden revelation, in adulthood, of Benny's exploitation and deception fits the classic early modern plot of *desen-*

gaño, becoming undeceived or disburdened of one's delusions. In recounting a time of relative innocence from the vantage point of experience, one discrete moment of revelation stands in for the inestimably gradual sediment of small discoveries that accrete to form adult consciousness. Above all, "Dos dreydl" is a story of betrayal: Benny obviously betrays the narrator, who in turn betrays his hardworking mother and the memory of his pious father. He can only end up betraying himself, a state of affairs he acknowledges in real time even if he can't quite account for it: "I had fooled my mother, and fooled her so miserably. I had sold my beautiful Siddur and lost the money playing *dreydl*. I had sold myself from top to toe."[28]

For his compulsion to gamble, the narrator feels deep guilt even in boyhood, but becoming aware of Benny's treachery only as an adult, he feels a proximate emotion: shame at having been duped. Benny's perfidy is all the more wrenching because he has always been his friend's loyal protector, a role he presumably continues fulfilling after the singular events of that Hanukkah, with the narrator none the wiser until they meet on the train decades later. It's one thing to have friends and enemies, another to have a blend of whom you are justly wary, and still another to have the difference obscured from your view. Whereas the *desengaño* plot usually figures the revelation—*caer en cuenta*, or becoming aware—as waking from the false world of dreams and delusions, Sholem Aleichem deploys the narrator's *desengaño* as the very model of maturation.[29] He passes in an instant not from dreaming to waking, but from the residue of childhood credulity to full, undeluded maturity.

This recognition scene is lopsided, however: The adult Benny Polkovoy, described as "the son of a rich man" and "now a rich man himself" has no idea—even in middle age—of how different the stakes of the game were for him than for the narrator, who has presumably become the writer Sholem Aleichem or a similarly situated member of the creative but impecunious class. Gambling necessarily meant something different to a poor boy than to a pampered one, for an orphan than for a child with his family intact. On the last night of Hanukkah, our narrator forfeits the few kopecks for which he has sold the prayerbook, and Benny repeats his empty words of comfort, this time in his own voice rather than ventriloquized through the narrator:

> "That's why it's a *dreydl*." Benny tried to console me, pocketing my last few kopecks. "If you were as lucky as I, *you'd* win. But since I'm the lucky one, *I* win."

> Benny's face was flushed. His house was warm and bright. The silver Hanuka candelabrum, with its handsome kindling candle, was filled with the finest oil. From the kitchen wafted the delicious aroma of recently rendered goose fat.
>
> "We're making pancakes today," Benny declared, imparting the good news while I stood at the door, my stomach rumbling with hunger.[30]

Decades hence, the narrator might well remember the deflection maneuver whereby Benny denies his own privilege, ascribing his winning streak to random luck. But the one who suspends this little bit of gaslighting in the sensory amber of Benny's flushed cheeks, his well-appointed, schmaltz-fragrant home—every detail of which is sharpened by the contrast with the narrator's chilly domicile with its menorah improvised of scooped-out potato halves—*that* can only be the mature Sholem Aleichem.

The author, who was personally devastated by the ill-timed bursting of a stock exchange bubble more than once, viewed the swindle or con as life's single most revelatory transaction, and children were by no means immune to its allure.[31] The innocent boyhood games of dreydl lay on a continuum with the blandishments of matchmakers and card sharps, the depredations of the bourse, and even the enticements of human traffickers. Many characters in and beyond the fictional shtetl of Kasrilevke struggle with gambling or the compulsion to risk valuables. Still, the narrator of this tale could have figured out that something was amiss with Benny's dreydl game. Perhaps he subconsciously defers the knowledge until such time in his life as he can process and contextualize this formative swindle. When all is said and done, is Benny's unbeatable dreydl essentially different from the unfair distribution of wealth and privilege? Capitalism itself is a stacked game for Sholem Aleichem; gambling only throws into relief the asymmetry of opportunity and outcome. The boy's fixation on the beautiful and comprehensive prayerbook—the *kolboynikl,* or "book that contains everything"—stands in for his relationship with his knowledgeable father. In forfeiting the book to his own avarice, he loses his father anew. Similarly, we might contemplate the long shadow that Meir Polkovoy's scrappy rise to wealth casts over *his* son's life, who moves his inherited capital far beyond Kasrilevke, where he need no longer brook any diminution of his status by dint of being a tailor's son.

Fittingly, the old friends meet on the train. The railroad is the very emblem of mobility, the counterpoint to the stasis of the shtetl Kasrilevke with its timeless institutions, chief among them the kheyder. This story begins as a school tale but then morphs into an *ayznban geshikhte*, a railroad story, a distinct subgenre that Sholem Aleichem developed not only to emblematize the fitful Jewish relationship to European modernity, but also to showcase the deceptions enabled by the train's easy-on, easy-off dissolution of knowable communities.[32] Between these two heterotopic spaces (after all, the sailing ship was Foucault's emblem of a modern heterotopia), and in relation to what each of them represents, we witness the *desengaño* of not only one writer's inner child but that of his entire civilization.

. . . And Spin Again

Fast forward half a century, to another kheyder full of the prosperous sons of upwardly mobile parents being observed by another smart boy on the outs. Given the nearly seventy-five years that intervene between the publication of "The Dreydl" and Bashevis Singer's "A Hanukkah Eve in Warsaw," it is remarkable how similarly their two khadorim are depicted.[33] This time, the setting is urban Warsaw, but the potent admixture of winter-holiday high spirits with quickening desire and dread-laced envy endures: "That morning, I had brought along a dreydl. Hanukkah is a holiday when you can play. But in order to play, you have to put down money, and my poor parents hadn't given me any. I wouldn't be receiving a groschen until evening, after blessing the Hanukkah candles. And what's more, some of the kids had ivory dreydls or colorful, fancy ones. But my dreydl was plain old tin."[34]

Even at his tender, self-reported age of "not yet seven," the narrator understands his place in the pecking order.[35] Knowing that hope of any windfall is probably futile, he nevertheless carries the plain dreydl in his otherwise empty pockets. Unlike Sholem Aleichem's narrator, his family has plenty of food to eat; his mother sends him to school with "second breakfast" and the anticipation of latkes that evening. Yet this security in an absolute sense doesn't shield him from the pain of his relative want. Witness the very next sentence: "I always felt ashamed when I came to cheder, and I often prayed to God to grow up fast and not have to go anymore."[36] Later in the story, he will fantasize about becoming rich and being able to hire a private tutor; he desires education but is tormented by the teasing of his hazily sketched peers.

Long before there was Isaac Bashevis Singer, the Nobel Prize–winning eminence who came to speak for all of Yiddish literature in winsomely (if calculatedly) self-deprecating tones, there was little Itshele Zinger of Krochmalna Street.[37] Itshele, as remembered midlife by the global literary phenomenon

Singer, was a dreamy child with a mystical bent and a deep curiosity about the world beyond the limited domain between home and school.[38] Based on the luster of his father's rabbinical reputation, he attended a kheyder with tuition costs beyond his parents' means; his classmates, by contrast, belonged to the rising merchant class and had the enviable schoolboy trifles to show for it. In "A Hanukkah Eve in Warsaw," he knits together the uneven social dynamics at school with the dramatic events of a snowy winter's evening.

From its opening sentences, the story establishes its pattern of oscillating between historically verifiable, hyperrealistic facts (including the addresses of home and school) and flights of magical realist fantasy.[39] In all his imaginings, Itshele is the heroic protagonist; at school, though, he seems to be relegated to the sidelines by the triple disadvantage of parental poverty, piety, and protection. The first two elements were inextricable: His father's rabbinical role answering Jewish legal questions and presiding at life cycle events for the common folk of Krochmalna Street was no pathway to affluence: "Coming to cheder was for me a daily trial. The other pupils quickly made friends with one another. They conducted all kinds of secret business transactions among themselves. One boy gave another a silver button and got a gold button in exchange. Quietly, so that the teacher wouldn't see, they traded pencils, pens, and sometimes chocolates and cookies they brought from home. Most of the students were sons of storekeepers or factory owners and were already little businessmen themselves. Their parents lived in the wealthier streets."[40]

Even at six, Itshele can connect the dots between his friends' caches of goods and their residence on the wealthier streets of Warsaw. His parents swam against the cosmopolitan culture of the city, eschewing urban smartness for their son and dressing him in old-fashioned, practical clothes that made him look "like a yokel."[41] His pronunciation of certain Yiddish words marked him as an outsider.[42] Heredity conspired against him too: As if the social isolation weren't enough, Itshele inherited his father's flaming red hair.

Standing on equal economic footing with his peers might have smoothed over the cultural differences, as it surely would have for Sholem Aleichem's ill-fated dreydl player. However, the engine that sets this plot in motion is the third disadvantage: The level of (overprotective) parental concern that led the rabbi and his wife to hire the assistant teacher to walk their son to and from school each day. This arrangement, though attested as common in many shtetl locales, shrinks the distance between pupil and teacher, on which more cosmopolitan peers' acceptance depends. More than his poverty or his two itchy woolen vests, this intrusion on Itshele's autonomy—"being escorted like a baby"—is the bane of his existence.[43] On the eve of Hanukkah, the assistant teacher asks the boy to make good on his frequent boasts that he can walk home alone (while keeping his parents in the dark).

Itshele doesn't even get the satisfaction of boasting to his classmates of his independence. In the English translation, the assistant puts his finger to his lips in warning, and, in the Yiddish, whispers punningly, "Pasekh shin-sha."[44] The *sha* does double duty as the sound produced by the consonant-vowel combination "pasekh shin" and as the onomatopoeia cautioning silence. With this utterance, the assistant blurs his twin roles as teacher and human school bus. His note of warning is playful but probably also tinged with a hint of menace, as when adults impress children into keeping their secrets. The boy begins his walk nearly intoxicated with the newfound independence: "I went out into the street, and for the first time I felt like a grownup."[45]

His drive to escape his schoolmates' snowballs and hazing diverts him from his usual direct route toward a busy commercial street, where the sounds, sights, and smells commingle in his kaleidoscopic imagination. Although he could not know it at the time, Itshele is part of an international and multilingual cadre of fictional fellow sufferers in modern Jewish fiction (e.g., David Schearl in *Call It Sleep*), whose heightened, personal relationship with biblical and rabbinic lore is similarly mapped onto a youthful protagonist's "real life."[46] Quotidian experience fuses with the narratives that form both the child's curricular and leisure reading. Scripture serves not only as an ethical guide, as the adults might urge, but also as a manual for the coveted magic of transmuting ordinary events into story.

Indeed Itshele's only source of social capital is his burgeoning reputation as a storyteller, which rests on suturing together his own imaginings with biblical episodes. He practices this art first and foremost on himself, and the rare opportunity for wandering in physical space afforded by his unescorted walk home becomes a chance for his mind to wander as well. The early winter sunset and an epoch-making snowstorm abet his fantasies, and the rather pedestrian experience of straying a block too far is transmuted into myth by the boy's overactive imagination, which has been richly seeded with Jewish folklore about what is called in the mystical tradition the *Sitra d'Akhra*, "the Other Side." No sooner does he realize he is lost than he perceives himself to be Lost. The electric trolley on this main thoroughfare, shooting its bluish sparks into the winter darkness, heightens the otherworldliness of the unfamiliar scene. It is the perfect space for the author's characteristic congeries of imps, demons, and other dark spirits to frolic unbridled:

That which I had always feared had apparently happened—the evil spirits had turned their wrath on me.

Now the wind thrust me forward, now it dragged me back. It blew up the skirt of my coat and tried to lift me in the air. I knew where the gale sought to carry me—to Sodom, to beyond the Mountains of Darkness, to Asmodeus's castle, to Mt. Sair, where the ground is copper and the sky is iron. I wanted to cry out to God, to utter some prayer or incantation, but my mouth had gone numb and my nose was stiff as wood. The cold penetrated through my coat, and through both vests. My eyelids became swollen and I could no longer see in the white maelstrom.

Suddenly I heard a shrill clanging and shouts. Someone sprang, and seizing me from behind, half dragged, half carried me off. Was this a demon, a wraith?[47]

Itshele is not, in fact, being spirited away by a malign demon but rather rescued by a well-meaning passerby from being struck by a passing trolley car. While the events are prosaic, his perceptions are enchanted. By the time he published this story, Bashevis had already made a whole career writing for adults about the exploits of demons and imps. Playing with the artistic possibilities of enchantment and realism, he freely employed the dark hosts of the underworld as a figural vocabulary in supernatural and realistic settings alike.[48]

During a 1976 visit to a college class on children's literature, the author acknowledged, "I wrote always about demons and sometimes sex, and I didn't think that this was really the material for children."[49] Much of *Bashevis's* fiction for adults, written and initially published in Yiddish, leaves the reader gripped by an existential malaise; however, *Singer's* stories for children, written in Yiddish but many of them only ever published in English translation, fashion a wholly different literary world wherein Jewish religious heritage is an accessible source of ethical inspiration and sensory comfort, virtue is rewarded, and no vice lies beyond amendment. Like Sholem Aleichem, albeit with greater artistic subtlety, Singer assumed that children require morally serious plots with happy, redemptive endings. Whether because he was a more practiced storyteller by the time he turned to writing for young audiences or because he simply lived more years of his life under the governing cultural script of "happy childhood," Singer does not usually have to resort to the kind of sudden pivot whereby Sholem Aleichem wrests his lachrymose tale "The Flag" to a cheerful conclusion. Across several subgenres—fairy tales, fauxktales about the Wise

Men of Chelm and other folkloric motifs, and memoirs like this one—virtue and grace prevail. It is always possible to go home again.

At the core of "A Hanukkah Eve in Warsaw" is the parable of a Jewish prodigal son. The darkness, literal and metaphorical, that surrounds Itshele as he lies and bumbles his way toward home, hours late, only emphasizes the light and warmth that envelop the boy upon his safe return, a reception crowned by the holiday indulgence of his usually stern father. Expecting the very worst after prolonging his absence with a visit to his neighbor Shosha (herself the preternaturally mild subject of an eponymous novella), Itshele is welcomed and even gifted—with a beautiful prayerbook imported from the Land of Israel. His older sister, destined to be a protofeminist author but on this occasion just a put-upon daughter who has spent the evening of her brother's wanderings dutifully helping with the labor-intensive potato latkes, observes acidly, "The worst dog gets the best bone."[50] That asymmetry is precisely what the parable demands. And in some sense, Isaac Bashevis Singer's turn to writing for children is its own sort of prodigal tale, one worth telling.

Altruism Pays Off: An Icon "Returns" to Childhood

It might seem inevitable in hindsight that Isaac Bashevis Singer would become a globally renowned children's author, given his fourteen volumes of stories for young readers. However, although he published his first adult novel serially in 1933 in Warsaw, he did not release his first children's book, *Zlateh the Goat and Other Stories,* until 1966 in New York. Bashevis was often asked to account for this time lag, and the fact that he answered in various ways over the years complicates our understanding of his journey toward writing for children. It is inarguable that he was the most commercially successful Yiddish children's writer ever; what is arguable is the extent to which he was a "Yiddish children's writer" at all. He worked outside—and gleefully against—most of the existing institutional structures that had given shape to the rest of the juvenile corpus in his mother tongue. To paraphrase another American-Jewish immigrant upstart, he made the record in his own way—and on his own terms.

Here is how Isaac Bashevis Singer told his origin story as a children's author in English in 1984:

> I never believed that I could write for children. I always had the false impression that those who write for children are not real writers, and those who illustrate books are not real painters. It is true that as a child I read the

> Brothers Grimm in German and also translations of Hans Christian Andersen's stories and I loved them. I will never forget the great joy I felt reading a Yiddish edition of Sherlock Holmes stories by Arthur Conan Doyle. Just the same, the idea of writing for children never entered my mind.[51]

The import of the first sentence is ambiguous: Is it a confession of humility ("I lacked the special knack of writing for children") or the boastful opposite ("I never imagined I'd deign to write for children")? The second sentence confesses to overcoming a "false impression," his long-held but unfounded disdain for children's literature. Singer then shifts to his own childhood literary menu of foreign classics and relies on the bland phrase "just the same" to carry the load of distinguishing between works written in other European languages and what originated in his humble native Yiddish. He goes on to acknowledge the pivotal role played by editor and translator Elizabeth Shub, who "was convinced that I could write for children." Somewhat demurely, the already much decorated author resisted her entreaties. "She was after me for a long time" before he capitulated and wrote the initial volume *Zlateh the Goat and Other Stories* and the "dozen other books for youngsters" that followed.

The question of young Itshele's literary diet is an important one for understanding Singer's subsequent beliefs about children's literature. As a child growing up in Warsaw, with a brief wartime stint in his mother's rural hometown of Bilgoraj, he certainly read the Hebrew Bible, rabbinic narrative interpretations (midrash), and storybooks (*mayse bikhelekh*). Khone Shmeruk doubts his claim to have read classic European works, as these would have been barred from a strictly religious home like that of the Singers and decried as "a superfluous and harmful pastime."[52] He did not read Yiddish children's literature either, for overlapping and contradictory reasons: "It did not exist among the Jewish people in my time," its political aims and aesthetic tendencies were at odds with his own, it lacked prestige ("those who write for children are not real writers"), and classical Jewish texts were more wholesome fare for Jewish children.[53]

It is true enough that the very earliest Yiddish children's publishing projects were just getting underway during the first decade of the author's lifetime. But the idea of a special literature for young readers was hardly unknown to Bashevis; indeed, we may infer that Itshele understood the commodity value of literature from his elementary years. The 1984 collection *Stories for Children* includes another memoir of his childhood, a more explicit portrait of the artist as a young man, set when he was eleven. His understanding of economic inequality has crystallized into something even harder and sharper than before, as he relates, "Until just a few weeks ago I had attended cheder on Twarda Street, but I had stopped going because my father couldn't afford the two rubles a month tuition." The young storyteller has money on his mind and a plan, in cahoots with his best friend, to earn some and even to reinvest in the business:

> I would soon publish my first book—all of sixteen pages long. Its price would be two kopeks. Feivel and I had figured it all out with precision. There were at least fifty thousand boys and girls in Warsaw who liked to read storybooks. If every boy and girl bought my book, we would take in a hundred thousand kopeks, or a thousand rubles. With this sum we could buy our own printing shop and publish additional books.[54]

These aspirations partake of the charm, familiar to his audiences, of childhood remembered at midlife by a master storyteller. Less known to English-language readers, though, is that Bashevis was in fact invited, quite seriously and just a few years after the time when he harbored such fantasies, to write for children. The educator and editor Yoysef Rotenberg, a friend from the renowned Warsaw Yiddish PEN Club, heard of the young writer's penury and promised the emerging talent a good rate if he would contribute stories to the *Kleyner folkstsaytung* (Small People's Press), the children's pages of Warsaw's Bundist organ, the *Folkstsaytung*. Bashevis, as the editor related to critic Khone Shmeruk, "sharply and categorically refused," exclaiming with his typically broad Warsaw vowels and swallowed consonants, "'Yakh shraab nish fa ka kindo!'" (I don't write for kids!). His vehemence, as Rotenberg recalls the incident and Shmeruk, with phonetic precision, transcribes it, suggests that Bashevis was insulted by the very offer. Citing the 1984 author's note, Shmeruk concludes, "What emerges most clearly from these memoirs is the fact that the adult Bashevis regarded children's literature as an inferior genre, and like many of his colleagues, he thought that creating for children was a humiliation for a writer."[55] Even as a hungry youth, Bashevis was determined to establish his literary bona fides for serious adult audiences.

What is more, the budding anticommunist had little desire at that time to see his work in a Bundist paper. (Obviously he would overcome scruples about supporting himself as a writer—or as several writers, given his liberal use of pseudonyms—in the socialist pages of the *Forverts* over several subsequent decades.) Rotenberg taught in the secularist TSYSHO schools during the interwar period in Warsaw, and the newspaper supplement he edited for children was governed by a spirit of iconoclasm corresponding to that of the modern, coeducational Yiddish schools.[56] Insofar as Bashevis thought about what children ought to read before he began writing for them, he favored Bible stories.[57] In a 1949 essay published in *Forverts*, he urged, "If we want our children to have a good taste for literature, we must raise them on the Bible, whether in Yiddish or Hebrew. Teaching schoolchildren exclusively easy poems, watered-down sketches, and pointless stories [*puste geshikhtes*] corrupts a child's taste and makes him into a reader of trash [*shund-lezer*]."[58] Were children to remain in Yiddish school longer, Bashevis reasoned, they might begin with lighter material and move sequentially to more challenging reading, as they do in public schools. But given that "most pupils in Yiddish schools don't stay long enough," they needed high-impact, highest-quality reading material right away. Modern Yiddish children's literature was brought into being, as we saw in chapter 2, to turn children away from reading *shund*; Bashevis asserted that it did precisely the opposite. His concerns about writerly prestige dovetailed with what Shmeruk calls his "principled negation of specialized literature for children."[59]

Bashevis began to reconsider at least some aspects of this opposition almost a decade before publishing his first volume of children's stories. In 1957, he visited Buenos Aires for the first time, receiving a royal welcome among the city's Yiddish institutions. These included a children's periodical edited by Zelik Mazur, *Argentiner beymelekh* (Little Argentinian Trees), which devoted a special issue to the author and his work. Since he had not yet published any stories especially for children, the monthly reprinted the chapter "A Day of Pleasure" from the memoiristic collection *In My Father's Court*. Mazur recounts an interview with the visiting author, who gratified his hosts with a stop at the local Yiddish school: "Acquainting himself with the children and seeing their proficiency in Yiddish and Hebrew studies and their deep understanding of Yiddish literature and history is of colossal value. And if there are such schools as these with children—he exclaimed joyfully—then there's someone to write for, because Yiddish literature and the Yiddish language have a future. Whoever doesn't write specially for children will from now on *also* dedicate himself to children's literature."[60]

Bashevis promises to become a frequent contributor to *Argentiner beymelekh*, a promise he is not known to have kept. On a visit to Canada in late 1962 or early 1963, he is similarly impressed with the local Yiddish schoolchildren and once again "convinced of how important it is to write for Jewish (Yiddish-speaking) children."[61] One of Montreal's premier Yiddish educators, Shimshen Dunsky, published a Yiddish translation of rabbinic midrash aimed at young readers, which Bashevis reviewed warmly in *Forverts* in 1963, alongside a collection of poetry for children by Mates Olitsky.[62] In both works, he saw a salutary reorientation of Yiddish children's literature away from universalism and toward culturally and even religiously specific Jewish content. Shmeruk maintains that when Bashevis registered this change, it marked a principled turning point in his attitude toward children's literature and what it might offer contemporary Jewish communities.[63]

The most charitable reading of the author's trajectory is that he gradually worked himself up to writing for children, especially once he could see his way clear to doing so in his own style and from within his own ideological habitus. The established Yiddish children's publishers were all linked to leftist educational projects for which he had little use, but by 1966, Bashevis Singer commanded enough publishing cachet to create a market for a new branch of his work, especially through translation. As has been well documented, Singer succeeded commercially by harnessing the power of translation—what he famously, or among Yiddishists notoriously, called the creation of "a second original"—in order to transcend his fate as a storyteller in a backwater minority language and enter the select company of name-brand "world" writers.[64] A more skeptical way of understanding his late arrival as a children's author was that he followed the money, which did *not* flow from publishing locally for the Yiddish-speaking schoolchildren of Buenos Aires.

Elizabeth Shub, the editor who pestered Isaac Bashevis Singer to try his hand at writing for children and then translated several of the stories she coaxed out of him, was uniquely positioned to nurture this particular talent. Singer employed scores of translators over his decades in America, from Saul Bellow to his nephew Joseph Singer, but only Shub envisioned him as a children's author and pressed him to become one. Not coincidentally, she was the daughter of Shmuel Charney, the long-time editor of the *Kinder zhurnal*, the children's periodical associated with the Sholem Aleichem Folk Institute, the least doctrinaire of the New York–based Yiddish educational networks. She had known Bashevis since he immigrated to New York in 1935 and could tell him candidly, when his first attempt at writing for children yielded stilted verse narratives, that he needed to go back to his writing desk.[65] Shub worked as a freelance reader and then an associate editor at Harper & Row, for which she acquired *Zlateh the Goat and Other Stories*. Singer's usual publisher, Farrar Strauss, and Giroux, was initially willing to let him take his children's stories elsewhere; who could predict the marketability of his new venture? When it came to subsequent works for children, they did not repeat the mistake. "Well, I admit that

I approached this field without too many ideals and too many messages," Singer recounted to a group of college students. "I just wanted to satisfy a friend of mine who was after me for a long time. The net result was that she translated many stories into English from Yiddish and now, whenever I get a check, she gets a check. Which proves that sometimes altruism pays off."[66] For both Shub and her prize author, altruism aligned with market savvy.

Isaac Bashevis Singer did not share in the "gestural tendency" that inspired so many of his elite peers to contribute to the commonweal of Yiddish cultural nationalism by writing now and then for children. He was no nationalist, and he managed simultaneously to do far more and far less than Sholem Aleichem, Y. L. Peretz, or Meyshe Kulbak did for young Jewish readers. He wrote children's stories in numbers few others matched and to levels of acclaim others could scarcely imagine. The "sad paradox," as Shmeruk terms it, is that by the time Bashevis turned to writing for children, there were no longer enough Yiddish readers to sustain the juvenile presses that had flourished before and immediately following the Holocaust.[67] The only infrastructure for disseminating his work was the newspaper, particularly the *Forverts*, which addressed itself to adults. In his analysis of Bashevis as a children's author, Shmeruk acknowledges distressingly often that he doesn't know where or whether a Yiddish original was published.[68] Many of Bashevis's novels and stories for adults languish unpublished in book form in Yiddish, demanding that the determined reader brave temperamental microfilms in dusty library basements; a large number of the children's stories never appeared in Yiddish print at all.

Bashevis's adult fiction might traffic in seduction and betrayal, violence and existential despair, yet his stories for children licensed an equally essential optimism for which he saw no other outlet. Quite simply, writing for children allowed him a measure of hope. Consider this question and answer from one of his visits with the emerging adults in the college course in Connecticut:

> Q: When asked why your stories for children always have happy endings you have been quoted as saying, "If I have to torture someone, I would rather torture an adult than a child." In what other specific ways do you alter your writing for children?
>
> A: I try to give a happy ending to a story for a child because I know how sensitive a child is. If you tell a child that a murderer or a thief was never punished and never caught, the child feels that there is no justice in the world altogether. And I don't like children to come to this conclusion, at least not too soon.[69]

Children grow up best in a world they believe to be ruled by a moral order, the storyteller asserts, and what is more, they have an innate tendency to seek justice. If nurturing this tendency entails some measure of *engaño*, delusion, then so be it.

Bashevis crystallized these attitudes in the summative essay, "Are Children the Ultimate Literary Critics?" which closes out his omnibus collection *Stories for Children*:

> Children think about and ponder such matters as justice, the purpose of life, the why of suffering. They are bewildered and frightened by death. They cannot accept the fact that the strong should rule the weak.
>
> Many grownups have made up their minds that there is no purpose in asking questions and that one should accept the facts as they are. But the child is often a philosopher and a seeker of God.[70]

Adults are resigned to the world with all its injustice, while children are innately nobler if also in need of protection to maintain their illusions just a bit longer. This Romantic view of childhood mapped directly onto Bashevis's characterization of Yiddish itself as articulated during the same "golden" phase of his career. He construed his Nobel Prize as "a recognition of the Yiddish language," which he described in his Nobel Lecture as possessing a childlike innocence: "a language of exile, without a land, without frontiers, not supported by any government, a language which possesses no words for weapons, ammunition, military exercises, war tactics." The "Yiddish-speaking people of the ghettoes," innocent of geopolitics, lived in a world apart, preserved in his fiction and outside history.

Childhood and Yiddish both represented Romantic ideals, exotic realms, to which this particular storyteller maintained privileged access. On the world stage, Singer cultivated a persona as the warm and wry Old Man Yiddish, relying in no small part on his identity *as* a children's author in league with the future. He made the linkage explicit in his Nobel Prize banquet speech two days after the conferral of the prize, when he enumerated ten of the "five hundred reasons why I began to write for children."[71] Child readers, as he explains, are primitives in the best sense: eschewing formal experimentation in favor of traditionally plotted stories, and impervious to critics' opinions or authors' reputations.[72] "They don't expect their beloved writer," he concludes, "to redeem humanity. Young as they are, they know that it is not in his power. Only adults have such childish illusions." Among such deluded adults, Bashevis would almost certainly number the ideologically engaged majority of Yiddish children's authors.

As part of the top-ten list Singer read off in Stockholm, he proclaimed that children "don't give a hoot about the critics." Some of those pesky critics have traced how, in consultation with his translators, I. B. Singer removed the distinctive linguistic markers encoding deep-seated cultural attitudes that imparted a truly Yiddish flavor to his writing and connected him to the mother-wit of his origins. As his international horizons widened, his locutions grew blander. David Roskies puts the turning point at about 1960 for the pivot toward American tales that "lose little in translation because there is nothing much to lose."[73] By then, Singer was a thoroughly American writer, active on the world stage via translation.

The continuing globalization of his artistic brand is inextricable from his self-refashioning as a children's author: "Henceforth, the stories tell us, when a Yiddish writer reaches a certain advanced age, he becomes a saintly figure by default. . . . Then all of Yiddish culture perforce becomes a take for children."[74] Like many Yiddish writers working after the Holocaust, Bashevis feels the need to imaginatively preserve, or even to reconstitute, some of the civilization that was obliterated. He evokes the streets and schoolrooms of his youth as a kind of auto-ethnography. He intersperses memoiristic stories in among the folktales and Chelm stories as if to say that he has traveled so far from his family of origin, *made himself up* so thoroughly, that he can treat life-writing as one more shade of fiction. Writing about his boyhood formation is at once a way of measuring that distance and of going home again.

Civilization in Little

Before the kheyder initiation ceremony fell by the wayside, leaving such a palpable absence in these stories, the rite symbolically adhered the individual to a larger-than-life collective experience. The pietists of medieval Ashkenaz fashioned rituals that would enact and reinscribe the idealized trajectory of Israel's journey in the person of each (male) constituent. This was especially true in locales where the initiation was conducted jointly for all members of an age cohort and pegged to the holiday of Shavuot with its celebration of the Law's Revelation. As Ivan Marcus notes, "The individual Jewish child's personal 'entry into Torah study' symbolically recapitulates the paradigmatic biblical story of Israel's journey from Egypt to Sinai. At another level, the child's rite of passage merges with the local Jewish community's own remembering of the biblical narrative during the spring holiday cycle from Passover to Shavuot that describes the formation of the Jewish people and its arrival at

Mount Sinai. In this way, the child's public gestures mimic the community's celebration of a remembered sacred past."[75]

Recapitulation orients itself toward the past to reaffirm the present, merging the child into the mighty stream of shared communal life. Although the story arc differs, the same essential pedagogical impulse animates the secular sabbatarians who spurred each young reader to retrace the Jewish people's journey from devout belief to principled freethinking. Recapitulation was a widely held nineteenth-century educational ideal. In 1861, when Shimen Frug was in diapers, the English philosopher Herbert Spencer observed, "If there be an order in which the human race has mastered its various kinds of knowledge, there will arise in every child an aptitude to acquire these kinds of knowledge in the same order. . . . Education is a repetition of civilization in little."[76] But unlike the secular Sabbath tales of the previous chapter, the kheyder stories we've considered are deeply ambivalent about the past and uncertain about the future. Sholem Aleichem and Isaac Bashevis Singer scramble the paradigm of education by recapitulation because they have no coherent program or developmental arc they hope for child readers to trace, no telos at which they would see Jewish children arrive. Unlike the founders of Yiddish children's literature, Bashevis especially did not believe in progress, but neither did he believe that traditional piety was possible in the modern world.[77] To judge by the fates of his agonized protagonists, what he believed in most keenly was being tormented ("tortured" in Singer's colloquy with the college students) by precisely this bind.

If Spencer is correct that the individual's education is civilization in little, then it is equally true that the civilization is the individual's education writ large. For centuries, Jewish education had sought to produce mostly continuity, with tolerably small divergences for the sake of adaptation to changing circumstances. The kheyder stories of Sholem Aleichem and Isaac Bashevis Singer, however, span a moment of radical rupture when the aims of education itself were coming into question. Would subsequent generations lead lives more similar to or different from the lives of the Jews who had come before? Within the formal miniature of a short story that is simultaneously a mythologized piece of life-writing, Bashevis wrestles with how to etch the arc of Jewish civilization on the cusp of the twentieth century.

On the surface of the text, little Itshele is deeply relieved, if slightly incredulous, at his parents' indulgence, their determination to keep the first night of Hanukkah free of recriminations for his disobedience. Father speaks softly to son, but beneath the surface, the adult author embeds the armaments of a battle that will endure throughout the boy's formative years. The combatants wield dueling metanarratives. Itshele's Big Story is only just taking shape in his mind as he plods through the snowy streets unsupervised, and it won't come to full expression for another decade:

> Suddenly I recalled a story my brother Joshua had told me about a boy who had been sent on Passover night to open the door for the prophet Elijah and had vanished. Years later he came home a grown man and a professor. He had walked from the town where his parents lived to Warsaw, and then on to Berlin. Rich people there had helped him obtain an education. That's what I would have to do, too—run away from home! I would read all the books about the sun, the moon, the stars. I would learn how mountains, rivers, oceans, and the North Pole had formed.[78]

His ur-tale, a miniature within a miniature, is a prodigal parable of venture and return. In fulfilling a Jewish ritual duty, a boy is exposed to the outside world and swiftly swallowed up by it. He comes back years later "a grown man and a professor." Becoming educated in this way requires him to leave home, but home awaits him unchanged. Significantly, this is also a story about plotting one's life course based on . . . stories. A heterodox older sibling has smuggled in a narrative of flight and return that is otherwise unavailable at home or school, and the boy has adopted it wholeheartedly as a roadmap. "That's what I would have to do, too!" The "click" is almost audible. So clear is the pathway and the destination that Itshele wishes he could skip over the rest of the childhood tedium that retards his progress: "The time of a child drags on slowly," he says in the Yiddish.[79] We are catching a glimpse, at six years old, of Hertz Dovid Grein of *Shadows on the Hudson*, or any of the other traditionally educated protagonists of the adult Singer novels who grow up to be tormented by modernity—unable to believe but equally unable to give themselves over to the modes of living that unbelief would seem to dictate.

His father also embraces a metanarrative of journey and return, but rather than adventure, he tells a tale by turns baleful and hopeful, of exile and eventual restoration. It is a version of *The* Jewish Story. As he hands his son the gift of a prayerbook, he urges:

> "Pray from this book. Everything that comes from the Land of Israel is holy. This Wall is a remnant of the Holy Temple, which the evildoers demolished. The Divine Providence reigns there forever. Jews sinned; that's why the Temple was destroyed. But the Almighty is all-merciful. He is our

> Father, and we are His children. God willing, the Messiah will come and we'll all go back to our homeland. A fiery Temple will descend upon Jerusalem. The dead will be resurrected. Our grandfathers, grandmothers, great-grandfathers, and all the generations will live again. The light of the sun will be seven times brighter than now. The saints will sit with crowns upon their heads and study the secrets of the Torah."[80]

Whereas Itshele imagines the triumphant return of the individual, the only redemption that has meaning for his father is the arc of collective return. He, too, sees in story a behavioral roadmap. A wayward child has angered an omnipotent parent so severely as to override the instinct to protect his offspring. But the Divine Father remains solicitous, ready to enact repair that will bring his children home. Even nature (the brighter sun) will ratify the eventual restoration, and in this ideal state, the saints will . . . do pretty much exactly what Itshele's father spends his days doing already. God is the model parent, and it is through imitating the gentle divine ways that Rabbi Singer arrives at the mildness he displays on this first night of Hanukkah. The parental gift of a prayerbook is always received in a different spirit than it was proffered.

The adult author shows how his father rummages through his conceptual storehouse in order to overlook his son's incipient waywardness and arrive at a sympathetic reading of Itshele's words and deeds. It is precisely the kind of paternal solicitude Sholem Aleichem's narrator struggles even to imagine. In the Warsaw boy's imagination, a sacred aura surrounds his friendship with Shosha, the simple and tender girl with whom he has spent the evening playing. Ignoring his wife's evident disapproval, the father is curious to know more about her, prompting the boy's earnest confession of love:

> "She is good. The boys at cheder call me names, but she is nice to me. When we grow up, I want to marry her." . . .
>
> Father smiled, but he promptly grew earnest. "Everything comes from heaven. It's said that forty days before a person is born, an angel in heaven calls out: 'This one's daughter will marry that one's son.' What's this girl's name?"
>
> "Shosha."
>
> "Shosha? I had an aunt Shosha."[81]

For story-addled Itshele, his miniature bildungsroman (lighting out for Berlin, returning as a professor) beckons alongside his romance plot with Shosha. The library of his mind holds many genres. His father, after indulging the gentle bemusement that adults usually bring to the matrimonial aspirations of six-year-olds, hazards a different conceptual pathway to the same desired union even if it requires some benevolent misperception. In accordance with *his* overarching story, such things are foreordained; in the boy's awakening desire might lie clues to the divine will. Itshele's dreams and his father's aspirations for him are not really reconcilable, but Bashevis's ultimate fantasy for children—or the fantasy that writing for children allows him to spin out for himself—is that these opposing life pathways might nonetheless lead to a convergence point so pleasant, so obviously salutary, that the opposition would cease to matter. Rabbi Singer's lexicon of tradition would yield the terms necessary for him to go on loving his son the Berlin-educated professor—or the Warsaw scapegrace author of scandalous novels.

With his mother, a similar transaction of feeling, of being "loved despite," is less enchanted and more direct:

> I showed Mother the shining new dreidel and she gave me a sharp glance.
>
> "You got lost, eh?"
>
> I wanted to deny it, but I could not speak from too much happiness. Besides, she knew everything, just like a prophetess. She often read my mind. Her big gray eyes seemed to say, "I know all your antics but I love you anyhow."[82]

Here the rhetorical polarities are reversed: The rationalist rebbetzin brooks no nonsense, while the prodigal son recruits an ancient grammar to elevate her maternal perceptiveness to prophecy. She sees him truly and loves him anyway: What more could a growing child yearn for?

Molodowsky's Kheyder Mayses

Sholem Aleichem and Isaac Bashevis Singer follow a trail back to childhood in tracing the genesis of adult problems like wealth inequality and the impossibility of traditional faith in the modern world. This was a logical, if not an irresistible, impulse when psychology was a novel discourse and framework for seeing the world. However, it yields child stories for mature readers rather than true children's stories. There *are* substantive yet simple kheyder stories that are truly for children. They reenchant the world, restore the hopeful romance of Jewish childhood. Kadya Molodowsky, writing from the vantage point of 1970s New York, evokes a nostalgia for the shtetl and its schoolboy milieu that is sweet without being cloying. Classmates rib and razz one another; they compete academically and envy each other's successes. Significantly, the storyteller takes his place at the center rather than the periphery of the social constellation. “Zelig the Rhymester,” whom “all the boys liked . . . because he told good stories and knew how to rhyme,” lures his classmates out on a starry night to wish upon falling stars with a particularly Jewish twist. As he explains to his rapt peers:

> “On a clear summer evening, when you can see each star shining, Elijah the Prophet goes out for a tour. He wants to check on whether kids are going to bed nicely and concentrating properly when they say the Shema prayer. He’s pulled across the sky by fiery horses harnessed to a carriage with four wheels made of stars, and a pillar of light follows the carriage. His ride lasts just one instant; but in that instant, he sees the whole world, from one end to the other, and he hears how every kid says the Shema. When his carriage shows up in the sky, the stars start to fall: ten stars at a time, five at a time, and then lone stars. Whoever looks up right at that moment and sees the stars falling can make any wish at all.”[83]

The boys wait for a clear night and slip out to a field. If they are to transcend the old social arrangements, the old emotional constraints of the room that is the kheyder, they must indeed do so out of doors. They fix their eyes on the heavens, breaking focus only when their rhyme-loving leader spots a rabbit and shouts after it, “Short-nose bunny, your nose is runny. Your ears are long and very funny!” The spell is broken, the boys lose their chance to wish, and they are annoyed at the distraction.

But one of the circle, little Shayele, has already assimilated the most salient childhood lesson about wishes: Always use your wish to wish for more wishes. In the split second when the sky lightens and the stars begin to fall, he calls out to Elijah to come back in a year: the animating spirit of the perpetual rallying cry “Next year in Jerusalem!” The story is at once mythopoeic and homespun. The boys’ immediate experience is plugged into the millennia-long saga of Jewish waiting even as it schools them, as modern psychology might, in coping with disappointment by deferring hope: “The boys agreed that the next year . . . they would call out their wishes as soon as Elijah the Prophet showed up in his carriage with the four star-wheels harnessed to fiery steeds, and then they would have all that they could wish for.”[84]

PART II

Contesting the Jewish Future

5

The Storm Within

THE MEDEM SANATORIUM AND THE INNER LIVES OF MODERN CHILDREN

"A TIRED, old wind dragged himself across snowy fields. He had already traveled through many towns and villages, creeping round over all the roofs, running his long, cold fingers along the windowpanes, and blowing into the chimneys, without finding anywhere to rest." So begins Meyshe Kulbak's 1921 story "The Wind That Got Angry," inviting the reader—or very young listener—to take a sympathetic interest in the fate of a wind in late winter. Spring has come too early this year, leaving our hero in mortal danger from "a sudden thaw in town, which could have spelled his end." Finding a safe place means finding a cold place. Assuming this unaccustomed point of view, we begin to identify with a force of nature that is usually dismissed as a nuisance at best and feared as a danger at worst. *This* wind is vulnerable, weary, desperate.

Above all, this wind is a refugee, and we tag along in his quest for shelter and rest. But after he tries lodging with the oak tree on the horizon, the rock down the road, and the little red inn beyond that, it becomes clear that his modest needs can't be accommodated. Dejected and overwhelmed, he reaches his breaking point:

> The wind started to feel angry at the entire world. Nobody would let him rest, and he felt terrible. He stood up, like a strongman, in the middle of a field, rolled up his sleeves, girded his loins, and began to blow with all his might. The snow flew off the ground and, like silver flour, began to fall anew. . . .
>
> The wind blew at everything, as hard as he could. Then he began to whistle, to blow and whistle, whistle and blow, until he had whipped up a whirling, whistling, screaming blizzard. And the snow began to whirl and

> throw itself about like white handkerchiefs flying in a gale. The wind began to cry. He cried like a child, without stopping. Then he began to howl like a dog, and with all the howling, hard-driving snow and screaming, it grew darker than the white snow had ever seen it. The snow scattered through the darkness, from the sky down to the ground and from the ground up to the sky. And the wind began to wail like a cat and to cry, as cats wail and cry on a dark night. It was a great blizzard.[1]

In other words, the wind throws a tantrum. Having conjured a storm for the ages, he disrupts the human world, halting coachmen in their tracks and terrorizing rich and poor alike. Of course, such tribulations always fall harder on those in cold, thinly insulated huts with threadbare blankets and hungry stomachs. At the edge of town, a poor woman and her two children tremble with cold and fear at the raging blizzard. "She had stroked their heads and tucked them in, but the wind knocked so hard against the windows that they couldn't go to sleep." The wind shifts from clattering the windows to howling in the chimney, further frightening the children. "This just made the wind cry more. It pained him that he had to spend his entire life outdoors, like a dog, and that small children were afraid of him."[2] Finally, after the mother appeals to him "for the sake of the little children," the wind is appeased. The storm passes, and the children spend the next day shoveling snow and restoring order.

For child and caregiver alike, Kulbak sympathetically channels the stormy emotional experience of an overpowering temper tantrum as a last resort for a figure with limited ability to make his needs understood. Such spillover events are akin to weather systems: They burst forth suddenly, for reasons keenly felt by the principal but obscure to onlookers, and once unleashed, their fury must simply be allowed to blow over. Tantrums might not be new, but a new understanding of them emerged as childhood shifted from being recognized as a default *social status* of incomplete agency—a state occupied by smaller, weaker, less rational, less cognitively complete humans—to a *developmental stage* along the formative pathway leading to adulthood.[3] This altered conceptualization was driven by changes in the lived experience of young people, as schooling became universal throughout the industrialized world and children came largely to be cordoned off from adults beyond their families and deemed in need of protection from exposure to sex, violence, and other potentially harmful phenomena of "adult" life.[4] Having their own distinctive reading materials could afford some of the necessary protection, while also shaping their attitudes in directions determined by adults.

Throughout Yiddishland, many adults set their hearts and minds on programs of utopian societal repair. When it came to educating children, they pursued collectivist aims through individualist means: seeking to raise healthy, public-spirited individuals who would, at every age, meld together successfully as a community. This meant navigating the tension that surfaces even in early childhood between one's own freedom and constraint for the sake of the common good. It meant teaching individual children to be curious, to try on the perspectives of others, to cultivate the empathy that made such prosocial restraint possible. Kulbak's tale is among the most elegant exemplars of how Yiddish authors used weather, animals, and other elements of the natural world to represent children's interiority and thus expressly to foster their empathy—both reflecting and helping to construct the emerging conception of child development.[5]

We might associate the 1920s with the *Yiddish* invention of childhood, to borrow Philippe Ariès's controversial yet nonetheless evocative phrase.[6] There are many useful critiques and reassessments of his "invention of childhood" thesis, which deployed the history of European artistic representation to argue for a major shift in how children were seen in the West from the period of early modernity.[7] Colin Heywood argues against a specific "discovery" of childhood in early modern Europe: "It would surely now be more illuminating to think in terms of an ebbing and flowing of interest in the young over the long term, and of competing conceptions of childhood in any given society. So, we should ask, when were the important turning points, and how did they relate to changing material and cultural conditions?"[8] Interest in the young flowed freely during the twentieth century, newly filtered through overlapping scientific discourses, such as psychology, pedagogy, and library science.[9] For those with utopian aspirations the world over, including Ashkenazi Jews in and beyond Europe, the blossoming scientific discourses merged with utopian political ideologies to engender a new degree of fascination with the inner lives of children.

This chapter focuses on two avatars of that fascination in the context of their respective "material and cultural conditions." Both composed by teachers in collective-minded institutional settings, these stories nonetheless diverge artistically while complementing each other thematically. Through the indirection of allegory, Kulbak's story animates the private, interior world of strong emotion. We will contrast this manifestly "literary" story with twin works that were written in an entirely different and less belletristic register that hovers in the space between fiction and nonfiction. Yisroel Biber taught at the storied

Medem Sanatorium, a facility established in 1926 at a location three train stops outside of Warsaw, for the prevention of tuberculosis among children of the city's Jewish working class. He wished to encapsulate the ethos of his institution, conjuring its essence for alumni and for the many thousands who would never enjoy the opportunity to experience the place in person. With a direct, reportorial tone, he wrote accounts titled *Winter in the Forest* (*Vinter in vald*) and *Spring in the Forest* (*Friling in vald*), both set on the piney acreage of Medem, a preventorium-cum-children's republic.

Meyshe Kulbak was born in 1896 in the town of Smorgon, near Vilna, descended from hardy stock that included a timber merchant father and farmers on his mother's side. His education was varied, including stints at a modernized kheyder, a Russian Jewish public school, and several yeshivas. He would become a giant of Yiddish modernism in poetry and prose, but his day job was classroom teaching. During World War I, he lived in Kovno and taught Jewish orphans in that city, using his free time to write poetry in Hebrew and then Yiddish. After the war, he moved between Vilna, Berlin, and Minsk. August 1920 found him teaching at the Y. Dinezon School in Vilna, sited at the Shnipishker Home for Orphans at 7 Khivinske Street.[10] He would marry fellow faculty member Zelda Etkin in 1924.[11] Residents of the home attended the onsite school, along with other day scholars who resided with their families. Kulbak appears to have written just this one story for children, and he dedicated it as "A gift to the children of the Dinezon Orphanage in Vilna": his own students.

The dreamy, lyrical story of the wind's anger shares thematic and stylistic elements that predominate in Kulbak's romantic poetry, including a preoccupation with alienated outsiders and a view of nature as vibrantly alive. He refers to the wind as a *geyer*, a wanderer, which echoes his poetry for adults, in which, as Jordan Finkin observes, "many poems are peopled by peripatetic souls, out on the road, in a tavern, by the wayside, or in a forest."[12] The city, which our wind must flee in order to survive, is treacherous, whereas unspoiled nature is "the site of true, authentic individual experience."[13] The opening lyric of Kulbak's poetry collection for adults, published in 1922, just a year after "The Wind That Got Angry," includes the following verse:

Kum ikh tsu a kretshme tsu
Klap ikh on in teyer[14]
"Ver bistu? Ver bistu"
Entfer ikh: a geyer

I come up to a country inn
And rap upon the gate
Who are you? Who are you?
Say I: "*Wanderer* is my fate."[15]

In reading the verse, situated in the first-person lyric "Ikh bin a bokher a hultay" (I'm a rogue of a fellow), as a manifesto for the lifestyle of the wanderer, Finkin draws insightfully on a tradition that emphasizes the laconic brevity of Kulbak's writing and the author's trust that the reader will make the necessary interpretive connections.[16] The sympathetic hero, like our weary wind, is a wanderer and a rogue by his own admission. Kulbak counted on his readers, even the youngest among them, to catch the allegory.

Given Kulbak's dedication of the story to his pupils at Dinezon, it is logical to assume that he conceived of them as his first addressees, penning the story he felt they needed. Many of those served by the orphanage and school were "half orphans" who had lost one parent. The image of two children living in poverty with a single mother would have resonated for many of them; reassuringly, that stalwart parent has the gumption to face down an angry wind for the sake of her children. For the "full orphans" who resided at the Shnipishker Home, even this representation of a precarious family life might have been an instance of "granting in fantasy" a domesticity they lacked in reality.[17]

It is notable that nevertheless in the congregate setting of an institution, which necessarily demands greater conformity than the nuclear family, Kulbak nevertheless approaches the wind sympathetically and honors the needs that drive his antisocial behavior. He invites readers to *take the perspective* of one who cannot conform, whose very existence stands athwart widely embraced ideals like "the coming of spring." Such perspective-taking is the bedrock underlying empathy, and Kulbak exposes this relational foundation to young auditors of his tale alongside the adult caregivers who may be reading it aloud to them. In crafting a story about emotional regulation—lost and regained—he reminds parents, teachers, and supervisory staff that the weary, sometimes angry young charges in their care are also sympathetic characters whose stormy emotions call for a wide berth and an understanding heart. And why stop at children? Surely the behavioral lapses we tolerate in children can occur in adults as well; a story that teaches empathy could be of use in understanding the motivations of adults who rage and blow like the wind. "Children are people too": The slogan would not gain currency until the 1970s, but the sentiment clearly impelled stories being written fifty years earlier.

Kulbak's inward-turned, atmospheric tale, with its limited cast of characters and rich layers of implication, is an intensely private one. Even though the wind's blizzard is acknowledged to affect society at large (wagon drivers must disembark and wait out the storm, and even the wealthy have their sleep disturbed), its effects are focalized through the viewpoint of a single family. A thriving society, the author seems to suggest, is composed of individuals who have been cared for in such empathetic and understanding ways. Although a combination of artistic, familial, and political considerations drew Kulbak to relocate from Polish-controlled Vilna to Soviet Minsk in 1928, his stylistic tendencies and thematic commitments put him on a collision course with the Stalinist regime.[18] In keeping with his wanderer persona, he was perceived as something of an outsider, an inherent danger to authoritarian control. Soviet literary critic Khatskl Dunets characterized Kulbak as bearing "a legacy not our own." In Minsk, Kulbak published his monumental comic novel of Soviet Jewish life, *Zelmenyaner*, and several works of drama and poetry, enjoying a productive decade until his September 1937 arrest and liquidation the following month. Though he was officially rehabilitated in 1956, the true details of his execution were not known until the opening of Soviet archives in 1990. Ironically, Dunets was also purged in 1937, accused of belonging to a counterrevolutionary organization.[19]

One aspect of "The Wind That Got Angry" that stood at odds with evolving Soviet aspirations was the messy turbulence of the wind's emotions. For the revolution to succeed, as we shall see in chapter 8, rational habits of orderliness and cleanliness would have to prevail. By the 1930s, no quarter could be given to the intensity and self-involvement of the wind's outburst. But while the nuclear family might have been able to contain and productively channel young children's emotional intensity, such outbursts were ill suited to institutional life, where order must hold chaos in check. Knowing that feelings and politics mapped onto each other and intermingled, what might it look like in the Yiddish heartland to honor children's strong, sometimes messy emotions while at the same time promoting a shared experience of calm? What would an institution look like if it strove to uphold both sides of this tension? It might look a lot like the Medem Sanatorium.

Situated seventeen kilometers southeast of Warsaw, near the townlet of Międzeszyn, Medem was as close as one might come to a literal heterotopia: an "other place" that was neither city nor shtetl. Like purely figurative heterotopias, its very existence shed new light on the ordinary spaces of city and town, school and family. The two children's stories that emerged from Medem during its existence offered a symbolic re-creation of the institution and its ethos. To appreciate the representation of the institution on the page and the significance of the discursive work these books performed, it will be useful to first offer an overview of Medem as an actual place.[20]

Unlike the TSYSHO schools, which ran as a coalition of the socialist and Zionist left, Medem was explicitly an institution of the Bund, at once a laboratory and a showcase for blending proletarianism and Yiddishism. Interweaving healthcare, education, athletics, and outdoorsmanship, the sanatorium responded with a duty of care to circumstances that jeopardized the well-being of children in Warsaw in the 1920s. The newly surging social sciences elicited raw data about prevailing conditions, and Jewish communal leaders sought to act accordingly. In 1925–1926, leaders of the Bundist youth group Tsukunft (Future) circulated a survey of its membership that indicated a growing number of young children entering the workforce. Journalist Pinkhes Shvarts analyzed the results in a series of articles, observing, "The younger the child is brought into the world of work, the more dejected and morally neglected he becomes. It is harder to organize these children than the older ones. The street, with all of its peculiar means of attraction, 'organizes' them."[21] The same poverty that propelled youth into unskilled labor was also responsible for endemic malnutrition and overcrowding, circumstances that left families and especially children vulnerable to the spread of tuberculosis. The city's poor children were used to sharing beds and making do in apartments without electricity, running water, or indoor plumbing.[22]

Even as these conditions grew increasingly exigent and demanded an organized communal response, the 1920s initially seemed to promise Polish Jewry greater room than before for political maneuver.[23] Poland had signed the National Minorities Treaty at Versailles in 1919, explicitly naming the Jews as one of the minority populations to be granted cultural autonomy in the newly independent state, with public monies allocated to support this autonomy. The Polish Constitution of 1921 neglected to mention Jewry outright but seemed to reinforce that autonomy, albeit without allocating funds for Jewish schools.[24] It seemed like a moment pregnant with pluralistic possibility for creating new political parties and institutions to meet communal needs and proactively advance communal aims. Although the hoped-for progress was slowed by the refusal of the government to support Jewish educational and healthcare institutions, the community continued its own fundraising. After some fits and starts, the Vladimir Medem Children's Sanatorium opened the doors to its first cohort of fourteen children on January 18, 1926. The population served ranged from ages six to sixteen, and though the average length of stay varied over the life of the institution, most children spent between a few weeks and a few months.

First and foremost, Medem operated as a preventorium, a healthcare facility dedicated to arresting the spread of tuberculosis among the children it served. Temperatures were taken daily, a dentist worked onsite, and there was a robust regimen of hygiene, including frequent handwashing, twice-daily bathing, and the practice, novel for many, of toothbrushing.[25] "One of our first tasks," wrote director Shloyme Gilinsky, "was to accustom the children to a hygienic lifestyle."[26] The leadership worked closely with the medical staff to maintain the necessary medical regimen while ensuring that "the institution not be ruled by a hospital spirit." The ethos may be summarized as *anima sana in corpore sano*: "The Medem Sanatorium came to be known in Poland and throughout Europe not only as a curative facility but moreover, and principally, as a curative-*educational* children's institution. . . . The whole attitude toward the child here was an educational one. You cannot separate the child's body and soul. If you want to heal the body, you must simultaneously heal the soul."[27] Medem's leaders fostered an ethic of integration that began with the inseparability of body and soul and carried outward toward the body politic. The soul could refresh itself in an atmosphere of respect, orderliness, and abundant access to the outdoors.

Ideals of the Institution

From its inception, Medem married increasingly international principles of progressive childcare, encompassing both education and health maintenance, with the socialism and Yiddishism of the Bund.[28] The discourse of pedagogy was already well developed throughout Western Europe and the United States, with eighteenth-century figures like Johann Friedrich Pestalozzi and his disciple Friedrich Fröbel delineating a set of aims that would be modernized at the turn of the twentieth century by theorist-practitioners like John Dewey and Maria Montessori in the West and Konstantin Venttsel in Russia. In its daily functioning, under the leadership of Bundist pedagogue Shloyme Fayvish Gilinsky, Medem sought to meld theory with practice. Thanks to Gilinsky's personality and pedagogical training, Medem was engineered to build upward and outward from the starting place of the individual child.[29] The urgency of meeting that child's needs was considered a precursor to fostering the collective aims bound up with socialism. Gilinsky, who fled east shortly after Hitler invaded Poland and made his way to the United States with his wife and son, described his and his colleagues' response to the varied life experiences and temperaments of the small humans placed in their care.[30] In his contribution to the omnibus anthology of first-person recollections of Medem published in 1971, Gilinsky recalled an environment of "constant pedagogical creativity" and a prevailing spirit of experimentation among teachers and medical caregivers alike, as they sought to meet the multifarious needs of the young *sanatoristn*:

> We had to find pathways to individual and collective education simultaneously: each child was a world unto himself, reacted differently to missing their parents and being in a new environment with hundreds of children; one was too passive, another too active; one was too bold, another too bashful and scared; one strove for "aloneness," isolation, while another wanted to be in the company of friends all the time; one enjoyed the basic habits of cleanliness and hygiene, while another was shocked at the "herd-like" discipline, the "primitivism" of the surroundings. . . . Children with a mix of traits: kind, gentle, hard, cruel, bitter; from different social environments; Yiddish speakers and Polish speakers. There could be no "machine-made" [*mashinove*] educational system here. Attention had to be paid to the individual, body and soul. Individual observations and adjustments had to come in here, adapting the singular child to the life of the collective.[31]

Gilinsky saw children as they were, without idealizing them as a Romantic educator might have done a century earlier. His evaluative language ("too" this or that) departs from the neutral descriptions of a child psychologist, but not by much. He is talking, after all, about the adjustment of children to their environment. He could acknowledge in young people, and in an encompassing context of love, uglier traits like cruelty and bitterness. Like Kulbak's wind, the children who seemed maladjusted to "the life of the collective" were expressing needs that had yet to be met. He strove to hasten their accommodation by viewing their struggles with both empathy and honesty.

Anna Gonshor correlates the wide variety of activities available at Medem with Gilinsky's theoretical commitment to individualization.[32] Introverts and extroverts, Yiddish and Polish speakers, preliterate children and independent readers all could be cheerfully occupied with nature walks, animal husbandry, gardening, playground time, story hours, leisure reading, language and literature study, arts and crafts, composition of a "wall newspaper," theatrical productions, and daily "radio" broadcasts. To these diversions was added the children's own involvement in the tasks of daily living, such as mending clothing, changing bedding, polishing shoes, and maintaining the library and children's co-op. Since stays were relatively short, it made sense to focus on experiential education rather than formal classroom instruction. Children could elect how to spend much of their time.

Utopian social relations underwrote the institution's approach to discipline, which was conceived, ideally, as self-discipline. Gilinsky sought to base all relationships, whether between adult and child or among the children, on reciprocal respect. He wrote, "In the sanatorium, *mutual trust* must reign—teacher in child and child in teacher. The child needs to believe the teacher. Without this belief, there can be no talk of a teacher's effect on the child. And if you want the child to believe you, trust you, you have to believe and trust in them. The first task of the teacher is to *win the child's trust*. And this isn't difficult, if you are honest, direct, friendly, and you relate to him as an equal."[33]

Arriving at the campus in Międzeszyn, children were inserted into an elaborate structure of self-governance with adult mentorship.[34] *Sanatoristn* were sorted into about thirty-five different committees of two to twelve children each that oversaw all kinds of tasks involved with housekeeping and caring for the physical plant, including the domestic animals and gardens. The committees reported to a Children's Council (*Kinder rat*), which kept a weekly log of its activities and was in turn elected for ten-week terms by the highest body, the General Assembly, whose weekly meetings were open to all children over age eight.[35] The *Kinder rat* included seven members alongside two educators who could also vote.

The methods were the message, and the group was the work. As *sanatorist(ke)* Bina Fridman recalled years later, no decision was too small to subject to the rigors of majority rule. "All provisions were voted on, committees elected. . . . Do we have to eat spinach or not? A mini-republic. Are we going to play today? Why should we be dressed in a specific manner [?]. It sounds quite funny now that I think of it. But we were taught how democracy worked."[36] The emphasis on self-governance was designed to obviate need for externally imposed or top-down discipline, at least in Gilinsky's formulation of the ideal: "The children's self-governance accomplished all the goals of collective coexistence, and the children, like bees each with its own place, upheld it religiously—each with his own little corner, his work that had been entrusted to him. And that's how they learned to keep everything in order and consequently themselves too."[37] Discipline was imagined not as a heteronomous, punitive force but as an exercise in self-regulation. When there *were* instances of recalcitrance, the children's own administrative structures took measures to hold the offenders accountable with compassion and firmness. Those measures might include mild forms of separation from the group, such as sitting at a separate table at mealtimes or sleeping in a separate bedroom. "The most severe sanction was to mention an unruly child during the morning show, 'Our Radio,'" recalls one former guest.[38] The goal was to prompt reflection and amendment.

Self-discipline and self-regulation were the necessary means to achieving the cherished value of freedom. Children's theatricals, both formal and informal, offered children opportunities to literally act out this message. The play immortalized in the fundraising documentary film *Mir kumen on,* "The Puppets" (Di lyalkes), tells the story of marionettes who escape their strings and taunt their erstwhile puppet master:

Enough of being locked up
Doing another's will
We all want to be free
To play just as we will

In addition to scripted and scored productions like this one, children put on parodies that poked gentle fun at peers and staff alike. At Medem, children could laugh *at* adults, *with* adults, and were thus taught to laugh at themselves—ventilating their potentially stuffy education in democracy.

It is not incidental that their laughter was prompted by songs and sketches in the mother tongue of Yiddish. Many aspects of life at Medem resembled progressive educational and public health experiments being undertaken under other auspices between the wars, but the combination of philosophy and its execution *in Yiddish for Yiddish* was unique.[39] Use of the language as the communicative instrument for the children's joy was not viewed as an incidental means to other ends but rather was an aim in itself. Between 1926 and 1937, only 38 percent of *sanatoristn* had attended the secular Yiddish-language schools of TSYSHO, run cooperatively by a broad coalition of the left that included Bundists alongside Zionists.[40] A further 41 percent had attended Polish-language public schools but, if Jewish, presumably spoke Yiddish at home. Likewise, another 7 percent attended religious schools of one kind or another. These numbers were adequate to seed a spirit of conscious Yiddishism among the children, with older children from Yiddishist schools reinforcing the Yiddishism of the teaching staff, and plenty of receptivity among competent native speakers to the notion of elevating Yiddish to a cultural ideal rather than just a practical means of communication. From the institution's opening, it had always hosted a cohort of non-Jewish Polish speakers; although they were accommodated in their native tongue, several of the memoirists of Medem recall those children starting to pick up some Yiddish quite organically in the immersive environment.

Gilinsky did not wish to extricate his work as an educational theorist from his commitment to Yiddishism. Calling on his classroom experience, he authored a pedagogical treatise so innovative that there was interest in translating it into Polish. Gilinsky insisted the book appear with a notice that it had been translated from the Yiddish. When the publisher refused, Gilinsky forewent the additional income and stuck to his principles, writing, "Only through the power of Yiddish have we elicited so much from the children. We won't be silent on this point. *Yiddish is our mother-tongue*."[41]

Inducting young children into a socialist consciousness entailed blurring the line between work and play. Nowadays, it is a truism among progressive early-childhood educators that "the work of childhood is play," but at Medem, it was almost equally true that the play of childhood was work, accorded the same dignity as adults' work. Work was not just an activity but an identity, and the *sanatoristn* were encouraged to identify as "children of the workers." Children pulled weeds and harvested in the garden and orchard, folded and changed bed linens, mended clothing, polished shoes, and carried out many other necessary tasks. This approach was not unique to Medem and in fact became quite prevalent in a variety of settings that extended from Montessori schools to Soviet kindergartens.[42] However, because Medem was also conceived as a preventorium for children at risk of contracting TB, many of whom were weakened by malnourishment and lack of regular exercise, the push toward labor was also balanced by a cultivation of rest and leisure.

Pleasure reading was celebrated as a leisure activity, and the library was one of the facility's most fondly remembered amenities. The collection of over one thousand Yiddish and Polish books, bolstered by gifts from visiting dignitaries, was supported by a nominal monthly subscription fee of twenty groszy, waived for those who could not afford to pay.[43] No books were to be taken back to bedrooms or to the dining room; however, children could enjoy them in the reading room or al fresco. They were encouraged to write reviews for the benefit of other *sanatoristn*. A careful system was put into place that allowed the children to run their library with maximal autonomy: When a book circulated, it was covered in a special jacket, while its usual book jacket held the volume's place on the shelf. This created a straightforward visual cue for reshelving, and when a book was returned "out of order," the lapse was announced on "our radio" at mealtimes. "Books seldom went missing," according to the booklet describing the sanatorium in minute detail to the families of prospective *sanatoristn*.[44] The library physically instantiated the orderliness and care that lay at the heart of the institution's values, and many children responded accordingly. "For me," recalled Hershel Shtrigler, who was among Medem's first group of guests in January 1926, "the library was the holy corner of the sanatorium. Here, on the shelf was gathered the 'whole of human knowledge,' and when I was assigned to the library committee, I had the impression that the Gates of Knowledge had opened for me."[45] The language of "holiness" further reinforces the spiritual dimension of secular utopian ideologies discussed in chapter 3 with respect to the Sabbath.

As with all the "extracurricular" activities, children were supervised and mentored by teachers with a special interest in a given pursuit. Gilinsky's wife, Lyuba Kantorovitsh-Gilinsky, recalled how "Teacher Yosl Katz, smitten with Yiddish literature, often read aloud the works of Peretz, Sholem Aleichem, Mendele, Asch, and fine poetry (*sheyne poezye*) in the sanatorium. He enthusiastically dedicated himself to work around the library, took care to have a good selection of books in growing numbers, introduced the new decimal system, taught children how to use various cataloguing systems, enlisting a group of older children in the work—they found, discovered a source of spiritual satisfaction, pleasure in reading books."[46] It was typical of Medem to recruit children into the behind-the-scenes administrative labor that made the library run, treating them as producers and not just consumers.

"We Become Friends of Nature"

Another teacher's area of specialization at Medem brings us back to the portrayal of natural phenomena in children's literature as a vocabulary for exploring children's inner lives. Now we turn to two works written by the biologist Yisroel Biber, who after directing the TSYSHO Teachers' Seminary in Vilna, came to preside over the sanatorium's encompassing nature education program. Aesthetically, his two children's stories, *Winter in the Forest* and *Spring in the Forest*, could not be more different from Kulbak's. Where Kulbak is allegorical and dreamy, Biber is direct and matter-of-fact. At first blush, his books might be classed as no-nonsense nonfiction, while "The Wind That Got Angry" is extravagantly literary. However, the aesthetic value of Biber's texts lies in how they braid together strands of emotion and information, feeling and knowing. Biber's In the Forest books, both published in Warsaw in 1937, exemplify the very task of integration that formed the heart of the facility's mission. Although they could be read by anyone anywhere with access to Yiddish, they signify particularly against the backdrop of the lived experience of the sanatorium, bringing the Medem experience to life on the page.

Biber gradually built up the infrastructure for teaching about the natural world, introducing a dovecote for raising pigeons, cages with rabbits and chickens, and even an incubator for hatching chicks. He brooked no distinction between literary arts and sciences, a sensibility his charges appreciated. In a brief, lyrical memoir of her days as a child at Medem, Shoshke Fligl-Erlikh asks, "Can you imagine a happier boy than a boy in charge of pigeons? Recognizing birds by their calls was a matter for child scientists and child poets alike."[47] Biber's first book, *Winter in the Forest,* chronicles a group of children's three-week stay. The story starts right in with the children being dropped off at the Bund office in Warsaw, whence they will travel by train to Międzeszyn. Many are local, but a few have traveled from other cities and towns. A motif running throughout the book is Gitl from Breslov's growing ability to understand the Warsaw dialect of Yiddish. In the course of her linguistic adjustment, we watch an outsider become an insider. Gitl's chatty letter home just a week before her departure from Medem (wryly juxtaposed with a boy's two-sentence missive) informs her parents that she's getting to be able to "speak like a Warsovian already."[48]

Biber's new arrivals quickly encounter an iconic image, reproduced across Medem publications including this one (see Figure 2). Labeled "Tree of children's self-governance in the Medem Sanatorium," the poster uses the organic imagery of a branching tree to map out the organizational structure whereby the facility thrives. At the root level is the children's General Assembly. The trunk is the more select *Kinder rat.* Thick branches represent domains, including "nature circle," "culture circle," and "housekeeping." The thickest branch is hygiene. Growing from these branches are thinner ones naming individual committees in charge of everything from emptying chamber pots to giving tours of the facility to visitors.

Biber likewise reproduces another sign that would have greeted new arrivals: a poster welcoming them with the rules of the institution written out as a numbered list. As with the original Ten Commandments, which may have inspired the format, the first item is a descriptive declaration rather than a directive: "1. This is the Medem Sanatorium. Everyone is friends here. The Medem Sanatorium was built by the Jewish Workers. It carries the name of the great labor leader, builder of the Yiddish secular school (*folkshul*) Vl.

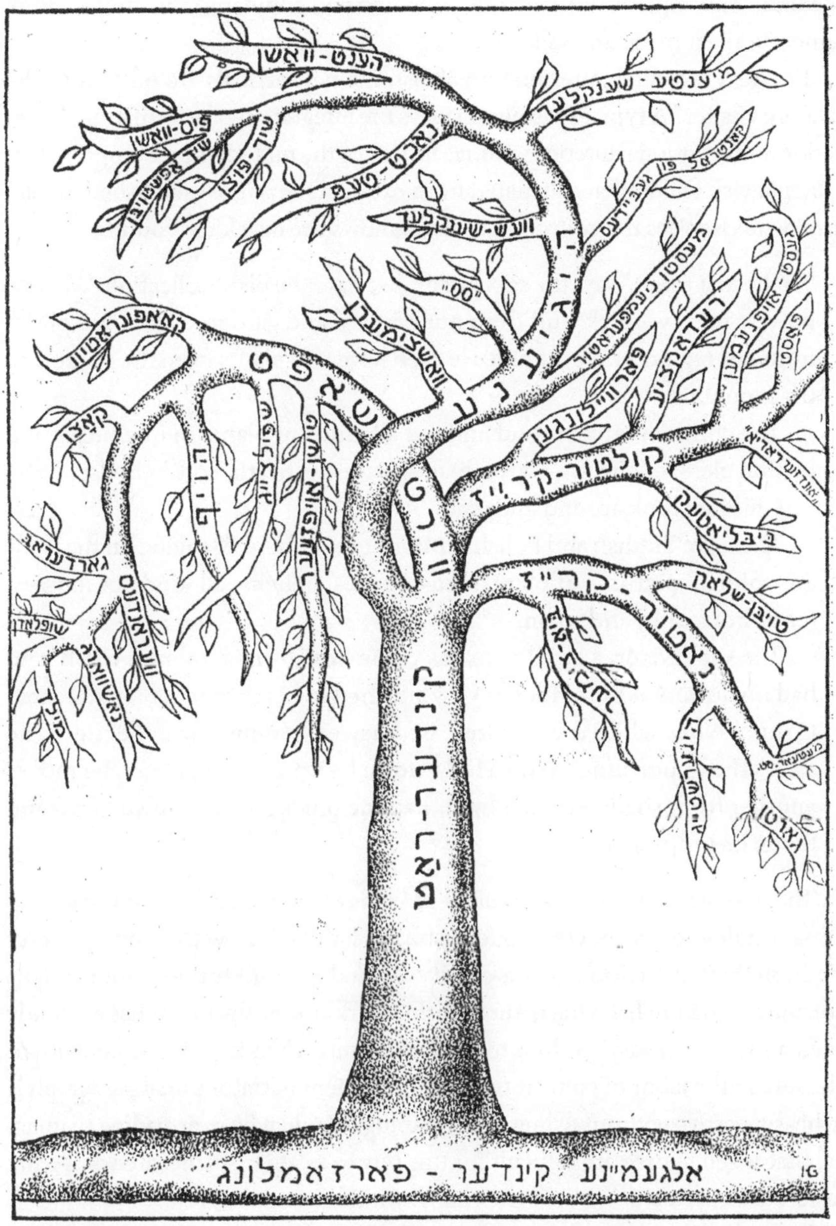

בוים פון דער קינדער-זעלבסטפאַרוואַלטונג אין דער מעדעם-סאַנאַטאָריע

FIGURE 2. A picture of a branching tree that is inscribed with the names of various committees staffed by the children of the Medem Sanatorium. Yisroel Biber, *Vinter in vald*, 1937.

Medem." Subsequent rules include "5. When you come into the dining room, remember: eat more and talk less."[49]

The next morning, after first breakfast, the new arrivals are off to tour the "Nature Center." A typical passage displays the integration of informational nonfiction and emotional interior writing, all against the underlying assumption that urban Jewish children are alienated from nature. One of the established *sanatoristn*, who oversees the collection of flora, shows the new kids around:

> "In the first room," says the supervisor, "we have the plant collection. We raise flowers here, we pick fruit from our orchard and garden, seeds, rare plants from our region, and over here we even have rare plants from the ocean and the mountains."
>
> The children look around and see all kinds of plants in fine boxes and behind glass: edelweiss, Carpathian sowthistle, heath, cotton bolls.
>
> Children look around and read.
>
> There are Yiddish and Polish captions everywhere. Hanging on the walls are colorful pictures of plants, mushrooms, lichens, all kinds of mosses, ferns, horsetails, and so on.
>
> The supervisor, a child who has come here from a Talmud torah, and had no flowers at his school, is very attached to his corner here in the sanatorium. Now, while the children are busy examining the collections, he seizes the opportunity to do a little work: he waters one planter, he moves another from shade into the light; here he plucks off a yellowed leaf, and there, he props up a stem.[50]

The passage moves between different kinds of discourse, inserting informational catalogues of species while gesturing lightly at how the boy's poverty (indicated by his schooling at a charity-funded Talmud torah) reinforces his previous alienation from the natural world. Work among the plants has evidently been a tonic. It is easy for him to be industrious when he takes such evident pleasure in the labor of cultivation. The omniscient narrator's final paragraph is richly suggestive without telling us everything. Would it be overreading to imagine that when people are difficult for this boy to relate to, plants are somewhat easier? That in nurturing their thriving, he finds his own?

Instead of dilating on these questions, Biber's text swiftly spirits off the children—his subjects and his ostensible readers—to tour the chicken and pigeon coops, to down their daily second breakfast, and to gather for a nature walk in the forest with their teacher. In the forest they will encounter a marten, a rabbit, and several fascinating birds. The last of these has been ensnared in a horsehair trap. "It was a pity to see the suffering of the little bird," reports an ambiguous first-person-plural speaker. "The bird looked at us so sorrowfully and helplessly, like a person tied up." When the teacher snips the loop around the bird's neck and it flies away, "The children breathed a sigh of relief as if they themselves had been freed from captivity."[51] The children are urged to *identify* with the animals, especially the vulnerable and harmless ones. Love of nature calls for them, insofar as possible, to insinuate themselves protectively into the lives of the animals around them, freeing trapped birds and preventing harm to prey from predators, especially other human beings.

Nature education at Medem was filtered through a robustly humanist lens. Seeing the mechanics of predation in action, the "armaments" of tooth and claw prevailing over tender fur and flesh, was designed to make the children into more compassionate people. Although such a theme is not made explicit in the text, it is not difficult to imagine children witnessing these small dramas of predation against the backdrop of antisemitic violence in Europe in the 1930s. "Nature class" oriented them in the struggle between strong and weak, predator and prey, and encouraged them to cast their lot with the more vulnerable. The children return from the walk empty-handed, but their teacher reminds them of their guiding ethos: "'Actually,' argued the teacher, 'we aren't hunters! We are *naturfraynd*, friends of nature; we don't want to catch animals but only to observe them. We want to learn about their lives. We even want to help them.'"[52]

"Nature," portrayed as a domain apart from the human, gives rise to the finer human feelings. The bridge connecting outward nature to inward emotion was the process of *baobakhtung* or "observation," which would offer up a wealth of details and cue the child about how to feel in response to nature.[53] Gilinsky recalled:

> The children of the sanatorium didn't just live amid nature, but rather *with nature*. There was awakened in them an impulse to observe and to research. Attention was paid to every natural phenomenon and change of weather, seasons: how the changes affected the vicinity and the life in the institution. Every important occurrence in nature—the arrival of spring or winter, planting flowers, picking the first fruits or vegetables in the garden—was transformed into a holiday, a holiday for the entire institution.[54]

Whether it was compassionate alarm at seeing an animal endangered or holiday joy at the change of seasons, the *sanatoristn* were encouraged to record the phenomena they witnessed so that they could respond as fuller, more emotionally literate people with richer inner lives.[55] Becoming attuned to the natural world held out the promise of self-discovery and of reintegrating selves that had been fractured by the grind of urban poverty. In his sequel *Spring in the Forest*, Biber explains in a brief introduction how "at the Medem Sanatorium, much effort and time is devoted to bringing the child close to nature." This is necessary because "the Jewish child of the city has been distanced from his nature-friends by walls and fences. Here, in the Medem Sanatorium, they get acquainted again."[56] Lurking in the background behind the immediate drivers of alienation, as Gonshor has noted, was the lasting damage of the Great War; by the time Biber published his books in 1937, the children of that war had become parents.[57]

Although Biber's books are superficially quite simple, they enact a subtle blending of fiction and nonfiction, fitting scientific and educational content into a unified relational frame. Both books may—arguably must—be read against the backdrop of the actual sanatorium and its operations. The Medem stay was immersive by design, focusing on the whole child, integrating care for the body with development of the mind and soul.[58] While few if any books can offer as encompassing an experience as a stint at an arboreal heterotopia, Biber conjured a plausible substitute both for the *sanatoristn* who sought to evoke and hold onto their visits, and for the many others who could not go in person to Międzeszyn. Naturally, he weaves themes of emotional self-regulation and democracy education into the more apparent nature "curriculum."

One important contrast that may be drawn between the In the Forest volumes and Kulbak's story has to do with the element of fantasy—utterly absent in the former while suffusing the latter. For the majority of children, though, a stint at Medem *was* a fantasy. As such, we might regard Biber's books in the light of a new kind of *skaz*, or oral, folkloristic storytelling that was being theorized in the USSR during this period. The revolution called for realistic works even as educators recognized that children craved a measure of fantasy, magic, myth, and whimsy.[59] "As a 'scientific' substitute for fairy tales," explains Lisa Kirschenbaum, "teachers proposed realistic stories" on the logic that "since 'fantasy has its roots in real events,' new *skazki* ought to revolve around the 'wonders of technology, the achievement of the radio.'"[60] Combining the aspirational values of the "children's republic" with a keenly humanist eye trained on the world of the outdoors, Biber's Medem stories register as a new kind of secularist Yiddishist *skaz*.

A Model(ing) Institution

The adults in charge at Medem were quite conscious of creating, with their children's republic, a model institution where a steady stream of visiting dignitaries—whether from the realms of medicine, education, politics, or the arts—might draw inspiration and shift their sense of what was possible for future generations. Gilinsky and his staff were proud of their tours, including the impressions of several prominent visitors in their booklet-length brochure about the sanatorium.[61] Medem presented itself to the world as a model institution, and it could do so with integrity because it presented itself to itself as a model*ing* institution—that is, a place whose pedagogical principles were thoroughly embodied by its staff and teaching was done by example. With their portrayal of the relations between children and teacher, as well as among the children themselves, Biber's In the Forest books seamlessly and subtly embedded the kind of cooperative interactions the leadership sought to foster. This was another form of the integration represented in Biber's work. As Gilinsky explains, "*Not with words, but with actions, with facts* must one approach children. In life, plain ideas, plain theories don't prevail. What prevails is embodied ideas, embodied theories. And if this is correct for adults, then it's one hundred percent true for children. Children must be shown the thing itself and not its shadow. Don't *talk* about comradeship [*khaverishkeyt*], don't *talk* about helping the weak, but practice it. And the same holds with respect to problems of order, cleanliness, labor, and the relationship with nature."[62]

Avrom "Amik" Brumberg, the son of Gilinsky's deputy Yoysef Brumberg, experienced the sanatorium over long periods as a faculty child. In later years, he recalled, "the sanatorium was the *embodiment*—albeit on a small scale—of all the ideals towards which the Jewish socialists strove. The purely humanistic and socialist values, as well as the Jewish principles on which the Bund was based, weren't expressed as clearly or carried out as successfully in any other institution or time period as in the Medem Sanatorium. The sanatorium itself represented a microcosmic 'society of the future.'"[63] Along with attempting to shift the direction of the future world to be more just and equitable, "more beautiful and better" (*a shenere un a besere velt*) in the Bundist locution, Medem's modeling was intended to dismantle some negative contemporary assumptions. As Magdalena Kozłowska points out, the promotional film *Mir kumen on* lavished attention on the physical fitness and joyful outdoorsiness of the *sanatoristn,* thus challenging "the stereotypical view of Jews as exclusively associated with religion, commerce, and the city."[64] Ultimately, the facility's patent cleanliness, orderliness, and artfulness made it a Jewish institution even a Nazi could grudgingly admire.[65]

A stay at the Medem, which was a heterotopia by design, was temporary—a short, high-impact intervention in the lives of its individual guests and, by implication, their entire families. Medem had a transformative effect when the *sanatoristn* reentered conventional domestic life. Shloyme Khayim Kazdan observes that "children brought with them into the poor cellar apartments of their parents new habits of hygiene, culture, aesthetics, language, and behavior with others," changes radical enough to constitute "a whole revolution in the home."[66] But the revolution wasn't necessarily frictionless. Shoshke Fligl-Erlikh, whose father, Henryk, led the Bund in Poland, and who probably often overheard grown-ups talking politics, summarizes the kinds of challenges that were posed to Gilinsky:

> "The Medem Sanatorium is an unreal world. It is too far from the children's homes. The sanatorium estranges children from their homes. They come back to the city and start to look down on home. He no longer likes the food, demands new customs; toothbrushes, separate towels, more frequent baths. Some parents can go along with this, while others can't. Why create conflicts with the home? The sanatorium is only for a little while after all; the home—for always."
>
> Shloyme Gilinsky responded:
>
> Nothing is too good for our children. There won't be any conflicts with the home because we, together with the children, actually *want* to introduce new things into the home. The parents, who send their children to us, have confidence in us, and they welcome what the children bring home from the Medem Sanatorium. The children are just the first swallows who announce the coming of spring. Together with them, we will improve life in their homes.[67]

The "unreal world" pointed to what was possible in the real one. Better hygiene would lead to healthier families; improved physical health would inexorably promote psychological well-being and the thriving of the body politic. Just as the various needs of every *sanatorist* had to be met in order to maximize the potential of their healing and education at the facility, so too each family's individual flourishing would constitute another building block of a thriving society. Echoing Gilinsky, Biber explains to his young readers that they should strive to fashion a world in which every child everywhere enjoys Medem-caliber living.[68]

Intersectional Childhood

Only at the dawn of the twenty-first century did it become possible to assess the galvanic changes in conceptions of children and childhood that had occurred over the previous hundred years. In 1997, sociologists Allison James and Alan Prout hazarded a "new paradigm" rooted in the idea of childhood as a *social construct* and noting that "the immaturity of children is a biological fact of life but the ways in which this immaturity is understood and made meaningful [are] a fact of culture." At the same time, they recognized the inseparability of "childhood" from any given combination of class, gender, and ethnicity—what today we might call the *intersectionality* of childhood identity. James and Prout recognized children's *agency*: that they were not just acted upon by adults but must rather be seen as "active in determining their own lives and the lives of those around them."[69] In seeking that which was distinctive about the early years of the human animal, they emphasized the study of children's needs and competencies, inflected as they were by time, place, available resources, etc. It is striking how closely the arrangements at Medem accorded with the paradigm that had crystallized by the 1990s.

Until the 1960s, as Colin Heywood underscores, Western researchers viewed childhood as mere preparation for adulthood. "What mattered," he observes, "was finding ways of turning the immature, irrational, incompetent, asocial and acultural child into a mature, rational, competent, social and autonomous adult."[70] Educators and writers in the Yiddish cultural sphere shared these lofty, Enlightenment-tinged goals for the children under their influence, but they pursued them in ways that, in retrospect, seem prescient. Kulbak understood that even apparent irrationality—the blind and blinding epochal blizzard—has its rationale. Before the weather can calm down, the need driving the emotional storm must be met. Gilinsky pioneered a different approach: assuming that children were mostly rational, competent actors already, in need only of the gentlest nudge or, better yet, example set by caring adults. When the vulnerability of children was ever more apparent, he sought to replace the tragedy of an impoverished upbringing with a glimpse, however brief, of a more secure, fully actualized existence. In proudly identifying as children of the workers, the *sanatoristn* were taught to push aside shame and draw dignity from their work. Children's empowerment was not a talking point but a bedrock assumption of the care they received and lavished on others during their time at Medem. Biber, of course, tried to broadcast these axioms through his books.

Perhaps the most radical aspect of the sanatorium was its enlistment of the children as creative partners for the adults. The social scientist Moses Kligsberg, distinguished for his research on Yiddish childhood, would review the landmark *Medem sanatorye bukh* in 1971, noting the inextricability of the material and the spiritual in the shared task of creating a flourishing republic: "When the children arrived at the sanatorium and their basic needs were met—adequate food, comfortable bedding—all their spiritual faculties quickly blossomed like wildflowers under the spring sun. The teachers and the children together created all that was great in the sanatorium; beauty was palpable in every corner. If you want to capture that greatness in a few words, you might say, '*In the Medem Sanatorium, the child felt like a whole person.*'"[71]

Kligsberg reminds us of when Medem must have seemed, to all witnesses, like the very harbinger of spring (akin to how Gilinsky figured the children as "the first swallows"). Of course there is a special historical piquancy to the idea of eliciting children's rationality and maturity at a moment when adults were pursuing increasingly irrational, bestial forms of violence.

Biber's *Winter in the Forest* closes with his cohort of lightly fictionalized *sanatoristn* on the train back to Warsaw after their stay in paradise, circa 1937. The mood is predictably glum. An older boy, Avreml, pulls out a brief but heartfelt thank-you note to Medem and reads it aloud. The travelers decide to affix all their names; one offers to mail the note from Warsaw. Avreml demurs, explaining that he'll dispatch the letter *then and there*. He rolls the onion skin paper into a tiny scroll and inserts it into an aluminum tube with the hint of a theatrical flourish. Then he pulls a carrier pigeon from a box, a resident of the dovecote that real-life Yisroel Biber had introduced, and affixes the tube to the band encircling its talon (a scientific diagram is provided). Biber had a genius for picking out the emotionally resonant physical detail, the tendril of outward events that burrowed most surely into the subterranean depths of inner life. Sometimes this ability verged on the uncannily prophetic. The children open the window to release the bird, which promptly wheels toward sunny Medem as their Warsaw-bound train enters a long, dark tunnel.[72]

6

Without

THE NEW GIRL AND THE POWER OF GETTING LOST

AFTER GIVING birth to Y. Y. Trunk's father, Grandmother Leah, whom we glimpsed reading by candlelight as a teenage newlywed in the first chapter, went on to bear another son and a daughter. The mother's steady diet of storybooks and novels opened a space in their humble synagogue-rafter apartment for a mild sort of waywardness: Her daughter became a lover of reading, even a book monster. With her mother's collusion and behind her father's back, Trunk's intellectually insatiable Aunt Itke studied Hebrew and Polish with the local proponent of Enlightenment. In a single night, she would "swallow up" each Hebrew novel her tutor lent her.[1] Thin, unpretty, uninterested in feminine adornments, unsentimental, mannishly intellectual, Itke was nevertheless the vessel for her mother's aspirations.[2] Grown at last into her own stature as a matriarch, Leah placed herself in league with the future: "Looking at Aunt Itke, her only daughter, Grandmother Leah quietly hoped that she, Aunt Itke, would win in life what Grandmother Leah had lost." It is difficult to gauge the extent to which Leah considered these dreams fulfilled. Mother and daughter alike dreaded the match that patriarch Meyshl had arranged to one Berish; upon her marriage, the girl's circle of enlightened friends regarded her as a tragic heroine, as if she'd stepped out from the pages of one of the novels they scarfed down. The last we hear of Trunk's studious aunt, she is filing for divorce; the union does not appear to have produced offspring.[3]

This chapter is about Leah's spiritual granddaughters and great-granddaughters on three continents: Olke, Khave, Norma, and Shprintse, girls who seem, when we turn the last pages of their stories, to be on course to "win at life" in ways that would have perplexed but perhaps also delighted pious

Grandmother Leah. One tenet of the progressivism that animated secular interwar Yiddish culture was a striving for greater equality between the sexes. On a literary landscape dominated by male authors writing about male characters, this cluster of fictional girls represents the kind of strong female protagonists with which cultural leaders sought to invite girl readers into the world of Yiddish letters. The Yiddish schools offered a natural and burgeoning female audience, with a large female-favoring gender gap across the various ideologically aligned school systems based in New York City.[4] Variations on the archetype of the prodigal daughter became centrally important in Yiddish children's literature. Descended from the protofeminist "New Woman" of the late nineteenth century, the "New *Girl*" is a dynamic character who bursts onto the scene early in the twentieth century, arriving in Yiddish in the late 1920s. The Yiddish New Girl reads, she pumps on a swing with the wind in her hair, she disappears without permission, she gets lost, she orates.[5] She has an attitude.

A creature of freedom and possibility, the New Girl's most subversive and defining move is simply failing to be where she is expected at any given time. Unlike kheyder boys, she is often on her own, depicted alone or pointedly as *not being with* others. She moves through the world as a *pícara,* becoming educated through the accumulation of experience.[6] The social world of girls among other girls is mostly left to the imagination. Whereas the Jewish boy ventures forth textually, through his growing Hebrew–Aramaic literacy, the Jewish girl wanders spatially. Like Kadya Molodowsky's six-year-old Olke (with her iconic blue *parasolke*), she dreams of escaping the domestic drudgery that's been imposed on her from earliest girlhood. For the New Girl, getting lost is perversely empowering: She elicits others' care as needed and finds that her internal resources exceed anyone's imaginings.

In addition to what the Yiddish New Girl stories represent directly, they resonate on a special frequency that is harder to hear. These apparently simple and lighthearted tales of adventure and return signify a great deal by virtue of what they *don't* say, especially when juxtaposed against the broader contemporaneous discourse of girlhood in Europe and the Americas. Approaching the turn of the twentieth century, the time between menarche and marriage was lengthening, at first gradually and then dramatically. Widespread schooling, whether optional or compulsory, industrializing economies, more robust child labor laws, and new occupational pathways all combined to create a distinct developmental and social phase between daughterhood and wifedom that Grandmother Leah had never known. New possibilities were shadowed by new dangers.

We cannot read fiction, of course, as history or sociology and must posit some distance between artistic representation and lived experience. But a corpus as consciously constructed as Yiddish children's literature offers an unusually clear portrait of its creators' aspirations and ideals, as well as their limitations. Simply put, culture—in the form of popular fiction—made promises that it could not always keep, especially to the poor and marginalized. "Whatever their actual circumstances," argues Sally Mitchell in her study of the New Girl, "girls' culture told adolescents at the end of the nineteenth century that their lives would be different from their mothers' lives and that they could mark out a new way of being in the world."[7] Although Mitchell's analysis focuses on England, the phenomenon had global reach: Hadn't Enlightenment satires of Hasidic life tantalized Itke with visions of a life different from Leah's?

The Changing Horizons of Girlhood

Girls had long been portrayed in literature as figures of singular vulnerability; whether in primitive fairy tales, Victorian novels, or masterpieces of modernist naturalism, most of the tales that centered their experiences were cautionary.[8] "For girls," notes Melissa Klapper in her study of female Jewish adolescence, "puberty brought physical, social, and psychological danger. For boys, puberty merely brought manhood."[9] The humiliation or "despoliation" of girls and women stood in symbolically for a host of other harms from the personal to the national in scale. The stories we will consider here all involve girls wandering, straying, or getting lost—but with none of the baleful consequences that such plots archetypically engender. Indeed the gap between most literary "girls in trouble" and the uniformly happy endings of Yiddish girl stories bespeaks both a shift in the meaning of girlhood in general and the insistently utopian worldmaking tendencies of this particular corpus. The authors of Yiddish children's literature were determined to construct a world in which it was safe for girls to adventure, err, and grow.

While our gaze remains fixed on fictional representation, it is useful to establish some grounding facts about the historical backdrop against which these fictions, and their silences, stand out. One of the hallmarks of modern childhood is a widespread belief in children's innocence, especially their sexual innocence, as an affirmative value.[10] Citing frank details from the diary of the French royal physician about the kind of sexual teasing and play engaged in by the family of Louis XIII, Philipe Ariès registers a shift in early modernity from assuming that children were *indifferent* to matters of sex to believing that children were *innocent* with respect to sex—an innocence that adults had a duty to protect.[11] In the modern period, Anastasia Ulanowicz observes, "Purity was constantly in danger of being corrupted by immoral influences."[12] Fears of sexual and thus moral corruption clung especially to girls and young women, for whom pregnancies out of wedlock were only the most visibly life-altering consequence of sexual activity.

Because girlhood was understood to be fraught with danger, cultural elites sought to create a network of overlapping protections that would eventually interweave education, social engagement, and literary-cultural fashioning within increasingly organized structures. But protection began with a single word. In Anglophone precincts, the cumbersome but common phrase "young lady" started to be replaced by the word "girl," a locution meant to desexualize the young female of the species. According to Mitchell, the word became "more dramatically visible" in English around 1880.[13] Steven Mintz, writing about American adolescence, marks the same phenomenon: "Toward the end of the nineteenth century there was a great outpouring of advice manuals, career handbooks, health guides, magazines, stories, and works of fiction featuring the word *girl* in their title." These works were set outside the home and depicted college friendships and white-collar workplaces as sites of "adventure, where young women could assert their independence and prove their mettle."[14] In Yiddish, traditional texts most often referred to a girl as a *yidishe tokhter,* literally a "Jewish daughter."[15] Her identity was implicitly imbricated with that of her parents; she was expected to carry herself in the world, honorably, as their daughter. Modern stories, however, almost exclusively use the word *meydl,* the word for "girl" that derives from *moyd,* or maid. Although the latter term carries a mildly pejorative whiff of "expired goods" on the all-important marriage market ("an old maid"), the diminutive *meydl* is value-neutral. If anything, the word might situate her in diminutive relation to a future self rather than to the parental lineage that had produced her.

While the English term "girl" was itself neutral enough, it was often preceded in Progressive Era America by a word like "incorrigible" or "wayward," or followed by the word "problem" or "question." As Crista DeLuzio explains, the "girl problem" was "the common euphemism for female juvenile delinquency during the Progressive era," a kind of social contagion that spread from the immigrant and working classes upward and outward to any girls "who failed to comply with the ideals of Victorian femininity."[16] The Progressive response, as was true of so many societal challenges, deployed both carrots and sticks in its efforts to "lift up" the "fallen" girls or steady those in danger of "falling" into sexual experimentation or domestic insubordination.[17]

Ruth M. Alexander chronicles how readily New York State collaborated with poor immigrant families in the ostensibly protective incarceration of their wayward daughters. Mining the inmate records of the Bedford Hills Correctional Facility, Alexander fleshes out the wage-labor-to-detention pipeline, including examples from the Jewish immigrant working class of "previously sheltered teenage girls" who "met young people who shared modern ideas about fashion, recreation, and sex," and who would spend nighttime leisure hours at "commercial dance halls, nickelodeon theaters, amusement parks, and other 'cheap amusements,' engaging in social rituals that celebrated feminine allure and heterosexual romance, the autonomy of youth, and the purchase of fun."[18] Norms around courtship and romance were changing, marriage was taking place later, and wage earners felt justified in reserving a portion of their pay to participate in an emerging mass culture of pleasure. Already fragile families, many of them experiencing the effects of geographic, cultural, and linguistic dislocation as migrants or immigrants, reeled under the social stigma and economic consequences of harboring a "wayward daughter" and might turn to the state to intervene in her rehabilitation. The year 1910 saw the passage of the Mann Act, legislation designed to eliminate prostitution that was often used in practice to prosecute participants in consensual sexual relationships and was enforced differentially with respect to race and class.[19] Female minors prosecuted under the law often ended up at Bedford Hills or a similar institution, designed to reform them under the watchful eye of propriety-minded matrons. Focusing primarily on the experience of Black female youth, literary and cultural historian Saidiya Hartman reads some of the same penal records of "wayward lives" and discerns in them a chronicle of "beautiful experiments" in freedom and "living otherwise"—beyond the narrow dictates of the bourgeois family and Victorian morality.[20]

Hartman's analysis emphasizes that the American Progressive amalgam of protection, control, and reform hinged on differences in race and class.[21] Consequences of sexual activity that would cost poor girls dearly could be more readily absorbed and even concealed from public view by more affluent families. On an individual scale, the same traits that were castigated in poor girls could be celebrated in middle-class and affluent ones. The chief difference between a stubborn, rebellious girl and a high-spirited, mettlesome one might well have been a couple of thousand dollars in her family's bank account or a quantum of melanin in her skin. Working-class girls who deviated from a narrowly Victorian path could be punished as prostitutes, while middle-class and affluent adventurers were heralded first as New Women and later as Jazz Age flappers. The New Woman, as Carroll Smith-Rosenberg characterizes her, was "single, highly educated, economically autonomous," and she used her relative privilege to eschew marriage and childbearing in favor of professional striving and advocacy for "innovative, often radical, economic and social reforms."[22] She was bourgeois and even genteel, as working-class minority women could only aspire for their daughters to become, and she trained her sights on political impact. She bicycled through the world with a modicum of moral gravity.[23] The flapper, more influential cultural symbol than statistically significant cohort, carved out an existence at the nexus of pleasure, consumption, and freedom—all imagined to be apolitical.[24] While her freedom would have appealed to the cultural leaders of the Yiddish left in the abstract, her hedonistic use of her liberty—to drive, to smoke, to dance—surely repelled them. They sought to depict alternate pathways to freedom, ones that would elevate solidarity and collective flourishing over individual pleasure.

The New Woman was ineluctably bourgeois, but the creators of Yiddish children's literature sought to secure the benefits that she enjoyed for the daughters of the working class. They promulgated a culture of wholesome girlhood, one bound up with educational and intellectual striving—albeit with a more radical twist than in the American mainstream. The protagonists that a set of mostly male authors placed at the center of their "girl stories" were daring, mischievous, insouciant, and courageous; they were also, as a matter of course, almost wholly desexualized. No special vulnerability clings to them by virtue of their status as female in a patriarchal world. They are never subject to harassment or unwanted sexual attention. They don't reckon with menstruation or infatuation with boys, let alone other girls. We don't see their peer relations depicted very often at all; the drama of their lives centers on the complex negotiation between breaking away from their parents toward greater freedom and remaining connected to the home and its sheltering protections. In the pages of books at least, girls could wander far away, sail over oceans, stay out all night and otherwise assert their independence—all without fear. For the duration of a story, poem, or novel, authors, unlike parents and teachers, could free them of the realistic burdens of being female. Such fictional girls inhabit a complicated literary and ideological space strewn with didactic tales of uplift and striving for respectability.[25] Yiddish children's literature often framed uplift as a collective project rather than a matter for individual cultivation, affirming that true respectability comes through hard work and solidarity rather than social prestige—and that there is dignity in belonging to the working class.[26]

Jewish Cultural Specificity

Given that Yiddish authors participated in the creation of a broader "wholesome girl" culture, it is natural to ask which elements in the worlds they fashioned were distinctively Jewish. The nexus of reading, education, and self-fashioning was certainly not unique to Yiddish-speaking Jews, but it was inflected in culturally specific ways. As Iris Parush has established, although Jewish girls in Eastern Europe were all but shut out of the traditional kheyder system, they had long enjoyed "the benefits of marginality" with respect to their educational institutions and independent leisure reading. Writing about families like Trunk's, she notes, "The 'woman's space' that allowed fairy tales to be present on the grandmother's bookshelf" enabled successive generations to move easily toward reading novels and maskilic periodicals. "The shift in reading habits was enabled by not only the intimate nature of the domestic sphere, concealed from the eye of society," but a more generalized disregard for female text culture owing to "the contempt in which traditional society held women's intellectual capacities."[27] The same indifference to girls' formal schooling marooned the least privileged educationally but allowed girls from middle-class and more affluent families to take part in dynamic educational experiments with more innovative pedagogy than their brothers could access. Eliyana Adler has found documentary evidence for 130 girls' schools operating in the Russian Empire between 1831 and 1881 and speculates that the existence of several more is implicit in the historical record. By the late nineteenth century, Jewish women were disproportionately well represented in secondary and higher educational institutions in Russia and even more strikingly so among those who ventured abroad to study medicine, dentistry, and other subjects.[28] After World War I, Orthodox education for girls spread to Galicia and Poland, thanks in large measure to the efforts of Sarah Schenirer, founder of the Beis Yaakov network of girls' secondary schools.[29] Before high school became compulsory in the United States, Jewish immigrant families showed a preference for sending their sons out to work if needed while keeping their daughters in high school.[30]

While earning a baccalaureate degree that could open the door to the professions was certainly not a mass phenomenon for women (or men) anywhere at this time, Jewish women's participation in the labor force certainly was. Although proponents of the Jewish Enlightenment had called on Jewish men to emulate the ideals of bourgeois European Christianity and provide economic support for their wives and daughters, long-standing Jewish ideals of women supporting men's Torah scholarship in higher social strata combined with economic necessity at lower socioeconomic levels to authorize women's continuing participation in the labor market.

Women's large numbers in the work force translated to their engagement in the political questions and organizations that increasingly defined Jewish life in Eastern Europe during the first decades of the twentieth century. Women were active in the Zionist movement and even more so in the Jewish Labor Bund, whose membership was one-third female.[31] An embryonic women's movement was taking shape in Warsaw by the 1920s, where a pamphlet published by the "Publishing House of the Jewish Women's Association in Poland" bore the title *Di moderne froyen bavegung* (The Modern Women's Movement).[32] Two women's newspapers, with primarily female authorship, also appeared briefly in the middle of the decade.[33] In their pages, we can discern an early articulation of what today, thanks to Kimberlé Crenshaw's work, we call intersectional identity: "The Jewish woman . . . must lead a double struggle as a woman from an oppressed and persecuted people."[34]

For most female Jewish immigrants to the Americas, the double struggle would continue in new environs, although the social science of the day had trouble honoring or even acknowledging it. The emerging field of psychology was deeply interested in adolescence but studied it under a "metric paradigm" that "preferred age and gender characteristics and differences at the expense of class analysis, identifying the universals of female psychological development as the primary motivators of all forms of adolescent social behavior."[35] In other words, researchers hazarded the procrustean assumption that being a girl mattered more to identity than being Jewish or belonging to the working class. For the psychologists of the 1920s, "white middle-class femininity" set the implicit norm and could then safely recede into the invisibility of imagined neutrality.[36] Adolescence was being newly described and tolerated because it was changing the lives of white middle-class families, even though "it was the working-class and immigrant teenage girl who took on newly heightened significance in the scientific literature as the changing circumstances of *her* work and leisure unfolded within a climate of anxious and idealistic social reform."[37] A period of domestic and economic independence was already customary for many working-class girls, but the arrangement came to be newly idealized as large numbers of middle-class and affluent families adopted it.[38] The young reader of Yiddish girl stories joined English-language readers of the same era in trying to "have it both ways: to entertain imaginative freedom while preserving the networks of affiliation at the center of their lives," but she did so with an increasingly urgent sense of class awareness and Jewish ethnic difference.[39]

Girls Lost and Found in Europe

The simplest and least radical Yiddish girl story of wandering and return is B. Oyerbakh's *Evie Gets Lost*, published in Warsaw by Farlag Mitspeh with no date recorded but likely from 1920. The very type of the "spirited girl," the eponymous protagonist gets lost in the big city of Warsaw when she tries to follow her older brother to school one day. Her disappearance throws the family into crisis, with each parent responding in predictably gendered ways. The danger of big-city living, getting lost, is counterbalanced by the kindness of strangers and the connective technology of the newspaper, where a classified ad directs the distraught father to his daughter after a single sleepless night for the parents. Although she meets no harm along the way, Evie's status as a girl provides the pathos; with a missing boy at its center, the story would not have held the requisite tension.

Shifting from a hyperlocal to a global canvas, we move to Buenos Aires in 1936 to consider "The Girl in the Mailbox," by Lit-Man, the penname of Simkhe Geltman/Freylekh. This is a charming trifle of a tale about a father who takes his daughter along to mail a letter and ends up pitching her into the mailbox instead by mistake. A mailman "none too clever" empties the box and carries the girl along with the letters to the post office. The enchanting conceit is that the girl *could* be delivered as a letter if only she bore an address and adequate postage, since letters "speak" just as people do ("Each letter had a different story to tell"[40]). Her lack of an address means that she can't be sent anywhere, so the letters take up a collection of their excess postage to underwrite her fare to Europe. She embarks on "a cheerful journey." Upon arrival, each letter proclaims its destination—Lithuania, Poland, Reb Joel's—but since the little girl has nowhere to go, she's sent back to Argentina posthaste:

> She was taken to the city square, where they asked, "Who wants to buy a little girl? A little girl from the mail? Cheap and inexpensive, she costs just a groschen."
>
> Soon the girl's father came running and said, "How much does the girl cost? A groschen? Here, take ten and give her back to me!"[41]

The story's conclusion may be read on two different planes of interpretation, depending on the reader's frame of reference. The naïve reader smiles at the merry adventure cheerfully concluded, while a more knowing one might wince at the representation of a Jewish girl sent from Poland to Argentina and auctioned off to the highest bidder—even if he ends up being her own father and she's had a rollicking good time. It is difficult *not* to read "The Girl in the Mailbox" against the backdrop of Jewish involvement in human trafficking, or "white slavery" as it was known in the contemporaneous discourse, especially in Argentina and Brazil.[42] The "legitimate" Jewish community in Buenos Aires struggled to cordon itself off, in actuality and in the popular imagination, from the parallel society of Jewish pimps, madams, and prostitutes, who were collectively known, from the biblical Hebrew term for ritual impurity, as the *tmeim*.[43]

Demographically disproportionate involvement in the sex work industry was understood as a blot on the honor of local (and worldwide) Jewish communities, and between the 1890s and 1930s, Jewish communal organizations like Ezres Noshim (Women's Aid) worked vigorously and often in cooperation with global Jewish relief agencies and local authorities to stem the flow of trafficked women into Buenos Aires and to incentivize "honest" work and "legitimate" (i.e., monogamous) marriages among those already arrived.[44] Prospective husbands and immigrant brides each had to furnish a "certificate of morality" before they could marry, so as to prevent sham unions that would give cover to sex work. Like the newspapers of modern Warsaw that help Evie's family to recover her, the mail and international shipping are inextricably linked technologies that effectively shrink the world. At the same time, those technologies enabled human trafficking on a global scale, ensuring that Warsaw poverty and degradation became Buenos Aires vice. As Mir Yarfitz observes, "The postage stamp serves as a crucial immigration agent" in that a letter home could invite subsequent chain migration by friends and family members in Europe.[45] "The Girl in the Mailbox" is a fanciful, literalized take on a real exchange whereby letters delivered to Europe summoned forth human passengers on the return ship.

By the 1930s, as Yarfitz documents, the sex trade was in retreat and Ezres Noshim shifted its efforts from fighting prostitution to overseeing Jewish marriages. Where the historical record is faint, let us speculate for a moment about a generations-long "rehabilitation" process whereby families whose constituents had been involved in sex work gradually passed into the "legitimate" Jewish communities of Argentina (despite the best efforts of Ezres Noshim to keep the "tainted" population separate). The imagined dichotomy between respectable and fallen never obtained in real life; prostitute mothers were considered the ultimate affront to communal norms of decency, yet they existed.[46] What if their Yiddish-speaking children or grandchildren subscribed to the children's periodical *Argentiner beymelekh* (Little Argentine Trees) or were gifted a copy of Lit-Man's collection *Mayselekh* (Stories) when it reached the New World from Warsaw, where it was published in 1936 and sold for just thirty groschen? Was the tale of the girl in the mailbox, the first of three in that volume, read as cautionary? As an innocent wish fulfillment? When a careworn grandmother, retired from the trade, giggled with her granddaughter over the feckless father who mailed his daughter instead of the letter, did she also wince at the tragic parental ineptitude that had endangered the girl in the first place? Her own youth a distant memory, perhaps she stifled a sigh, while the child squirmed on her lap, at the fantasy of the girl keeping the amiable company of letters home to Europe, exposed to such long transit but none the worse for the wear.

Teen on the Run

Seeking to raise the stock of Yiddish education in 1940s New York, Communist-aligned Yiddish educator Shloyme Davidman planned a series of twenty slim volumes set, as its projected title proclaimed, "In and Around the Yiddish Schools."[47] Only the first of these ever appeared, the 1952 collection *A Language Is Like a Garden*. The stories celebrate the leftist Yiddish school system and reinforce the value of transmitting the *mame-loshn* and secular Yiddish culture at a moment of galloping linguistic assimilation and widespread attrition of Yiddish fluency among American youth. Preserving Yiddish, Davidman knew, required dramatic acts of intentional cultivation—and he would turn that drama into compelling and exemplary storytelling. The titular character of "Norma Becomes an Orator" is a strong girl protagonist who runs away from home and remains estranged from her parents—yet suffers no ill effects during her self-imposed exile. The story illustrates masterfully both the political and psychological dimensions of the conflicts it portrays.

"People said she would grow up to be a doctor, an engineer, or even a professor."[48] From that opening sentence, the weight of others' judgment of Norma is palpable. Not only does her intellect elevate her above the typical expectations for a preteen girl of her time, but she possesses the artistic adornments expected of a *young lady*: she plays piano, dances "like a demon," declaims poetry, and cheerfully displays all those talents at family gatherings. What drives such an apparently thriving child to flee the natal home? Norma's parents labor together at their candy shop, rising at dawn to distribute newspapers to regular customers and toiling until long after dark to sell another glass of seltzer or one more pack of cigarettes. "And all for her sake," the story notes—so that they can provide for their daughter.

But in America, the gap between generations is unavoidable. Far from feeling gratified by her parents' self-sacrifice, Norma is ashamed of their mercantile status: "Her parents were incomprehensible to her. Her father himself had taken her to the Yiddish School. And there, they had taught her something different: *the worker is the builder of the world!*" As she grows into political consciousness, Norma wishes to express her solidarity with those "real" workers but feels that as the relatively pampered child of bosses, she lacks standing to do so. Her bid for authority, which must rest on authenticity, requires a sojourn in the proletariat: "She couldn't say, 'We, the children of the workers!' Her father was a businessman. So how would the workers' children look at her? She didn't want to go to school anymore. She wanted to go away to another city, start working, and then . . . !" Noting her disaffection, Norma's mother takes her to consult a doctor, who laughs off her distress: She is perfectly healthy, "just" unhappy about something. With her thirteenth birthday looming, precocious but misunderstood Norma runs away, leaving behind all her silk dresses and stockings in favor of hiking gear and a notebook. "Whatever she might be doing with her life," observes the narrator, "she was planning to write it down."[49] The girl's sudden departure is a source of shame, which takes on a distinctly feminine cast when the "neighbors whisper" and speculate that she will end up in the madhouse.

While her parents spin face-saving white lies to explain Norma's absence, the frame shifts dramatically, to an evening in an Appalachian mining town. Mothers watch over small children while the fathers are tied up at a meeting—perhaps to organize themselves against their exploitative bosses? A hiker comes over the crest of a hill, looking tired, as if his way has been long. But a surprise is in store for the miners' children: "Only when the hiker stopped, said hello and smiled, could they see that she was actually a girl—with white teeth, like pearls. Miners' children didn't have teeth like that. She had black eyes and hair, and when she broke out in a smile, did it cheer things up!"[50] The portrayal of Norma as a hiker, so intrepid as to seem sexless from a distance, cements her character's modernity. Physical fitness, justified as a preparation for the demands of motherhood, was one of the priorities of the reformers who aimed to lift the daughters of the working class out of poverty and into the American middle class.[51] Norma quickly ingratiates herself with the town's children, bringing tales of New York factory workers' solidarity with striking miners. She is a friendly alien, fomenting a bond between the downtrodden of Appalachia and their Jewish counterparts in the Big Apple.[52]

Once again, newspapers bridge the distance between worried parents and a runaway daughter, not only informing Norma's parents of her whereabouts but revealing to them her true essence. A single paragraph, with its liberal use of ellipses, covers almost the whole of Norma's adolescent years: "Days and weeks flew by . . . now and then she wrote a letter home . . . she had traveled to so many places . . . unemployment . . . you see? She was seventeen already . . . she spoke and spoke . . . her picture was in the papers . . . and the letters from home wouldn't let up . . . now they knew who she was! But she should come back at least for a single day . . . her mother begged of her, her mother! People were talking about her great contributions, beautiful speeches! . . ."[53]

Norma's accomplishments as a labor organizer are a source of pride, actualizing her parents' political sympathies. After the long separation, they want, in equal measure, to see their daughter and to have her be seen. When "the movement" allows her a two-day furlough to visit home, we appreciate how highly Norma's parents prioritize the social fact of their daughter's existence. After her four-year absence, the girl who always performed at family parties walks into . . . a packed house and a bustling party rather than an intimate reunion. Despite the generation gap, all family members implicitly embrace an existence focused on collective identity. They define the collective differently, of course, with the parents inhabiting a sociable yet private sphere bounded by business ownership, kinship, and close friendship, while Norma's vision erases the boundaries of privacy implicit in conventional family life. She belongs to the workers and places herself on loan to her parents and their social world.

As on past occasions, Norma is the cynosure of her homecoming party, but instead of singing, dancing, or declaiming someone else's words, she uses her own to reconcile home and away: "As usual, Norma gave a short speech, an intelligent one: 'We need to attract the small business owners to the side of the workers!'" The party guests, presumably the same circle of friends and family who were ready to consign the unhappy preteen to the madhouse, now marvel at her prowess and prognosticate sunnily about her future as a professor, a dancer, and an orator. Her success, forged on her own terms and unconstrained by others' expectations, is nevertheless a matter of communal investment and collective concern. While Davidman's doctrinaire message is that Yiddish school can effectively overcome the bourgeois tendencies of American family life and redirect its students toward proletarian consciousness, he affirms incidentally that Norma's hardworking parents have done pretty well by her. The scene of return at the story's end is nearly identical to its opening—Norma cleverly entertaining her extended family and parents' friends at a party—yet she has passed through girlhood out of view and is now an emerging adult.

Norma's age and life stage define her identity as much as her political commitments do. While many Yiddish girl stories do not specify the age of their protagonists, we know that this plot unfolds between ages thirteen and seventeen, the period that had been identified starting in the 1920s as sociocultural, self-individuating *adolescence* over and above biologically defined puberty.[54] In the history of adolescent Jewish girls, Melissa Klapper locates a window onto "the question of how individuals from traditional groups navigate between the twin shoals of cultural retention and cultural adaptation." In America, "adolescence and modernization emerged as parallel phenomena" around the turn of the twentieth century, with a new acceptance for "the idea that adolescents were an identifiable social group defined by shared activities, responsibilities, characteristics, and expectations that superseded family or community interests."[55] Davidman's leftist stories feature characters who participate in this process of separating from family even as their aspirations run counter to the culture of leisure and mass consumption that were commonly taken as the province of youth and the presumptive aim of youthful rebellion.

The radicalism of "Norma Becomes an Orator" lies less in its repudiation of small business owners (after all, the worldly-wise daughter eventually calls for a rapprochement between her parents' class and the true proletariat) than in its questioning of the bourgeois nuclear family as the basic unit of society—or at least the questioning how long into a child's life that structure should remain inviolable. Davidman's tale illustrates and only partially softens the claims of radical psychologist Samuel D. Schmalhausen, who advocated for children's "psychological weaning" from the nuclear family, that outmoded relic of Christian capitalism. The underlying aim, in Schmalhausen's own words, of "liberation from neurotic bondage" was "to be free—to be free—from those who would enslave and crucify us—with their love. . . . Especially mother love."[56] The attachment that sends Norma's mother into a faint upon discovering her daughter's disappearance threatens to stifle the girl's development as an independent actor. It is hardly surprising that during World War I, Schmalhausen was dismissed from his post teaching high school in New York on grounds of his "holding views subversive of discipline and of undermining good citizenship."[57] To subvert the authority of parents over children was to subvert the claims of the state upon its citizens.

"Norma Becomes an Orator" also plays with another, less radical form of American-Jewish fantasy: the special, gifted, extraordinary child—a desideratum for parents and children alike, although not necessarily at the same time or within the same family. Sixteen-year-old Marie Syrkin, a real-life Yiddish-speaking girl who would grow up to become an influential Zionist writer and scholar, confided to her diary in 1915 the fear that she was stagnating intellectually and becoming "common place." Her anxiety escalated a few days later with the admission that "all the time there is continually forcing itself more clearly upon my consciousness the terrible truth that I am absolutely 'ordinary.' Ordinary, what dismal pictures the word conveys."[58] Without actually relinquishing any of her charisma or ability, the manifestly extraordinary Norma "trades in" the adornments of upwardly mobile young ladyhood (music, dance, elocution, good grades) in favor of extraordinary achievement in another realm. She regains the admiration of her parents and their friends through her precocity as an orator and labor organizer. Her sex entirely subordinated to her work, Norma occupies a realm apart from female juvenile delinquency even as she turns literally wayward—bound toward *the way*, toward Appalachia. Her brief homecoming furnishes an occasion for her family to celebrate her excellent, overachieving form of "waywardness." Davidman's story is almost a jaunty burlesque of the social-scientific discourse on wayward girls, to say nothing of the Bedford girls' case files. What if nobody had to worry, the story posits, about policing or protecting girls' bodies? What if girls could light out for the territories and set off in pursuit of noble adventures, hiking unmolested across the years and miles? It would be nothing short of revolutionary.

An American Quixote in Mary Janes

The eponymous heroine of Dovid Rodin's novel *An Unusual Girl from Brooklyn* has such a talent for disappearing that her family nickname is "Shprintse-Where-Are-You" (*Shprintse-vi-biste*).[59] In the immature speech register of her younger sister, the phrase becomes a charming rhyme: "Shprintse-vi-bintse." But Shprintse's disappearances within the built environment of Brooklyn are only incidental, for her real precocity lies in disappearing into whichever book she happens to be reading, through her intense identification with its characters and their experiences, no matter how different from her own. A fantastical adventure tale set into realistic surroundings, Rodin's novel unfolds as a spiral of increasingly dramatic instances of going missing and being found. The girl is never without a book, and she struggles constantly to hold at bay the world's pesky intrusions—adults with their errands and chores, and the little sister who is sent as their emissary to retrieve her—so that she can read. Shprintse experiences bodily whatever is happening to the characters in her book; her "real" world merges with the fictive one, the story inside her story.

Although a scant readership existed for a Yiddish children's novel published in Tel Aviv in 1973, time and space are so elastic within the tale as to render it an instructive coda to the half-century American ascendancy of plucky New Girls. Set in one of the last cobblestoned and gaslit holdouts in a rapidly modernizing turn-of-the-century Brooklyn, Rodin's sophisticated text plays with narratorial reliability, reading as mimesis, and its own complicated temporality.[60] More important than the precise dating of the technologies and appurtenances referred to in the text (gas streetlamps and also electrification) is the recurrence of anachronism as a theme: Shprintse is a modern girl shaped by Victorian habits and an implicit sense of being out of step with her times.[61] The anachronism of her street fuses with the belatedness of her reading to locate Shprintse as an emblem of *pastness* even as she embodies a future-facing "girls' world." Just as the book is chronologically indeterminate, so too is Shprintse's own developmental stage left murky. She is meant to be "unusual"—the descriptor in the title could also be rendered as "strange" or "weird"—but some of her readerly rapture is surely a function of both her age and her Age, whatever they may be.

For an out-of-step daughter of the twentieth century, nothing in Shprintse's life is more Victorian than the intensity of her *relationship* to her reading material. The rising economic tides and technological advancements ushered in by the Industrial Revolution had liberated many girls and women still confined to the natal home from the burden of housework. Defining a specifically Victorian adolescence, as Jane Hunter explains, "self-culture was especially critical for girls for whom freedom from domestic labor left a good bit of free time during their impressionable years," and nineteenth-century advice givers recommended filling that time with edifying reading.[62] If such girls "drew on their surrogate reading lives" to help construct the "selves they would offer to the world," Shprintse's merging of text and self muddles our notion of what it means to have "real experiences" in the first place:

> When she was absorbed in a story, she would forget where she was and what kind of a world she lived in, because she imagined that everything she was reading about was actually happening to her. If she read that the little girl in the story was sitting, then Shprintse sat; if she read that the little girl in the story was standing, then Shprintse stood up; if she read that the little girl in the story was going over to the faucet and starting to wash the dishes, then Shprintse went over to the faucet, laid down her book beside it, and while continuing to read, started to wash the dishes. And if the little girl in the book had a plate fall out of her hand and shatter, then a plate also fell out of Shprintse's hand and shattered.[63]

Shprintse's consciousness fuses world and book. And because she is not of what Hunter calls "a certain class," she democratizes the practice of identificatory reading as she moves through the world. She participates in a culture of leisure reading that many real girls experienced as a liberation from the grind of school lessons and housework, and from parental or pedagogical oversight.

The Victorian intensity of Shprintse's passion for her reading is matched by its thematic content. Although we don't get much direct information about her books, certainly no titles or authors, we can make out in the tale of the lamplighter's daughter in the first chapter echoes of Dickens and Stevenson. It seems likely that she is given to indulging in "sensation" literature, a category akin to the popular Yiddish *shund* (pulp) novels, and one that called forth a similarly censorious critical discourse. As in the Yiddish cultural sphere, would-be guardians of youthful readers, including many librarians and educators, execrated the inebriating or taste-obliterating effects of dime novels, "that cheap kind of book pastry" that ruined one's literary taste as surely as sweet or rich foods spoiled the palate.[64]

Although the novel never says so directly, we might surmise that the books Shprintse read were in English, as the kind of reading material described simply did not exist in Yiddish at the time and certainly not in quantities to provide a steady literary diet. In her study of American Jewish female adolescence, Melissa Klapper describes reading as a critical aspect of Jewish immigrant girls' Americanization process insofar as it gained them access to a "literary idiom" that could be not only shared with their non-Jewish counterparts but tolerated and even encouraged by the adults in their families, thus bridging the generation gap both for driven autodidacts and those with access to superior educational opportunities.[65] But while the act of silent reading is a solitary one, most girls contrived to make the larger experience of reading at least somewhat sociable. Immigrants often did so under the tutelage of volunteer librarians, teachers, and philanthropists who saw library-based clubs as a form of uplift.[66] Given this historical reality, Shprintse's readerly isolation is all the more notable. Rather than drawing her closer to her family, her reading leads her to evade them.[67]

The bookish strangeness of the "unusual girl" is noted by everyone Shprintse encounters and often played for laughs. Detouring from her mission to harvest greens for dinner from her aunt's garden, a hungry Shprintse stops for a sandwich in a restaurant near the docks, frequented by sailors. After observing her peculiar behavior, the restaurant owner remarks, "You're an unusual girl. You look to me like you come from another world. Here, the way it works in our world, you eat a sandwich and you read a book. And you do just the opposite."[68] Numerous other characters hazard similar comments, to the effect that Shprintse is dreamy (*farkholemt*), doesn't live in our world, doesn't feel the ground beneath her feet when she walks but rather hovers in the air, and is impervious to her surroundings—the *luftmensch* become a *luftmeydl.*

She herself evinces awareness of her strange relationship with the world as mediated through her reading: "'It's strange,' thought Shprintse: when she read a book, it seemed to her that she could see the people from the book, hear their speech just as if they were talking to her, and stranger still, she could hear herself answering people, even though she kept her mouth shut."[69] The encounter that prompts this reflection is a conversation with a red fire alarm box on a street corner, which she mistakes for the red, fire-eating giant in her novel. Like Quixote facing the windmills, she clings to her error until she is at last persuaded—for just a moment!—to look up from the book.

After chatting equably with the fire alarm box (alive only in her head) and the restaurant owner, Shprintse leaves the restaurant and wanders into a park, where, riveted to a bench with book in hand, she experiences a "split": the division of herself into a sedentary reader and a mobile experiencer of the world that will dominate the book's next eighty pages. "Here Shprintse felt something strange happening to her: she was split in two! One of her sat there reading on the bench between two lanterns by the stream; and the other started to wander . . . over streets and alleyways until she reached the tall bridge suspended from cables over the water. How had she gotten to the bridge? She couldn't understand it."[70] Thus imaginatively suspended and still seeking a quiet, remote spot to read, Shprintse climbs a painter's ladder that leans against the suspension bridge's high tower, just as she climbed onto a lamppost in the first chapter. Distracted by her reading, she takes no notice when she runs out of ladder rungs and steps into thin air hundreds of feet above the East River. Onlookers' hearts beat in their throats. Just as her fall begins, a sailing ship passes beneath the bridge, and Shprintse tumbles safely onto the rigging, book still in hand. She has landed aboard the *Golden Dove*, a pirate ship of yore outfitted with a panopticon-like magic table that allows the captain to track everyone's whereabouts at all times.

Unlike the ship's complement of frightened child captives, Shprintse is overjoyed to find herself on board because something identical has just happened to the heroine of her book.[71] Her bookish absorption ensconces her in a protective cloud of unknowing, of radical innocence as dangers mount. While she admits that "these things could scare a child," Shprintse identifies less as a child than as a *reader*, notwithstanding Victorian-era advice which cautioned that reading too much melodrama would harm girls' nerves.[72] For a girl growing up in twentieth-century New York, Shprintse displays an arresting lack of street smarts, and although she moves among sailors and pirates and discovers that the ship is transporting captive children, she betrays no awareness of being in any specific danger *as a girl*.

But taken to its extreme limit, Shprintse's elision of world and book eventually endangers her both physically and morally. Late in the novel, the *Golden Dove* is sinking, while Shprintse sits on a coiled rope, placidly reading. A well-meaning pirate breaks through her absorption, urging her to escape: "He ran up to her and shouted, 'Shprintse, what are you doing just sitting there?' She looked up and said in her drawn out tone, 'H o w s h o u l d *I* k n o w?'" A sing-song tag line uttered whenever she is grudgingly interrupted, such casual nescience underscores her perversely scrambled priorities:

> "Oh, really? Just like in the book!"
> "What are you so happy about?" said Tsalke, "You're gonna drown!"
> "Really? Is that true?" asked Shprintse.
> "It's true! It's true!" screamed Tsalke, "and I don't want you to drown. Come quick!"[73]

Even a pirate can uphold the sanctity of life and make better moral decisions than the distracted bookworm. Rodin lodges a gentle critique of solipsistic reading, driven by total identification with the characters and leading to unheroic conduct. While the cerebral girl disappears into the book she is reading, she recedes from her own narrative as protagonist and girl-hero, leaving a conventional adventure tale with conventional gender roles, with the male pirates entirely carrying the inset story. Shprintse is an immoderate reader who does not take instruction from her books about how to act in the world.[74] At the furthest possible remove from the exemplary figure at the beginning of Bunyan's *Pilgrim's Progress* who transitions from book to world in purposeful reflection (and Christian duty), she merely moves gluttonously on to the next book.

However imperfect, Shprintse's reading is ultimately empowering. During a showdown in the ship's "chamber of horrors," a frightful witch shouts, "Take away that/the book! That/the book! That/the book is my enemy! That/the book is the end of me!" The meaning of the Yiddish definite article is ambiguous. Does it suggest that the antagonist knows that this particular book's plot demands her undoing, or is she susceptible to the apotropaic power of books in general? The confusion is not resolved by Shprintse's deduction: "Just look what power my book has!"[75] Her book has the power to bend the world to its plotting, and Shprintse perceives this to be true of her own life as well. Her reading material dictates what will happen, including what will happen to her: who and what she might become.

Shprintse's divided self comes back together again when the pirate ship sails to safe harbor in New York as night is falling. Yet poignantly, her reading habits have distanced her from her family, habituating them to her disappearances. As the other rescued children disembark and leave with their relieved, delighted parents, Shprintse stands off alone, unclaimed. In fact, her parents, together with her two maternal aunts, are traipsing all over Brooklyn in search of her. Her Aunt Dinah reiterates in concentrated form the assessment of all who have interacted with Shprintse throughout the novel: "She's a distracted angel, just like her father! She's probably holed herself up with her book somewhere and forgotten where in the world she is! Does she even live in this world?—Where she actually lives is in books! She doesn't live among us! Her feet don't touch the ground, she hovers in the air, climbs a ladder in mid-air on into the clouds!"[76]

With its perceptive blend of sympathy and annoyance, the phrase "distracted angel" captures the peculiar supernal disembodiment of the bookish girl's existence, freeing her of the burdens of moving through the world as a *young lady*. It would be the mother's sister who observes archly how Shprintse's defining trait is inherited from her father—perhaps the object of the mother's exasperation, although that has not been depicted outright. The bemused emphasis on a temperamental quirk shared between father and daughter bespeaks another aspect of the text's modern, American sensibility: It disrupts the template for Ashkenazi psychosexual reading practices, wherein girls naturally follow their mothers while boys enact a transit from mother to father after achieving basic literacy.

No matter how loving the family, the American twentieth century still imposes an unbridgeable gap between generations, a mutual incommunicability of experience. The adults cannot convey to Shprintse the toll of fear, anxiety, and sorrow that her disappearances exact. The girl does not notice her mother's tears. And in the end, the grown-ups never learn of her adventures on the pirate ship. During her afternoon and evening spent reading in the park, she has sailed over seas, "in and out of weeks," in Maurice Sendak's resonant phrase, but her family has just spent yet another anxious night searching for their daughter. They see a girl reading in the park, while Shprintse has seen much of the world. The essence of growing up in modern America is venturing to places, including places of the mind, that your parents cannot follow and that you cannot explain. Shprintse remains an inscrutable puzzlement to her mother and aunts, united in their maternality and speculating darkly that her father seems to be "missing a little wall in his head." But the father-daughter bond, like the mother-son bond invoked at the end of "A Hanukkah Eve in Warsaw," engenders an unspoken pact to stay close despite the chasm between generations. Spotting his daughter on that bench, book in hand, the father "broke into a wide grin, lifted Shprintse tenderly from the park bench, hugged her, kissed her chin, her eyelids, and her forehead, and said, 'Come daughter, let's dance our way home.'"[77] She is not quite a prodigal daughter: Rather than tracing an arc of return home, her family goes out and finds *her*.

Reading Toward the Way

Like the intrepid Norma, Shprintse's character seems almost to offer a winking spoof of Progressive Era anxieties about her sex and time of life. She is a charmingly imperfect, altogether wholesome "incorrigible girl." One of the thoroughly modern, as opposed to Victorian, aspects of the novel is that Shprintse isn't made to "learn a lesson" about how to be a more moderate or sophisticated reader. She remains frankly unashamed of and unapologetic about her enchantment with the written word. This detail is particularly salient against a Victorian discourse of girls' renunciation and guilt "about the passions and the obsessions that their reading invoked."[78] The convergence of Shprintse's sex and literary taste mark the novel as modern in the context of Jewish culture as well. An ocean away and a generation or two earlier, her level of immersive textual preoccupation would have distinguished a boy of Shprintse's age as an *iluy*, a Talmudic genius in the making. Rodin has secularized and feminized the paradigm of textual wandering that had long been encouraged for Jewish boys. Shprintse's proclivity toward consuming (non-Jewish) fiction is her wholesome vice. Yet her story is captured in the *mame-loshn*, converting the reader's own potentially shallow identificatory reading into the virtue of Yiddish linguistic preservation. Reading about pirates and witches may be indulging "that cheap kind of book pastry," but doing so in Yiddish marks a heroic stand against assimilation into the majority culture.

The girl stories of Yiddish children's literature feature literally but not actually *wayward* protagonists, those drawn from home toward "the way." With this tendency established, it is an opportune moment to return to Kadya Molodowsky's six-year-old Olke, whom we met in the introduction, resolutely brandishing her blue *parasolke* against the relentless heat of parental task-setting. When the buttons she is meant to sew finally mount their rebellion, they turn into all manner of wheeled conveyances, including the velocipede of the New Woman. At the poem's conclusion, one of these vehicles transports her, perhaps into a future as a poet:

> Then Olke hitches all the wheels in a harness
> And makes a long train to go farther than farness
> Then the train whistles, and Olke travels away,
> Far, far away on a glowing, white way[79]

It is exceptional that Olke does not trace a prodigal arc of return homeward, and indeed her trajectory furnishes a bracing contrast with the girl stories written by men considered in this chapter. Molodowsky bestows upon her heroine a one-way ticket out of the patriarchal, impoverished Jewish family.[80] *Avek*, "away," means toward the way, as opposed to *aheym*, toward home. At a moment of widespread anxiety about wayward girls, most Yiddish culture honors the impulse toward *the way*—toward adventure, agency, independence, and novelty—while returning girls to the safety of the home. They wander temporarily and unharmed that they might eventually come back to the care of the natal family, returning transformed and improved. Carefree girlhood is a brief interlude before maturation and maternality assert themselves; the journey and return finally affirm the durability, or at least the necessity, of the nuclear family.

Because girlhood is fleeting, girls could be celebrated for asserting a degree of power and agency unlikely to accompany them into adult womanhood. Girl power doesn't necessarily demand a comprehensive revision of social norms. We might well read about the escapades and derring-do of the New Girls of Yiddish children's literature and wonder, "Are we feminist yet?" These stories are not quite feminist by our lights, but they make some substantial gestures toward promoting the equality of girls. Most importantly, they developed a set of images for girlhood that were not oriented around vulnerability and victimization. This represented a real departure from the norms, taken as neutral, of Progressive Era American Christian whiteness. In this deviation, we discern the legacy of European Jewish women's long history of working outside the home and being full economic partners with men. Against the general darkness of female delinquency, vulnerability, and sex trafficking, these stories make lightness visible. They also endorse a vigorous life of the mind for girls, whether it is the literacy hunger of preschool-aged Evie, the immersive reading of a young Shprintse, or the alchemy whereby Norma's good grades and personal magnetism give rise to an accomplished new labor leader. Travel of the mind is always encouraged. Yiddish children's literature celebrates cerebral waywardness and corporeal return home. These stories recast the plot of being lost as a plot of adventure, a distinction that turns on the girls' own agency and a salutary outcome. The happy endings of these tales proclaim a new hope, aspiring to reshape reality by imagining new possibilities. So no, the tales of the Yiddish New Girl are not fully feminist by twenty-first-century standards, but they certainly set Grandmother Leah's daughters well *on their way*.

7

Questions for *Mame*

EDUCATING FOR EMPATHY

UNDER THE unpronounceable yet fetching title "???," the Polish Canadian poet and novelist Ida Maze evokes a young child's longing in just a few strokes:

> If you were me
> And I were you,
> I'd be in
> Your shoes.
>
> *I* would be eight,
> And four's what *you'd* be;
> So then would you
> Play with me?

The poet voices a preschooler's unrequited desire for the attention of an elementary schooler who presumably scorns "baby games" in favor of playing with the big kids. The sidelined younger child resorts to a strategy of marginalized people everywhere: imagining that the tables were turned. It is easy to conjure a scene in which the poem's speaker gazes through the window at the addressee, who is busy outside with older friends. Whether or not the would-be narratee is physically present to listen, the simple verse lodges a direct appeal for empathy: *Imagine how you would feel in my place! Act accordingly!* The poem offers a universally accessible portal to "feeling as another feels"; after all, most who read the poem have experienced being four years old. It is relatively easy to remember one's former self and revisit, from the new perspective granted by greater maturity, one's own forgotten feeling. However, fellow-feeling across lines of immutable difference—race, sex, physical ability—can be more challenging to cultivate, and doing so became one of the most pervasive and enduring concerns of Yiddish children's authors.

What about a form of difference that was mutable in theory but glaring in fact? The single most common theme in the Yiddish children's corpus is the persistence of wealth inequality and the exigent demand it imposes on people of conscience. Although this topic isn't present in every work for children, it is explicitly centered in a great many stories reaching all the way back to the first Yiddish children's tale ever published, Mordkhe Spektor's 1889 "Kinder," about two elementary schoolers who raise money on Purim to help relieve the poverty of Old Shmerl, the water carrier. Eighty years later, when Kadya Molodowsky looked back nostalgically toward prewar Europe from the vantage point of a relatively prosperous New York City, she would echo that early focus on social repair through philanthropic giving. The theme of ameliorating poverty is the natural starting place for analyzing how Yiddish children's literature sought to cultivate readerly empathy, the mechanism for creating "a shenere un besere velt" (a more beautiful and better world). But the focus on empathy didn't end with economics; indeed it encompassed other forms of marginalization, including racial injustice, especially in the United States and especially on the Left. Taking others' perspectives was a skill that young readers could practice across remediable disparities in wealth and then harness to imaginatively straddle other divides.

Textual "mirrors" might reflect Jewish children's own experiences with marginalization, ranging from garden-variety poverty and casual bigotry to antisemitic violence, but the "windows" in much of the fiction they consumed gave onto the suffering of others and invited readers to try on perspectives different from their own.[1] Disparities in wealth posed a unique narrative opportunity, for they are subject to change in story, even as the lived experience of poverty was often difficult to transcend in fact. Readers might be as poor as the characters in the stylized, often nameless *shtetlekh* of yore, but for the duration of a tale, they were invited to implicitly assume the position of benevolent donors without surrendering their reflexive identification with the needy. The unspoken hope was that no matter their eventual socioeconomic status, these readers might grow up to lead lives organized around solidarity and generosity.

Over decades and across oceans, Yiddish children's literature kept a singular focus on cultivating its readers' empathy despite—or precisely *in light of*—the intransigent differences in human circumstances. The ethical transaction at the core of the corpus was an appeal to readers to sympathize with, and ultimately to act on behalf of, those who were suffering. The systemic emphasis on altruism can help us understand what the creators of Yiddish children's literature thought their project was *for*: They educated children to be *eydl* (refined), *hartsik* (kind), *breythartsik* (generous), *rakhmonesdik* (compassionate), and *mentshlekh* (humane). They trusted their stories to turn *vildekhayes*, the ungovernable "wild things" that Maurice Sendak imported into the English lexicon, into specimens of ethical humanity capable of *mitlayd* (compassion, but literally, "suffering with").[2] Very often, they composed stories that dramatized the process of *acquiring* empathy, or they represented already-empathetic actors whose kindness could serve as direct exempla for young readers.

Many of these stories are beautiful and affecting. Maze's economical miniature gestures at her debt to a European artistic tradition, especially well developed in England, that emphasized the fusion of ethics and aesthetics.[3] Authors who trafficked in moral sentiment had long recognized the power of narrative specificity to elicit fellow-feeling. "Appeals founded on generalisations and statistics," observed George Eliot, "require a sympathy ready-made, a moral sentiment already in activity." Bare statistics merely preach to the choir, whereas art, being "the nearest thing to life," offers "a mode of amplifying experience and extending our contact with our fellow-men beyond the bounds of our personal lot." The task, Eliot asserted, was to transcend one's limited point of view, and art is just the thing that "surprises even the trivial and the selfish into that attention to what is apart from themselves, which may be called the raw material of moral sentiment."[4] While the Yiddish children's authors of a century ago intuitively crafted plots that sought to nurture fellow-feeling, today we can gain new insight into the mechanics of these stories by turning to recent research at the nexus of child psychology and literary studies. Cognitive narrative theory has rendered a rich account of how authors cultivate readerly empathy, and both psychology researchers and literary scholars have begun to extend these insights to young readers, with their marked neuroplasticity and consequent potential for ethical refinement through their reading. Suzanne Keen defines narrative empathy as "the sharing of feeling and perspective-taking induced by reading, viewing, hearing, or imagining narratives of another's situation and condition," noting that such sharing plays a role in every phase of a work's composition and reception.[5]

Applying this framework to the specific domain of Yiddish children's literature not only helps us to understand the task of these stories at the deepest level but also furnishes an especially resonant archive for testing some of the insights of cognitive literary theory. Following the trail of narrative empathy leads us to a set of terms and concepts that didn't exist when this literary corpus was being created but can nevertheless help us reconstruct how the texts set out to create "mensches." While analyzing authors' output in terms of the political movements and institutions with which they aligned themselves (Bundist, Zionist, etc.) allows us to appreciate the subtle gradations of ideological *difference* among them, these newer discourses can render an equally important *unified* account of how Yiddish children's authors approached their singular task. It is therefore worth translating the authors' humanistic vocabulary into the terminology of more recent science and gauging their efforts against a more universal account of how children are formed morally as readers. While a certain degree of anachronism dogs my effort to apply a discourse that had not yet been invented when the works in question were published, I would argue that the reward outweighs the risk. After all, I am interested less strictly in the intellectual history of Yiddish children's literature than in its strategies of representation and how it worked upon its intended audience.

In a landmark article, Raymond A. Mar and Keith Oatley prise apart the felicitous jumble of strands that make literature such a powerful tool for promoting empathic growth. They isolate the ability of literary fiction to offer "the simulation of social experience," which rests in turn on the efficiency of abstractions, noting that "individuals who have been exposed to more fictional literature tend to exhibit better empathic abilities." Just as a flight simulator allows a pilot-in-training to encounter challenges and respond to dangers, learning through serial trial and error that would be fatal in real life, literary fiction "allows us to experiment in a controlled and safe manner with intentions, emotions, and emotion-evoking situations that would be impossible and often highly undesirable in the real world."[6] War and hunger, orphanhood and illness all can be tried on as borrowed realities without actual danger to life and limb.

As Eliot postulated, empathic growth occurs by extending our understanding of other people's beliefs and emotions, helping us to construct an ever more nuanced theory of what goes on inside their minds. Over the last two decades, psychologists and literary theorists alike have come to recognize in fiction a rich resource for studying this kind of "mind reading" or "theory of mind," two terms that are often used interchangeably to describe "our ability to explain people's behavior in terms of their thoughts, feelings, beliefs, and desires."[7] The simulation of social experience that literary narratives afford provides an opportunity for empathic growth. It trains us to extend our understanding toward other people, to embody (to some extent) and understand their beliefs and emotions and ultimately to understand ourselves.[8] As is often true in scientific study, the normative case is pieced together by studying deviations. The recognition of what has come to be called autism—and the ability to study its physical manifestations through brain imaging—has helped scientists and then cognitive literary scholars to formulate a detailed account of how a neurotypical reader "just knows" that a character is trembling, to use Lisa Zunshine's example, due to nerves or desire and not because of a neurological disorder.[9] Simplifying the linkage between two distinctively human "social skills," theorist of children's literature Maria Nikolajeva characterizes empathy as an "ability to understand how other people feel," while theory of mind (often abbreviated as ToM) is "the ability to understand how other people think."[10] Youthful reading, she maintains, is essential to training both abilities.

Psychologists have established that storybooks color children's understanding of which emotions are idealized in their culture; intriguingly, the axis along which researchers differentiated between the various societies under study was the degree of their individualism versus collectivism.[11] The idealists who authored Yiddish children's literature sought to foster a more collectively oriented, empathetic society in the midst of Europe and then the United States, each with its dominant post-Enlightenment philosophical and cultural traditions centered on the individual. At the turn of the twentieth century, this individualist focus was couched in newly scientific language, in the ascendant discourse of evolution. Charles Darwin was famously puzzled by the phenomenon of altruism, as an act of self-sacrifice on the part of any member of a species might cost the opportunity to reproduce.[12] In fact, as far as evolutionary biologist Stephen Jay Gould was concerned, the existence of altruism raises the question of whether evolution always operates solely at the level of the individual organism or whether some sort of "cultural evolution" rooted in the uniqueness of human consciousness might prevail among *Homo sapiens*.[13] To Bundists and other leftists, though, it seemed intuitive that (human) society flourished best when people were habitually conditioned to perform acts of generosity and even selflessness.

The task of the author-educator was to help children overcome a selfish state of nature, and literature naturally aided in these aims by granting deep access to the subjectivity of others, making their minds more knowable. Empathy fluctuates with variables, including "perceptibility, trust and attachment."[14] It is easier to empathize with someone when their suffering is perceptible and when one feels a degree of trust in or connection to them. Narrative renders human emotion visible where it might otherwise be concealed, and by *simulating* responses, as Mar and Oatley theorize, it ends up *stimulating* feelings of trust and attachment. Yiddish children's authors had a marked tendency to thematize these empathy-producing elements. Whereas Western cultures privileged master genres such as romance and the dramas of family formation ("and the king and queen lived happily ever after"), many Yiddish writers chose to foreground stories of social repair where a character's generosity is motivated by sensing another's travail.[15]

Yiddish children's authors advocated for a wide variety of strategies for redressing economic inequality, but a unity of purpose underlay these diverse approaches. Broadly speaking, they subscribed to what psychology researchers call the "empathy-altruism hypothesis": "the claim that empathic concern produces altruistic motivation."[16] In other words, when people experience strong fellow-feeling, especially in the face of another person's (perceptible) suffering, they will act, even against their own interests, to alleviate that suffering. A curious paradox lodges in the binding of the child's Yiddish book then: The reading experience, which turns ever more solitary with a young reader's growing literacy, is increasingly mobilized to serve the communitarian ideals of generosity and solidarity.

Fairy Tales of Philanthropy

Literary narratives, according to Mar and Oatley, can simulate complex interplays of intentions and behaviors that would take decades to unfold in real life, helping readers to perceive linkages between cause and effect. Which kinds of stories do this work best? It stands to reason that if abstraction creates effective simulations, then an especially abstracted—or, in the language of literary analysis, *stylized*—genre would excel at modeling social emotions.[17] In Yiddish children's literature, empathy in its most concentrated form—as a theme within the text and a readerly response to the text—is represented as a kind of fairy tale. "A kind of," I hasten to qualify, because these stories hew to some fairy tale conventions even as they resist others. Ruth Bottigheimer describes the genre as "brief narratives in simple language that detail a reversal of fortune, often with a rags-to-riches plot that culminates in a wedding. Magical creatures regularly assist earthly heroes and heroines achieve happiness, and the entire story exemplifies a proverb . . . or demonstrates a moral point."[18] While the stories highlighted here are built around reversals of fortune and ultimately demonstrate a moral point, they do not culminate in a wedding or enlist magical creatures. More specialized categorization schemes might refer to them as "moral tales" rather than fairy tales.[19]

By other accounts, though, magic is entirely beside the point, and the fairy tale designation remains apt. In a trenchant paper about the economic principles implicit in the genre, Dorothy Noyes maintains, "The fairy tale is our touchstone for articulating the normative life course of the individual. As many scholars have concluded, its magical elements are mostly window dressing; the world of the fairy tale shares our own mundane preoccupations with family life, work, sex, property, power, and identity." Centering a "continual reworking" of these familiar plots, Noyes accounts for the progression from the originally oral "classic" fairy tales that were collected and written down in the eighteenth and nineteenth centuries to "modern," artistically rendered retellings composed near the turn of the twentieth century and beyond. Insofar as "classic" fairy tales dealt with economics, they did so in relation to romance plots, by engaging questions of "social class and economic possibility, critical constraints on the ability to marry and form a new family." As the fairy tale "moves from European peasant communities into increasingly capitalistic and liberal societies," it often expands in scope from the choices constraining individual families to broader collective concerns, evincing a new "emphasis on neighborly reciprocity, collective action, and labor migration."[20] Noyes sees in a set of modern Italian fairy tales of the 1870s "models for action" whose real-world effects are discernible by the 1890s. At roughly the same time and in response to the Industrial Revolution in Britain, utopian writers of fairy tales "took a resolute stand against materialism," and opposed "class domination and the crass exploitation of the 'little people,'" according to Jack Zipes.[21] In this sense, Yiddish fairy tales for children were in step with their time. But for Eastern European Jewry, labor organizing and global migration were well underway as mass phenomena before a cohesive children's audience came into being. Yiddish fairy tales are saturated with themes of social redress; families, which tend to be already formed by the time a story's action begins, are the intimate sphere wherein social inequities that plague the larger society become visible.

While both classic and modern fairy tales played an important role in projects of nation-building, many educators around the globe bristled at the element of fantasy such stories imported into children's consciousness. The genre traveled with few encumbrances between the nations of Western Europe but was "conspicuously absent" in colonial American schools and lending libraries, where magic was regarded as "contradictory to the enlightened rationalism that underlay and guided American political thought."[22] The most significant American revision of the European fairy tale tradition was the series of Horatio Alger novels, which idealized succeeding economically by pulling oneself up by the bootstraps, thus placing the burden of redressing wealth inequality on the individual—an idea anathema to the Yiddish Left of the early twentieth century.[23] Not entirely dissimilar aesthetic controversies played out in the world of letters for Jewish children, with an Enlightenment-inflected preference for realism holding sway in Yiddish literature throughout the nineteenth century and a Romantic backlash developing in the early twentieth. In fairy tales constructed especially for young readers, we can detect the mutual tempering of these two impulses, whereby Yiddish writers revise the fantastical fairy tale in the service of a rationalist vision of social amelioration.

Although morally oriented wonder tales typically share the dreamy indeterminacy of fairy tale locales, they appear downright realistic when compared to the animal fables and other forms championed by heirs to the Jewish Enlightenment. With elements of fantasy that invite closer inspection of what might otherwise pass unremarked, these tales depict a heterotopian off-world that reveals otherwise inaccessible truths about the more familiar "real world." Fairy tales address anxieties about various forms of social change, including the advent of romantic love as the basis for marriage and the shifting economic arrangements that accompanied industrialization and urbanization. Whether writing for adults or children, a figure like Sholem Asch "was able to satisfy the increasing demand of Jewish and non-Jewish audiences for an undisturbed rural idyll," quelling anxieties about modernization and how it might overturn an economic order that was inextricably bound to a prevailing system of religious authority and piety.[24]

Sholem Asch's 1929 volume of short stories, *For Youth* (*Far yugnt*), includes several simple tales, their plots accessible to naïve readers, that nevertheless plumb psychological depths of interest to more sophisticated readers as well. At the start of "Rich Man, Poor Man" (Der oremer un der raykher), the protagonist epitomizes contented virtue and even supererogation.[25] When we meet him, he is known as the Magnate of Jerusalem, a prosperous merchant who manages to oversee his business interests while reserving ample time for Torah study. He attends to the diverse needs of others, directing his wealth toward charity and his mind toward an informal psychotherapy practice avant la lettre: "All those who were heartsick or suffering from bad thoughts or whose minds wouldn't let them rest" consulted him and received "sound advice" or "a kind word from his generous heart." Asch portrays the magnate's wealth, generosity, and ritual devotion as seamlessly interwoven and mutually reinforcing. His home is decked out with the trappings of lavish but tasteful piety: rare manuscripts copied out at his direction, specially woven curtains to cover his well-stocked bookshelves, an ornate silver spice box, and "silken garments that gladdened his heart whenever he donned them, for they had a bright silver sparkle and a happy song woven into them." A focus on the luxuries' provenance and ritual functions promises to elevate them beyond crass materialism. The narrator, edging close to the character's own consciousness, often dilates on the origins of a given ornament, like a waiter at a farm-to-table restaurant waxing poetic about the provenance of the various ingredients. The pervasive spirit of repletion redounds to the credit of the heavenly Provider:

> The magnate was very pleased with himself and with the Master of the Universe, his Creator. He'd had a day full of good deeds and charity, with study and prayer, and he'd had nothing to record in his book of sins. He thanked God in his heart that he'd been chosen as his emissary and that he was the giver and not the recipient of charity. But on this day, the rich man was even more cheerful than usual, for he had performed a great mitzvah, a commandment, that can seldom be fulfilled. His accountant, who had just returned from a trip with the caravans that carried spices from India to Turkey, had informed him that while in Izmir, he had performed on the rich man's behalf the commandment to redeem the captive by releasing Jews from the Turks, who had brought them as captives from the Slavic lands. The magnate was overjoyed with the mitzvah, and he heard that his caravans had arrived safely at the seashore and their cargo had been loaded onto ships.[26]

The nameless rich man is almost childlike in the direct causal link he draws between his fulfilment of the commandment to redeem the captive and the worldly success of his merchant trade. The burden of the story is to grow him up a bit. Throughout Asch's fiction, as Mikhail Krutikov argues, wealth ratifies the prevailing order: "Money signifies stability and respect. Money establishes a person at the center of discourse and provides him with the authority and the means to express and execute this authority. The wealthy merchant is the master not only of the economic, but also of the moral, the religious, and even the natural order in the shtetl universe." Krutikov does not discuss Asch's tales for youth, but many of the tropes and certainly the attitudes toward wealth are similar to those found in his fiction for adults, including the rich man's place atop a hierarchy that is "represented as part of the eternal natural order, where each element has its fixed place and function."[27] The "economic side" is indispensable to Asch's portrayal of a "full-blown shtetl romance," and here, the material abundance finds its psychological analogue in the righteous man's assured self-satisfaction.[28]

But were the pleasant homeostasis to continue, there would be no story. The aura of righteous joy at having redeemed the captives dissipates with the entrance of a poor man, a wretch: "The foul odor that preceded him overpowered the good smell of the spices, and the rich man felt weak because he was fastidious and couldn't stand bad smells." Despite all the scaffolding the magnate has built into his daily life to support the doing of good, he is overcome by his creaturely disgust at the beggar's odor. The violation is exacerbated by a further breach of decorum, when the alms seeker enters and approaches the magnate confidently, "his hand outstretched in a hearty greeting." Predictably, the refined *istenis* (the Greek loan word meaning "weak," whereby rabbinic culture labels the fastidious or overly sensitive) cannot endure the visitor's smell, to say nothing of his effrontery. He calls a servant to lead the alms seeker away for a bath and some new clothes. Asch chooses to present the scene from the point of view of the magnate, wallowing in the grotesquerie that engenders his disgust: "The hand was full of grime and other ugly things that aren't nice to talk about and especially not to write about in detail. His whole body was wrapped in filthy clothing from which bits of his naked flesh poked out, soiled with dirt, and locks of hair were matted onto his face and crept forth from his head. His was not the face of a human being but rather of an ugly animal, God help us, with swollen lips, broken teeth, and bulging eyes."[29]

Little does the would-be benefactor realize that in having the unpalatable visitor led away to the kitchen, he has tugged the first thread in the unraveling of his own life. He has set in motion a riches-to-rags fairy tale that will culminate not in a wedding, but in an enhanced understanding of his own insensitivity and of God's ways.

The rich man is disquieted by the encounter, losing sleep that night and lodging his complaint with "the Master of the Universe, who had created such outcasts and wretches." Despite all his conditioning toward material generosity, his reflexive disgust overwhelms compassion; if it were up to him, he reasons, "he would have created only beautiful and clean people and not allowed such wretched outcasts into the world." It isn't clear whether the greater portion of the rich man's sin lies in humiliating the beggar to his face or willing his kind out of existence in his thoughts, but creeping catastrophe ensues. By turns, he loses wealth, and then health, and finally the daughter "to whose soul his own was bound and whom he loved more than ten sons." At last the message has penetrated: "He was seized by a great terror before God's judgment, to which he was being called, with no idea of how he had sinned."[30]

The magnate's pious resignation is so deeply ingrained that only his severely mounting losses can breach the impregnable fortress of his virtue, pierce the inner ward of his reflexive piety, and incite the spiritual crisis necessary for growth. He is a paragon of Aristotelian habituation to virtue, a philosophical ideal that Maimonides imported into medieval Jewish discourse and grafted seamlessly onto rabbinic modes of introspection and behavioral amendment. As he writes in his philosophical treatise Shemonah Perakim (Eight Chapters)," "Know that these moral virtues and vices are acquired and firmly established in the soul by frequently repeating the actions pertaining to a particular moral habit over a long period of time and by our becoming accustomed to them."[31] The otherwise unpredictable internal process of introspection is systematized through a practice of daily stocktaking.[32] If bad actions are recognized and rooted out, and good actions are repeated consistently, Aristotle reasons, then a person will come to choose the good almost effortlessly, out of sheer habit.

But this very effortlessness troubles a Romantic like Asch: The magnate's generosity is too automatic.[33] After all, if your kindness is automated, are you really acting virtuously at all? Shouldn't virtue rely not on some abstract, legalistic notion of The Good, but rather on the power of another person's suffering to spontaneously call forth fellow-feeling? Moreover, traditional conceptions of Jewish ethics are implicitly routed through the demands of an exigent God. Insofar as interpersonal interactions like charitable giving are mandated by the divinely stamped Torah, they involve more than just human goodness. Asch's deeply humanistic vision of charity centers the exigent claim that resides in the drawn, troubled face of the other. Rather than systematized compassion, which begets complacency, he seeks to restore the aleatory spark of individual encounter, the radical wholeness of the other person's messy, smelly subjectivity. If the relationship between donor and recipient is reduced to a purely formal one, the very act of philanthropy threatens to unmake the beneficiary's humanity. The only way the magnate can internalize this lesson is by having his own humanity unmade.

Like the Yiddish Romantics who preceded him, notably Y. L. Peretz, Asch drapes his humanism in shrouds of divinity: "One night, when he was lying down and thinking over why bad things happen to good people and why good things happen to bad people, it occurred to him that he should go out and wander the world, and perhaps God would take pity on him and let him know his reasons. This thought was actually from God, who, in his mercy, could no longer bear the man's suffering." The magnate sells off his valuables to provide for his wife and remaining children, dons sackcloth, and sets off as an itinerant beggar. Subsisting on the kind of charity he used to dispense, he joins the ranks of the nameless, faceless poor: "Very gradually, his name faded out, as is the way of the world; one soon forgets what was—and he was forgotten." His undoing is a mystery to him, and he wanders in search of the solution. Over time, he hears about the rise of a new magnate, this time in Damascus, and resolves to visit the man and seek his advice, perhaps finding an explanation for "why God had taken away his wealth and given it to another." Only he perceives the continuity of his personhood—*he* still feels like himself—but in the eyes of others, the magnate has been transformed into a source of disgust. The omniscient narrator is unsparing: "His body gave off a stench, like the body of a corpse, God help us, and his face was swollen and full of dirt—just like the face of the poor man who had come to him when he'd been the magnate of Jerusalem. But he didn't notice any of it, because it was his own body and not a stranger's."[34] The narration lingers on his altered appearance and malodor, revisiting the grotesque imagery three times over four pages.

The erstwhile Magnate of Jerusalem, an ironic moniker assigned by his fellow beggars to poke fun at his fastidious ways, must himself be reduced to a wretch before he can perceive the humiliation he visited upon another so long ago. Arriving at the home of the now-ascendant Magnate of Damascus, he recognizes his own familiar surroundings in the sparkling rabbinical chamber, outfitted with curtains inset with gemstones, perfumed with exotic spices wafting from ornate spice boxes. Time and hard experience melt away, as surely as his personhood has dissolved: "He thought that he had come back into his wealth, which he had just now lost—so he walked with an outstretched hand to greet the magnate of Damascus, his peer." Only when he is dismissed exactly as he dismissed another—"The room is full of a foul odor"—can he understand and finally ratify the justice of God's ways.[35] The reader, meanwhile, apprehends the cycle starting again and surmises that the wealthy man of Damascus might be coming in for some hard times. The cyclicity of these events is left implied, so the reader infers the state of the original beggar's mind when he strode into the study of the Magnate of Jerusalem.

The reversal-of-fortune plot simplifies the practice of theory of mind by breaking down what is usually a simultaneous transaction ("I am in my position, but I can imagine how you would act from your position") into a *sequence* of events and perceptions ("You now occupy the position I used to"). This boon to thinking-as-another predictably yields an advantage in learning to feel-as-another: a plot arc perfectly crafted to elicit what psychology researchers call projective, or role-taking, empathy.[36] Asch's story draws on another potent source of emotional instruction: the dramatic irony, or "audience superior position," whereby the reader possesses more information than a character. In this case, the omniscient narrator positions the young reader to know important details the adult protagonist does not, like the fact that his fortune must unravel because of his treatment of the beggar. In consuming fiction, children may experience degrees of power and authority unavailable to them in real life, even coming to sympathize with a highly advantaged adult. As Patrick Colm Hogan notes, "We have greater pity for someone to the extent that we infantilize them, to the extent that we view them as experiencing the emotional intensities, inhibitory limitations, and behavioral incapacities of children."[37] For youthful readers, stories like this one offer not just a reversal of fortunes, but a reversal of roles as well, whereby a reader who is usually disadvantaged with respect to knowledge vis-à-vis adults attains a high enough perch to be able to gaze down at a suffering magnate with pity and cultivate empathy for grown-ups who turn out not to know everything after all.

Generous Baker, Striking Birds

Toward the end of 1917, Kadya Molodowsky was hungry. A twenty-three-year-old teacher who had left home a few years earlier to complete her education, she was living in Kiev and waiting out the fighting between the Reds (Bolsheviks) and the Whites that would come to be known as the Russian Civil War.[38] Food supplies were a perpetual problem. One day, an acquaintance recommended her to a local baker who sought a Yiddish and Hebrew tutor for his children. Thus ended a prolonged period of malnourishment. Once hired, Molodowsky would stride energetically through the snowdrifts on her way to work, knowing that at the bakery attached to her pupils' home, she would receive "plenty and comfort" in the form of abundant bread. It is hardly a stretch to imagine that baker, whom she describes as "good natured," as the model for one of the titular characters in her 1970 reversal-of-fortune story "The Baker and the Beggar," which portrays a generous and humble yet increasingly prosperous baker who always distributes baked goods to the needy. Over the years, he forges a bond with one specific beggar with radiant eyes and gentle ways, taking care to personally hand the man a challah every Friday.

Eventually, though, the fictional alms seeker stops coming. "Perhaps God had helped him," reasons the baker, "and he no longer needed to beg." The baker inquires after the man, but nobody knows his fate, and eventually he is forgotten. "Who keeps thinking about a poor man?" muses the narrator, pointedly.[39]

The baker prospers, building a house with a large oven, acquiring "little luxuries" like shoes for the children, and "drinking glasses and spoons by the half dozen." But no one's luck lasts forever: One Friday, a fire consumes the bakery just hours before the Sabbath, and the family is left destitute. "*Just then*," in the near-fairytale parlance of the story, the erstwhile beggar returns as benefactor.

Crucially, he does not offer reciprocal charity to the newly indigent baker; he appears specifically and emphatically to *pay his debt*. The formerly poor man has kept a careful tally of all that he ever received at the bakery. Rather suddenly, he has come into money, and his errand is to repay the precise monetary value of several decades' Sabbath loaves. As luck (and fairy tales) would have it, the sum he furnishes is exactly enough to make the family whole again. This transaction draws on a deep-seated rabbinic understanding of philanthropic giving that owes less to the Latin *caritas* (charity as coming from "care") than to the Yiddish-Hebrew *tsdoke/tzedakah*, derived from a Semitic root meaning "justice."[40] So-called charity is really the discharging of a debt, the accurate balancing of the divinely inscribed ledger that is usually shrouded from human view.

The young reader is implicitly invited to identify with the prosperous and generous baker. Fairly or not, the protagonist has always favored the poor Jew with the beaming eyes: "The baker liked him best of all, and each Friday, he would give the man an entire challah for Shabbos." The baker may be said to be acting prosocially (doing good) but not altruistically (at cost to himself). Is he any less generous with the passel of other needy Jews, the ones with ordinary eyes, offering them only smaller rolls? If so, might his favoritism be the germ of a peccadillo that causes his later ill fortune, as when the magnate of Jerusalem shoos the smelly beggar into the kitchen? Is he meant to learn a lesson? Molodowsky gives no hint that the baker's adversity is a punishment; it is simply bad luck, acknowledged by his neighbors as undeserved. However, the reader, through identifying with the baker, takes a lesson from this exemplum of reciprocity and care.

If Yiddish authors were nearly unanimous in seeking to redress wealth inequality, then they varied widely in the approaches their work celebrated—from personal, one-on-one aid as is highlighted in the reversal-of-fortune fairy tales, to more systemic methods of philanthropic giving, to radical forms of collective action that bear on large social systems, including labor organizing and even revolution. Some stories depict the awakening of a character's empathy as a process, while others simply model empathic actions for the reader.

Some feature adult characters like those analyzed above, others focus on children, and yet others make their point with anthropomorphic animals.[41] As early as 1918, Judah Steinberg's "Questions" (Fragen) isolates the moment when an elementary schooler's class consciousness begins to dawn. Through posing a series of questions to those less privileged than he is, he begins to grapple with the arbitrary, unearned quality of the material advantages he enjoys: Why does his friend, the carpenter's son, live in a home without furniture? Why does the washerwoman who cleans his clothes go about in dirty rags? Why do the geese whose down fills his pillow sleep naked on the ground? Why does the cow have nothing left for her own calf to suckle on? And so he goes on, posing his insistent "Why?" to the donkey bereft of his jenny, her hide destined for shoes, and to the sheared sheep, its fleece woven into his woolen suit. When his mother heaves a sigh but cannot answer his queries about the reigning world order, he resolves to write them down and find out the answers when he grows up. The story is far too earnest for a fairy tale, and but for the talking animals, it is an entirely realistic account of how a young person begins to understand the demands that his very existence imposes on others with far less privilege. Perhaps the middle-class boy will grow up to be a revolutionary.

Empathic concern spurs the action in Lit-Man's 1936 story "The Birds Go on Strike," specifically the free, forest-dwelling birds' concern about their urban brethren living under human dominion in cages. Rather than dwelling on the emotional interactions, though, this tale offers a blueprint for labor organizing, wherein the avian activists undertake a general strike: No bird will chirp until all birds go free. Unbeknownst to humanity, the rising of the sun depends on the stimulus of birdsong. Without the sun, trees and plants wither, and the children find no joy. After a full week of cheerless days, the children appoint a delegation to negotiate with the striking birds in the forest. The humans accede to every demand—cages are burned, nests left unmolested—to the benefit of all. Animals figure in much children's literature the world over, perhaps because both children and animals enjoy less complete agency than human adults. But here, the children hold the power to harm or protect the birds, and they are the natural interlocutors for those seeking to advance social justice. The trappings of the story, with its talking birds and outsize importance accorded to birdsong, are fanciful, but the allegory is serious. These narratives of dawning class consciousness and collective action might be classed less as fairy tales than as political wisdom tales, a modern form of wisdom literature whose earnestness is communicated through anthropomorphic animal characters.

Empathy Across the Color Line

"Mainstream" and leftist Yiddish writers in the United States differed on the question of whether reparative empathy extended to race. For Sholem Aleichem and his wide-eyed immigrant protagonist Motl, the Cantor's Son, "Negroes" were a scenic part of the exotic urban landscape of New York, to be disregarded or played for mild laughs.[42] However, avowed communists and many socialists could not ignore the imbrication of class difference with racial disparity, and they sought to mobilize children's fellow-feeling to counter white supremacy. As historian Eric Goldstein demonstrates in his valuable study *The Price of Whiteness*, Jews' negotiation of the American racial landscape was complicated, varying by location, historical period, and level of acculturation to American behavioral norms. Until World War I, "whiteness remained a highly unstable category of identity for American Jews," and in the interwar decades, "Jews largely remained torn between their empathy for blacks and their aspirations for full acceptance in white America."[43] If this sympathy was reluctant or inconsistent among rapidly acculturating immigrants, then it was more full-throated among leftists who continued to embrace Yiddish as a kind of "safe space" for radical thought. Goldstein observes, "Not surprisingly, it was in Yiddish that the most assertive statements of identification with African Americans were made during the 1920s and 1930s. In their own language, unintelligible to a non-Jewish audience, Jewish writers could afford to express their deeply held emotional identification with blacks."[44] Goldstein analyzes these tendencies in the Yiddish press, but it was no less true of children's publishing, especially given the tightly woven networks that bound together newspapers, fraternal organizations, Yiddish schools, and publishing houses.

We will focus on a revealing outlier, Yankev Kreplayak's explicitly antiracist story "Shvarts un vays" (Black and White), published by the Kinder ring arm of the socialist Workmen's Circle in 1939 and likely aimed at upper-elementary-aged or young teenage readers. It is a wholly realist text bent on verisimilitude. As with Meyshe Kulbak's story "The Wind That Got Angry," readers are immediately invited to identify with a figure whose reality is remote from their own. But unlike the wind, a natural element equally familiar to and distant from all human beings, this character is a human being on the other side of New York's racial divide. We meet her first as a worker, then as a woman, and finally as a mother. Encountered in a different context, like a movie theater, muses the narrator, her "big, intense eyes would surely be taken for the expressive 'vampish' [*vempishe*] eyes of a Bette Davis or other movie actress."[45] But no such glamor here: The setting is a gloomy warehouse block of Lower Manhattan's Pearl Street, befouled by the smell of tanning leather, and the expressive feminine eyes belong to a Black custodian who has bequeathed them to her young son, Jimmy.[46] A long opening sequence shows the mother cracking up at her boy's antics, as he mimics swimming on the sidewalk and driving a car. But as fondly as she relishes the capers of her one and only *zunyu*, "sonny boy," his joking has a serious edge: The pair share a dank cellar apartment, and come summertime, there are no safe, appealing places for Jimmy to spend his days. All he can do is mime the diversions he yearns for. The solitary child craves company, activity, and sunshine, which seldom penetrates the "iron web" of the elevated tracks that shadow the street. For safety's sake, his mother restricts him to the sidewalk outside the buildings where she works.

But Pearl Street isn't safe for him either. Small in stature and delicately dressed, he is not socially legible as masculine and remains insensible to the dangers that pervade his urban environs, whether from adults of questionable intentions, the speeding vehicles his mother fears, or the racism of other children playing in the streets of New York.[47] Like Olke in her Warsaw slum, Jimmy fantasizes about escape to somewhere more exciting, even if just to the faraway public pool or the more colorful blocks where other children hitch rides on the backs of fast-moving buses and cars. After hours of restless idling on the sidewalk, he ventures impatiently to the street corner and then . . . hops onto the rear bumper of a shiny green car with red stripes that's hugging the old shoreline curve of Pearl Street to precincts north and east, where bright traffic lights catch the sun. Jimmy has ventured that way before, seen how the other children grab onto the speeding vehicles. Lonesome for playmates, he seems not to "see color" or have any inkling that he will be shunned and worse by lighter-skinned, older children eager to police the boundaries of "their" streets.

Here Kreplyak's narrator turns urban ethnographer, detailing the prevailing order whereby the neighborhood boys have organized themselves into three distinct "kingdoms" according to the ethnic enclaves along the east-west thoroughfare of Madison Street: "Greece," "Italy," and "Yidnland." The demarcation keeps a fragile peace, founded on an aspirational whiteness. The unofficial law of the land is that a boy can hitch a ride within his rightful identitarian empire, relinquishing his hold on the back of a car or bus at the first safe opportunity once it crosses into the next zone, where a denizen of that kingdom is then free to take his place. Failure to abdicate means he's fair game to be pulled down, possibly subjecting him to being run over by motorists who never agreed to abide by any of these uncodified laws of the urban jungle. Summers, with everyone prowling the streets, could be singularly dangerous—but there were idyllic days, the narrator explains, when the boys would don their roller skates, grab each other's belts or suspenders, and form long chains pulled along by buses and cars, irrespective of borders. How could Jimmy know that on the particular day of his ride, "there was no such peace in the world, and even if there were, it still probably wouldn't have helped him"? As soon as his ride crosses into "Greece," Jimmy's Blackness incites the fury of the other boys, and the cry goes up "A *negerl* sitting on a car! A *negerl*! Pull him down!"[48]

"Shvarts un vays" is a story about where Jews fit into America's, or at least interwar New York's, racial and ethnic landscape. When the story was published in 1939, Jews were increasingly being identified by others as a distinctive "race," a term that many Jews accepted even as they strove to be considered white. Until "ethnicity" came to predominate after World War II, the category of "race" offered an appealing alternative to the procrustean options of identifying American Jews as either a "religion" or a "nation." But multivalent Jewish identity did not fit neatly into any of these categories, a fact underscored by the only-partial symmetry between "Greece" (Grikhnland) and "Italy" (Italye) on one hand and "Yidnland" on the other. The locution encapsulates the dilemma: "Jewland" is nowhere on the map of this world. Kreplyak's story illustrates what it means to pay "the price of whiteness," as when Goldstein observes, "Although there was little they could do to soothe the underlying social anxiety that made them figures of uncertainty among white Americans, many Jews hoped that they could assuage the doubts of the dominant society by affirming their place as unqualified whites. Central to this effort was demonstrating a clear social distinction between themselves and America's principal racial outsiders, African Americans."[49]

As long as there was relatively little contact between white Ashkenazi Jewry and African Americans, the former proved "more resistant than other immigrant groups to adopting antiblack feelings," but when migration and shifting residential patterns brought the two groups into sustained proximity, that tolerance was tested.[50] For many light-skinned Jews, the assumption of racist attitudes formed part of their acculturation into being fully American. Prejudices that would have been anathema to a generation that formed its political identity through the pages of leftist Yiddish newspapers became socially instrumental and therefore palatable to their children.

This is the historical backdrop against which Jimmy, holding on for dear life to his perch on the bumper of the green car with red stripes, speeds into

"Greece," where the children are so astonished by the boldness of his intrusion into their "kingdom" that they don't manage to pull him down. "Greece" shouts to a similarly flummoxed "Italy," and fumbling the opportunity, "Italy" alerts the denizens of "Yidnland" to carry out the cruel errand. The three minority ethnicities form a coalition in their bid for a whiteness that coheres only in its effort to repel the incursion of Blackness. In Yidnland, the cry reaches Davey, the leader of the Jewish "gang," whose members are occupied with prying a rubber tire off a wheel. Heeding the alarm, Davey and his crew rush toward Jimmy and his precarious perch. From Jimmy's perspective, "this big white boy . . . running across the sidewalk" is not any kind of nuanced ethnic minority member but only a hostile older kid on the other side of a racial chasm, a source of terror. Davey catches the interloper by one foot, and the narrator pulls back from Jimmy's cry "full of horror and mortal terror" to the more distant perspective of an appalled witness: "A Jewish mother from Madison Street had seen how the boys were pulling down the Black boy by his little feet, how he wasn't letting go. And there—just at that moment, he was getting tangled in the wheel, and let out that inhuman-human shriek."[51] The car's driver stops, scoops up the injured boy, described as lying coiled and twisted like a trampled snake, and asks for the nearest hospital. "Straight to Beth Israel!" comes the reply, shouted from all directions. If Davey's embrace of the prerogatives of white supremacy represents to Kreplyak the specter of the worst Jewish selfishness, then Beth Israel hospital represents the altruistic ideal trajectory of Jewish New York. Founded by a group of traditionally observant Jewish garment workers in 1890 because most Manhattan hospitals refused to treat those of the Mosaic faith, the institution grew in size and stature over the ensuing decades, transmuting the particularistic history of discrimination against one people into indiscriminate compassion for all in need of medical care.[52] This resonant if romanticized history probably would have been familiar to the parents of Kreplyak's original readers if not to the children themselves.

At this point, the center of narrative consciousness shifts to Davey and his family, never revisiting its earlier proximity to Jimmy and his mother. They remain present as characters but become mostly objects to be spoken of rather than subjects speaking. When Davey goes home for an early dinner after the incident, we surmise how little his parents know of their son's life on the streets. We learn about the aftermath of the violent incident through the eyes of Davey's father, a self-proclaimed socialist, and his mother, an immigrant *alrightnik*. The father, suspecting nothing of his own child's involvement, has passed by the hospital and witnessed the spectacle of Jimmy's mother sobbing over her critically injured child, her "one and only," uncertain of his recovery. Part and parcel of the father's socialism is his empathy for Black suffering and his instinctive recoil from the dehumanization of the Black mother, who is escorted out of the hospital for "carrying on" and left to tear out her hair and harrow her own flesh in public view.

"You already know what I'm going to say," the father admits, sitting down to eat. "If he wasn't Black, those white runners never would have pulled him down." He had always assumed that Jewish mothers held the winning hand in misery poker, but the sight of Jimmy's mother has made him reconsider whether profuse maternal grief might be universal after all. Exasperated, Davey's mother waves away her husband's distress, asking, "Oh what are you talking about, aren't they all dragging each other around? You, always with the socialism." No sibling is mentioned; isn't Davey *her* one and only, her *zunyu*? While she minimizes her husband's well-founded charge of white supremacy, her son has tapped into the raw social power that flows from whiteness—a historically accurate representation of intergenerational attitudes, as Goldstein acknowledges: "Those most susceptible to the desire to identify with whiteness . . . were the children of Eastern European immigrants who were either born in the United States or came of age here."[53] The garden-variety street bigotry that kids like Davey likely experienced in the 1920s and 1930s was not sufficient to inoculate them against prejudice as turn-of-the-century European antisemitic violence had done for so many of their parents.

But Davey is not without moral feelings, and the day's events haunt him. Squirming at his parents' candid discussion of empathy, with its comparison of Jewish and Black mothers' suffering, he is eager to grapple with his culpability away from their gaze. His conscience struggles to break through the wadding of denial:

> Davey went out to the street, stubbornly thinking he wasn't guilty: that guy had resisted being pulled down. If he'd just gone along with it, nothing would have happened—he would've given him a hand up. And Pa was wrong, he would have done the same with a white kid. . . .
>
> It suddenly dawned on him: with such a small white boy, would he really have done the same thing?

The ensuing guilt directs Davey's steps to Beth Israel, where he learns that the injured Black boy needs blood and presents himself as a donor. A nurse, presumably non-Jewish and schooled in the neighborhood's prevailing racial order, is puzzled as to why a Jewish-looking boy would offer blood to a Black child.[54] Nevertheless, she summons her supervisor, a Dr. Kohn, who ushers the boy onto the ward and questions him closely about his motivations. If Beth Israel is the ideal institution, then Dr. Kohn is its aspirational avatar, with his reflexive humanism, deep compassion for Jimmy, and readiness to chastise Davey in loco parentis. When the youth confesses his involvement and consequent desire to rectify his earlier misdeed, Dr. Kohn lights into him unsparingly, shouting, "Before, you pulled him down, and now you want to come give him blood? You ought to be whipped and flogged. What sort of business is this, hanging off cars and pulling one another down?!" Instead of accepting the proffered blood donation from a minor, Dr. Kohn forces Davey to look in on Jimmy and confront the consequences of his violence. When the sight of the bandaged boy takes Davey's breath away, the doctor softens and observes, "Remorse is a great thing." The young Jewish *gengster* has learned a lesson, but not one as thoroughly penetrating as the moral Kreplyak hopes to convey to his reader. The tale ends with this equivocal near apology:

> Davey began to leave the ward when suddenly he turned back, crossed to Jimmy's bed, and, carefully touching the bedspread with a finger, asked: "Does it hurt?"
>
> The small Black head with the wide-open eyes nodded: "Yeah."
>
> "Did you have to let yourself be pulled down?"
>
> Davey said even more quietly, "I didn't mean . . ."
>
> Davey wanted to say more, but not finding the words, he turned and walked slowly out of the ward.
>
> Dr. Kohn stood and watched.

Compassion flickers in Davey, but he doesn't take full responsibility for his own actions. Working in the didactic genre of moral sentiment, Kreplyak nevertheless commits to the messy realism of an incomplete apology and boyish inarticulacy. His refusal of guilt is a lesson of its own, a negative exemplum rather than a parable of repentance and full amendment. Surprisingly, the final sentence is focalized through Dr. Kohn's viewpoint; its indeterminacy offers an opportunity to refine one's theory of mind. The reader doesn't know whether the doctor feels hopeful that Davey will reform or rueful at the limited extent of his own influence. But we do know that the story likely humanized figures who might have otherwise remained invisible to young readers of Yiddish.

The Limits of Empathy

Beyond pulling Jimmy and his mother out of the shadows over Pearl Street, would Kreplyak's story have sufficed to overcome the so-called similarity bias and induce empathy for the suffering of people so unlike his presumptive readers?[55] Several of the literary theorists mapping the contours of narrative empathy have sounded notes of caution, both about the extent of literature's power to induce empathic concern and about whether that concern translates into "ethical interventions in the real world."[56] The experience of reading might not yield "moral efficacy" that spurs "altruistic action" in real life, and what's more, reading might lure us into a false and therefore dangerous belief that we are perforce becoming better "world citizens" just by virtue of turning the pages.[57] Keen, attuned to the many ways the activity of reading can fall short of the ethical claims made for it, catalogues various critiques of empathy itself as a mistaken goal, including the damning idea that as a Western philosophical ideal, empathy imposes itself "on cultures and peoples that it scarcely knows, but presumes to 'feel with,' in a cultural imperialism of the emotions."[58] Kerry Mallan, in applying Keen's analysis to children's literature, offers this trenchant critique of self-congratulatory narrative empathy:

> To consider ourselves empathetic makes us feel good about ourselves, but often in a simplistic way that still requires binaries such as victim and saviour, superior and inferior, and that acknowledges individual and often one-off acts of empathy while failing to address institutional, corporate, systemic abuses of power that are much more toxic, powerful, and oppressive than anything an individual can individually commit or, conversely, repair. So, in valorising the Western cult of the individual, empathy, which takes as its base actor the individual, must always, necessarily, overlook and underestimate the place of the individual within their historical and national contexts, and the vast and powerful forces that bring him or her to the moment which is simplified in empathy narratives down to a simple choice between empathy or not, self or other, good or bad, right or wrong.[59]

Although Kreplyak carefully portrays Davey's moral reckoning in the aftermath of his harming Jimmy, the author might have sensed what Mallan describes explicitly: how much prehistory had been layered into the decisive moment of violence, how daunting were the structural forces arrayed against any sort of racial reconciliation. Perhaps the shift to Dr. Kohn's silently observing perspective is Kreplyak's way of keeping his own authorial counsel and resisting a pat, optimistic ending that would ring false. Yet the text is also deeply invested in the decisive power that resides in individual actions: It is impossible to argue that Jimmy and his mother would not have been far better off had Davey desisted, in that split second, from violence.

One meaningful response to the limitations of literary empathy is to think about the activity of reading not just as a solitary transaction between author and audience but as taking place within a social context. "Questioning the causal link between altruism and narrative empathy," argues Keen, "devalues neither narrative empathy nor the widespread hope in the socially beneficial yield of novel reading. It shifts the emphasis to what people choose to do with their reading experiences, how they share them, and how they encourage themselves and others to act on feeling responses." In her earliest work, Keen argues that *discussion* is essential to the operation of narrative empathy. In a later revisitation of these ideas, she highlights Changing Lives Through Literature, a program that exposes prison inmates to the study of literature with college faculty and in the company of their parole officers. It is the shared social engagement around the text, with all reader-discussants on an equal footing, she argues, that accounts for the efficacy of the program in reducing recidivism.[60]

The originator of the empathy-altruism hypothesis, C. Daniel Batson, argues that "the most plausible evolutionary account of the origins of empathy-induced altruism seems to be generalized parental nurturance."[61] In the modern world, the evolutionary functions of parental nurturance might be shared among several parties whose complementary efforts sustained children's commitment to reading and subsequent moral formation. The conversation *around* the reading experience is transformative: "Parents, teachers, librarians, reading-group participants, and enthusiastic book-recommenders everywhere are too ready to erase their own contribution, giving all the credit for impact away to the books themselves."[62]

In the Yiddish cultural sphere, in addition to being embedded in their families, most children interacted with several institutions, including schools (public and supplemental), youth groups, summer camps, and libraries, to say nothing of synagogues.[63] The Medem Sanatorium, discussed in chapter 5, was an extraordinary example of a comprehensive if temporary integrative web that bound together the production and reception of reading materials, all with the aim of fostering democratic values that were understood to include empathic identification with the disadvantaged. While overlapping and mutually reinforcing "prompts toward prosocial action" serve as confounding variables that make it more difficult to isolate the effects of reading in the research laboratory, these layered experiences surely aided in the goal of most Yiddish children's authors: the production of mensches.[64] Individual families played a role, of course, in mediating the institutions with which a child interacted. There is something subversive—of callousness, that is—in the representation of parents who don't know what their youngster is up to on the streets within a book being published by a socialist fraternal organization and distributed through its school network. Child readers might recognize familiar intergenerational alienation, but they consumed this work of fiction as part of a culture that was being handed down (or over) by the adults closest to them. Kreplyak manages to stand "in league with the future" while binding a new generation of readers to a humane legacy of fellow-feeling.

Shprintse, Revisited

It is worth revisiting Dovid Rodin's portrait of the highly unusual girl, Shprintse, in light of the ideas about reading in relation to empathy and theory of mind elaborated in this chapter. On one hand, she may be imagined as an ultra-empathetic, highly responsive reader. She experiences bodily whatever events befall the main characters of her books, and if we could slide the fictional Brooklynite into an MRI machine, we could probably witness the activation of her mirror neurons in response to the text. Her identificatory reading tracks with the cognitive model described by Mar and Oatley, whereby "imagined settings and characters evoked by fiction literature likely engage the same areas of the brain as those used during the performance of parallel actions and perceptions."[65] In this view, she suffers an excess of empathy. On the other hand, this facile self-projection into the text may be regarded as a deficit of empathy. As Nikolajeva observes, "Projection reveals an immature, solipsistic position that, in real life, we encourage young people to abandon." Immersive reading stands in tension with the cultivation of empathy and should be subordinated to it in her view: "Novice readers who identify with characters and apply projection, that is, life-to-text strategy, will uncritically share the character's goals and thus emotions. They feel happy because the characters feel happy. Here, educators have vast potential to prompt young readers to be empathetic rather than immersive."[66] Shprintse is a cautionary portrait of the excesses of a novice reader.

Shifting from evaluation to description, we might note that Shprintse experiences her reading as *transportation*: being taken out of her own consciousness and reimplanted in the world of the story.[67] Seeking always to escape the pull of her family toward domestic responsibility, Shprintse's life as a reader is defined by its solitude—but might her solipsistic disappearances into story nevertheless promote a prosocial if not fully altruistic experience for real-life consumers of her story? Even a bibliomaniac Shprintse, who is so transported by her books that she reads solipsistically as a character *within the text,* might nevertheless be construed as awakening altruistic values *beyond the text* in those who read her story.

An Unusual Girl from Brooklyn is an unapologetic fantasy tale, and researchers posit that escapism and "fantasy empathy" may be as effective as "perspective-taking exercised across barriers of difference."[68] The less realistic a text is, whether fantasy or fairy tale, the more potential it has to unlock the benefits of "protective fictionality," or "releasing readers from the obligations of self-protection through skepticism and suspicion." Real pirates might stimulate fear, a smelly beggar in real life might evince readers' disgust, and so might the sight of an injured little boy, writhing on the street. But the distressing or off-putting traits of characters encountered at the remove of a fictional world can be overridden by readerly empathy "with possible later real-world responsiveness to others' needs."[69] The desensitization that may allow us to hurry down a city block past the outstretched hands of several abject panhandlers can be safely neutralized while reading.

Mar and Oatley discuss psychological experiments involving "high-prejudice" elementary schoolers who exhibited a greater reduction in bias after hearing a story with sympathetic African American characters than after hearing a story about white characters or cooperating on a shared task *with actual African American children.* "Perhaps mediated contact (i.e., indirect contact with stigmatized others through the medium of fictional stories)," they theorize, "allows individuals to approach these individuals with sufficient psychological distance and feelings of control to promote true empathy and perspective-taking. Direct contact may be experienced as too threatening or otherwise emotionally arousing for a great deal of empathy or even sympathy to take place."[70] Whether in fairy tales that walk readers through a character's reversal of fortune or realist fictions that dramatize the development of empathy, reading creates a zone "safe" enough for readers to let their guard down and be transformed. Young readers practice *thinking as* and *feeling as* diverse others, however similar or remote those characters may be to their own experience. Many educators' ultimate goal, of course, is to cultivate empathy and deepen readers' theory of mind beyond the page.

The intensely transporting experience of reading is paradoxically solitary and communal in nature. In Yiddish, that collective experience was bound up in the language itself and in the contingent history of social networks in which its young speakers would have encountered stories written just for them. A corpus written in a minority language and developed as an outgrowth of politically tinged cultural work, Yiddish children's literature blossomed on an ideologically saturated landscape. Through the tales they told, authors and teachers on the secular Yiddish left demarcated a particular zone of safety for reading and feeling, from which certain kinds of self-fashioning were expected to ensue. Yankev Kreplyak means for his readers to feel proud of Davey's father's socialism, bound up as it was in what today we would call an antiracist disposition. In equal measure, those readers are meant to feel ashamed of Davey's truculence, a mortification safely contained within the relatively homogeneous and bounded community of Yiddish speakers. Centering plots of social repair, whether in reversal-of-fortune fairy tales or narratives of empathy-driven realism, Yiddish children's authors sought to catalyze a conversion in the reader toward greater generosity and selflessness. They intuitively understood that "empathy," a term that originally translated the German "Einfühlung," or "feeling into" a text, accords with how children read: They feel themselves into new experiences and inhabit them viscerally.[71]

In the next chapter, on explicitly communist children's literature, we will note the presence of similar underlying concerns about economic and racial disparities, albeit with less of an emphasis on the awakening of empathy, which spurs greater generosity. In Yiddish communist children's literature, inequality is less frequently a direct stimulant to plot than in socialist or more broadly leftist, secular work. George Eliot spoke of "a sympathy ready-made, a moral sentiment already in activity," which seems to capture how communists imagined the children in their midst. Whereas socialists and politically unlabeled writers of a general secular Yiddish Left challenged children to reckon with unfairness and suffering through the simulated model of fiction, communist authors assumed that a political identity had already crystallized and that the task of the next generation was to advance, in soldierly fashion, the program it dictated.

8

Who's Your *Tate*?

THE STATE AND THE FAMILY ON THE FAR LEFT

A SOVIET boy's soldierly aspirations might take shape very early in life, while he's still young enough to wear short pants and swoon over the foals in the stables of the Red Cavalry. Such is the case for the first-person narrator of *Ah, When I Grow Up!* (*Akh, az ikh vel oysvaksn*), an undated verse picturebook by the foremost Soviet Yiddish children's author, Leyb Kvitko (1890 or 1893–1952).[1] Equally enthralled by the large, gentle horses and the vigorous stable hands who care for them, the boy dreams of joining the elite ranks of Marshal Budyonny's "Cossack" cavalry division.[2] As the story-poem ends, the narrator imagines meeting with the illustrious Marshal Semyon Budyonny himself, who assures him that if he studies hard, he will indeed be on course to join the cavalry someday.[3] To readers of Isaac Babel's story collection, *Red Cavalry*, this invitation sounds so comically improbable as to be almost sardonic. The Jew riding among Cossacks—immortalized "with glasses on his nose and winter in his heart"—was meant to be an oxymoron, the very definition of irreconcilable differences. But in (propagandistic) children's literature, Kvitko overwrites the tensions between Jewish and Soviet identity, conjuring impeccable specimens of communist youth culture—who happen to speak Yiddish.

Kvitko's protagonist is the youngest in a series of solidly proletarian siblings; his older sisters work as a pilot (described as a *fliern*, pictured as a parachutist) and a weaver, and one older brother is a poet. Yet the parents who produced this productive, occupationally diverse little legion are never mentioned. The marshal stands in loco parentis, doling out fatherly advice and encouragement. His counsel to study typifies a Soviet emphasis throughout the 1920s on the "moderation, discipline, and rationality" required to build up a communist society on the foundation of the political power that the Bolsheviks had wrested in 1917.[4] While "the bold and brave child as a symbol of the radical new Soviet state" was celebrated in the immediate aftermath of the revolution, by the time of the Third Komsomol Congress in October 1920, Vladimir Lenin was exhorting the nation's youth, "Before all else learn"—hardly a radical message for young revolutionaries.[5]

For a society actively remaking itself, the question of "what to tell the children" was politically acute, but so was the question of "how to think about children." By vicissitudes, and sometimes simultaneously, seemingly unprecedented hope for the very renewal of humanity as well as terrible anxiety about an uncertain future were projected onto the abstract figure of "the child." Children were assumed to be more plastic and receptive to new ideas than adults, and the significance of childhood transcended biological development to evoke, as historian of Soviet youth culture Anne E. Gorsuch points out, an idealized "'youthful' state of mind . . . a kind of social optimism." Yet precisely because the processes of maturation yielded such unpredictable outcomes and the stakes for the future were so high, enormous resources and pressure were brought to bear on guiding children's development, molding their education and leisure. These pressures were especially acute in the first phase of the revolution, with the Communist Party promulgating eighty resolutions on youth between 1918 and 1932 (as opposed to just fifteen in the thirty years thereafter).[6] The children's literature that flourished during this period, whether in Russian or minority ethnic languages within the USSR, was designed to craft the ideal revolutionary childhood and thus build the ideal revolutionary citizenry from within.

The individual's development, understood in increasingly scientific terms, could be synchronized with the growth of the nation.[7] Kvitko's dreamy narrator, who harnesses together emotional sensitivity and muscular ambition, is in turn tightly harnessed to the Bolshevik cause. Aspiring to grow into a good and disciplined soldier, he instantiates the tension at the heart of a revolutionary childhood: The past was suspect, and older generations were broadly assumed to represent regressive forces, yet children needed to obey, to be guided and educated by their elders.[8] The revolution called for obedient disobedience, for children to dutifully disrupt every institution, including those that governed their everyday lives, such as family and school.[9] What was to become of parental authority on one hand and the parental duty of care on the other?

Like other institutions, the patriarchal, bourgeois family was ripe for revision. While young children were understood to require structure and guidance that had traditionally been imposed by parents and other trusted adults in a family's intimate sphere, the rebellious spirit of adolescence synchronized perfectly with the Marxist spirit of world-historical revolution. Declarations like this one likely would have stirred Kvitko's narrator even if he was too young to articulate it himself: "Our generation has October as its birthday. It is the first generation in Russian history not to have ancestors. We are children without fathers."[10] In the earliest years of the Revolution, fraternity seemed likely to displace paternity in the Soviet imagination. "Vertical" ties rooted in parental authority seemed to dissolve in favor of "horizontal" bonds of fraternity, as when Kvitko's narrator places himself in relation to his biological siblings but only truly *defines* himself in relation to the confrerie of soldier-workers whose ranks he longs to join. Leading revolutionary, Marxist theoretician, and feminist pioneer Aleksandra Kollontai, who embraced the dismantling of the traditional nuclear family in favor of more communal, labor-based affinities, envisioned "a big, universal working family, in which those who work, men and women, will be brothers and comrades above all."[11] And until the youngest revolutionaries were ready to take their places alongside those comrades, the state would assume some of the functions traditionally performed by parents and other relatives.

Whereas Bundists and other Western socialists sought to transform individuals and thus eventually the collectivity, the Bolsheviks operated directly on a mass scale.[12] They had little choice, given that in 1914, a third of the Russian population was under age twenty-one.[13] The government established a large, state-sponsored apparatus of care that encompassed education, residential placements where necessary, healthcare (physical and mental), and leisure.[14] Seeking to shore up the next generation's commitment to the principles of the revolution, this apparatus entered every realm of children's experience, including their reading materials, making children's literature an arena for political contestation and an unprecedentedly "crucial genre," as well as a rich resource for understanding the reformation of childhood and family life under the red star.[15] Ideological mandates came to govern both the production and reception of children's literature in Russian and the languages of several ethnic minorities.[16]

In its first decade of existence, the USSR was hospitable toward cultural production in the "national languages" of its multiethnic empire, and Yiddish children's publishing flourished in Moscow and Odessa, Kharkov and Kiev. During the 1930s, Russian-language hegemony would begin to assert itself gradually in education and publishing, but a Yiddish press for children still thrived throughout the interwar years. Although Kvitko might have liked to find greater success writing for adults, he continued to publish for children, including during the delicate years after an internecine squabble with other Soviet Yiddishists jeopardized his prestigious literary career.[17] Kvitko would survive that episode and confront other political and artistic challenges until the infamous Night of the Murdered Poets on August 12, 1952, when he and a dozen other Soviet Jews, several of them writers and members of the Jewish Antifascist Committee, were shot dead on Stalin's orders.

To understand the tenor of Soviet Yiddish children's literature as it developed under Stalin in particular, we can look to Kvitko, who returned in 1926 from a sojourn in Berlin to take up residence in the paradise for Yiddish promised by the new Soviet Union.[18] He was a pivotal figure insofar as he helped to create the culture of a revolutionary childhood in Yiddish and, through translation, Russian. Like a clandestine message stitched into the squares of a quilt, his picturebooks weave in a subtle account of family transformed; under Stalin, the paradox of revolutionary childhood found its blunt resolution. Instead of a wholesale obliteration of the traditional structures of adult authority over children, Soviet youth were expected to transfer their filial piety, their political and emotional allegiance, from the superannuated biosocial parents who had produced them to a single superparent and his authoritative surrogates. Again and again, Kvitko depicts children with absent or incompetent parents. The young must overcome this deficiency by falling back on their own internal resources as well as those of the Soviet state, the ultimate dispenser of care and guidance.

This motif is thrown into prominent relief when we contrast Kvitko's work with that of another Yiddish children's author, who shared fully in his communist commitments but articulated them in a radically different cultural context. Gershon Einbinder (1901–1964), who wrote under the pen name Chaver Paver (meaning "bosom buddy" while evoking the abbreviation for "Communist Party"), made his own fateful move in 1924: from his native Bessarabia to New York. After about a decade there, he would decamp to Los Angeles, meeting a far gentler end than his Soviet counterpart. These two writers were avatars of the Soviet- and American-Yiddish communist address to youth; they shared an ideologically tinged tendency toward realism and a willingness to engage political themes, although Kvitko usually did so less directly. Yet in one key respect Kvitko and Chaver Paver very nearly inverted each other. Kvitko showed how the state could be newly reconfigured as a child's family, while his naturalized American counterpart depicted the traditional nuclear family—consisting of father, mother, brother, sister, and one very famous dog—as the very microcosm of a cheerful, democratically functioning state.

From Nanny Goat to Nanny State

Once he began writing for children in the 1920s, Kvitko was dizzyingly prolific, with seventeen books appearing in 1928 alone.[19] We will focus on three representative texts published between that signal year and 1940, placing them in dialogue with some of the animating concerns and ideals behind the broader Soviet approach to children, childhood, and the management of children's reading. Illustrated by A. Sudamara, *A Nanny Goat with Seven Kids* (*A tsig mit zibn tsigelekh*) appeared in Kharkov. At the outset of the tale, the traditional family unit is thriving if slightly short of "perfect":

> Once upon a time, in a clearing in the wood, lived a billy and a nanny goat with all that was good.
>
> Their home was happy, its own little heaven, and as for kids, they had seven.
>
> Six of their kiddies were healthy, athletic—but the seventh one was truly pathetic.[20]

Yet the seventh kid, described as thin and limping, has compensatory strengths: "But where he *could* be, he was the best: more clever and cheerful than all the rest." These internal resources prove useful when the nanny goat is widowed and must leave her children to forage for food. She strictly admonishes her latchkey *kids* to open the cottage door only for her, and they listen for the song that announces her daily return from the forest.

But a bear lurking nearby soon learns to mimic her singsong and tries to pass himself off as Mother. Initially, the clever but lame kid prevails on his siblings not to open up for the hoarse, presumably masculine voice singing their mother's song. But the ursine predator disguises his voice, and the kids tire of heeding their cautious, know-it-all brother. Once they admit the bear, he snatches six of the seven siblings, promising to return for the cripple cowering behind the oven. Following undetected, the clever kid discerns the location of the lair. When Mother returns and despairs at the loss of her kids, her young son entreats her to stop crying and instead lay a bear trap that will enable them to rescue the others before they are eaten. The parent provides the muscle, but the wise child provides the brains and initiative to save the day. The combination of clueless parent and savvy child typifies the Soviet children's literature of the first decade and a half of the USSR, according to Catriona Kelly. The Russian-language canon was "often pro-child and anti-adult (or at least hostile to private adult authority as represented by parental power, which was seen as shoring up the undesirable social attitudes of the past)."[21] Though physically compromised, the seventh kid displays the wisdom and initiative to rescue his able-bodied siblings.

Kvitko's latchkey kids represent a tempered version of the orphanhood crisis that overtook the USSR in the early 1920s. Known as *besprizorniki* (literally "unattended" or "unsupervised"), these parentless children came to occupy a large place in the cultural imaginary. They constituted the ideal human clay to be refashioned by the revolutionary state; even before the war, as Tara Zahra notes, "orphans seemed to offer the ideal raw material for nationalist movements."[22] Marina Balina draws the connection between the social reality of unattended children as "much-desired raw material, as it were, a human *tabula rasa* on which the Soviet government could write its glorious and happy future" and the utopian depictions of orphanhood in Soviet children's literature. The unsupervised child, accustomed to hardscrabble street life, perforce "collectivized" as a matter of survival, could be romantically portrayed as the vanguard of a revolution that sought to overturn the autocratic power structure of the bourgeois family. Indeed the Marxist pedologist Aron Zalkind (1886–1936) claimed, "The communal bands of *besprizorniki* are *closer* to the collective comradely ethic than is the 'normal' morality of self-love that children from a bourgeois environment have."[23] Through the rosy lens of revolution, the orphan—already inured to privation—was imbued with a fraternal, collective consciousness that exceeded the contingencies of mere blood relations.

Yet Kvitko's lame kid is—overwhelmingly—a child *apart* from his siblings. Urging them against admitting the bear, he calls them "fools." His care for them is quasi-parental, not peer to peer. He instantiates the "high-achieving" child who is ultracompetent but not necessarily likable. As such children and their exploits on behalf of the revolution came to be widely idealized, a backlash ensued. Catriona Kelly pinpoints an anxiety about the "callow arrogance" that might overtake such children should they be "given too much attention as a result of their achievements."[24] But the combination of physical deficiency and high intelligence suggests another allegorical reading in the Soviet Yiddish context: It is difficult not to discern in the well-justified vigilance of the seventh kid the situation of the Jewish child on the Soviet ethnographic landscape. While the new nation proclaimed pride in its ethnic and linguistic diversity, at least in its first decade of existence, old stereotypes about defective Jewish masculinity and the combination of superior brainpower and inferior physical strength were difficult to dismantle.[25]

More universal interpretations of the allegory are plausible. As Mikhail Krutikov observes of another Kvitko tale, "In many ways those cute domestic and wild animals—pigs, cows, dogs, hares, squirrels, foxes and bears—underwent the same fate as ordinary Soviet citizens. They were either domesticated and put under full control by humans, or isolated, tortured and eventually killed." Kvitko's animal allegories harbor a strain of complicating and ultimately enriching political ambiguity. Writing about a far darker 1937 tale of Kvitko's, also in rhyming verse, that narrates the extermination of a dog perceived to have gone mad, Krutikov notes that the allegory is given to conflicting readings and "is certainly not typical for Kvitko's generally rosy portrayals of the idyllic world of children and animals."[26] While Kvitko generally contrives a happier ending than the stoning of a child's beloved pet, the rose tones are often overlaid with shades of mauve. The protagonist of *A Nanny Goat with Seven Kids* is equivocal. The mother's absence exposes her children to danger, but she is so paralyzed by grief that her return home would do little good were it not for her cool-headed offspring. Yet together, they trap the bear and rescue the other six kids. Kvitko concludes with insistent cheer, "Once again they were happy."

The Soviet Discourse of Happy Childhood

"Happy childhood" was a slogan that expressed an ideal central to the Soviet social project, a "sacred value."[27] Conceiving of children as "the only privileged class" in the newly egalitarian socialist paradise, the state presented itself as "uniquely humane" in fostering the well-being of its youngest citizens. Catriona Kelly places the "heyday" of that sentiment in the mid-1930s, tracing items in the adult and youth press and noting the emergence of September 1, the start of the school year, as a "festival for 'happy children.'"[28] The thriving of the nation's youth, measured scientifically and celebrated in the cultural discourse, attested to the success of the revolution and its evolving aim of eliminating class privilege.[29] According to Kelly, "All Soviet children, irrespective of their parents' occupation, enjoyed—so the myth went—a perfectly happy childhood, while Western children were either pampered bourgeois brats or workers' sons and daughters groaning in poverty."[30] The requisite "happiness" implicitly entailed everybody's having just enough, and occasionally a bit more besides.

But what did happiness actually look like from a child's perspective? Might it entail a vision of degenerate *excess*? Maybe happiness inhered in some combination of unlimited access to treats and never having to take a bath, Kvitko suggests in his mischievous, exuberant narrative poem of 1935 "Buts un di sanitarn" (Boots and the Bath Squad). A realistic tale insofar as it features human actors, the protagonist is an elementary-school-aged boy who, like some forerunner to a Shel Silverstein character (or latter-day *Struwwelpeter*), eschews activities favored by adults like reading and bathing while devouring an endless stream of carbohydrates. *Somebody* obviously had to fry up the dumplings and pancakes and procure the jam on which he gorges, but no adults are in evidence when the poem opens on a hungry Buts raiding the kitchen and overturning pots to lick out the last morsels of sweetness.

The protagonist's name evokes the Hebrew word for "mud" (albeit with a slightly different vocalization), and a dirty residue clings to him. Without warning, a detachment of three *sanitarn*, state sanitation agents, bursts into the home uninvited, seizes the recalcitrant youth, and hustles him into a bath. Although they are not necessarily targeting Buts *as a Jew*, they do justify their public health measures in relation to a cold circulating in the shtetl before moving on, rhetorically, to an indictment of the boy's personal grime. The mandate for forcible bathing seems to be informed by an admixture of germ theory and a subtle Dirt Libel:

The Bathman
Sang out shrill as trumpet's metal:
"A cold is going 'round the *shtetl*
What a punk!
What a craw!
Such filthy funk!
His dirty maw!
Grab that Boots, that grubby schlub!
Drag him over to the tub!
Turn on the taps!
No time to cosset,
Hurry, get him to that faucet!"[31]

The head bathman's two henchmen ("Neither smaller than the other") are drawn as preternaturally elongated figures in the sinuous illustrations of Boris Fridkin, and they swiftly set about extirpating Buts's "filth." Although the forcible bathing is by turns traumatic and comical—Buts's socks are so caked onto his feet with sweat that they must be soaked off and left to float to the surface—the lad comes to revel in his new state of cleanliness. Even a "grubby schlub" of a boy comes to appreciate the order and discipline imposed by the state's apparatus of care. Once clean and dry, he manfully shakes the hand of his smock-clad erstwhile oppressor:

When they took him from the bath,
He beamed with pride, began to laugh;
He didn't recognize himself
Sitting on a chair so grand.
He reached to shake the Bathman's hand.

Absent parental interference, the state transforms the dirty, little Jew so thoroughly as to render him unrecognizable to himself. Dramas of bathing fit into a larger revolutionary discourse of cleansing filth and pollution from the body politic and the body personal.[32] Discussion of crime, hooliganism, and "defective" youth often called on the vocabulary of contagion, disease, and impurity.[33] In Korney Chukovsky's 1923 Russian-language narrative poem, "Moydodyr" (Wash 'Em Clean or Wash 'til Holes), an anthropomorphic washstand chases down a recalcitrant boy who initially refuses to bathe.[34] The ablutionary drama illustrates on a homey, intimate scale the state's capacity to transform its people into the most sparkling version of themselves. Marina Balina identifies a "'reforging' genre" linked to creating "new happy Soviet citizens" which developed in 1930s Soviet children's stories even before it overtook the adult literary sphere.[35] With respect to the lived experience of hygiene, the revolution expanded on a strong tsarist-era foundation of monitoring and measuring by a growing army of experts in healthcare and education.[36] Bolsheviks understood sanitation as the linchpin of physical and mental health and thus a natural arena for state involvement.[37]

While the bath-as-metamorphosis motif might have enjoyed currency throughout the Soviet Union, it is worth examining the particular valence in Kvitko's Yiddish version. The shtetl-dwelling Jew, backward and implicitly unclean, is remade into an ethnically unmarked Soviet citizen. Yet in this light, the poem's ending seems rather subversive of Soviet discipline. While it's true that a cleaned-up Buts gratefully shakes the head Bathman's hand, the poet reserves the last word for the insouciant boy:

"Hey, thanks!"
Then, facing the men who (as you'll recall)
Could neither of them be said to be small,
And taking his time lazy and sweet,
He chirped,

"*Now*
I could go
For a bite
To eat!"[38]

Authorized by their mandate to promote public health, agents of the state have entered the home and arrogated one of the most intimate tasks of parental care—but the transformation they effect is skin deep, destined to last only until the boy's next encounter with some errant glob of raspberry jam. Does Buts's hunger, driving his inexorable recidivism, owe more to his age (and possibly sex, as the prerogatives of boyhood were then understood) or to his entrenchment in specifically Jewish "filth"?

While this question may not be susceptible to a definite answer, the science of child study, pedology, which began under the tsars and gained in prestige and reach throughout the interwar period, stood ready to weigh all these factors and to assemble them into an encompassing profile of pathology.[39] The flip side of a universal ideal of "happy childhood" was a similarly widespread anxiety about imperfect or "defective" children (*defektivnyi*).[40] A set of disparate behaviors, all frowned on by adults—gluttony, resistance to bathing, lack of interest in reading—assume a threatening coherence once placed into the unifying framework of "deviance" or "imperfection." If multifaceted problems could be understood in singular fashion, then the response could be similarly unified. Pedology was a "framework of integration" whose multifarious disciplinary domains—pedagogical, juridical, and medical—merged in their efforts to "rationally manage" the nation's youth through a disposition toward therapeutic intervention and cure.[41] Against this *disciplinary* backdrop, in the senses of both converging scientific disciplines and the state's efforts to correct youthful waywardness, Kvitko's messy snacker stands out as a highly equivocal figure. In rollicking rhyme, the poem narrates the particulars of his fresh start in the cleansing waters, almost a scene of secular baptism, before reversing that "progress" with his persistent hunger. Nothing suggests the newly bathed Buts will become a neater eater.

Although Kvitko seems to have been thoroughly devoted to the party line, it is tempting to wonder whether, even on an unconscious level, Buts's tale might stand as an allegory for the author's own experience of transformation.[42] He had, after all, run afoul of the Yiddish party establishment and been "sentenced" to two years of proletarian labor in a tractor factory. He was rescued by a pivot from Yiddish to Russian facilitated by the celebrated children's author Korney

Chukovsky.[43] The story of how Chukovsky, whose father was Jewish, came across the Yiddish stories in the first place speaks to the multilingual landscape of Ukrainian society. At one point, Kvitko taught Yiddish to his neighbor, the Ukrainian modernist Pavlo Tychina, who in turn translated the Yiddish poet's work from transliterated texts into Ukrainian. These were the texts that Chukovsky read and hailed at the 1933 Kharkov conference on children's literature. The most celebrated Soviet children's author had undergone his own revolutionary metamorphosis, embracing writing for young audiences as "a safe haven in the stormy sea of Soviet cultural politics" where he might preserve a greater "degree of aesthetic autonomy" than by writing for adults.[44] With Chukovsky's championship and the translation into Russian that followed, the typical print runs of Kvitko's works grew from a few thousand copies to several millions. *Leyb's* "reforging" as *Lev* may be reflected in the metamorphic drama of the bath. If so, what are we to make of the subtle strain of regressive nonconformity that endures after the state has worked its sanitizing magic?

Comrade Stalin and the Happy Childhood

By the mid-1930s, the generalized Soviet ideal of "happy childhood" came to be fixed specifically on Joseph Stalin as the protector and patron of the nation's youth. The phrase "Thank You Dear Comrade Stalin for a Happy Childhood!" began to be "emblazoned over the doorways of nurseries, orphanages, and schools," splashed across print media, and chanted by children at festivals. As Catriona Kelly chronicles, an evolving visual iconography represented Stalin in cheerful, benevolent communion with ethnically diverse groups of Soviet children, or with young citizens of visibly minority status (although not usually Jewish ones). Girls were accorded especial prominence.[45] If Buts's state-sanctioned cleansing ultimately betrayed a persistent spirit of incorrigibility in the young glutton, then a 1940 tale focusing on the Stalin cult for children admits no such ambiguity. "To whom do the nation's children belong?" is the question embedded in the title of Kvitko's picturebook *Vemes iz es meydele?* (Who's Little Girl Is This?). Published in Moscow by Melukhe-farlag "Der emes" (The Truth), the story enjoyed a print run of ten thousand, one of Kvitko's largest in Yiddish.

Alternating between verse and prose, the tale opens with a rhyming frontispiece that might gesture at Molodowsky's Olke with her blue *parasolke* as it conjures the *meydele inem bloyen kleydele* (the girl in the little blue dress), who looks forward to chasing butterflies when her family vacations in the countryside. But in the train station with her mother and baby brother, she is transfixed by the crowds of other dacha-bound families. In the hubbub, she becomes separated from her mother, who mistakes another little girl for her own and hustles that child onto the carriage, leaving her distracted daughter behind. At first the abandoned girl is so paralyzed with fear that she can neither move nor speak, despite the best efforts of the passersby to identify and care for her. Growing increasingly upset, she hovers on the verge of tears when she spots a familiar face. The onlookers follow her joyful gaze—to the portrait of Stalin hanging between two windows, toward which the girl now makes her way. She has located a paternal presence to substitute for the missing maternal one. Encouraged by the familiar face, at last she is ready to address the gathered crowd, confidently stating her name, age (nearly three), and address. Her precocity charms the onlookers, who rush to aid and engage her. "The girl lit up with laughter, felt nary a care / By the Great Friend of Children everywhere!" At just this happy climax, Maya's harried mother returns to claim her.

Fawning praise of Stalin and other revolutionary heroes, often voiced by an omniscient narrator, was a staple of Soviet children's literature.[46] Here, though, Kvitko depicts an individual child's vibrant, reverential response to the portrait, a kind of secular icon. Soviet youth were "encouraged to regard the leader as a protector and patron, an all-powerful paternal figure" with whom each child enjoyed a relationship that was "intimate but not exclusive." In fact, this "power asymmetry between ruler and adoring subject," argues Kelly, was the paradigm for Soviet citizens at large; ascribing this attitude first to dependent children paved the way for adults to hold their leader in the same esteem.[47]

Stalin's designation as benevolent patriarch was overdetermined. On one hand, the widespread imagery of (older) children's delinquency necessitated the discipline of a stern father.[48] On the other, the cult of "Papa Stalin" was further enabled by depicting biological parents, especially mothers, as woefully incompetent. A 1925 Russian-language story, "Mommy Will Be Looking for Us" (*Mamka iskat' budet*), portrays the death of a brother and sister, beggars abandoned by their mother at a Moscow train station.[49] Kvitko's tale seems like a sunnier rewrite of that tragedy, perhaps with Stalin himself figured as the sun that has risen over the intervening decade and a half to illuminate the lives of Soviet children. Whether it is the nanny goat in panicked paralysis at the abduction of her kids, or the human mother who absconds with the wrong little girl (the story makes no mention of *that* child's fate), mothers could not be counted on to provide steady care under stress. Even as Soviet media questioned parents' reliability as caregivers, a growing culture of scientific expertise turned parents, especially mothers, into "the subjects of both surveillance and enlightenment and, as such, the targets of moral and rational critique, orchestrated by the growing body of experts in child development."[50] Mothers were encouraged to regard themselves as "researchers," or at least data collectors, furnishing teachers and doctors with the fine-grained information about their children's lives to which they had the best access.[51] Stalin, however, was depicted as a "wise father" who knew *intuitively* how to protect children and solve their problems, with a capacity to act beyond the scope of ordinary parents.[52] Of course Stalin's nearly limitless power to act capriciously on his own changing perceptions and preferences engendered U-turns and pendulum swings, many of them fatal to others. By the late 1930s, the "state science" of pedology had been discredited as a "pseudoscience" shaped by bourgeois norms.[53]

The arc of the Bolshevik science of childhood, with its span from the 1917 revolution to its decisive reversal twenty years later (the approximate length of one childhood), sharpens a set of questions relevant for anyone with an ideological interest in children's development—which is to say, anyone with an interest in the political future. In chapter 3, we considered the recapitulation theory implicit in leftist Sabbath tales, wherein young, secular readers were invited into a symbolic encounter with traditional religious observance that would ultimately reaffirm their (parents') secular identity as the apex of human progress. The development from traditional observance to secularism was not centered within the tales but was implicit in the reading context. Soviet children's literature foregrounded the transformation from capitalist and bourgeois to revolutionary and proletarian. As Catriona Kelly observes, "The crucial model of identity in the early Soviet period had, after all, been expressed in a 'conversion narrative,' where the thinking subject progressed gradually to enlightenment from social deprivation and cultural backwardness. In this model, the actual moment of being broken and remade, and the sense of humility and gratitude to higher authority that it inspired, held as much importance as adherence to political orthodoxy in itself."[54] As surely as Buts was changed from dirty to clean, young Soviet readers in the first years of the revolution were encouraged to move from the corrupt old order to the new.

The conversionary message, however, quickly becomes irrelevant to members of subsequent generations, who are ostensibly born into the workers' paradise. Instead of transformation, they needed only preserve the gains already secured, perhaps by studying hard and excelling in the existing system, as the imagined Marshal Budyonny counsels the horse-smitten boy. If the experience of being broken and remade is no longer central to Soviet identity, then what replaces it? For that matter, how is it possible to create a *second* generation of children's literature—privileging continuity over rupture and reformation—for anyone whose political vision is bound up in transformative change?

The revolution had to be perpetual, the state reimagined as the family. The visual and literary representations of Stalin with children, especially those belonging to ethnic minorities, underscored a "symbolic filiation" insofar as "the child was not and could not be the actual offspring of the leader, the product of ordinary, banal, and 'selfish' reproduction within the family."[55] The civic bond transcended the selfishness of the gene, equably affording parental care and protection to all the nation's diverse children. Elevating ideological affiliation over biological lines of filiation constituted a strategy for revising the irredeemably bourgeois nuclear family.[56] At the same time, it is illuminating to place the Soviet experiment, with its messaging about children and families, in the context of a broader global revision of the Victorian and Progressive Era ideal of the nuclear family.[57] Leftists of many stripes were eager to recognize childcare as labor, which might be shifted to sources outside the home in the overlapping interests of efficiency and fairness. In the Jewish world alone, consider the immersive nature (albeit for brief periods) of the Medem Sanatorium or, over the far-longer term, the Children's House that was a staple of early Israeli kibbutz life, wherein children resided separately from their parents under the round-the-clock care of designated workers. Instead of being presided over by the maternal "angel in the house," children's lives could be overseen—to varying extents—by a range of expert and efficient adults, including educators and medical caregivers.

But not in America.

Labzik: A Tale of Adoption

Labzik: Tales of a Clever Pup, published in 1935, was distributed through the Yiddish *shules* of the International Workers Order, the most communist-aligned of the four secular Yiddish school systems functioning in New York City—and its proletarian sympathies are vividly clear. In his 1948 capsule review of *Labzik*, Khayim Shloyme Kazdan critiques the impoverished Yiddish and flagrant propaganda of the quintessential children's text of American Yiddish communism. However, he acknowledges the power of the book's jazzy new idiom, acknowledging that the charming mutt and his author had proven that proletarian literature could compete for young readers and that children's literature didn't have to be an inherently bourgeois phenomenon.[58] An even more radical conclusion is that these stories demonstrated that a nuclear family as American as apple pie (or *sendvitches*) doesn't have to be inherently bourgeois either. It is a testament to the sophistication of Chaver Paver's text that the stories gesture simultaneously in the directions of both filiation and affiliation. Filiation because the mutually supportive biosocial family constitutes the safe base from which every adventure is launched, and affiliation because *Labzik* centers on a tale of adoption. The family circle can even enlarge to accommodate another species.

When we meet the doggie Labzik, he is frolicking in a basket on the elevated train, little suspecting that his kindly but impoverished owner has dragged him on the long journey from Brownsville, Brooklyn, deep into the Bronx only to abandon him far from home. She turns him out of the train at the Jackson Avenue Station, where he cowers on the platform during evening rush hour. A note hung round his neck explains the family's predicament: the Depression has left the woman's husband unemployed, and they've even had to send their own daughter to live with relatives in Boston. They cannot afford to feed a dog but hope that some other good family will; his name is Labzik. As he shivers in the rain, the mutt's whimpering attracts the attention of tender-hearted Berl the Operator, who decides to take a chance and delight his children with the gift of a pet.

Dwelling in the heart of a bustling working-class neighborhood in the Bronx, Berl the sewing machine operator, his wife, Molly, their son, Mulik, and daughter, Rifke, offer a sympathetic portrait of Depression-era secularist Jews who confront life's adversities and adventures as a family. They're sketched in efficient if predictable stereotypes. Berl's gruff demeanor is offset by his reassuringly merry black eyes. He punctuates his speech with the mild curse "*A kapore*!" which seems to signify a range of protestations and dismissals, from "Gosh darnit" to "What the hell?!" His wife, Molly, is cheerful but no pushover. She manages the household and enforces standards of decent behavior, like making Berl greet her and the children properly on the night when he comes home sulking over an impending strike. Rifkele is all sweetness and affection, especially where Labzik is concerned. In between cuddling him like a baby doll and gently chastising his occasional bit of mischief, she explains to him the world and its political order—in terms that a bright pup or an elementary-school–aged reader can readily understand. Mulik is brave and decent, selflessly leading a protest at his public school on behalf of his hungry classmates (who are ethnic Polish Americans). His two best friends are Hymie, another Jewish boy, and Noyekh (Noah), who is Black and not Jewish.

Like a situation comedy or radio play, each chapter features its own conflict, rising action, and resolution—usually involving Labzik's heroism. With the stories structured episodically, you can almost hear the laugh track punctuating the dog's antics. The canine savant delivers contraband leaflets calling on the public school to subsidize lunch for hungry children, prevents the slashing of a portrait of Lenin, tags along to protest marches, and fetches the doctor for an ailing Rifke when the adults are out looking for work. He sniffs out trouble, literally, and rescues Berl from the *gengsters* that his sweatshop bosses have hired to break a strike. Due to his limited repertoire of gestures and responses, Labzik's heroic interventions are sometimes initially misconstrued as harmful—as when he must lead the doctor to Rifke by tugging at the hem of the gentleman's coat with his clamped jaw. At other times, his deeds are unapologetically mischievous, as when he exposes the mayor of New York as a liar by stealing the official's hat from City Hall when he has falsely claimed to be off in Albany advocating for his constituents.

Chaver Paver was centrally concerned with economic and racial justice, leaving unexamined assumptions about gender that now feel regressive. Mama Molly is a *berye*, a skillful or efficient housewife, and she clearly reigns undisputed in the domestic realm. She comes to terms with the family's boarder, revising Berl's hastily scrawled advertisement for a room to rent. While she holds the purse strings of the domestic economy, the implicit preference is that she not seek work outside the home until forced to by financial necessity. She joins Berl in searching for a job during the bleak period when the worst of the Depression collides with the cyclical slack season that perennially overtook the garment trade. While the man of the house obviously feels empowered to decide for himself on the spot to adopt a dog, his partnership with Molly on picket lines and at protests is displayed more often than his autonomy. Husband and wife quibble over sundry domestic trivia, but there is no daylight between them on political questions. They inhabit a milieu thick with leftist culture, sustaining and being sustained by its institutions. After public school each morning, the children's secular Yiddish *shule* highlights various leftist causes and participates in rituals such as the daily singing of "The Internationale."

But while embedding plenty of explicit references to ideology and historical events, Chaver Paver manages to subordinate the doctrinaire to the personal, emotional, and affective. The stories resonate nearly a century after their original publication because they offer such a rich portrait of the canine protagonist's interior life. While Labzik is generally cheerful, two fears threaten to plunge him into despair. The first comes to pass in the book's initial episode, when the unsuspecting pup is abandoned. During the uncertain interval when Labzik has been left on the platform at the mercy of strangers, he starts to "feel very sorry for himself and to whimper like a small child," fearing that "he might even die."[59] The melodrama wears a comical tinge: We surmise from the jaunty cover and promise of eleven more chapters that Labzik is bound for better days.

His second fear comes on more gradually, dawning as an inexpressible malaise. At the beginning of chapter 2, right after his successful adoption, the dog begins to question his cozy domestic surroundings: "One day, Labzik got it into his head that something wasn't quite right. What could that something be? He was given food to eat and water to drink, a little bed to sleep on at Berl the Operator's, but he wasn't really *doing* much of anything. He lounged about, an idle loafer. No, he needed to *do* something, or else he might be taken for lazy."

How to be productive when you're a house pet? One after another, Labzik tries to join in the various family members' activities: the kids' homework, Berl's perusal of the leftist newspaper *Morgen Freiheit*. Alas, he's pushed away at every turn. Maybe the answer is to seek an education, so Labzik tags along with Mulik to afternoon Yiddish school, hoping in this way to "become a mensch." The quest for productivity carries over to the next chapter, when Labzik finally finds a sense of purpose in waking the family's boarder so that Mama Molly can catch a few more winks on cold mornings. "The doggie was so happy to be thanked that he didn't know what to do, and he stopped thinking his sad thoughts about being a loser, etc. Now he thought, 'Oh, how good it was to be alive and to accomplish something!'" For Chaver Paver, the initials of whose penname proclaim his political loyalty, productivity is happiness. To be a monad, cut off from society, is intolerable; to be a mere parasite on others, catastrophic. Labzik's fears mirror his yearnings. He hungers first for a family to call his own, and then for a meaningful way to contribute to that family's welfare. In this sense, Labzik's situation resembles that of the child seeking to connect and to contribute to the common weal. Is this not the heroic quest of the ideal worker in search of solidarity and utility? The child's "job" might be to attend school (and *shule*), but even from the elementary years, the young person's *identity* is fused with that of the worker.

Labzik and the International Workers Order

By 1930, American Jewish communists had formalized their educational commitments, founding the network of *shules*, or after-schools, whose publishing arm brought out Chaver Paver's *Labzik: Tales of a Clever Pup*. The *Ordn-shuln* were named for their parent organization, the International Workers Order

(IWO), which between its founding in 1929 and its dissolution in 1954 served as a mutual aid society providing health and life insurance, medical and dental care, health clinics, newspapers, education, summer camps, and burial plots to its members.[60] When *Labzik* was published, those members numbered sixty-seven thousand, although their ranks would swell, at their post–WWII peak, to two hundred thousand.[61] The IWO eventually comprised fifteen sections, organized by language and ethnicity at a time when the working class included many immigrant laborers who had not yet acculturated into speaking English. The Jewish section, which transacted its business in Yiddish, was by far the largest. The organization had originally split off from another Jewish laborers' organization, the democratic-socialist inclined Workmen's Circle. The rift took place gradually, over the course of nearly a decade. At issue were questions about how political opposition was being handled in the cynosure of global leftism, the fledgling Soviet Union, as well as closer-to-home questions about the New York–based newspaper *Morgen Freiheit*; the schism unfolded against the backdrop of debates about how explicitly political these fraternal organizations should be.

At that time, most communists in the West looked with unalloyed admiration on what would later be termed, more ambivalently, "the Soviet experiment."[62] Yiddish cultural figures like Kvitko, enjoying unprecedented state support during the revolution's first decade, signed on enthusiastically to the project of refashioning the citizenry from within. The mandate came from on high to eradicate illiteracy while forming a proletarian consciousness from the cradle. Vladimir Lenin's wife, Nadezhka Krupskaya, was an educator who used her prominence to promote children's librarianship. When Stalin came to power after Lenin's death in 1924, he embarked on a program of rapid agricultural collectivization and industrialization that still held great promise at the end of the 1920s. He was not yet the absolute autocrat whose name would become a byword for capricious political violence. The first catastrophic consequence of Stalin's economic policies, the famine of 1932–1933, had not yet entered Western consciousness as Chaver Paver wrote his *Labzik* stories. The facts pertaining to that decade's Great Purge (1934–1935), which liquidated seven hundred thousand political enemies, would seep out slowly.

Several aspects of this political history are reflected in the *Labzik* stories. While other secular Yiddishists viewed the preservation of Yiddish as a worthy end in itself, communists tended to view the language as an instrumental means toward the aims of class struggle and eventual revolution. Chaver Paver's text is dotted with English vocabulary and phrases, especially when his characters have reason to interact with English speakers, such as a policemen, fellow strikers on a picket line, or fellow marchers in Washington, DC. The text also adheres broadly to the aesthetic norms of Soviet children's literature, including a preference for realism over fantasy and a rejection of the supernatural, even under the heading of whimsy. Labzik is highly intelligent and quite expressive with his limited gestural vocabulary, but significantly, he cannot talk. The omniscient narrator sometimes grants us access to his thoughts and vocalizations, but while the former are fairly sophisticated, the latter take the form of growls or onomatopoeias like "vuuu, vuuu" (wherrre, wherrre).[63] The characters express loyalty and admiration for some of the heroes of global communism. The children take a charity box to the busy area outside the elevated station in order to raise funds for the legal defense of Weimar-era German Communist leader Ernst Thälmann.[64] Mulik surprises his sister with a poster of Lenin, intended to anchor their family's "Lenin vinkl"—the semidevotional "Lenin corner" with which many Soviet-era families replaced their religious icons. This very portrait becomes a magnet for the ire of the bourgeois Boy Scout who lives in their building. Pointedly, though, Stalin is never mentioned.

As a class, the Depression-era workers are beleaguered yet defiant; it is a given that mainstream institutions like the police force, the public schools, and local government are arrayed against their political interests. Mulik's public school teacher, Miss Crane, who is not indicated to be Jewish, identifies as a worker but fears for her job should the principal learn she is a "Red." Like the family's unquestioned Jewishness—expressed primarily in their use of Yiddish at home and enrollment of the children in a Yiddish supplemental school—their communism is offered to the reader as a minority identity that can invite discrimination and even danger but nevertheless a source of pride. Nor is communism the only secular religion on display in these stories. Virtually no Jew in Europe would have regarded a dog with anything other than suspicion, but the kind of emotionally enmeshed pet ownership that turns Labzik into a family member is a quintessential sign of Americanization and constitutes its own distinctively American creed.

Jewish Leftism and the Racial Question

For the International Workers Order, antiracism was a function of economic solidarity and mutual aid. The 1936 IWO manual proclaims:

> Most fraternal organizations in the field appeal to the workers of the same nationality, of the same religion, of the same political faith or of the same color. The International Workers Order appeals to all workers irrespective of

> their religion, race, color, sex or political beliefs. Insecurity is a problem faced by all workers. The more workers are united, the more effective will be their mutual aid efforts. It is for this reason that the I.W.O. strives to break down the artificial barriers which today serve to separate the workers along lines of race, color, nationality, religious or political beliefs.
>
> The most harmful barrier is that of white chauvinism (theory of white supremacy), which is designed to separate the white workers from the Negro workers. The I.W.O. strives to break down this barrier by uniting in its ranks both Negro and white workers.[65]

Eighty-five years on, the phrase "white chauvinism" rings slightly quaint, but rooting many of America's stranger fruits in the "theory of white supremacy" sounds downright contemporary, as does highlighting the intersections between race, religious identity, sex, and economic inequality. To Chaver Paver, economic and racial justice are indivisible.

Heroic and intelligent as Labzik usually is, he holds some reflexive internal biases that must be examined and finally eradicated. His lowest moment comes when, during a playdate, he bites Mulik's friend Noah just because he is put off by the dark color of the boy's skin. Right away, a horrified Mulik metes out ten lashes, but corporal punishment isn't adequate to really teach the lesson. When a third friend, Hymie, hears of Labzik's misdeed, he labels the dog a "vayser shovinist" and insists that Mulik convene a tribunal of kids from the block to enact more fitting discipline. Is Chaver Paver gesturing, whether with admiration or a gentle smirk, at the conventions of Soviet justice? The children determine that Labzik must be ostracized for a full week, a punishment so hard on the social animal that after a few days, Labzik wishes he could drown in a river instead. When the week is up, the lesson has been learned—never again, the omniscient narrator avers, would Labzik bite a Black child who'd done nothing to him, even for a whole house full of *lembchops*. A canine protagonist allows Einbinder to have it both ways: On one hand, Labzik displays preternatural intelligence, but on the other, "a dog is just a dog"—unintelligent, unenlightened, and literally inhuman when it comes to the scourge of racism. Labzik's task is indeed to "become a mensch."

In the very next chapter, "Labzik and the Pioneers," Labzik returns to his heroic mode, demonstrating that he has internalized the lessons of solidarity. When Noah, Hymie, and Mulik lead their public school classmates in a peaceful strike agitating for subsidized lunches for their hungry classmates, the dog enrages the school principal by delivering contraband pamphlets to agitate the students. Carefully trained by the three boys, Labzik is predisposed to succeed at special operations: He's fast and loyal, and he cannot squeal. The villainous administrator arrays every source of institutional power available to him against the movement's leaders, calling in by turns the police, the dog catcher, the fire department, and the school board. He is not above psychological torture. Responding to the principal's call, a venomous and unmistakably racist police captain assails Noah as a "Black Bolshevik" and raises his club, ready to strike. He stops only when an angry swarm of neighborhood mamas come running into the schoolyard, threatening to tear him clean in two "like a herring" should he harm the boy. Their solidarity across the race line stands in pointed contrast to Yankev Kreplyak's portrayal of Davey's mother, as she pulls her family toward the bourgeois embrace of white privilege.

Not only does Labzik's biting incident with Noah teach a lesson against racial bias in negative terms, but Berl's easygoing solidarity with a broad coalition of diverse workers sets a positive example of the kind of coalition-building that Chaver Paver regards as necessary to foment social and economic change. The book's final chapter, based on the Hunger March on Washington that actually took place in 1932—albeit without significant participation by a dog attested in the historical record—highlights the multiethnic, multiracial nature of the alliance that converges on the nation's capital to demand the president's attention to plight of the unemployed. Berl is proud of being chosen to represent the workers of Jackson Avenue. In his typical fashion, he entrusts the packing of his suitcase to Mama Molly, and naturally, on the morning of his departure, they bicker as usual:

> He picked up the bag and exclaimed angrily, "What did you pack in here for me? Why is the satchel so heavy?"
>
> "See for yourself," replied Mama Molly, "What did *I* pack in there? *Your* underwear, a sweater, two shirts and a few other little things."

The astute reader has probably already guessed what's making the bag so heavy. It isn't the sweater.

Once Berl and his heavy bag arrive at the rendezvous point in Union Square, he takes care to introduce himself to fellow protest marchers, who represent the ethnic, racial, geographic, and occupational diversity of the (unemployed) American worker. Kinley is a farmer from Massachusetts, Tom Lincoln is a miner from Pittsburgh, a "black man with large eyes." One significant subplot of the chapter is Tom's susceptibility to a respiratory illness in the cold weather. With his large eyes and wide nostrils, the characterization of him comes uncomfortably close, for the modern reader, to minstrel stereotypes; however, the emphasis is clearly on Berl's solicitude and advocacy for Tom to receive the medical care he needs.

Seamlessly inserting the heroic antics of the precocious pup, the larger plot arc of the final chapter also includes many historically accurate details. Berl is full of admiration for Bill Foster (William Z. Foster, 1881–1961), the radical labor organizer and eventual general secretary of the Communist Party USA. "All over America," explains the narrator, "people knew who Foster was. The wealthy hated him, and they always sent policemen especially to beat him up. The workers loved him a lot, and they never let the policemen hurt him." The nonviolent hero identified only as "Carl" was most likely Carl Winter, the Communist Party official who in 1949 was convicted under the Smith Act, the legislation used to imprison ranking members of the party after World War II. Documenting the Hunger March for *The Catholic Worker*, Dorothy Day observes, "Drama was what the Communist leaders of the march wanted, and drama, even melodrama, was what they got. They weren't presenting their petitions to Congress with any hope of obtaining cash bonuses and unemployment relief. They were presenting pictorially the plight of the workers of America, not only to the countless small towns and large cities through which they passed, not only to the Senate and the House of Representatives, but through the press to the entire world. And in addition they were demonstrating, to the proletariat, the power of the proletariat."[66]

The sought-after drama unfolds when the caravan of buses reaches the capital and is refused entrance to the city by a cordon of police, who have set up barricades. Newsreel footage documents how three thousand delegates from the National Unemployment Councils were denied a march permit and diverted by a squadron of police for two days and three nights.[67] The events in Chaver Paver's story are nearly identical—until an irrepressible mutt bursts forth from Berl's satchel to save the day. Labzik's intelligence and bravery help the workers make their way into the capital and all the way to the White House, where their pleas fall on deaf ears. Chaver Paver does not sugarcoat this failure, but the remedy is clearly articulated: All the marchers must return to their communities and broadcast the callousness of the incumbent administration. The workers and all Americans of good conscience will simply have to vote the phonies out of office.

Labzik, Yiddish, and *Yidishkeyt*

Berl and Molly's family doesn't go to synagogue or observe the Sabbath. Keeping kosher is never mentioned, and Berl reads the newspaper rather than studying the Mishna. What is the significance of the family's Jewishness, or of this work's composition in Yiddish? This question takes on a special poignancy nearly a century after the book's publication, when *mameloshn* is no longer the vernacular of a bustling world of secularizing, acculturating immigrants. I'd like to hazard an answer by looking closely at Berl's catchphrase. Starting with his mild grumbling about some rainy weather in the first chapter, and continuing in almost every episode where he makes an appearance, Berl resorts to the gentle expletive "a kapore!" The most accurate, neutral translation I could alight on for the phrase is "gosh darnit!"—with its gently blasphemous harnessing together of God and damnation, albeit in softened form. Small annoyances and pleasures, as well as large disasters can elicit "a kapore!" from Berl.

With extraordinary efficiency and emotional charge, this phrase offers a study in how the fusion language of Yiddish makes meaning in a modern, secular context. The term harks back to a ritual performed on the eve of Yom Kippur, the Day of Atonement, in which either a chicken or a sum of money is designated as one's expiatory substitute. The individual's sins are symbolically transferred onto the *kapore* object so that the human being might be spared even well-deserved punishment. After a brief recitation to that effect, the chicken is slaughtered and donated to a needy family, or the money is given to charity. The generosity helps to shore up the case for the atonement being sought. Colloquially, then, any bad experience can be wishfully assigned such an expiatory role, even after the fact: May this bad weather/financial reversal/professional or personal setback serve as a redemptive *kapore* that I might evade a worse fate. "A sheyne, reyne kapore—a nice, clean kapore!" is the Yiddish idiom for "serves 'em right!" The expiatory suffering can even contain an admixture of pleasure. To be a *kapore* for someone is to be madly in love with them.

After eleven chapters of tetchily or delightedly declaring this or that "a kapore!" in his Yiddish-saturated surroundings, Berl finally lets slip his habitual phrase in English-language conversation with his new friend Tom Lincoln, the miner:

> In each city, the local workers came out with songs and music, with sandwiches and coffee, and the hungry workers ate and drank and felt very cheerful. And the most cheerful of all was Berl the Operator from the

Bronx. In fact, he grew hoarse from cheering. He always kept nudging Tom Lincoln from Springfield and said, "*A kapore*, you see what good comrades we have in every city! They're giving us coffee and sandwiches."[68]

The Black man replied, "*A kapore*? What's that?"

Berl couldn't explain what "*kapore*" meant, so he said, "Oh, a *kapore* is nothing [*nating*], but the sandwiches and coffee, now. . . ."

"Ah," said the Black man, "Sandwiches and coffee, that's right, that's right."

Bent on making common cause with the other workers, Berl understandably focuses on the sandwiches and coffee, the universal language of hunger and satiety. But in failing (or refusing) to explain "a kapore," Berl consigns to oblivion the linguistic fossil that is also the living marker of the civilization that has produced him and led him to this moment of shared humanity and justice-seeking. Tom asks in a spirit of sympathetic curiosity, inviting Berl to explain himself. *A kapore* may be hard to understand, and even harder to explain on the fly, but it certainly isn't "nating." The 1930s found Yiddish-speaking, Ashkenazi Jewish workers like Berl at a liminal moment. They were immigrants positioned between European and American identities; pale-skinned newcomers who had been persecuted as perennial Others in Europe but were now poised to enjoy the privileges of whiteness on the American racial landscape; subsisting in Depression-era poverty but about to see their children lifted by a rising economic tide after the Second World War.

If you had even these provisional forms of privilege, Chaver Paver and his allies insisted, you were duty bound to agitate for those who had less. And if you could agitate through stories and have fun doing it, so much the better and more effective. The Labzik stories are rooted in an artistic vision that honors children as political actors, speaking their language and introducing them to the grammar of democratic political life. These tales exude a lively energy without talking down to kids. They promulgate an unsparing view of economic inequality and its corrosive effects, albeit one leavened by lighter moments. Ironically, the most lighthearted episode in the book, in which Labzik falls in puppy love with Tootsie, the pretty lapdog who lives in a big house on the other side of the park, conveys the most discouraging message: No solidarity or even sympathy will be forthcoming from the rich. The people in power will cave only when they have to, and yet the power of the workers united (and especially their children) is a force to be reckoned with. Politically progressive, racially enlightened—these are the values that Einbinder puts forward as both Jewish and American, seamlessly joined. And the place where those values are both modeled and discussed is the home of the Jewish worker. The functional, involved family provides the site where identity is formed.

Leyb Kvitko needed parents out of the way so that the state could be shown to nurture its youngest citizens directly. In story after story, the nuclear family is temporarily compromised or permanently dismantled to create space for a nationalized parental presence; "Papa" Stalin figures as the only father who can give effective care, and thus the only parent who ultimately matters. The loss or vitiation of parents goes unremarked or is even celebrated rather than mourned. In contrasting American fashion, Berl and Molly's functional, involved family provides the fertile soil where their children's political identity is cultivated: Brother and sister learn by *imitating* their parents' politics. The family's sympathies and habits are bound up in their Jewishness, their *yiddishkeyt*, but not constrained by it. Communism is just as much their religion as Judaism—and, like a traditional religion, the gentle American version of this political faith guides them to seek justice and pursue ways of kindness. The family overcomes any internal dissension to present a united front to the world—unambivalent in their stance against racism and poverty, resolute in their disdain for the bourgeoisie. While the Labzik stories focus tightly on the portrait of a single family, it is meant to be a broadly representative one—with all members acting, as a nation might, on high-minded commitments and robust democratic norms for the betterment of humanity.

PART III

Cataclysm and Creativity

9

"We May Have Sinned Thereby Against Child Psychology"

METABOLIZING CATASTROPHE

IN THE singsong trochaic pentameter of nursery rhyme, poet and schoolteacher Szyfra Werber sketches a prewar paradise that might as well be antediluvian for its remoteness, at least from the vantage point of her poem's 1950 publication in Belgium.[1] In the city of Brussels lives a boy named Nisl with his mother, Tsipe, and father, Lipe. They dwell together in *freydn* (peace) as if in their own *gan eydn* (Eden). But a bellicose *keyzer* (kaiser) rules over a faraway land, and he demands that (adult) Jews be rounded up and sent to him, to be placed in "Camp Number Four"—an instance of a made-up detail so oddly specific that it reinforces the poem's dreamy, fairy tale quality. When his parents are taken away, the boy sobs, bereft. One of the many tears he sheds cannot abide his sorrow and loneliness. She resolves to venture forth and bring back his parents.

Over the next thirty pages, the omniscient narrator follows the tear's picaresque adventures as she travels the world to advocate for the *tate-mame*'s return. First to London and then Washington, DC. It's the same story everywhere: there's a war effort on, the tear is told, and tears won't help. Reaching Israel, the weary traveler is recognized sympathetically as "our brother's tear," and her needs for shelter and sustenance are met. Israel can't bring home the missing parents, however, and as Nisl's tear prepares to forge ahead to Russia, every kind of worker rallies to outfit her with food and clothing for the journey. A girl offers a material object designed to meet a spiritual need: a small brush inherited from her grandmother, proffered so the tear can clean herself up to look nice. In Soviet Russia, "the land of justice," the tear receives the same admixture of sympathy and dismissal as in the Allied capitals of the West.

The only hope, the tear realizes, is to head straight for the *lager*, the concentration camp where the parents are being held. On the way, the traveler meets countless other tears, shed for the same reason and now on the same mission. Collectively, they form a river "bright and shining as the snow" and flow right past a sleepy guard and into the fearsome Camp Number Four. The captives recognize their children's tears, but as Nisl's parents explain to the visitor, they can't escape the high walls and ubiquitous guards. Dejected, the emissary prepares to carry the parents' loving, wistful regards back to their son, pausing to pull out the little brush and pretty herself up a bit for the journey. Then it happens: The brushing-up causes the tear to shine bright as a diamond, bedazzling the guards so completely that Tsipe, Lipe, and all the other parents escape unnoticed. In the poem's final stanzas, the families are reunited and their paradise regained. The diamond tear, the crystallized remnant of the family's suffering, now hangs on the eastern wall of the home; thus is the memory of the recent destruction incorporated into a traditional emblem of ritual remembrance. The narrator closes with a strong claim for her omniscience:

> I was there too,
> For myself saw it all
> Even the diamond
> On the fair eastern wall[2]

This final stanza is no mere throwaway line: Unlike most of the authors who wrote about the Holocaust for Yiddish-speaking children, Werber was indeed there in Nisl's Belgium. Born in Vilna in 1908, she had emigrated in 1926 to attend university in Brussels. With her husband, Abusz, she spent the war years underground, working as a teacher, involved in child rescue efforts, and aiding in the publication of a secret Resistance newspaper, *Unzer vort* (Our Word). The narrative poem "Nisele's Tear" is dedicated to her son Michel, who would survive in hiding with a Walloon family.[3]

Every aspect of Werber's poem is profoundly counterhistorical: the deportation of *only* parents, with children left relatively unmolested; the very survival of the separated family members, let alone their successful reunification. What else might we expect from a whimsical confection starring a tear who can travel, speak, and spiff herself up with a brush? Not only does the plot of Werber's fantasia swim against the flow of the historical river of tears, but as a narrative poem attempting to contain unimaginable barbarity within a strict and even rollicking rhyme scheme, it also runs counter to prevailing literary stylistics. Szyfra Werber, a survivor and a heroic one at that, seizes the prerogative to depart from rhetorical norms and boldly rewrite history. It is hard to begrudge her. Unsurprisingly, she approached her imagined audience of child survivors, greatly shrunken by the war, with great tact. The children in her ambit already knew enough of the unvarnished truth. I read "Nisele's Tear" not as an instance of "lying to children" but rather as a bold case of "granting in fantasy" the kinds of wishes that were brutalized in reality.

Of the million Jewish children who perished in the Holocaust, it is difficult to estimate how many were the natural addressees of "modern Yiddish children's literature," that is, the books published for the pupils of the various Yiddish school systems of the secularist Left. While we can tally the enrollees in the secularist Yiddish schools that operated in Eastern Europe, we cannot know precisely how the books produced for them might have circulated across lines of ideology and religious identity. Thus it is impossible to attach specific numbers to the decimation of those books' intended audience in Europe. What is clearer is that most of the fiction, poetry, and drama depicting the Holocaust for Yiddish-speaking children was aimed at those who spent the war years on the safety of other shores—particularly in the Americas and Palestine. The authors who wrote for them had different artistic predilections and political priorities than Werber, and the stark contrast between her work and theirs throws into relief the aims and methods of most Yiddish Holocaust literature for children.

Consider the story "No Man's Land," published, like Werber's, in 1950, by the proletarian Moyshe Shifris, who had emigrated to the United States as a teenager in 1914.[4] In this grimly realistic story, the dazzling-unto-blindness motif cuts the other way, when ten-year-old Hershl is roughly shaken awake in the wee hours, opening a hesitant eye to the "blinding" sight of a black swastika on a circle of white. Intruding Nazi soldiers drive his family from their apartment and into the streets, where they join a crush of Jewish humanity being herded to the train depot and into overcrowded freight cars. Separated from his parents and younger sister in the crowd, Hershl is packed onto a train echoing with the shouts of other lost children. The train's rhythmic clacking stops at the Polish border, where the human cargo is decanted onto a barren field as a Nazi soldier shouts, "Germany doesn't want you anymore. You've infected our country. Go! Whoever returns will be shot like a dog. March!" In a debased echo of the biblical Book of Ruth, the omniscient narrator describes the boy's primal consciousness of belonging to the Jewish collective: "Hershl ran with everyone else. Even though he had no parents with him, he could nevertheless feel that he was one of thousands of Jews, and whatever they were doing, he must do, and wherever they were going, he must go."[5] At the border, Polish soldiers greet the human tidal wave with guns, admonishing them to go back where they came from. Plodding back toward the German side and the empty freight cars, the stateless refugees meet a wall of machine guns and German derision. The story ends with Jews huddling "like sheep" in the field of "no man's land," soaked by a chilly rain. The only resolution is the delayed completion of the interrupted night's sleep: "Before daybreak, Hershl fell asleep—and a dream reached him in No Man's Land. Hershl was no longer homeless: he was back at home. His father sat at the table playing chess with a neighbor. From the kitchen, he could hear the gentle clatter of dishes. His mother was washing up from dinner. Hershl played with Saraleh. His friends ran in and called him, 'Hershel, wanna come and play?'"[6]

Hershl's fate is not disclosed explicitly, but as with "The Little Match Girl," his dream is the paltry consolation available on the hard, cold ground where he lies at story's end. In this tale, Shifris's priority is to convey to a new generation of readers the stark truth of "The Way It Was," in the formulation of a section heading for an anthology of Holocaust literature that would appear decades later.[7] "No Man's Land" is the ninth of fourteen stories in *The Canary Bird,* a collection whose story settings ricochet from the Jewish poultry-farming communities of southern New Jersey to Modi'in in the time of the Maccabees to the Warsaw Ghetto.[8] Whereas several postwar short story collections cordoned off their Holocaust-related content under its own heading, Shifris embeds bleak, realistic Holocaust narratives among cheerful tales of American Jewish life.[9] He implicitly seeks to minimize the distance between the subject and his readership, suggesting that sheer, dumb luck determined whether a child was born into farming chickens in Toms River or died of exposure on the German-Polish border.

Children and the Holocaust: Fiction and Fact

Shifris's Holocaust stories speak from the midst of a postwar corpus that grew up to explain the tragedy to children an ocean away. Taken in the aggregate, as a *cultural project,* this postwar literature implicitly wrestles with how to raise the first generation of post-Holocaust Jews. What did children growing up in New York, Buenos Aires, or Montreal need to know about the events that came to be referred to as "the (third) Destruction"?[10] How could they best assimilate the knowledge? What did they need to feel? What did they need to *do*? For the most part, Shifris adhered to a playbook that had already been roughed out during the war. While many American families struggled with the question of when it might be developmentally appropriate to begin educating children about the atrocities unfolding in Europe, the secularist-Yiddishist world and its trusted teachers felt they lacked the dubious luxury of waiting for some optimal imagined moment: The wreckage was all around them.[11] Shortly after the war, educator, scholar, and children's author Yudl Mark would insist that "the children of the Yiddish school may be said to have lived through the happenings themselves."[12] For Mark, this immediacy was by design. In an editorial published early in the annus horribilis 1943 in the *Pedagogical Bulletin* that he had founded two years earlier, he offered Yiddish teachers detailed instructions about how, vividly and unsparingly, to represent current events in Europe.[13] He urged storytelling over independent or shared reading, offering a menu of fourteen events and phenomena that teachers might relate to students on an escalating scale of horror, from "burning Jewish books" to (encased in protectively distancing quotation marks) "Jewish 'soap.'"[14]

Along with the dire facts, Mark insisted, children must be offered "an element of heroism" that might partially redeem even the most unspeakable tragedies: the self-sacrifice of the teachers who accompanied the children of the Medem Sanatorium to their deaths; the courage of the Krakow Bais Yaakov schoolgirls, whose collective choice of suicide over Nazi sexual slavery Mark reveres as "the one and only protest that remained at their disposal."[15] Other heroic themes were more straightforward: the partisans, the underground movement, non-Jews who sheltered Jews or wore the yellow star, and tales of revenge against the oppressor.[16] Reflecting in 1947 on the prerogative of real-time candor in the Yiddish schools, Mark acknowledges, "It may be that we sinned thereby against child psychology"—a supposition raised only to be dismissed as he continues, "Nevertheless we permitted ourselves to be influenced by the urge to take our children in as partners in our harsh fate, and to arm them with firmness and to brighten their spirits with the luster of the recent martyrdom of fellow Jews. There is no doubt that the pupils of the Yiddish schools are more nationally minded now than they were before."[17] Children, Mark asserted, were part of the Jewish body politic and could not be spared knowledge of harm to that body. Despite their identity as Americans (for the most part), the nation that now lay most urgent claim to them was "dos yidishe folk," the Jewish people.

Mark saw clearly the tension between this "national" Yiddish interest in arming children with fuller knowledge and a private, individual interest in protecting children's well-being by sparing them that knowledge for as long as possible. He understood parents' devotion to the new, liberal American creed as an obstacle to be circumvented by educators:

> Our parents are progressive or liberal young people who speak only English amongst themselves, who have only a secondary, not an active position on Jewish matters, and do not even have a sufficiently lively interest in Jewish education for their own children. . . . National survival and the continuity of Yiddish culture or of the Eastern European heritage are not the slogans that speak to the hearts of our parents today. . . . For them it is much more understandable to talk about the mental health of their children, about preventing painful psychological conflicts, about preparing them for the life and fate of a Jew. . . . We must, first of all, convince the parents that a Jewish education—any sort of Jewish education!—is a necessary thing. We are talking, after all, mainly to those whose religious impulse is weak and whose national instinct is obscured by all sorts of misconceptions that Americanism and Progressivism will heal all possible wounds.[18]

Indeed, the fourth item on Mark's 1943 listing of "typical events under Hitler" that teachers might narrate to their students is "di negishes kegn kinder," the persecution of children. Mark felt that schoolteachers should override American parental instincts toward safety if that safety was premised on ignorance of what every European Jewish child was forced to know.

That said, ideas about children's impressionability and susceptibility to harm were so widespread that the canon of children's *khurbn* literature, even at its most raw, observes certain representational limits. Despite children's documented historical circumstances, authors were concerned to provide a layer of psychological insulation for their young readers, especially with respect to violence and sex. Most centrally, Jewish children in Yiddish children's literature suffer alongside their parents and other caregivers as members of the Jewish nation, whereas in fact the Nazis targeted children with special venom as "useless eaters" and made strenuous efforts to inhibit Jewish reproduction, childbearing, and child-rearing.[19]

Perhaps the greatest deviation between the historical record and children's literature had to do with the destruction of the nuclear family as the container for children's care and nurture. Children in literature are often shown becoming separated from their parents, but they usually remain under the care of adults in substitute, improvised family-like structures.[20] In fact, the orphanhood crisis was acute in the ghettoes, and, to many, damning. In introducing the cache of documents collected in Emmanuel Ringelblum's Oyneg Shabes archive to English-language readers, David Roskies observes that among the nearly fifty thousand school-age children incarcerated in the Warsaw Ghetto as of January 1942, "orphaned, helpless, sick, and abandoned children were a ubiquitous sight," prompting the Central Organization for Orphan Care, Centos, to set up day care centers. Children's "anguished faces and emaciated bodies" pricked the conscience perpetually and represented opposite possibilities in the eye of the beholder: "an indictment of the community at large, proof that Jewish solidarity has collapsed and that Jewish agency is impotent; or evidence of Jewish loyalty, resilience, and boundless courage."[21]

Children are portrayed—accurately—in Holocaust literature for adults as smugglers par excellence, but this is not a common trope in literature for young American readers.[22] Nor is the imaginative play of ghetto children, which ran toward dark themes and surely helped suffering children process their fear, anger, and grief.[23] Occasionally they made for unobtrusive spies. Although teenage boys and girls fought as partisans and members of the resistance, younger children in fiction are depicted providing humanitarian aid and even logistical support for those engaged in armed struggle—without directly taking up arms or killing anyone.[24] Jewish children in the literary canon are often frightened, their lives revealed as precarious, but seldom is a child's death frankly depicted, unless heroically and usually then only in the background, perhaps as part of the Warsaw Ghetto Uprising. Even the implicit demise of the protagonist in "No Man's Land," warmed by his dream, lies at the thematic edge of what these stories represent.

Likewise, children are depicted in fiction as wholly desexualized, while the Lodz Ghetto reportage of Josef Zelkowicz documents the precocious onset of sexual activity among eleven- to fourteen-year-old children who had disrobed to preserve their garments while digging for "coal"—flammable materials to be burned for fuel—in the streets of the ghetto.[25] Left almost totally unrepresented in literature for children was the fusion of eros and violence, as when Emmanuel Ringelblum documents the legend of the "Jewish Maid of Orleans" (a reference to Joan of Arc), "a beautiful eighteen-year-old girl dressed in white . . . seen firing a machine gun at the Germans with extraordinary accuracy, while she herself was invulnerable." While her existence was a "popular fantasy," Ringelblum acknowledges that it rested on the "authentic facts" that girls active in youth movements, particularly the Zionist Ha-Shomer Ha'Za'ir and Hehalutz, fought alongside men and "completely outdid the men in courage, alertness, and daring."[26]

Vehi she'amda—What Has Stood by Us

Since their origins in the interwar period, the Yiddish school networks had been stratified by political ideology, and each was closely associated with its respective children's periodical. In all four of the main publications produced in New York, cultural leaders represented the dire events to children as they unfolded. During the lead-up to the war and its early years, these magazine's approaches to treating the Third Reich were as ideologically varied as Yiddish children's literature generally. Gradually, an artistic consensus emerged in keeping with Mark's prescriptions: factual candor, typically expressed through literary realism; themes of uplift, resistance, and redemption; a spotlight on Jewish suffering; and an invitation to the reader to identify with young Jews in Europe.[27] After the Warsaw Ghetto Uprising began in April 1943, just two months after Mark encapsulated his pedagogical program, the rhetorical frame narrowed, and the "luster" was furnished by the valor of those who resisted, whether physically or spiritually. Tales of heroic resistance came to predominate. A volume of *khurbn* stories published in Buenos Aires in 1953 bore the frankly declarative title *Kinder heldn*, or *Child Heroes*.

This volume typified how the wartime stories and poems published in the periodicals of various educational movements were repackaged into books, often joined by new compositions reflecting on the recent history. In the decade and a half following the war—the culturally significant span from liberation of the camps to the English-language publication of Elie Wiesel's *Night*—the Holocaust corpus for Yiddish-speaking children took distinctive shape. Across all languages, as Jeffrey Shandler explains, the preponderance of children's literature on the destruction was "written well after a master narrative of the Holocaust as a discrete historical event was established."[28] In the ways they contained and contextualized the horror, these Yiddish works modeled how young readers were meant to make sense of the events in their bewildering scale, simultaneity, and viciousness; they invited readers to identify with the victims and survivors and called on the living children to imbue their own existence with meaning in response to the national tragedy. These books delineated a distinctive children's Holocaust poetics that juvenilized adult literary approaches to representing the destruction. We may understand their particulars by delving into how they treat Jewish time and *khurbn* space—and the interplay between the two.

Throughout a long history of withstanding persecution, Jews developed a sophisticated cultural technology for acknowledging and metabolizing violence. The time-tested strategy for responding to a new catastrophe was to fit it into a stylized pattern of historical events that the community had endured, to locate fresh traumas on "a scale of archetypes."[29] With respect to time, that meant the flattening, blurring, or elision called panchrony.[30] The violent events of linear time could be reckoned with—contained—by their insertion into the eternity of Jewish cyclical time, which always stood ready to incorporate fresh sorrows and newly sprung heroes. Since biblical times, liturgical poetry has reinforced the patterns of cyclical threat and salvation in concentrated form.[31] Medieval martyrdom motifs could be retrieved and newly secularized to describe modern horrors.[32] But prose, especially that written for children, worked by the same logic. Forest-based partisans *were* the guerilla Maccabees; Jews being deported on trains *were* the exiles from Jerusalem, driven out by the Babylonians and the Romans; the liberation of Bergen-Belsen *was* the Exodus. Moyshe Shifris can bounce from Toms River, New Jersey, to Second Temple–era Modi'in to wartime Warsaw because these times and places are meant to exist on a single continuum in the eyes of the Jewish child. The past is prefiguration, the present is echo, and intertextuality is the norm.

We might think of this approach to history as "seder logic," following the liturgical construction of the Passover Seder, which is designed, paradoxically, to alarm and reassure, to provoke and solace. Participants are invited to regard themselves as if they personally had been redeemed from bondage in Egypt—that is, to identify with Israelites and imaginatively project themselves into the text, feeling viscerally the ignominy of an abject nation. At the same time, a key passage, sung aloud joyfully, proclaims, "Vehi she'amda": that although in every generation, malign actors have sought to eradicate the Jewish people, *this* (albeit debatable and indeterminate) has stood by our forebears and us, allowing the continued flourishing of the nation in toto.[33] If the assaults are perpetual, runs the reasoning that undergirds this elaborate preemptive coping strategy, then they already constitute what Yiddish speakers would dismiss as "a story with a beard," nothing new. Thus are the fangs of any fresh historical harm blunted. A Hitler who is naught but a mustachioed Haman has been cut down to size.

Of course the novel Nazi system of mechanized murder stretched this logic to its breaking point, but for the authors of Yiddish children's literature, the *ordering* function—"seder's" literal meaning—of narrative eked out a narrow victory over despair. Moyshe Shifris's mimetically drawn story "In the Warsaw Ghetto," also included in his 1950 collection, describes a family—or the surviving remnants thereof—sitting down to the seder meal together in 5703 (1943).

The action is focalized through the eyes of ten-year-old Yisroel, who "sighs like his grandfather" as he huddles in sparse candlelight with his mother, older sister, and the aging patriarch. Just as they are about to begin the ritual meal, in bursts older brother Borekh with two friends, a cache of weapons, and the news that they intend to meet the imminent German *aktion* with bullets. God is not coming to deliver the people, so grandfather, mother, and sister take up arms for themselves and join the newly begun uprising. Yisroel, deemed too young to shoot, will serve as water carrier and courier for food and ammunition. They are *living* the Haggadah; to merely recite it would be superfluous.

For Yudl Mark and his colleagues, such representations were ethically imperative. In the adult cultural sphere, would-be writers of Holocaust literature had to contend with Theodor Adorno's declaration that to write poetry after Auschwitz was barbaric—or more accurately, with the attitudes it was meant to convey. As Alan Mintz glosses the philosopher's scruple, "There is no art, no matter how severe, that does not create some beauty or pleasure, if only at the level of form rather than content; and beauty and pleasure, it was averred, should not be derived from atrocity." Moreover, the artifice of art was repugnant in the face of a primary duty to "document that horror rather than transfigure it in any way."[34] But these cautions presuppose an audience who knew the basic facts; children, and especially the Jewish children who would be called upon to carry on and regenerate Jewish life, would better digest and incorporate the facts in the alembic of narrative. Whereas Adorno sought to honor the world-abolishing singularity of the Holocaust, the presence of children asserts the primacy of continuity, the pressure of the quotidian toward making worlds and remaking abolished ones. Primo Levi observed this sociological fact in extremis in his memoir:

> All took leave from life in the manner which most suited them. Some praying, some deliberately drunk, others lustfully intoxicated for the last time. But the mothers stayed up to prepare the food for the journey with tender care, and washed their children and packed their luggage; and at dawn the barbed wire was full of children's washing hung out in the wind to dry. Nor did they forget the diapers, the toys, the cushions and the hundreds other small things which mothers remember and which children always need. Would you not do the same? If you and your child were going to die tomorrow, would you not give him to eat today?[35]

Mark, a male pedagogical expert thrust into a "maternal function" by virtue of his proximity to the young, demonstrates the cultural equivalent of such solicitude for the immediate needs of his charges. Children need storytelling to process the barbaric. In the very midst of the unspeakable, Mark catalogues the available tropes, topoi, and archetypes, but he leaves implicit the expectation that teachers' stories will have beginnings, middles, and endings: the "beauty and pleasure"—the solace—of story.

Engendering a Sense of Coherence

Despite Mark's half-rueful admission that "we may have sinned against child psychology," his candid, narrative-based approach comported with insights from research that would be conducted only later, emerging from the study of the longitudinal arcs of survivors' lives. Aaron Antonovsky was born to working-class immigrant parents in Brooklyn in 1923. Growing up in the Labor Zionist Hashomer Hatzair youth movement, he imbibed the tenets of socialism. Stationed in New Guinea, he served in the Second World War and then lived out his youthful ideals by spending 1948 as a founding member of a kibbutz. He completed a doctoral program in sociology at Yale before returning to Israel permanently in 1960. His subspecialty was the sociology of medicine, and after a stint in Jerusalem, he relocated to Beersheva and helped set up a new medical school there.[36] His research had always focused on minorities and marginalization, immigrants and victims of discrimination. In the late 1960s, while interviewing a group of postmenopausal women about the role of stress earlier in their lives, he located a subset of Holocaust survivors who thrived despite their exposure to what he called a *horror* (rather than a garden variety *stressor*).[37]

Over the 1970s and 1980s Antonovsky would promulgate a new approach to conceptualizing human flourishing and its absence. Whereas most medical practitioners, whether of physical or behavioral health, treated an ordered state of good health as the given and disease as a deviation from the norm that required reversal (treatment), Antonovsky saw the "the human organism as prototypically being in the state of heterostatic disequilibrium," or disorder.[38] If the conventional approach to medicine was to interrogate how disease comes about, or pathogenesis, then the new approach would reorient researchers' energies toward understanding *salutogenesis*: how good health arises. When Antonovsky shifted toward viewing "dis-ease" as a continuum and recognizing that some subjects thrive despite terrible adversity, he accounted for these outcomes by theorizing the central importance of a *sense of coherence* (SOC) that could counter entropic forces and promote well-being.[39]

SOC develops, he further theorized, when adverse events can be rendered comprehensible, manageable, and meaningful. What might otherwise be a trauma-inducing experience may be withstood if one can understand it, manage or mitigate it, and/or make sense of it. As we consider two distinct populations of Jewish children affected by the Holocaust—those directly under Nazi attack and those witnessing the events from afar—Mark's pedagogical framework and Antonovsky's therapeutic one converge. While "managing" the myriad overwhelming events that constituted the *khurbn* was out of the question, *story* made those events at least somewhat comprehensible and worked vigorously to fit the horror into a shapely structure of meaning.[40] Reflecting in 1990 on his "odyssey" toward the salutogenic orientation, Antonovsky practically makes the case for "seder logic," the ordering function of narrative: "The phrase 'the world makes sense,' if understood in the emotional sense, is quite distinct from the cognitive perception of order. It refers to a way of looking at life as worth living, of seeing stressors as perhaps painful and yet worthy of being coped with rather than anaesthetized. Seeing life in this way provides the motivational force which leads one to seek to order the world and to transform resources from potential to actuality."[41]

Although Antonovsky's initial insight grew out of work with Holocaust survivors, he had not selected his sample based on this identity. Indeed, he tried to formulate his conclusions as universally as possible: "My argument was that seeing the world as comprehensible, manageable, and meaningful would facilitate the selection of culturally appropriate and situationally efficacious resources and behaviors."[42] But subsequent researchers have built on his work to investigate more directly whether the SOC model could explain the absence of posttraumatic stress in some survivors. Indeed, a team of Dutch psychology researchers found that "even six decades after the end of the war, for child survivors who endured the most severe Holocaust survival exposure their sense of coherence moderates the association between traumatic experiences during the war and posttraumatic stress."[43]

Antonovsky succumbed to a brief illness at seventy-one, still very much in the midst of empirical research intended to solidify his far-ranging theory. One of the questions he marked out for further study was whether the SOC model could operate at a collective level, beyond the individual.[44] Culture, for Antonovsky, was one source of what he called generalized resistance resources, which are the tools that strengthen an individual's sense of coherence.[45] Could a culture purposefully promulgate a sense of coherence in its participants? Reading Mark's reflections on *khurbn* pedagogy, both during and immediately after the war, it is clear that this is precisely what he and his colleagues in the Yiddish school systems and children's publishing arena aspired to do.

Ghetto and Forest: Metonymic Topoi

The cyclical patterns of archetypal Jewish history—violence, mass death, survival, rebuilding—gave coherence to time, while a similarly patterned evocation of a few metonymic topoi gave coherence to space. These places stood in for myriad others beyond the textual frame. This is not to say that the sites overwhelmingly depicted in Holocaust literature were mere archetypes; railroad and forest, ghetto and camp were indeed the real sites of historical events.[46] But the predominant literary representation of those spaces thickens them like the overlapping brushstrokes of many different painters of the same scene. Time and space meld into nodes of memory, and eventually memorialization: "Mainz was to the Crusades as Nemirov would be to the Khmelnitsky massacres, as Kishinev would be to the tsarist pogroms, and as the Warsaw ghetto would be to the Holocaust."[47] History is an armature for memory.

The substitution of one place for several also solves a problem posed by the limits of human cognition. The scale of the Nazi destruction exceeded the capacity of memory such that "the task of remembrance threatens to eclipse all else."[48] If this was true for survivors, or for their contemporaries, then how much more so was it necessary to enshrine a limited set of images and events for the children of those contemporaries! While a fine-grained analysis of children's *khurbn* literature could easily fill a book of transnational scope, the balance of this chapter will adopt a similarly metonymic strategy and focus on a single exemplar. *Kinder heldn* (Child Heroes) was published in Buenos Aires in 1953, under the auspices of the leftist YKUF (Yiddisher kultur farband, or Jewish Cultural Association). At just under fifty printed pages, the collection includes prose by Itshe Goldberg and M. A. Suhl, both of whom arrived in New York long before the war, as well as one poem each by the bard of the Jewish resistance, Hirsh Glik, who died a hero, and Binem Heller, who survived.[49] As the title indicates, the collection explicitly centers children's heroism, which aligns with the Soviet framing of World War II as the Great Patriotic War. But each of the included works focuses unapologetically on Jewish experiences during the *khurbn*, bearing out a trend toward Jewish particularism that grew over time.[50]

Because of Hitler and Stalin's nonaggression pact, the communist Left remained silent about atrocities perpetrated against the Jews until Hitler attacked the USSR in 1941, freeing them to speak out.[51] But by the early 1950s, Goldberg and many of his fellow travelers had grown disillusioned, disgusted even, with Stalin's purges. The Night of Murdered Poets in 1952 had been a watershed for Yiddish cultural leaders and progressive Jewry at large. Leftist educators sought to merge into a Jewish mainstream that was more attuned to specifically Jewish suffering and heroism. After all, if the leftmost Yiddish schools didn't impart a Jewish historical consciousness, then their pupils would have little reason to cling to Yiddish, even in its most secular manifestations. They formed modern Yiddish literary culture into a bridge to the mythic Jewish past, casting the *klasikers*, the foundational authors of the modern Yiddish literary efflorescence, as secular prophets to inspire and console the Jews suffering under Hitler.

In Itshe Goldberg's story "Yitskhok-Leybush Wept," Y. L. Peretz is brought back from the next world (he had died in 1915) to bear witness to the Warsaw Ghetto Uprising and its terrible cost. First appearing in the communist-affiliated *Yungvarg* in April 1945, the tale is set during the fateful seder night in 1943 Warsaw. As in Shifris's story, three generations gather quietly around the table, but this time, the focus is on Yitskhok and Leybush Hurvits, twins who are marking their somber bar mitzvah at the Passover meal. They had been born precisely on the fifteenth *yortsayt*, or death anniversary, of the literary titan and named in his memory. If the core aim of the Passover Seder is for individuals to inscribe themselves into the long arc of mythic Jewish chronos and so fuse lifetime with nation-time, then this story represents that process four times over: (1) the seder (long Jewish time), (2) the *yortsayt* of Peretz (recent, historical Jewish time), (3) the bar mitzvah (a life-cycle event superimposed on historical time), and, for the reader, (4) the start of the Warsaw Ghetto Uprising.[52]

The literary caliber of the story is compromised by the tendency of both the twins' father and the narrator to speechify, but it is hard to miss the theme of the Haggadah coming to life as the family assumes positions at their apartment house's windows and on its rooftop to "end this year's Seder with guns in our hands." The adults take up arms, while the boys run dwindling stores of bullets, bread, and water to the fighters. Over several days, the fighters dwindle too, until at last a low-flying German plane strafes Yitskhok and the boys' father. Only Leybush remains, sitting vigil over the bodies of the departed. Suddenly a man appears, his walrus mustache unmistakable: Yitskhok Leybush has come to weep over the dead and comfort his namesake. Beckoning to the survivor, Peretz escorts him down from the rooftop, past the ghetto's ruins, through Aryan streets to the very banks of the Vistula. They direct their gaze—as the narrator proclaims, showing questionable omniscience—"to the east, where the sun will rise." The ending is hard to countenance, given the realities of what Stalin had perpetrated in the east during just the five years between the story's initial appearance in a periodical and its republication in book form.

Given the standard communist commitment to mimetic realism in literature, it is extraordinary that Goldberg would portray such a "supernatural" occurrence as the revivification of the dead. But such was the extent of his desire to tap into the Jewish mythopoeic and incarnate the restorative possibilities of continuing the secular Yiddish literary culture that Peretz represented. Like many other stories that deal with death, a bisemic reading is possible: The child reader might see a beloved *klasiker* come back to life, while a more sophisticated reader might recognize his being pressed into service as a benevolently ministering Angel of Death, sent to escort his young namesake back with him to the beyond. Even so, the rhetorical gesture toward any kind of afterlife is notable, given the source.

Goldberg's other contribution to the collection, "A mayse mit a tsviling" (A Story of Twins), also set during the early days of the Uprising, opens onto a primitive underground bunker, where a woman cradles the boy-girl twins she has born on the first night of the fighting. As she and "an old grandmother" snuggle the newborns to shush their first cries, their father is on the roof "snuggled up to his gun." By the fifth day, we learn that the mother is not well, and the father has died in action; the older woman appeals to the commander of the street's ragtag company for assistance. He calls two of his trustiest young fighters, eleven-year-old Sholem and twelve-year-old Don, and charges them with rescuing the babies by sneaking them out to the partisans in the forest. Sholem is vexed at being turned from soldier to nursemaid, but the commander explains that they are guards, responsible for protecting two lives; besides, it's a direct order. The more mature Don accepts the charge on both of their behalf, acknowledging their collective responsibility for the babies with the phrase "A people remains a people" (*A folk blaybt a folk*). The family circle must stretch to include the nation. Though the text makes no mention of their identity other than their names and ages, the woodcut illustration by an unnamed artist depicts the boys with their heads covered and visible sidelocks.

Before setting out, the boys secure the necessaries for a celebration, and the twins' weakened mother uses her waning strength to pronounce their names Moses and Miriam. After a few weeks, the older boys depart with the infants, entering the sewer system and following its pipes and their commander's directions over countless days and nights. The babies instinctively refrain from crying; the older boys are terrified, standing still sometimes for hours at a time. At last, they exit to the forest beyond the city and are picked up by a partisan patrol on their second day out of the sewers. As they are escorted to the unit's commander, narratorial restraint prevails. Sholem and Don unwrap the rags and present their bundles with the laconic announcement "This is Moyshe. This is Miriam." The commander holds the babies aloft. A rising sun steals through the forest boughs; the couriers permit themselves a smile. A postscript explains that since the war ended, Moyshe and Miriam have lived at an orphanage for Jewish children, where they pride themselves on sharing their birthday with the Uprising.

National identity is strong enough to uphold the familial duties of care through a series of surrogates: the "old grandmother" who is not necessarily related to the birth mother, preadolescent heroes Sholem and Don, the partisans who presumably care for the twins throughout the war years, and eventually the orphanage established by the Jewish community in peacetime. Sholem and Don save the Jewish future by rescuing a brother and sister whose names evoke the deep Jewish past. Biblical Moses also required rescue as a baby; the historical resonance is unmistakable. Equally prominent is the centrality of their teamwork. Indeed, several of the stories in *Kinder heldn* stress themes of interdependence, mutual answerability, and cooperation. Twins represent two halves of an integral whole: Yitskhok and Leybush, Moshe and Miriam.

Boyhood friendship as the basis for effective alliance figures among the several thematic elements and tropes present in both Goldberg's and Suhl's contributions to *Kinder heldn*. M. A. (known as Yuri in English) Suhl emigrated to the United States in 1923 from Galicia and taught in the communist-affiliated Ordn schools while building a career as a proletarian poet. In "Der kleyner Sholem Aleykhem" (Little Sholem Aleichem), he too depicts the transit from ghetto to forest during the Uprising, and the child's mandate to "save" *yidishkeyt* by rescuing a metonymic representation of secular Yiddish culture in the form of a classic author. This story also originally appeared in the periodical associated with the IWO schools, *Yungvarg*. Like Goldberg, Suhl is ready to blur some of the identifying markers that would have pinned down his character on the sociological map of Polish Jewry. Protagonist Shloymele wears a caftan (old, torn, black, and shrunken), which suggests he is religious, but mention is made of his *lerer*, the teacher in a modern *shule*, rather than the *melamed* or *rebe* who would have taught in a *kheyder*. What matters is what's under the garment: During the final days of the Uprising, as bullets whiz through the smoke-choked air, the boy keeps the ghetto's last remaining volume of the *Collected Works of Sholem Aleichem* tied around his frail frame. Shloymele is a child apart, partial heir to the artist-as-a-young-man discussed in chapter 4 insofar as he sees much but goes largely unseen: "In the great tumult of the battle, nobody even noticed him. Nobody so much as looked his way as he ran from one hiding place to the next. Even his friends, the boys his own age, and his teacher, were too busy with the battle to even give him a thought. Only he, Shloymele, kept his large eyes alert to all that was going on around him."[53] It's not clear what role his peers are playing in the fighting, but it is apparent that Shloymele's role is different, and he represents a different way of being a boy than most of his peers.

When the fighting is done and Jewish bodies lie strewn in the streets, a classmate of Shloymele's named Velvl is tasked by a partisan commander with checking for signs of life, determining who might yet be evacuated to the partisans in the forest and saved. By that time, one of the inert bodies belongs to Shloymele, who appears to have taken a Nazi bullet to the chest. Velvl spots his fallen friend and appeals to the partisan leader for help:

> "Come quick, quick!" he said, pulling the man by the hand.
>
> "You find someone?" the man asked.
>
> "Yes," said Velvl, "Sholem Aleichem."
>
> "What kind of Sholem Aleichem?" the partisan rested his eyes on the boy. "The writer?"
>
> "Yes," said Velvl, "the writer."
>
> "Are you out of your mind?" the man was getting annoyed at Velvl. "You've picked some time to joke around. Sholem Aleichem the writer has been dead for years. He died in America."
>
> "Yeah, yeah, I know that, but this is the Little Sholem Aleichem."
>
> "Well congratulations!" the man shouted at Velvl. "The little Sholem Aleichem? Maybe next you'll discover the medium Sholem Aleichem!"
>
> "On my life, I'm not joking," Velvl swore. "I recognize him. This is the little Sholem Aleichem. And if you won't help me, I'll drag him by myself," said Velvl, bursting into tears.[54]

Velvl has said a mouthful, for he *recognizes* his friend in both the superficial sense of his physiognomy and in the deeper sense of understanding how his apparently quixotic mission of book rescue is essential to securing the Jewish future. Velvl's esteem for Shloyme stands out in sharp relief against the schoolboy tales set in the prewar *kheyder*, wherein the dreamy artist is dismissed if not actively disliked by his undifferentiated group of more rough-and-tumble classmates who embody boyhood conventions. The two friends cannot be neatly ranked on a scale of "manliness," for Shloymele stoically forces himself to stifle scream and cry alike for fear of giving away his hiding place, while the "brave, courageous" Velvl sobs next to his unconscious classmate.

Once Velvl successfully commandeers the commander's attention to examine Shloymele, no heartbeat is audible—although his nostrils flutter with breath. To inspect more closely, the partisan unbuttons the boy's caftan and discovers the book strapped to his body, muffling the sound of his still-beating heart. Sholem Aleichem's portrait is etched in gold on the cover; one eye has been pierced by the German bullet. Like some outrageous version of the traditional Talmudic pin test, secularized and adapted for the brutalities of modern warfare, the partisan leafs through the volume and sees that the bullet's tip has lodged at the story called "Baranovich Station."[55] This yarn forms part of Sholem Aleichem's 1909 *Railroad Stories*, a collection of short, finely crafted tales told as if orally in a third-class passenger train and recorded by a "commercial traveler" who stands in for the author. In this volume, the taut space between a frame story and what it enframes often vibrates with tension. In "Baranovich Station," a skillful narrator wins the attention of his distractible traveling companions by retelling a provincial saga he has heard directly from his grandfather, one of the principals. He recounts the blackmail of a whole town's Jewry by an audacious ne'er-do-well, but the action is interrupted just at its climax by the train's arrival in Baranovich, the (internal) storyteller's destination. He hops off, leaving all his listeners in shocked dismay at the abrupt interruption, the rude but inevitable dangling of a tale unfinished. Especially distraught is the commercial traveler, who hurls a curse to close out the frame narrative: "I wouldn't mind if Baranovich station burned to the ground!"[56] A critic's dream narrative, the story meditates on narratorial power and its limits.

The bullet's stopping at "Baranovich" is at once a simple, almost random signifier of "secular Yiddish literary culture" and a more sophisticated and specific instance of Jewish intertextuality. A story about interruption has interrupted a Nazi bullet. As the most radically open of the *Railroad Stories*, this choice gestures at the power of children in shaping the future narratives of the Jewish people.[57] After all, an outside force (whether the capricious dictates of train travel or the accursed Nazi foe) might interrupt the telling of your story, but anyone inside (the train carriage or the culture) can seize the prerogative of narration and make a fresh start—or loop back into a never-ending story.

Astonished at the latter-day miracle, the adult partisan says simply, "Sholem Aleichem saved his life." Of course there is a compact, even a covenant, at work: Shloymele has devoted himself to saving Sholem Aleichem, and it is only right that the tragicomic genius return the favor.[58] As Kadar observes, "In the framework of this tale, his physical rescue is transmuted into the spiritual ideal. The story suggests that as a people cares for its spiritual treasures, even in the face of annihilation, so do those cultural assets safeguard the shared heritage and values of that people."[59] This ethical transaction may be read as another secularized echo from the deep well of Jewish ritual, in this case the poet Ahad Ha'am's (1856–1927) postulate that "More than Jews have kept the Sabbath, the Sabbath has kept the Jews." Shloymele's ultimate act of heroism lies in stepping up as the guarantor of Yiddish culture. While his classmates do what they can to save the Jewish body, he has fought alongside them to save the Jewish soul.

While Shloymele's preservation work is sacred, it is, as noted, largely invisible to the dwindling population of his community. It is Velvl's stubborn insistence that renders his friend's heroism visible to the adults in charge. In and through the boys' friendship and mutual esteem are the twin prerogatives physical and spiritual preservation united. Once they have escaped to the forest and are sitting around the campfire, it is left to Velvl to explain the still-recovering Shloymele's special duty in the now-destroyed Warsaw Ghetto. With just one volume of the master's *Collected Works* remaining intact, Velvl recounts, the "quick, agile" Shloymele was tasked with carrying the book from school to improvised school in the final days of the ghetto's existence.[60] The schoolchildren recognized the carrier of tales and nicknamed him "Little Sholem Aleichem." Now living in the partisan encampment, Shloymele remains the keeper of the book, which the fighters borrow to gain spiritual sustenance for their ongoing struggle. They dignify the boy with an update to his nickname. No longer *Little*, he is now hailed with the honorific *Panye* (Mister) Sholem Aleichem, just as the author had styled his narratorial alter ego half a century earlier and an irrecoverable world away.

The Arboreal Domestic

If "The Little Sholem Aleichem" revises the boy story for wartime, then Suhl's longer contribution, "Reyzele," revisits the prototypical girl story. The story opens in medias res, with its disoriented seven-year-old protagonist's head pounding as she struggles to regain her bearings in a rain-drenched field under a moonless night sky. Gradually, she recollects how her family was herded into an airless freight car, how the train stopped unaccountably, and her mother improvised a risky plan. Cautioning her daughter neither to fear nor to cry, she heaved her into the darkness with instructions to hide until the train started moving and then find the partisans in the forest. They would protect her. Tired and hurting from her fall, the girl's progress is slow, but she reaches a patch of forest and is quickly intercepted by an armed patrol who asks her in Polish where she's headed. When he asks directly whether she is Jewish, she clams up, but when asked her name, the whispered "Reyzele" bespeaks her identity and engenders the Jewish patrolman's care. He takes her to base camp deep in the forest and, since the commander of the unit is sleeping, tucks her in to nap on a pile of comforters, covered by gunnysacks, murmuring to her in Yiddish, "Sleep, little girl, sleep . . . and don't be afraid."[61] The patrolman leaves Reyzele in the care of the commander's bodyguard, a brave soldier named Berko, whose leg injury in an earlier skirmish now keeps him from more active duty. A bodyguard is needed because the Nazis have put a steep price on the commander's head, and any one of the many peasants on whom the partisans depend for supplies could betray them.

Berko watches her sleep and remembers his own little girl, Khavale, of whom he has heard nothing for two years. He recalls how terribly he used to miss her and her mother at first, how he used to push deeper into the forest all alone so the other partisans wouldn't see their battle-hardened comrade "cry like a little child." Gradually, his wounded heart has scabbed over; "he exchanged his deep longing for his family for a burning fury against the Germans." It's a combustible fuel. The arrival of this little girl reawakens his longing for his own, spurring all the man's domestic impulses: "'I'll take care of her,' Berko said to himself. 'I'll be to her like a father is to his own child. I can't go into battle anymore anyway. I have enough time to devote to her.'" His mind races ahead: He'll put up a tent for her, surround it with a garden, source the supply of fresh milk and eggs every child needs to grow properly. The only rub is that commander Anatol might not allow a child to remain in camp.

As it turns out, though, Anatol's reaction is *not* the only rub. For as we know from chapter 6, the one thing that a girl in a Yiddish story can be reliably counted upon to do is go missing. With the lightening of the sky, Berko goes to check on her, and . . . she's gone! He panics, tears into Anatol's tent proclaiming the disaster of the girl's sudden disappearance. Anatol only now hears of her existence and swiftly reassures his deputy that if she couldn't get into the forest undetected, she won't get out either. She must be nearby. They'll have to go find her and turn her over to a gentile peasant woman; after all, "A forest is no place for a little girl."[62] Crestfallen, Berko nevertheless hurries to keep up with Anatol on the search because locating Reyzele *now* is more important than planning her future. Meanwhile, the commander reconsiders, musing to Berko that if the girl is brave and speaks good Polish, there might be a way for "your little girl" to live in the partisan camp after all. Anatol's plan is to request two goats from a peasant and outfit Reyzele as a goatherd so that she can move around freely, keeping an eye on the railroad tracks and German troop movements without attracting notice. The girl can't remain in the forest as just a pet or a morale-boosting mascot, but if she can do useful work, that's another matter. But where *is* she?

When a branch rustles overhead, the partisans spot the ragged girl in the early morning light, looking like "a giant bird or some kind of strange little creature" crouching on a large tree limb. They call to her, but, eyeing their rifle and revolver, she stays mum. After a brief standstill, Berko reaches up and lifts her down from the branch, asking why she ran away. Reyzele explains that she didn't "run away"; seeing light in the sky but not the partisans, she had followed her mother's instructions to "always hide from the Germans." Impressed at her bravery and determination, they invite her to become a *partizanke* and carry her back to base camp in time for breakfast.

The eldest partisan, a man of around sixty, jokes that they must administer the Partisan's Oath for her to become a proper partisan; she repeats the formula word for word "with her head held high." The oldest comrade is dispatched to fetch the two goats from the village, and Anatol explains that Reyzele will begin her intelligence work and shepherding duties the next day; meanwhile, she is to rest up in the relatively comfortable bed in his tent. "And this time, you won't run away and hide in a tree, eh, Reyzele?" he chides gently while tucking her in. "No," she replies. "I'm a *partizanke*, and I'm no longer afraid." The story could end there, on that note of domesticity established, dignity regained. But Suhl is keen to emphasize the effects of Reyzele's presence on the other partisans, so Berko enters the tent to make sure she is well covered and soothes her with the incantatory, "Sleep, Reyzele, sleep."

It is a testament to the durability of the "Yiddish girl story" that its arc of wandering and safe domestic return can be transposed to a Holocaust setting where there is no safety for children or their parents, and the hearth is a campfire at a military base in the forest.[63] But where the nuclear family has been destroyed, the Jewish nation reconstitutes itself as a symbolic family, complete with the comforting rituals of bedtime. The pathos of male nurture signifies in contrast to peacetime gender roles: Men, including family men like Berko, are pressed into service as brave soldiers and then further pressed into service as nurturing caregivers. A small girl, concealment her only defense, demonstrates bravery in her readiness to adapt to circumstance. "Reyzele" extends the ethos of the Medem Sanatorium, wherein children are citizens first and foremost, dignified by their substantive contributions to maintaining the community in which they live—objects *and* reciprocal givers of care. While the girl cannot remain in camp as a mere token, the simple fact of her presence rehumanizes the fighters, unblocking Berko's access to his feelings of grief, love, and longing for his own family.

In prewar Yiddish literature, the forest setting often bespoke liminality, uncertainty, and danger—even if the uncanny could solidify into a marble edifice of reassurance, as in the tale "A Sabbath in the Forest" (discussed in chapter 3). In wartime, though, when the most dangerous predators were human, the unfamiliar, immersive world of flora and fauna figures as a refuge. Indeed one of the remarkable true histories to emerge from the Holocaust was that of the Bielski brothers, partisans who focused on rescuing vulnerable Jews from ghettos and whose forest encampment grew to include gardens, a bakery, laundry, infirmary, tribunal to adjudicate disputes, prayer space, and a makeshift jail. One historian refers to the encampment as a "shtetl" in the forest.[64] When Soviet liberators arrived in the summer of 1944, the forest camp was home to 1,236 Jews, 70 percent of whom were women, children, and the elderly. Although the Bielskis' rescue effort was the largest and most successful, partisans are documented to have cared for children in other instances too.[65]

For the readers of these stories, ghetto and forest are rendered sites of Jewish continuity, albeit in extremis. Even a young reader who has never visited Europe begins to feel located in time and space. The cumulative effect of these *khurbn* stories is to shade in a schematic mental map and timeline, locating the recent tragedy in Jewish history. They were also meant to demand something of the reader, to awaken "both compassion for the anguish and loss of the Jewish people and a sense of responsibility of individual Jews toward *klal yisroel*" (the Jewish collective).[66] In other words, *Kinder heldn* and all its sibling texts fostered a sense of coherence.

Holocaust Literature as an Ethical Transaction

I close this chapter by elaborating more fully on the transaction whereby Holocaust literature provides something to its readers and demands something of them at the same time. Much has been written about the manifold dimensions of survivors' trauma, including those who were children during the Nazi years.[67] But the events of the Holocaust also inflicted upon world Jewry a more diffuse *moral injury*, a term that clinical researchers have developed to describe the effects of "perpetrating, failing to prevent, bearing witness to, or learning about acts that transgress deeply held moral beliefs and expectations."[68] Yudl Mark was rightly concerned that he and his colleagues might have "sinned against child psychology" insofar as we now understand "bearing witness to the aftermath of violence and human carnage to be potentially morally injurious."[69] But the harm followed from the events themselves, and failing to discuss and contextualize the evil for the youth of "the Jewish nation" could scarcely limit the damage.

A logical solution was to structure a therapeutic dimension into the very exposition of the harm. The same stories that exposed children to moral injury would also help to bind up their psychic wounds, offering redemptive storylines full of heroism (on however small a scale), meaningful metanarratives about Jewish resilience in the face of historical violence, and a sense of self-efficacy in being able to cognize the overwhelming events by situating them on a mental map (however stylized) and timeline (however streamlined). Literature could affirm the community's deeply held values and individual readers' sense of belonging and importance to the collective. The history in which they were implicated was brutal but coherent.

As a collective project, these stories, poems, and dramas enacted a therapeutic alchemy, transforming their readers from passive bystanders to active, ethically charged witnesses.[70] The psychoanalyst Dori Laub characterizes the Holocaust as an event "that produced no witnesses":

> It was not only the reality of the situation and lack of responsiveness of bystanders or the world that accounts for the fact that history was taking place with no witness: it was also the very circumstance of being inside the event that made unthinkable the very notion that a witness could exist, that is, someone who could step outside of the coercively totalitarian and dehumanizing frame of reference in which the event was taking place, and provide an independent frame of reference through which the event could be observed. One might say that there was, thus, historically no witness to the Holocaust, either from outside or from inside the event.[71]

But the readers of *Kinder heldn* and the dozens of other *khurbn* stories sprinkled throughout periodicals and anthologies *were* outside and *could* observe. They could add their tears to the currents of Jewish history and so grant their decimated cousins the dignity of their bearing witness.

10

Should I Be Pope Someday?

JEWISH EUROPE, AMERICAN TEENAGERS, AND THE CHOICE OF LIFE

IN 1930, M. A. Nasiram took to the pages of the New York–based educational journal *Shul un heym* (School and Home) to complain that the cheaply printed Yiddish juvenile books coming from Eastern Europe were wholly unsuitable for American children.[1] Not only were the print and paper quality poor, but the characters were unfamiliar, and the plot lines unenticing to New World readers. Whereas an adult might overlook a volume's physical trappings, "for a child, the appearance of a book is the most important stimulus to starting to read it." The available fare was especially paltry for teens aged thirteen through fifteen, who had outgrown the literary kiddie menu.[2] Young teens, Nasiram muses, are generally known to be big readers (ah, 1930!), and "a book that happens to appeal to them will sell like candy." But the entire existing corpus, drawn mostly from the ranks of the canonical Yiddish classics, would last a voracious leisure reader no more than a couple of months.[3]

Corresponding from Warsaw that same year, in the pages of the Vilna-based literary review *Literarishe bleter*, Dovid Roykhl used a review essay of two new American works to underscore the fact that Europe's burst of publishing activity for children had gone quiet, and "dry, businessed-up" America (*farbiznister*, in his charming neologism) and its cultural capital "city of iron and concrete, of gigantic skyscrapers" were now exporting the most exciting Yiddish titles for young readers.[4] Moreover, they were "solid" artifacts.[5] In both Europe and New York, those in the business of educating Yiddish speakers and readers knew that the onus was on them to keep the customer satisfied. They met this demand through more handsomely printed books: clearer print on better paper and in larger trim sizes. These reader-friendly accommodations arrived during a period of cresting consumer power for American teenagers, whose desires would influence the market just as women's leisure reading practices had driven the rapid rise of fiction in the nineteenth-century Yiddish sphere and earlier in Western Europe.[6]

But concentrating the material resources necessary to print beautiful Yiddish books didn't necessarily coincide with—and in the aggregate, may have even run counter to—children's desire to read them and remain engaged with Yiddish. After all, the pathway to the kind of upward mobility that made such books affordable—both to produce and to consume—led *away* from Yiddish. In 1937, the director of the Arbeter Ring education department, Fishl Gelibter, acknowledged to the Vilna-based pedagogical theorist and children's author Shloyme Bastomski a disquieting truth: "The majority of American Jewish children don't speak any Yiddish and have no desire to read Yiddish books. If we want our children to read Yiddish books, we must serve them the books on a golden platter."[7] Once the Holocaust had begun, the main dish to be served on that platter was Jewish history. Working "against the apocalypse," Yiddish cultural leaders took especial care to contextualize historical violence against Jewish communities and to impart the "Jewish values" they considered most relevant to their respective ideological frameworks. Their approach to history was essentially realistic but with pronounced mythic and fantastic elements. Throughout the 1940s and 1950s, the highest priority became helping young readers metabolize the violence in Europe and relate it to their own Jewish lives and choices as emerging adults, all through the medium of Yiddish. Knowing Jewish suffering might motivate young readers to choose Jewish joy.

While some authors went about this task through direct, mimetic portrayals that explicitly juxtaposed the resilience of Holocaust survivors to the resilience of earlier generations, others depicted episodes of anti-Jewish violence at a more distant and thus "safer" historical remove. Examining the ambitious fare served to adolescent readers, we discern a common exhortation to American Yiddish-speaking teens to choose—affirmatively, robustly, and joyfully—Jewish identity and continuing engagement with Yiddish culture. The motif of electing Jewishness stands out with especial prominence against an older idea of "ineluctable Jewishness" captured in the phrase "dos pintele yid": an indestructible kernel of deep Jewishness that might lie dormant through a long winter but would inevitably blossom forth under the "right" conditions—be they exceptionally favorable or hostile.[8] The teen novellas of the wartime and postwar eras posited a core of similarly ineradicable Jewishness, but they made the case to their readers for having to choose *yidishkeyt* actively and intentionally, and with redoubled vehemence when acting in defiant spite of antisemites.

A Scholar on Horseback: Don Isaac Abravanel

The most straightforward kind of historical fiction is the biography or hagiography of Jewish historical figures, such as the life of Don Isaac Abravanel written by Isaac Metzker (1901–1984) and published by the Workmen's Circle–affiliated Kinder Ring in 1941. Readers follow the birth of a boy destined for scholarly excellence and political prominence, to parents who are pious, learned, and cosmopolitan. From earliest childhood, young Isaac is depicted as intellectually curious, the very type of the "gifted child." His contented innocence is punctured by the arrival of a tattered refugee from Spain, fleeing an episode of church-endorsed forced conversion. Religious and political consciousness arrive inextricably for the precocious six-year-old, who hears the stranger's account and questions his father,

> "The priests want there to be no Jews left? All of them should convert together at once?" Isaac asked of his father in a sorrowful voice, like that of an adult.
>
> "That's what they want," his father replied. "But this isn't the first time that someone has tried to alienate the Jews from their faith by force. They have always resisted and not capitulated."
>
> "And did they take everything away from the stranger from Spain? He has no home left?"
>
> "No, they didn't take everything away from him. They only robbed him of his worldly goods, but they couldn't take away his courage or his steadfast faith. They couldn't take those things away from my father and your grandfather, Samuel Abravanel, either, when he fled from there."
>
> "My grandfather? Did he also have to flee from Spain?"
>
> "Yes, my son. The same thing that happened to the stranger from Spain happened way back when to your grandfather."
>
> Isaac moved over closer to his father, looked up at him with sad, intelligent eyes, and peppered him with questions. He wanted to know everything about his grandfather and his ancestors.[9]

Metzker's Isaac Abravanel is instinctually invested in the Jewish past, connecting on a personal level to Bible stories and a genealogical line the family traces back to King David. As a teenager, he is uninterested in the fleeting pleasures available to him as part of the upper echelon of Lisbon society, and yet he is influential among his peers. Abravanel is not, the author takes care to show, a wet blanket.

While lives of the saints for adult readers tended to focus on figures in the Hasidic world, hagiography remained a major didactic genre for children across a wider swath of global Jewry. It was an ideal vehicle for the broad shift from teaching by means of fear and negative examples to instruction by modeling the good. Intellectual voracity and curiosity about the Jewish past are qualities for young readers to emulate. Scholarly, courageous, and quite comfortable on horseback, the fully grown Abravanel undergoes one displacement after another, from Portugal to Spain to Italy, borne on the winds of shifting political fortunes and rising intolerance for Jews in Iberia. He serves as finance minister to the Crown. After being warned that the young Portuguese king (Joan II) plans to blame him for an unsuccessful war, he flees to Spain and rebuilds his life, shifting his focus to the biblical scholarship his heart craves. He sets down his quill only to enter the service of Spain's Catholic monarchs, attempting to secure his people's safety in that kingdom by helping the Crown to finance the interminable Reconquista. Jewish Iberia, in the person of one of its most distinguished sons, was ripe for romanticizing.[10] Metzker's Abravanel stirs the envious fury of Torquemada, who figures, panchronistically, as a latter-day Haman: "All the courtiers in the royal palace and even the rulers kissed the hem of Torquemada's holy robes, but not Abravanel. While everyone piously bowed to the court priest, Abravanel sat by serenely and thought of Mordecai, a pious Jew of ancient times and the only man in the royal court of the Persian King Ahashueres who did not kneel and bow before the wicked Haman."[11] For the teenager reading in New York, this gloss reinforces existing knowledge as well as proclaiming the timelessness of Jewish resistance to genocidal threats.

In the court of Ferdinand and Isabella, Abravanel brushes shoulders sympathetically with Christopher Columbus, whose imminent voyage, the text takes care to point out, has been financed by Spain's Jews in hopes that the fortune to be imported might placate the fickle Catholic monarchs.[12] The Jewish sage dares to muse (again, in a book published in 1941) that perhaps Columbus really *will* discover a new land, where the Jews might one day take refuge from European violence. Of course, no fortune will suffice to thwart Torquemada's will, bent on the dispersion, conversion, and destruction of Spain's Jewry. Although he is welcome—even required—to remain at his ministerial post, Abravanel resolves to accompany his people into exile. Metzker's text situates the expulsion in the long arc of cyclical Jewish time: "In one day, around three hundred thousand Spanish Jews were left without a home or a roof over their heads, for no other reason than that they had remained Jews. This was on the ninth of Av, the day when both Temples were destroyed. The expelled Jews recorded that sad day as the day of a third *khurbn*, or destruction, and a third exile."[13] In 1941, Metzker employs the term that will come to dominate Yiddish discourse about the Holocaust. Implicitly, he teases out the message that Sephardic Jewry suffered its *khurbn* (destruction) with a surviving remnant, and now the Ashkenazic Jewry that found itself plunged into another *khurbn* would similarly endure—thanks to the commitment expected of the story's readers.

Joseph in Rome: The Jewish Pope

By 1492, Isaac Abravanel is grandfather to a one-year-old, the child of his son Judah. Ferdinand and Isabella are so determined to hold on to their clever Jewish finance minister and Judah, their court physician, that they scheme to have the baby kidnapped in order to detain his prominent relations. Told of the plan, the family spirits the little one off to Portugal in the care of a nursemaid, but "pious soul snatchers," as Metzker writes, intercept the nurse and her charge. "They immediately converted the little Abravanel and dragged him off somewhere to a Portuguese church, and the Abravanels never again saw their child, the apple of their eye."[14] As the family enters exile, their mourning for the lost boy never abates.

The theme of Christians snatching and converting Jewish children, ancillary in the biography of Don Isaac Abravanel, is brought to the center in a different work of historical fiction published in New York just after the war, in 1947.[15] *Der yidisher poyps* (The Jewish Pope) represents a departure for Yudl Mark (1897–1975), a renowned Yiddish educator, pedagogical theorist, grammarian, philologist, translator, and author of textbooks and straightforwardly factual historical books for children.[16] This novella, which today might be marketed to young adults, appeared as part of the Kinder Ring Library's series titled Historical Figures, but its title page proclaims a more complex truth when it touts the book as "a web of legend, history and fantasy."[17] It is not surprising that Mark would have dug deeply into Jewish history, for he understood himself as a "Folkist," belonging to a small Yiddishist party in Eastern Europe that eschewed the socialism that defined the Bund. As Alec Burko explains, "Mark was by temperament a traditionalist, not a revolutionary."[18]

In 120 gripping pages, *The Jewish Pope* offers an account of the 1130 succession of Pope Anaclet II to the throne of St. Peter; it is rife with intrigue and chivalric romance and told through an unapologetically Judaic lens. The novella reiterates and expands on a polymorphous motif in the Jewish cultural imaginary, namely, the recurrent fantasia of a Jew who ascends to a status "more Catholic than the Pope" or even to the papacy itself. Dating back at least to the Talmudic period, and rooted in the biblical Joseph cycle, the most persistent version of this story arc is the narrative of the Catholic pope of Jewish origin.[19] One of the notable aspects of this malleable and evergreen fantasy is the way it combined and recombined with the other terms on the book's title page: legend and history. The papal motif surfaces in a variety of eras and places and always has the potential to illuminate, through the special European Jewish role as consummate insider-outsider, historical tensions (papal schism, imperial expansion) that implicated but did not fundamentally originate with or depend upon the Jews. In the shadow of the Holocaust, the Jewish boy's ascension to the papacy and reclamation of Jewish identity suggested to young American readers that they could take a strong hand in shaping their own destinies.

The story opens with a sympathetic view of Theresa, an impoverished Catholic woman taking confession for the "sin" of working as a *shabes goy* (a non-Jew who lights the oven fires and does other tasks prohibited to Jews on the Sabbath) in local Jewish homes, labor that is formally interdicted by church law. Her confessor, Father Thomas, insists that the only measure that will compensate for her blemished soul is to deliver him a new soul—that is, a Jewish child who can be converted to Christianity. Overcoming her qualms, Theresa dutifully abducts Elchanan, the sickly six-year-old son of Mainz's distinguished rabbinic leader, Rabbi Simeon the Great. During a daring midnight escape attempt, the boy falls ill. He awakens recaptured but now entrusted to the care of Father Felix, whose compassion and delicacy begin to wear away at Elchanan's dogged resistance to proselytizing. On the way to Rome, the priest instructs the boy in Latin and catechism.

In Rome, Elchanan is adopted by the wealthy and powerful Pierleoni family, themselves Jewish converts. Rechristened Petrus/Peter, Elchanan witnesses the schismatic violence between the Pierleonis and the rival Frangipanis, as well as Urban II's initiation of the First Crusade, with its unintended (as the text presents them) consequences for German Jewry. As a twelve-year-old boy, Elchanan/Petrus learns of the decimation of the Jews of Mainz and other German communities, including, presumably, his birth parents. The ostensibly orphaned Petrus journeys to France to study (with Peter Abelard, no less) and enters the church, rising to the rank of cardinal while still a young man. Traveling to Germany on a papal diplomatic mission, his carriage is stopped by a poor Jew who begs his assistance in rescuing his daughter, Rebecca, from the rapacious Knight of the Red Plains. He does so heroically. The first half of the novella closes with Petrus's election as the "legitimate" Pope Anaclet II in Rome, while his peers clandestinely elevate one of their number as the "illegitimate" Pope Innocent II.

The novella's second half focuses on the pull that the Jewish pope feels toward the faith of his forbears. Father Felix, now blind and impoverished, makes a pilgrimage and begs forgiveness for his involvement in the abduction, revealing incidentally that Elchanan's father is still alive. Increasingly drawn to his coreligionists, the Jewish pope attends the Kol Nidre service incognito, recognized only by Rebecca, who has arrived in Rome with her father. The pope resolves to summon the leaders of Mainz Jewry in the hopes that his father will be among them. To compel his aged father's attendance, Elchanan-Petrus-Anaclet promulgates an extravagantly harsh decree against the Jews of Mainz that no bishop can overturn but that must rather be rescinded only by the pope himself. The ruse has its intended effect, and Rabbi Simeon arrives in person to plead for his community. The obligatory anagnorisis follows, with Anaclet, Joseph- or Odysseus-like, disclosing his identity to his father. Ultimately, the Jewish pope devises a strategy to escape his station undetected and return to the home and faith of his parents in Mainz—with the resolute and beautiful Rebecca as his bride.

The Events in History and Legend

Until recently, there was no secondary literature on Mark's novella.[20] As a literary product of the twentieth century, *Der yidisher poyps* is marked by a high degree of narratorial omniscience and access to several (though not all) of the characters' feelings, thoughts, and motivations. The historical plot is interwoven with a suitably medieval romantic one, and the whole is subordinated to the overarching drama of Jewish identity compromised, forfeited, and then joyfully reclaimed. The folk and historical sources on which Mark drew were more circumspect albeit thoroughly recognizable in his embroidered text. The "legend" to which the title page alludes is first elaborated in Yiddish in the *Mayse bukh*, a collection of rabbinic and folk material published in Basel in 1602. Totaling eight pages (in Moses Gaster's English translation), the *Mayse bukh* presentation of

"The Jewish Child Who Was Stolen by a Servant and Later Became Pope" is considerably more bare-bones than Mark's novella, but quite prolix relative to the rest of the *Mayse bukh* collection.[21] The early-modern version claims wide-ranging narratorial access but uses this omniscience to offer a very cursory, exterior view of the early events of Elchanan's life and character formation, eschewing any account of the various characters' inner motivations except to justify the Jewish pope's predictable decision to remain among the Christians, "as one may well imagine, considering that it went well with him and that he was held in high esteem."[22] The 1602 text gives only glancing treatment to Elchanan's boyhood, either in Mainz or in Rome.

Most of the *Mayse bukh*'s emphasis (six of the eight pages) rests on the father-son reunion, which recapitulates several aspects of the biblical Joseph's reunion with his brothers and then with their father, Jacob. Chief among these is the lopsided nature of an encounter in which a long-lost son, not only acculturated but having succeeded to fabulous power within his adoptive surroundings, lures his father to a meeting through a manufactured crisis; son knows father's identity, but the reverse is not true. Recognition is established gradually by signs and tokens, such as the pope's uncannily deep facility with Talmudic argumentation and his knowledge of an idiosyncratic and masterful chess move transmitted early on in life by Rabbi Simeon to Elchanan. Not only does the pope rescind his harsh decree at the encounter, but in its aftermath, he authors a polemic against Catholicism, which he orders every subsequent candidate for the papacy to read; then he escapes Rome in order to return to Mainz and become "a good Jew again." His father, in turn, authors a liturgical poem (*piyyut*) commemorating the story, which the *Mayse bukh* proffers as an attestation of the events' facticity: "Therefore do not think that this is mere fiction."[23] The legend thus accounts for the provenance of a composition still recited on Rosh Hashana.[24]

Perhaps the most poignant moment of the reunion comes just after Elchanan's disclosure of identity, when the son asks his father, "Can you advise me how I can atone for my sin?"—the sin, he means, of retaining his Christian identity and practice into adulthood, while knowing of his Jewish parentage.[25] His father's reply invokes the pertinent rabbinic legal designation, consonant with the kidnapped boy's lack of volition: "You need not worry, it was against your will, for you were only a child when you were taken away from me."[26] The concept of the "captive child" originates in Talmudic argumentation and grows into a capacious legal category for unwitting sin that still figures prominently in Jewish legal discussions of the status of nonobservant Jews.[27] The leniency that the rabbis carved out entailed an implicit recognition of the overwhelming power of coterritorial—non-Jewish—societies and religions in general, and then in medieval Europe, of the Catholic church specifically. The resonance of the papal motif comes through its promise of Jewish power, consolidated under adversity but then benignly exercised: "For its part," writes Joseph Sherman, "impotent Jewry invented a fantasy that there might one day be crowned a truly Jewish pope—not an apostate, but a crypto-Christian—who, by remaining true to the faith of his people, would help to reverse that people's powerlessness."[28] In fact, the most realistic hopes for Jewish attainment of power in the real world lay precisely in unidirectional and unrepentant apostasy.

The historical record of the turn of the twelfth century reflects a schismatic moment in which a family of recent Jewish extraction played a pivotal role in papal history. Banker to Pope Leo IX (1049–1054) and other high church officials, the Jewish Baruch/Benedictus was converted (along with his son Leo) under the direct sponsorship of the Supreme Pontiff. Leo's son, Peter Leo/Pietro di Leone, lent the family its surname and continued to offer financial support to various popes and church elites. He and his brothers were supporters of Urban II (1088–1099), who died in one of the family's homes, near the Trastevere, Rome's Jewish quarter. A son—not adoptive—of Pietro Pierleoni who shared his father's name entered the church, rose to cardinal in 1120 and pope in 1130, reigning in Rome as Pope Anaclet II until his death in 1138. Meanwhile, a rival faction of cardinals regarded Anaclet as an antipope and instead designated Innocent II (1130–1143), who fled to a far more hospitable France after the contested election.[29] Although his family history raised no objections during his tenure as cardinal and papal legate, polemics against Pope Anaclet II dwelled heavily on his Jewish heritage, imputing to him a racist panoply of "Jewish" sins and impurities, including avarice, usury, gluttony, and even incest with his sister Tropea.[30] Mark's novella seems to play with these rumors about the relationship with Tropea, figuring her as a warm, sisterly presence who teases the new addition to the family during their childhood, and as an older teenager sighs with her adoptive brother in a moonlit garden at the prospect of her looming departure for Sicily, where she is to be married off to King Roger.

Passing Up Passing: An Assertion of Agency

We might concur with David Levine Lerner that in its medieval manifestations, the papal legend was "an expression of Jewish defiance in the face of political subordination to the Church."[31] However, when the motif is addressed to young readers in the late 1940s, it comes to represent defiance of Nazi racial doctrine as well. By the 1940s, the Jews of Europe had been trapped by a European imperial conflict on the grandest scale yet. The Nazis revived the racialized dogma of *limpieza de sangre* that had taken hold in fifteenth-century Spain: Once again, any quantum of Jewish blood constituted an ineradicable taint. But what if Jews were not damned to insuperable alterity by their very biology? What if it were possible to assimilate into (Christian) normalcy by some combination of coercion and suasion, as Elchanan does? The Jewish pope motif located the possibility of conversion within Christian theology itself and so implicitly deracialized religious categories. The papal abductions of children implicitly affirmed the plasticity of affiliation and therefore of identity, averring that religion was a matter of mutable faith rather than of immutable genes.[32] Yudl Mark was not the only author to make the case for Jewish identity as contingent. As Jeffrey Shandler points out in his essay on Yankev Glatshteyn's ultrarealistic novella for young adults about the early days of the Anschluss, *Emil un Karl*, a pair of best friends are indistinguishable to the Nazis, even though one is Jewish and the other Christian. At various points in the text, observes Shandler, "each of the boys is mistaken for what he is not," a confusion that serves to "flout assumptions about the intractable nature of Jewish or Aryan identities as argued then by race scientists."[33]

But the destabilization of racialized identity categories is only the first step for Mark, the necessary prelude to choosing Jewishness. Yiddish cultural leaders wanted more for Jewish children than the possibility of safety through ceasing to be Jews, and indeed, Mark dilates on the story's end, where Anaclet chooses to resume his existence as Elchanan. Anyone who *could* live as a Christian but chose not to was affirmatively electing Jewish identity rather than merely defaulting to the lachrymose fate dictated by the "wrong" ancestry. Perhaps, Mark and others suggest, the Jews could pass up the need for passing altogether. The preadolescent and teenage audience for his novella—being reared to read or at least to comprehend a fairly ornate narrative in the Yiddish language, immediately after the decimation of Europe's Yiddish speakers—found themselves in a threshold position similar to Elchanan's at the moment of his abdication and return to Mainz. If there is no *limpieza de sangre,* and apostasy and assimilation are viable choices, then so is Jewishness.

For Mark the grammarian and educator, choosing Jewish meant choosing Yiddish. The hybrid tongue had always competed for its speakers' loyalty; as Shandler elaborates in his account of postvernacular Yiddish, "the choice of speaking in Yiddish (or not) has always been charged with meaning"—and never more so than in a cultural space reconfigured by mass migration and genocide.[34] Yudl Mark had reached the United States in 1936, arriving as part of an outrageously fortunate trickle of would-be refugees rather than with the torrent of two million European Jews who had immigrated to the United States in the four decades preceding the Immigration Act of 1924 and established an infrastructure of Yiddish cultural and educational institutions. By the mid-thirties, there could be no doubt that the relocation was irrevocable.

By the time Mark's novella appeared, Eastern European Jewish culture found itself in redoubled exile: The age-old Jewish exile from the Holy Land was now trebled by the further displacement of most remaining Yiddish speakers to the Americas or Palestine. For the multilingual speakers and readers of a newly American Ashkenaz, was Yiddish to be a repository of precious cultural distinctiveness or a gloomy linguistic catacomb? Over the course of his prolific career, Mark cultivated bright, sunny spaces where Yiddish might plausibly rebuff the assimilatory pressures coming from both English and Modern Hebrew. He refused to disentangle the Yiddish language from his vision of robust cultural Jewishness, *veltlekhkeyt*. Just as the papal plot demonstrated how Jews might pass as Gentiles and even rise to the top of Gentile power structures before ultimately electing Jewishness, so too Mark hoped to inspire his students' embrace of Yiddish as the freely chosen language of homecoming. He wished for his juvenile readers to affirmatively engage with all elements of the religio-cultural-linguistic complex to which they were heir. Passing up passing meant not only staking a robust claim on Jewishness but passing up the seemingly inevitable process of linguistic assimilation and the abandonment of Yiddish.

Just a year after publishing *Der yidisher poyps*, Mark took to his periodical *Shul pinkes* (School Register) to lay out a vision of *veltlekhkeyt* (literally, worldliness) over and against the lure of Anglicized "sekularizm," which he derided as a deracination so total that it edged into apostasy.[35] While *sekularizm* came only to negate, he argued, *veltlekhkeyt* carried affirmative content and the materials to create anew, to grow new fruits on a four-thousand-year-old tree while liberating Jews from the walls of a "spiritual ghetto."[36] Even after the war, there was reason for its most loyal devotees to hope that the fortunes of Yiddish might rise in the refuge of the New World. After the murder of six million Jews, there remained five or six million Yiddish speakers, "more Jews than spoke English at the time, and five or six times the number that spoke Hebrew."[37] Mark therefore viewed holistic Yiddish education as a "mission" (*shlikhes*), one that grew all the more urgent for its increasingly apparent futility.[38]

Historical currents that implicated Jews in distinctive or unique ways, such as secularization, modern antisemitism, and unprecedented levels of global migration and mobility, inflected cultural and educational leaders' understanding of the ostensibly universal experience of human growth and development that was being elaborated by the rapidly diffusing field of psychology. Mark's close associate and fellow founding figure at the YIVO Institute, Max Weinreich, devoted great energy to the study of Jewish youth from a psychological perspective and indeed coined the term *dervakslingshaft* to capture the sense of "adolescence."[39] In interwar Eastern Europe, to "grow up Jewish" was to align with a political identity crystallized in one or another youth movement.[40] Jewish youth experienced their developmental milestones in and through these affiliations, as became amply clear in the hundreds of responses submitted to a series of autobiography contests sponsored by the fledgling YIVO Institute.[41] Political intuitions or commitments suggested an answer to the most elemental questions, such as where to live (answered variously by Bundists and Zionists), which in turn might dictate an occupational pathway and determine the shape of one's prospects for love, marriage, and reproduction. Political alignments also conditioned choices about how to spend one's leisure time, money, and emotional energy.

Weinreich's account of Jewish youth centered the psychological harm resulting from antisemitism. For those at the center of YIVO's founding, the best remedy was a thriving Yiddish culture, which could act "as a compensation for the damage done to Jewish youth by general society in place of religion."[42] Mark's Jewish papal novella illustrates how these aspirations worked on a minute level. He portrays the child's core reality as narrowly constrained agency in the present and immediate future, offset by the imagined prospect of limitless agency in adulthood, the hazy and remote time to come. The actual process of maturation is a gradual reckoning with the limitations of that eventual agency. Thus does Mark emphasize Elchanan's powerlessness, desperation, and fear during the early phases of his abduction, contrasting them with his eventual power as pope; the ultimate manifestation of that power, of course, is abandoning the papacy for a life of his own choosing.

A Story of Sticking—and Getting Unstuck

While many texts aimed at older elementary and teen readers represented resonant themes at a "safe" historical distance in the Jewish past, others portrayed the Holocaust directly, recruiting its events and tropes as exempla to prove the urgency of ideologies such as Zionism or communism. *The Story of a Stick*, a finely wrought 1958 novella by Zina Rabinowitz, follows four generations of a single Jewish family's history across Europe and culminates with a son of Warsaw surviving the war and "replanting" himself in the Land of Israel as a teenager. The book traces an arc of journey and return to Zion and typifies a set of "transitional works that yoked the travails of the Holocaust with the hope presented by the establishment of the State of Israel."[43] Born in Bessarabia in 1895, Rabinowitz benefited from an unusually sophisticated education that culminated in her attending university in Moscow. She identified early as a Zionist, spending 1913–1914 in Palestine. In adulthood she moved between the Land of Israel and New York, working as a Hebrew teacher and building a writing career in Yiddish. She visited the fledgling state with some frequency, and late in life, she resettled in Tel Aviv for good. Her children's books were popular in Latin America, and *The Story of a Stick* was originally published by the Yiddish School in Mexico.

Set in Frankfurt's Judengasse in 1858, the novella opens onto the travails of wealthy merchant Jacob Guttmann, whose pious home is shadowed by his wife's seemingly incurable illness. He donates generously to every kind of charity, large and small, subscribing to the rabbinic idea that charitable giving can avert an evil decree from on high. When a delegate from the Holy Land visits the city's main synagogue to solicit gifts, Guttmann donates as usual and itemizes the gifts for his wife. Giving through an emissary is good, she avers, but it would be even better for her husband to dispense philanthropy himself in Jerusalem. Though he hesitates to leave during her illness, she allays his fears by promising to await his return.

Arriving during the wintertime tourism lull, he immediately spreads the word that he's come to support local institutions. Among those lining up at his hotel for a handout is an impoverished scribe, who invites Guttmann to visit his home and see how his sons work alongside him copying out Torah scrolls. The youngest but cleverest of these sons wishes to receive some of Guttmann's largesse without suffering the indignity of begging. He decides to offer the visitor a souvenir, hoping that it will prompt a reciprocal gift of coins. After musing about what he might be able to bestow upon such a distinguished traveler, the boy alights on the idea of carving a stick of olive wood with a biblical verse, a portable and meaningful memento. After preparing the wood, he engraves the first part of Leviticus 19:23, "When you come into the land and plant." The rest of the verse relates the rule about waiting three years to eat fruit planted in the Land of Israel. However, rabbinic tradition reads the first half of the verse as an imperative unto itself: When you come into the land, *you shall plant*. The young carver-scribe presents his gift with an exegesis along these lines, explaining his choice of verse thus: "Because all over Jerusalem, they say you've come and 'sowed' much charity. A donation, my good sir, is like a planting. . . . Some benefit for Jerusalem will grow from it."[44] The European visitor proclaims himself awed by the precocious children of Jerusalem.

The Guttmann family's relationship with the stick begins with an ethically complicated encounter. Rabinowitz makes no secret of the boy's selfish motivations in contriving his gift, but at the same time, his handiwork takes on a life of its own that transcends his transactional intentions. Seeing the carving turn out to his satisfaction, the boys kisses the stick and thus becomes the first of a chain of young men to do so in moments of joy, relief, and general emotional plenitude. In every generation the stick will save the Guttmanns' lives over the course of three different wars—but always and only through rational rather than supernatural means. Jacob Guttmann, for his part, is not a wholly altruistic actor either; he hopes for his wife's healing in exchange for his generosity. Yet he does not truly expect it: He is shocked, upon returning to Frankfurt, to find a party gathered at his home, and an alluring woman in blue silk its cynosure. His wife has made a full recovery.

They do not live happily ever after, though, for in the next chapter we learn that the Guttmanns have a young adult son, Joseph, who is being conscripted into the German Army to fight the French in the War of 1870. In light of his wife's recent illness and general fragility, Jacob hopes to exempt his son from military service. Guttmann's rabbi counsels against using his wealth and influence to extricate his son from danger; after all, military service is the price of the citizenship that has been newly granted to Jews, and to shirk civic duty would be both unfair and unseemly. The lad should report for duty, the rabbi enjoins, with his tefillin, prayer shawl, and the special stick from the Holy Land, which might offer him some ineffable protection.

Young Joseph Guttmann wishes to dispose of the burdensome stick, but he realizes it won't be simple: Any Jew who chanced upon it would return it to his father, and the young man is loath to let it fall into Gentile hands lest Christians make fun of the Hebrew letters. Thus does the stick become a sentimental burden, a metonym for Jewishness itself. Unable to stash it or throw it away, Joseph reports for training with the stick concealed under his shirt. This gives him ramrod posture, which draws the favorable notice of his commanding officer. Later, in the fog of battle, Joseph tumbles into a deep ravine and uses the combination of his rifle and the carved olive branch as walking sticks to stabilize his footing on the long, lifesaving climb out of the chasm.

Finding himself in Strasbourg at the conclusion of hostilities, Joseph seeks out the local rabbi so that he can follow his parents' advice to make a charitable donation in gratitude for his survival. The rabbi studies Talmud with the impressive young man, rejoicing when his daughter marries Guttmann and settles with him in Alsace. There the couple raise their precocious son Benjamin, who has mastered the Five Books of Moses by age six and is studying at a Parisian university when the Great War breaks out. Benjamin is pressed into service, but since his father is German and his mother French, he struggles with which side to enlist on, which side of his heritage to risk betraying. What does it mean, the novella asks, to belong to a nation other than, or in addition to, the Jews? This question can only be resolved for Rabinowitz by the creation of a Jewish nation-state, wherein Jewish identity and loyalty can be seamlessly united. In the meantime, the generations cycle, with the son taking the place of his father, and the father's old thoughts springing to life anew in his son:

> It wasn't long before Benjamin left his parents' home. But before he had to depart, his parents made him a holiday banquet, just as Joseph's parents had done for their son when he left for the army.
>
> After the meal, Joseph took down from the bookshelf the stick carved with the verse, "When you come into the land, you shall plant." He hadn't given the stick back to his parents when he'd returned from the war.
>
> "Do you recognize this stick, my son?" said Joseph Guttmann to his son, Benjamin. "When you were still a child, I used to tell you about how this stick had saved me from a slippery, muddy ravine in wartime, in the year 1870. Take this stick and keep it with you until the war's end, until you come safely home."[45]

Benjamin reasons that while the stick might have been useful in his father's quaint nineteenth-century conflict, it obviously has no place in modern tank warfare. Now the pesky stick is *his* burden to dispose of, and he tries to ditch it in the Great Synagogue of Paris. But an eagle-eyed caretaker notices the finely carved piece and reunites it with its owner. So Benjamin reluctantly resorts to the same strategy as his father did: keeping the stick on his person. It saves his life twice. First, a detachment of Germans manages to isolate him from his company. Running from their bullets, he trips over the stick and falls. Seeing him go down, they turn their attention elsewhere rather than wasting bullets on a fallen enemy. Later, he awakens in a German hospital after a fierce firefight in the forest. His life has been spared because the soldiers who found him assumed that the letters carved into the stick were some kind of code, and they have pegged him as a high-value spy. Hearing that he's been nursed back to health only so he can break the "code," he grows fond of the olive wood.

The doctor who treats Benjamin is a highly assimilated Jew, with—needless to say—a pretty daughter. They befriend the enemy soldier and, after the war, invite him to visit them in Warsaw. When he does so, Benjamin Guttmann marries the doctor's daughter and makes a life with her and his in-laws in the Polish capital, overlooking his doubts about their professed dislike for the Jews and devaluing of his Jewish education. They clash over the stick and what it signifies; disgusted by his "idolatrous" attachment to the relic, his wife tries to dispose of it quietly. When their son is born, the conflicts intensify. She prevails in naming the boy Stefan and calling him Stefek; nevertheless, his father quietly appends the Hebrew name Ya'akov, after the boy's great-grandfather. The question of his education is another flash point for the unhappy couple:

> Benjamin requested of his wife that they invite a Jewish tutor into their home several times a week to teach the child Yiddish. But his wife and her father laughed at him.
>
> "Our Stefek has no time to learn a language that's written from right to left. . . . What would he get out of Yiddish?" Benjamin's wife asked sarcastically.
>
> "Stefek doesn't need to know any of the 'Holy Tongue'! Stefek needs to learn European languages: English, French, German, but not these foolish things that are more suitable for old Jews and country bumpkins. Stefek lives in Warsaw, among Poles, so he should grow up as a Pole. Our neighbors ought not suspect that he is a Jew."[46]

The mother prevails, and the day the boy turns thirteen is darkened for his father not only by his son's ignorance of his heritage but by Hitler's march into Warsaw. While Stefek's mother and grandfather are certain that no harm will come their way, Benjamin is less sanguine. Noting an unusually large crowd milling about the Great Synagogue at midweek, he enters and listens to a young man's appeal to parents to rescue their children by smuggling them out of Warsaw before it's too late. Benjamin knows his wife would never consent, and for that matter, his newly teenage son would never elect to leave home. After struggling with the question of how to "kidnap" his own child, he bends his steps toward the apothecary and requests a remedy for insomnia. At home, he feigns good cheer and mixes cocktails in honor of the boy's birthday, drugging everyone in his household and allowing him to sneak the sleeping teen to the wagons gathered outside the synagogue. Benjamin tucks the carved stick into the beltloops of the boy's coat, along with a word of explanation. The boy comes to, perplexed to find himself in a wagon in the company of several other children, and is directed to his father's understated note:

> Stefek, our son, we're parting from you for a while. The fire of war has caught all of Warsaw. If with God's help we see each other again, I will tell you all about why we chose this path for you. We are going on a different road, but we are sure that the road down which we have sent you is best. In the belt of your coat, you'll find a stick with carved letters. You've never learned those letters. A long time will go by before you will learn to understand what is engraved on the stick. But remember one thing: guard the stick until the war ends, and when the land calms down, do all that is engraved there.[47]

The young orator in the Great Synagogue accompanies the fleeing children and becomes Stefek's faithful friend—until the youthful rescuer perishes in an air raid in the forest. His parents' fate unknown but likely grim, Stefek survives the war and is sent to a children's village in Palestine with only the stick to accompany him. He clings to the totem, passed lovingly through the generations of his forebears, to remind him of the home and family he has lost. Having learned Hebrew, he can now parse the stick's charge to come into the land and plant, and he commits to carrying out its charge literally, in the most public way possible.

The novella's final chapter recounts the celebration of Tu Bishvat, the Jewish Arbor Day, when visiting dignitaries are invited to the children's village for a festive planting of saplings, accompanied by music and followed by refreshments and speeches. With great fanfare, the transplanted boy steps forward and declares, "I, Ya'akov Guttmann, the son of Benjamin Guttmann, the grandson of Joseph Guttmann, and the great-grandson of Reb Jacob Guttmann of Frankfurt-am-Main, am now fulfilling the instruction of my father to do what is engraved upon this stick: I am planting it together with a new sapling in honor of the New Year of the Trees."[48] The repatriated branch is clearly a metonym for the people being replanted in their "native" soil according to the narrative logic of Zionism. The stick regenerates symbolically in the form of the fledgling nation, the children's village, and the teenage survivor of a genocidal war. The novella's redemptive ending concentrates an array of Zionist tropes pertaining to agricultural, psychological, and national flourishing.[49]

Afforestation efforts constituted a nation-building activity with a transformative effect on the landscape and deep symbolic resonance.[50] Hizky Shoham chronicles the emergence of tree plantings as the central ritual of a modernized,

Zionist, child-centered Tu Bishvat holiday, elevated since the Mandatory period by a shared Jewish and British "perception of Palestine as the arena of the struggle between cultivation and barrenness," as well as a European-oriented preference for dense forests of tall trees over the mixed vegetation native to the Levant.[51] As Yael Zerubavel notes, the planted forest served at once as a living memorial to the dead (including Holocaust victims) and an "icon of national survival" in a young country whose children and trees would mature together.[52] The festivities in Ya'akov Guttmann's fictional community reflect several features of a ceremony, typically organized by teachers, designed to underscore the correspondence between flourishing forests and the newly muscular Jewish body. The historical record shows how educators showcased planting trees alongside children's vigorous physical activity and martial trappings that included "parades, trumpet fanfares, flags, military drills, and so on." Later, the presence of honor guards and the recitation of biblical verses were added.[53]

Significantly, the tree-planting ceremony originated with the same figure who pioneered the immersive Hebrew language pedagogy that came to be known as *ivrit be'ivrit* (Hebrew in Hebrew), Chaim Aryeh Leyb Zuta (1868–1939).[54] Twin acts of nation building, the "revival" of supposedly ancient forests (which were in fact an importation on the European model) corresponded to the "revival" of an ancient tongue that had been consigned to reliquary status but would now blossom forth anew. Rather than emphasizing the tension between Hebrew as the language of Israel and Yiddish as the language of exile, the novella positions both as languages "written from right to left" and scorned alike by deracinated Jews like Stefek's mother. While Benjamin had rued his son's ignorance of "the Jewish alphabet," it is the boy's growing Hebrew literacy in the children's village that prompts him to "do what is engraved upon this stick."[55]

The Tu Bishvat tree-planting ceremony, which began in 1907 at the Mikveh Yisrael agricultural school, helped mediate an intensifying tension between urban and rural identities. Although such tensions were enacted throughout the industrializing world at the turn of the twentieth century, they were inflected for Jews by a particular set of anxieties that stemmed from Jewish underinvolvement in European agriculture. More than any other sector of economic activity, successful agricultural production heralded the arrival of a physically robust and economically independent New Jew. Tu Bishvat became a day to celebrate the romantically idealized (re)attachment of the Jewish people to the land by means of its cultivation. Most of the holiday guests in Rabinowitz's novella likely drove out to the children's village from cities. While most actual Tu Bishvat ceremonies took place in urban settings, literary sources were keen to represent them as rural phenomena that underscored the "bond to nature" and the sanctity of green spaces.[56] Stefek-Ya'akov, as an urban child turned rural, is an especially fitting figure to reinvent himself in and through the tree-planting ceremony.

Because the children's village is organized as a kibbutz, the final chapters of *The Story of a Stick* offer a kibbutz tale, albeit an unusual one. Until the 1950s kibbutzim almost uniformly pursued a radical experiment in collective living, with children under the care of designated childcare workers from infancy so their parents could maximize agricultural production, among other reasons.[57] Subsequent practices varied, but the children's house remained on some kibbutzim for another three decades. This arrangement necessarily entailed "marginalization of the traditional role played by parents in raising and educating their children." As in so many other immigrant narratives, "the fantasy of sweet orphanhood" solves the "problem" of having to answer to parents and their outmoded legacies.[58]

Reading Rabinowitz's novella alongside Hebrew-language children's literature set in Israel in the decades before and immediately after Statehood, I note in the Yiddish text a striking lack of ambivalence about the Zionist "cure" for Stefek's exilic pathologies.[59] Whereas before the war, his deracinated family is urban (dwelling in a fashionable Warsaw apartment) and bourgeois (Mom reads fashion magazines and supervises the servants; Dad has a nondescript office job), Stefek's arrival at the children's home as an orphaned refugee offers the curative powers of agricultural labor in a collectivized, rural setting. In a community of similarly orphaned children, the nuclear family recedes in importance, and caring teachers impart the Labor Zionist ideology that both flows from and will help to further build a state as benevolent as it is strong.[60] The children themselves are the agricultural kibbutz's ultimate "produce."[61] In his rebirth from Stefek to Ya'akov, the boy bridges the divides between urban and rural, diaspora and homeland, wartime trauma and peacetime normalcy, and exilic languages (Polish as his spoken language, Yiddish as his suppressed heritage) and Modern Hebrew, which is presented as continuous with the biblical Hebrew inscribed on the olive-wood stick. It is unsurprising that Rabinowitz's novella was translated into Hebrew in 1960, but it is curious that it was published not in Israel, where some have discerned a post-Holocaust softening toward Yiddish culture and diasporic history, but rather in New York under the auspices of the Board of Jewish Education.[62]

In the war's immediate aftermath, Yiddish children's literature was ready to represent something that Hebrew was not: the child survivor, in *survival* rather than *heroic* mode. Unlike his father and grandfather, Stefek fights in no war. Over the course of his long, geographically vague trek through Europe, he is weakened by hunger nearly to the point of perishing. His last memory before blacking out is of someone slapping his head and seizing his stick; he awakens in a hospital, where he recovers until he can be transferred to an orphanage and thence to Palestine. As Shai Rudin explains, Hebrew literature—for both adults and children—seldom depicted Holocaust victims until after the Eichmann trial in 1961; the Holocaust in his formulation was "present-absent," and cultural representation focused on the heroics of the Partisans and ghetto fighters. Only in the late 1970s did children's literature focus on representing the emotional lives and psychological struggles of heroes and survivors. When survivor-children started to appear in fiction and poetry, their Holocaust experiences were a mere prelude to their rescue and constituted the ultimate justification of the Zionist project.[63] Stefek is not a Holocaust hero, but the text strongly suggests that he will lead a heroic life through building and defending his reclaimed and regenerated homeland.

Orphaned Stefek-Ya'akov is the idealized, protean Israeli. The multigenerational novella allows us to compare two boys inhabiting the Land of Israel. Whereas the unnamed son of Jerusalem who had carved the stick almost a century earlier was crafty, Stefek-Ya'akov is guileless, wholly innocent. His wartime education in the school of hard knocks has imparted only the skills of defense; he is no aggressor. If 1939 was his bar mitzvah year, then he turns twenty-two in 1948. Although the book ends long before his conscription, Ya'akov seems an ideal recruit for an army that will style itself a *Defense* Force. Describing a kibbutz educational regime that combines book learning (including Hebrew language of course) with physical fitness, Rabinowitz leaves completely unremarked the pressing reality that the transplanted boy will likely soon have to use his skills to defend his new home. This omission is in keeping with a tendency Darr identifies in Israeli children's literature to imagine children as eventual combatants only in works for far younger readers, for whom the eventuality of combat is a more distant prospect than it is for adolescents.[64]

Choosing (a) Life

The novellas discussed in this chapter were addressed to teenage readers on the cusp of making what Samuel Johnson called "the choice of life." Johnson's own novella *Rasselas* depicts a young prince trying to make a similar choice by undertaking a journey. His poet-friend Imlac advises, "Do not suffer life to stagnate; it will grow muddy for want of motion: commit yourself again to the current of the world." Yiddish speakers approaching adulthood in the 1940s had been thrust into the choppiest possible current of the world; stagnation was not an option. What wisdom were they to draw from their reading?

It is notable that all the protagonists face severely limited choices. "There is no other country," in the slogan of Russian-born Hebrew novelist Yosef Haim Brenner. Where else could Stefek have gone? Isaac Abravanel might have avoided exile in a narrow sense, but could he have unchosen it in a broader one? Elchanan has the widest range of options available to him, but then again he wears the golden handcuffs of a life not his own, and his unconstrained choice of Jewishness is precisely what renders the papal myth such a potent fantasy. The key message about Jewish history that these texts, collectively, imparted to their readers is that one's agency is always constrained, and yet it is always possible—and preferable—to choose knowledge over oblivion of the Jewish past. Thus the centrality of plots of voyage and return, even if the return takes several generations. Every literary portrayal reinvents the past as a resource for the present and the future. The community was always making itself up: invented pasts for imagined communities. This didn't mean that everyone had to become a historian, but rather that everyone had to commit to knowing what you could only come to know by reading Jewish books.

Conclusion

THE JEWISH TIMELESS: REGENERATION

SECULAR YIDDISH children's literature was a historically bounded phenomenon whose fortunes tracked closely with those of Yiddish itself, flourishing in the first half of the twentieth century before receding in the decades following the Holocaust. While this trajectory was shaped by historical forces, I want to conclude by considering how Yiddish children's authors sought to transcend linear time and re-embed young readers in the Jewish eternal, a discursive space-time safely beyond history. Their work offered Jewish children two main templates of transcendence: time and language. By *time*, I refer specifically to the rhythms of the Jewish liturgical year, wherein holidays and their themes fuse, or stand pointedly at odds, with the cycle of the seasons (in the northern hemisphere, at least) to dictate a liberatory spring, a joyful early summer, a doleful high summer, a solemn early autumn that gives onto sacred joy as the season progresses, a quietly glittering, candlelit deep winter, and a brief, carnivalesque release as winter turns back into spring. Yiddish holiday tales and poems taught children to *feel* their way into these rhythms even while adapting them to commemorate more recent tragedies and triumphs.

The other template, offered to orient the youngest readers, was instruction in the Jewish alphabet that was used to encode both the Hebrew of the holy books and the Yiddish of the ideologically diverse adults all around. A classic children's form was the abecedary, or book meant to teach the alphabet. No matter how apparently straightforward, this didactic genre was not immune to politics. Seemingly narrow questions of orthography trawled up to the surface more bracing ideological dilemmas about the relationship between Hebrew and Yiddish. Opinions differed on which letters or letter combinations counted as part of the Jewish alphabet, let alone the question of which words beginning with a given letter might be highlighted as typical or held up as exemplary. The texts and paratexts (illustrations, etc.) of the Yiddish abecedaries, which might also be placed in productive conversation with Ladino *silabarios*, deserve an entire book of their own.[1] Built on half-concealed armatures of ideology, abecedaries were often very playful texts that trafficked in visual and aural puns and whimsical personification of the letters.

An Ambivalent Son of Mother Yiddish

One of the joys of writing this study has been the occasional arrival of books unbidden. A Yiddish culture bearer living in Israel sent me a parcel that included two volumes of holiday stories by Levin Kipnis (1894–1990), *Under the Fig Tree* (*Untern faygenboym*), which spans the half year from Passover to Rosh Hashana, and *Under the Carob Tree* (*Untern bokserboym*), which covers the winter months round back again to Passover. But for their brightly illustrated, full-color covers, these handsomely printed volumes seemed perfectly continuous with what I had previously taken to be Kipnis's only book-length Yiddish volume for children, the 1961 collection *Under the Date Palm* (*Untern teytlboym*), published in New York with Matones Press and discussed in the introduction. But these successor volumes, which I have come to think of as "the twins," appeared posthumously in 1993 with the Tel Aviv publisher Yisroel Bukh, long associated with Yiddish and the Ashkenazi Left. By that time, Kipnis had been fondly memorialized as a founder of Israeli children's literature, with over a thousand stories and poems to his name—all in Hebrew.

Both volumes are prefaced the same way: with Kipnis's portrait, identical acknowledgments and an introduction by his widow, Devorah Kipnis, and an essay by the author about his lifelong relationship with Yiddish, "Mayn mameloshn" (My Mother Tongue). It seems fitting that the retrospective essay is undated because it appears somewhat out of time; its temporal stamp is simply "after." A deeply personal reminiscence, Kipnis begins by explaining that for the first three years of his life, he did not speak—or more precisely, he communicated in what he called *shtumer-loshn*, "mutespeak."[2] Kipnis reminds us that the child's process of learning to talk in ordinary language represents an accommodation to adult norms and expectations. An emerging self, usually in the body of a toddler, is pulled and prodded, lured and jostled into concourse with others, enacting a complex negotiation between heteronomy and autonomy. Kipnis contrasts his singular early mode of communication with the sudden blossoming of his Yiddish, inexorably relational, wherein he began to speak "*mame-loshn* with my mother, with my brothers and sisters, with my friends, with everyone." Benjamin Harshav pointedly translated *mame-loshn* as "mama language" rather than the more formal "mother tongue," noting that it evokes not just generic native fluency but "the specific set of cultural characteristics and stereotypes associated with the Eastern European Jewish mother."[3]

Yiddish was the medium of instruction in kheyder, of course, but the content being delivered plunged Kipnis rapidly into the accreted layers of Jewish multilingualism: *khumesh-loshn* for the study of the Pentateuch, *Akdomus-loshn* for the study of Aramaic liturgy and soon thereafter, Talmud.[4] In the thoroughly masculine space of the kheyder, where the ill-tempered teacher stood in loco parentis for his milder father, a cantor, the Yiddish vernacular stood in the place of the protective, sympathetic mama whose ambit lay elsewhere:

> "Hashoyleyekh get leishtoy"—when Reuven sends a writ of divorce [*gett*] from Zhitomir to his wife in Berdichev by means of an emissary, Shimen, also from Zhitomir—Shimen goes from Zhitomir with the *gett* to Berdichev to the wife of Ruvn of Zhitomir, who lives in Berdichev. . . ."
>
> We children got lost between Zhitomir and Berdichev, and the rebbe hit us, and we cried, and *mame-loshn* cried right along with us.[5]

Kipnis traces his development as a reader: from the trashy novels by Shomer that his sister brought home, to the early holiday tales by Mordkhe Spektor (likely an enduring influence on his own holiday tales), to the introduction of fiction by Sholem Aleichem, at which "the shtetl began to laugh!" Even his pious father—identified as "a real-life Peysi the Cantor," after the canonical humorist's most exuberant novel—accepted the ritualistic reading of Tevye's monologues at the Shabbos table. Kipnis's *mame-loshn*, he reports, was delighted with him: She *kvelled*.

But the development of these tastes could not withstand the forces of linguistic change overtaking the shtetl: The community sees its kheyder "reformed," and suddenly Yiddish finds itself vying for its speakers' loyalty. An awareness of the complicated language politics cannot but accompany Kipnis's emergence into adult consciousness:

> My town slept—deeply—and suddenly awoke and didn't recognize itself. The intelligentsia spoke Russian conspicuously, the young men of the study house became Zionists and broke their teeth to speak Hebrew. Even Jewish girls learned Bible [Tanakh], a *segule* [talisman] for a marriage match,

[worth] half a dowry. The "kheyder" became a "reformed kheyder"—Hebrew [instruction] *in* Hebrew.

Yiddish was spoken by Jews in shul among themselves at prayer times and in the shops, for business. Women adorned their Yiddish with Russian words—*mame-loshn* was declining, *mame-loshn* was *jargón* . . . shameful to speak. . . .

One fine day, a young fellow appeared in town, from the big city, with a white tunic with an embroidered collar, fastened with a string—a socialist. He'd come to hold a "talk for the youth." He was handsome, his voice, charming, and his tongue, sharp. But he spoke little about socialism. He quickly turned to making fun of Hebrew, of "the Holey Tongue." If not Russian, one must speak Yiddish. Yiddish is our national language [*folkshprakh*]. There had just been a conference in Czernowitz, and the great writer Peretz had spoken, and they had decided such and such. . . .

I was a passionate Hebraist. I'd established courses to study and speak Hebrew. I had been writing in Hebrew and also published poems in the children's periodical *Haperakhim*, "The Flowers."

I became a fierce opponent of Yiddish.[6]

Kipnis describes his emigration to the Land of Israel, where the streets of Jerusalem teemed with "all the [world's] seventy languages." During the years of the Great War, he observes, Palestine was blockaded from Europe, and Hebrew flourished as the fledgling nation turned inward. He threw himself into writing for the first generations of Jewish children to be raised in Hebrew in centuries. Kipnis and his social circle maintained a nostalgic fondness for Yiddish, gathering to sing and tell jokes in the familiar *mame-loshn*, purely for their own recreation without a thought for the propagation or preservation of their native tongue. But New York Yiddishism came calling: Would Kipnis contribute something to the *Kinder zhurnal*? His *mame-loshn*, resurgent, wouldn't content herself with second fiddle, wouldn't—in a locution suggested by a component of the Yiddish word for "translation," *iberzetsn*—sit still: "So I started to translate one of my little things from Hebrew to *mame-loshn*. But instead of being translated ['sitting still'] . . . something [new] actually wrote itself . . . and quite differently than in Hebrew. . . . It wrote itself so easily, so clearly. I was amazed. Whence came to me the Yiddish words after years without my speaking them, hearing them, or even having them in mind? Something like butterflies, birds, doves, came flying and fluttering, begging me, 'Take me! Grab me! Write me into the story.'"[7]

Before he knew it, Kipnis was publishing regularly in Yiddish children's periodicals from New York to Buenos Aires. His contributions depicted the ideal life of children in the Land of Israel, capturing in Yiddish for diaspora children the lives being lived by young Hebrew speakers: "I 'Israelized' [*'eretsyisroeldik' gemakht*] all the children's periodicals and children's corners [of adult periodicals]." But the sunshine of the idealized, blooming land couldn't dispel the shadows cast on Yiddish by the accumulated catastrophes of the twentieth century.

Fittingly, the dark drama that unfolds between the lines has a Freudian dimension. Biological mother and mother tongue are ultimately inseparable, and their intertwined fates are overdetermined. Late in life, Kipnis recalled his mother, Rachel, as just literate enough to read the Tsenerene but poetic enough to speak in rhymes. He had dedicated his 1961 collection of Yiddish tales to her, but now the fate of his Yiddish writing is uncertain; no natural readership remains. To register the loss, let alone to mourn it, demands the simultaneous superimposition of a biblical matriarch, his own mother, and his neglected mother tongue:

> *Mame-loshn* wanted to write herself, needed to write herself, was missing and remembering the good times, and weeping.
>
> Write . . . for whom? "Give me children!" pleaded the Matriarch Rachel. . . . No children for my *mame-loshn.*
>
> What shall I do for you, my *mame-loshn*? Shall I seat myself upon a little mourning stool and lament, bewail you? Shall I write a "Scroll of Lamentations" with verses in alphabetic acrostic and pour into my tears the best, most beautiful words in my *mame-loshn*?[8]

The condition of Yiddish "*after*"—after Hitler, Stalin, Roosevelt, Ben Gurion—was fundamentally a condition of maternal bereavement. Kipnis compares *mame-loshn* to the Matriarch Rachel ("give me children, or else"), who figures in biblical and rabbinic literature as "weeping over her children," a genius of grief whose instinctual capacity for pathos serves as lesson and rebuke to the facile mourning of the patriarchs and the lawgiver Moses.[9] Whereas Mother Rachel demanded children in her lifetime and returned from the dead to witness their descendants' humiliation through destruction and exile, Mother Yiddish, *mame-loshn,* admits an anguished Kipnis, has no children left to console.[10] While some degree of grief and loss accompany the ordinary vicissitudes of children growing up, Kipnis grapples with the unnatural shock of a child predeceasing a parent. Without questioning his investment in Hebrew—the only logical outlet for his prodigious literary energies—he gauges, with unsparing candor, the cost of such choices for Yiddish.

Imagining a counterhistory in which Yiddish might yet flourish among young (secularist) readers, Kipnis closes his essay with a mawkish, fantastical poem. As Leonard Prager observes, "His prose-poem ending imagining future readers of his Yiddish stories abandons reality in favor of a fantasy vision—in which he does not believe."[11] The poem imagines "leftover Yiddish words" entrusted to golden nutshells, unlocked by angels, all to the telltale strains of a lullaby. The poetic skill displayed in Kipnis's many Hebrew lullabies is not evident here. Yet his writing "as if" there were a sunny future for Yiddish authorizes his presentation of the twin story collections to new, unknown audiences. If the task of his introductory essay is to synchronize the workings of time's *arrow* in his own life's course and that of the historical moment during which his lifetime has unfolded, almost concurrent with the twentieth century, then the burden of the stories themselves is to recruit time's *cycle* as a consolation. Like authors publishing in the diaspora, Kipnis reckoned with the decimation of Eastern European Jewry by teaching children—even the youth of the secular Left—about the Jewish holidays and their associated motifs, firmly reimplanting his readers in Jewish liturgical time even while celebrating their families' secularist identities.

Home *to* the Holidays: Postwar Cultural Preservation and Consolidation

The emphasis on holiday tales was a feature of postwar Yiddish children's literature the world over. The Jewish Education Committee (JEC) was formed in June 1939 as a central body to coordinate administrative, curricular, and financial activities among a wide range of Jewish school systems in New York City, including Yiddishist schools. In 1958, the JEC published its first collection of Yiddish children's poetry, a volume by New York–based professor of Hebrew and Jewish education Elkhonen Indelman (May 22, 1913–April 21, 1983), which moved through the liturgical calendar and was called, fittingly, "Gut yontef, kinder" (Happy Holidays, Children). In introducing the volume, educational leader and JEC consultant Yudl Mark notes, "Indelman was principally a Hebrew writer. But he belongs to the great Pleiades of Hebrew writers who are, at the same time, also Yiddish writers." As in the case of artists like Levin Kipnis, Yankev Fichman, Kadya Molodowsky, and Zina Rabinowitz, a warmth toward Hebrew accompanied a Zionist orientation. Mark also notes that the collected poems reflect Indelman's output "over the last several years," and his efforts to help children metabolize the legacy of the Holocaust is evident on the page. The holiday cycle was his strategy and solace.

Consider, for example, how he ushers the reader through the transition from Passover to the Feast of Weeks. This period of anticipation, during which the days are literally counted, overlaps traditionally with a period of light mourning for the death of the Rabbi Akiba's students in the time of the Talmud. Over the seven pages he devotes to Passover, Indelman treats a range of conventional themes connected to the Seder's liturgy: the four questions, the four sons, a grandfather's Haggadah booklet, infant and youthful Moses, the "lone kid" of the *chad gadya* song, and the prophet Elijah and his wine cup. But now this solemn time span must also incorporate a new liturgical moment: commemorating the Warsaw Ghetto Uprising. Thus does a brief interlude of three poems, labeled starkly as "Ghetto," intervene between the two biblical holidays. One lyric imagines incorporating a stone from the ghetto walls into a new house in the "sunny," "distant land" of Israel, while a second describes a monument consisting of two "Jewish hands" sculpted in stone. Finally, Indelman situates "Elijah the Prophet in the Ghetto" as a wizened, desolate figure, traversing the ash heaps of Ashkenazi civilization "with burning footsteps" and bemoaning the absence of children's voices. The Holocaust has changed him from ageless to aged, "petrified." Passover arrives, and there are none left to fill Elijah's cup. The poem's stanzas are divided by a stylized graphic depiction of a burning shtetl. But the vagaries of pagination dictate an end to grief, and the reader literally turns the page from the woe of ancient Elijah to a lyric poem for Shvues, the biblical Feast of Weeks (see Figure 3). Entitled "Rejoice, Kids!" the four rhyming stanzas decisively replace paralysis with energetic movement:

Rejoice, kids! Our green *yontef*s here
We've counted up the hours
Summer's spread out everywhere
Its foliage and flowers

The fields have donned their festive garb
In *yontef* greens they're draped
And even ruins, tombstones
In viridian best are caped

The sky has just out-blued itself
Sunbeams poke forth warm and mild
And with wondrous, babbling sounds
The streams are running wild

פרילינג

פרייט זיך, קינדער!

וואס איז פרילינג

דער פרילינג איז געקומען

38

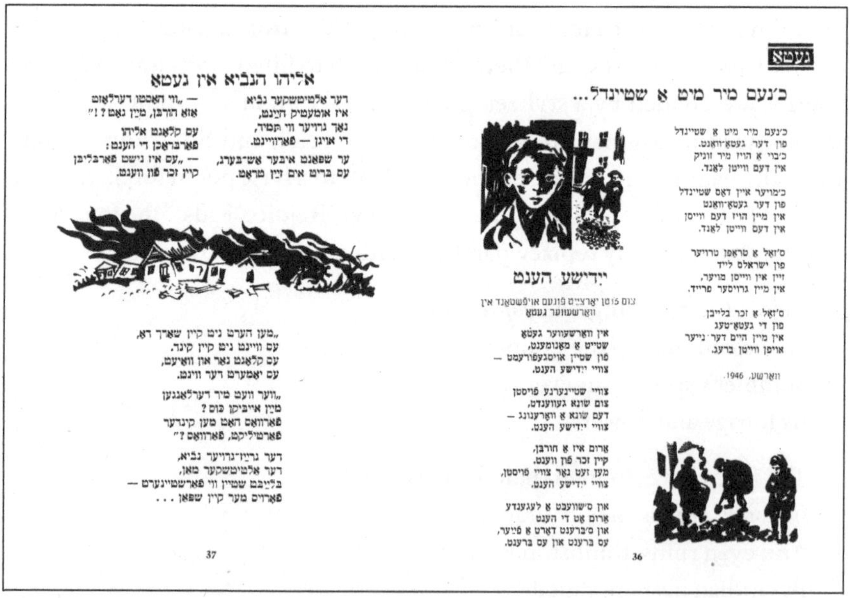

געטא

כ'נעם מיר מיט א שטיינדל...

אליהו הנביא אין געטא

יידישע הענט

37

36

FIGURE 3A AND B. Interior pages from an illustrated Yiddish children's book of holiday stories show the abrupt transition from Holocaust commemoration to welcoming spring. Elkhonen Indelman, *Gut yontef, kinder*, 1958.

May summer with its greenery
Our sadness cover over
With wondrous sounds awaken hope—
Fresh hope—amid the clover.[12]

The greenery associated with the early-summer holiday blankets ruins and tombstones and promises to cover over sadness itself. Even as late as 1958, this literature retains a strong Romantic bent. The solace of the liturgical calendar is synchronized with the natural cycle of the seasons.

The postwar bloom in holiday tales and poems included Mashe Shtuker-Payuk's 1957 *Gut yontef* (Happy Holiday), published in Buenos Aires, and Zina Rabinowitz's 1958 *Der liber yontef* (The Precious Holidays), appearing in New York with Farlag Matones. Both these works orient themselves markedly toward Zion, albeit usually from the perspective of diasporic locales and settings drawn from recent Jewish history. Rabinowitz emphasizes that Jewish identity rests on "doing Jewish," upholding ritual practices. In "A Jew Remains a Jew," a Nikolai-era conscript in the Tsar's army is restored to robust physical and spiritual health by regular meetings with a Jewish doctor, who helps "cure" his pathological assimilation with chicken soup, together with ritual education and engagement. "A Sukkah on the Pampa" describes the curious sight of a sturdy house with a retractable roof on the southern plains of Argentina; during their first Sukes season, the newly arrived agricultural colonists' conventional sukkah had blown down during the kiddush blessing. The "Jewish gauchos" subsequently learned to balance the exposure and vulnerability the holiday celebrates with the demands of their windswept environs. Rabinowitz often focuses on the theme of Jews detecting and recognizing one another in settings where they constitute a tiny minority or where the boundaries of the Jewish collective are fuzzy at the edges. Set in Casablanca, her "Mute Princess" describes how a young girl traumatized into transient mutism by the loss of her parents in a pandemic is received into a Jewish orphanage—her identity confirmed and her silence broken by her enthusiasm about kindling Sabbath candles.

An Alphabet Sustains Us: *Alef-Beyz* and Yiddish Language Instruction

In his anguished appeal to "Mother Yiddish," Levin Kipnis asks, "Should I write a new Eykho?" It is not incidental that the urtext of Jewish mourning he invokes, the biblical Book of Lamentations, is distinguished rhetorically by its chapters of alphabetic acrostic. According to Jewish mystical traditions, God fashioned the universe out of the letters of the Hebrew-Yiddish alphabet. The letters capable of registering the extent of successive waves of Jewish destruction (*khurbn*) are the very materials for cultural regeneration. As did Jeremiah, the hoary prophet of yore, the authors of Yiddish children's literature saw in the alphabet powerful tools for transcending mundane history. This alphabetic preoccupation underpins three children's genres: the true abecedary, whose task is to present each letter in alphabetical order, together with the sound it makes and, usually, exemplary words that begin with or include it; literacy primers, many of which begin with the (re-)presentation of the letter before moving on to letter combinations; and stories and plays that assume basic knowledge of the alphabet and recruit the letters as major characters.

An awareness of Jewish time doesn't necessarily lead to an awareness of Jewish language, but the Yiddishists picking up the shards of Jewish civilization at midcentury strove to make it so. Elkhonen Indelman concludes his holiday cycle, *Gut yontef, kinder,* with an abecedary in rhyming verse, "Mayn alef-beyz," that is typical of the genre. Some verses play with the letter's appearance, as in the stanza for *giml*:

> *Giml* wears a
> High boot—look!
> It's strolling right there
> Through your book.[13]

Giml is often depicted in boots, due to the echo of *gume* (*gime* in Polish pronunciation), the rubber favored for shoe soles. The shapes of the letters could be harnessed as mnemonics, and the memorization was reinforced through rhyme:

> Final *mem*
> Is shut up tight
> Like a garden
> Late at night. . . .
>
> *Nun*'s shaped like
> A phone that's ringing
> Pick up and hear
> What **n**ews it's bringing[14]

Other verses pun on the sound of the letter's name *and* its appearance:

Daled—**d***eles*
That means **d**oor
It's open; come see
What's in store.[15]

In Indelman's Polish Yiddish, the name of the tenth letter is homophonous with the word for Jew, *yid*; he toys with this longstanding identification (*dos pintele yid*, the tip of the letter *yud* understood as a kernel of "essential Jewishness") by winkingly describing both the letter and the prototypical European Jew as "short and pointy":

Yid—a yidl
Kirts un shpitsik.
Vilsti? Rif im . . .
Rif im: Itsik.[16]

Accounting separately for final letters and continuant (*veyz, fey*) and noncontinuant forms (*beyz, pey*), Indelman's alphabet contains twenty-eight letters. The 1947 *Alefbeys* published by Leyb Kvitko in Soviet Moscow includes twenty-nine, but there are only twenty-one letters in common between the two books. Yiddish was just one of the heritage languages that formed part of the Soviet Union, and like the others, its orthography was part of a highly politicized program of language reform leading up to and following the revolution. The concept of "a modern language for a modern people" required that Yiddish decouple itself from German by eliminating silent *h*'s and bringing the spellings of verb prefixes into conformity with most Yiddish speakers' actual pronunciation. More controversially, Soviet Yiddish strove to distance itself from the "regressive Hebraic past" by stamping out the residue of the language's ancient Semitic component: distinctive final letters and the phonemically redundant *khes, sin,* and *sof* that occur only in words of Hebrew-Aramaic origin.[17]

Kvitko's *Alefbeys* thoroughly Sovietizes Yiddish, counting as "letters" diphthongs, the consonant of the doubled *vov* (*tsvey vovn*), and sound combinations that represent phonemes common in Slavic words, such as *zsh* and *tsh* (see Figure 4). He omits all final letters and ends the alphabet with *shin*. He blends mnemonic details about the shapes and sounds of the letters with an alphabetical catechism of Soviet heroes, aims, and attitudes. The page devoted to *alef* is typical:

An alef hot fir ekelekh
A shtekl mit tsvey flekelekh

FIGURE 4. A chart shows the Yiddish and Soviet-era Russian alphabet. The Yiddish letters are shown in printing and script, omitting the "redundant" letters that occur only in words derived from Hebrew-Aramaic. Leyb Kvitko, *Alefbeys*, 1947.

—
Aleksander Matrosev iz a held
A denkmol vert dem held geshtelt

—
Arbeter un poyerem
Arbetn banand
Aleyn tsu zey gehert
Ale giter funem land[18]

An alef has four legs:
A stick with two pegs

Aleksander Matrosev is a hero[19]
A monument is erected for him

Workers and peasants,
Together they band
To them alone belongs
All the bounty of the land

Kvitko, of course, was dispatched by Stalin in 1952, and the abecedary is one of his last works to appear during his lifetime. Perhaps the alphabet, buttressed by propaganda, seemed a relatively safe redoubt.

Kvitko's *Alefbeys* typifies the fuzzy line between many abecedaries and the literacy primers meant to carry a child through the process of decoding words. An early, unadorned volume published in Vilna in 1912 takes a phonics approach (which predominated in the Anglophone West until about 1930), while the frankly proletarian *Arbet-kinder alefbeyz*, published in 1930, rejects phonics in favor of the whole-word method.[20] In 1921, the distinguished fabulist and lifelong educator Eliezer Shteynbarg published a richly illustrated *Alef beyz* that, true to form, utilized strongly rhythmic rhyming fables to smooth the transit from syllable to syllable. Many of these early readers were aimed at teachers as much as parents, and their authors and editors often include an introduction laying out the pedagogical theory and assumptions undergirding a new work. David Hochberg's undated primer *Di naye shul* proclaimed the "sounds method" (i.e., phonics) superannuated, while in 1937, Dvoyre Tarant's IWO-affiliated *Mayn alefbeys* (My Alphabet) explained diplomatically that her book could be used for "visual, phonetic, and ideally, eclectic" methods.[21] Tarant notes that special pages are devoted not only to similar-looking letters but also to the sound *kh*, which was more difficult for American students to pronounce.[22]

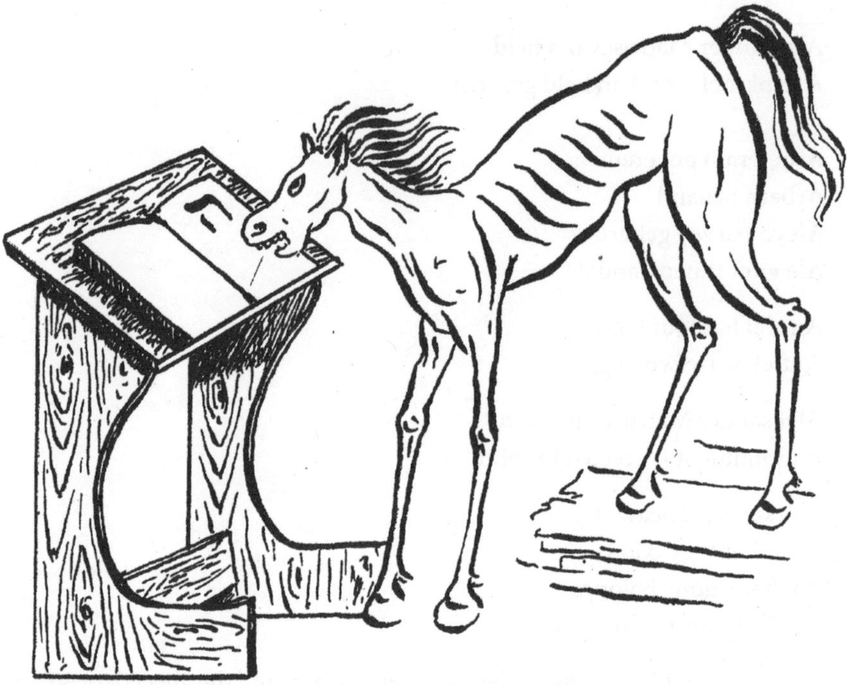

אַ פערדל מיט מאָגערע גלידער
זוכט אַ ביסל „ה״ אין סידור.

FIGURE 5. "What's he to do, / This skinnybones horse? / Look for some 'hay' in / The prayer book of course!"
An illustration from a children's book shows a skin-and-bones horse looking at the letter hey in a book displayed on a wooden lectern. Alef Kats, *Fun alef biz sof,* illustrated by Joseph Schoor, 1939.

In the work of New York–based A. Kats, we can trace how one author registered the Holocaust's destruction through an alphabetic cataclysm.[23] On the eve of the war, in 1939 he published an abecedary called *Fun alef biz sof* (From Alef to Sof), delightfully illustrated by Joseph Schoor, that presents twenty-three letters in straightforward fashion. Very few of the objects exemplifying the various letters are politically or religiously charged, although the uniquely

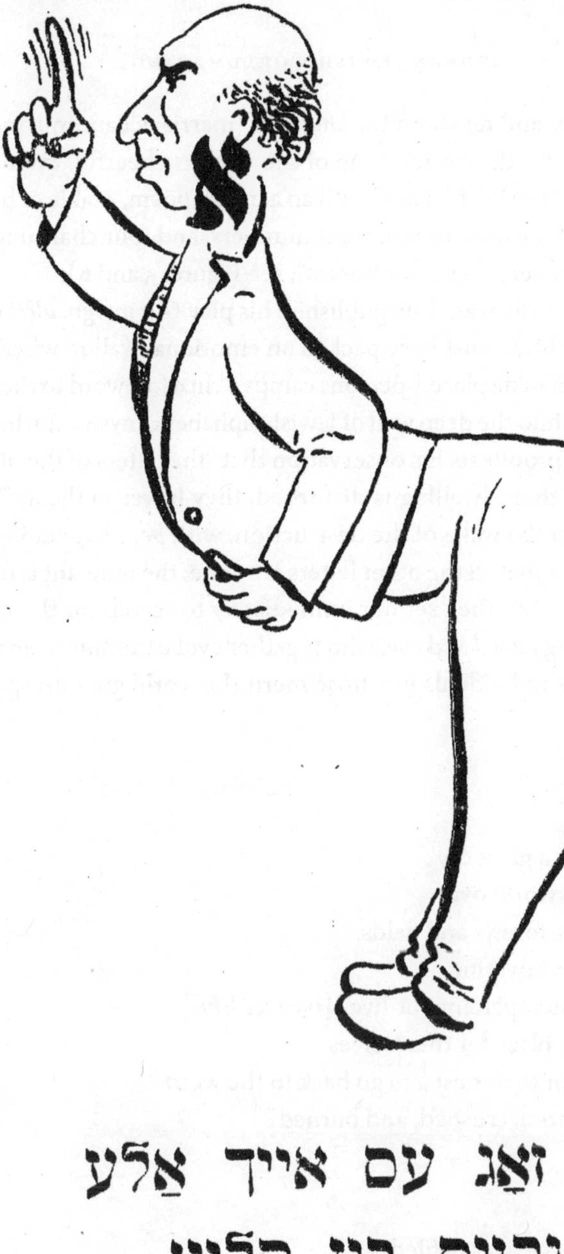

FIGURE 6. "I'm telling you all, / Great and small: / When there's an alef in 'lo,' / It means no, no, NO!"
A drawing shows a man whose posterior protrudes so that his body is bent into the shape of the letter lamed, wagging his finger. The letter alef is superimposed on his neck so that he spells out the word *lo* [no]. Alef Kats, *Fun alef biz sof*, illustrated by Joseph Schoor, 1939.

Hebraic letters *khes* and *tof* stand for *khuppah* (marriage canopy) and *toyre* (Torah), respectively. The overall tone of the work is cheerful, even comic. Kats supplements these "alef-basics" with an acrostic poem, a table of how the letters are traditionally used to represent numbers, and four charming mnemonic cartoons ([letter] "*hey* is for horses"; see Figures 5 and 6).

Immediately after the war, Kats published his play *Gut morgn, alef!* (Good Morning, Alef!), which must have packed an emotional wallop when it was first staged, in German displaced-persons camps.[24] In a foreword to the script, Katz explicitly taps into the deep well of Jewish alphabetic mysticism, buttressing with Talmudic prooftexts his observation that "the letters of the *alef-beyz* are eternal. When their dwelling is disturbed, they hover in the air."[25] The bleak play begins in the wake of the destruction, with *beyz* happening upon *alef* and alerting him that all the other letters are gone; the remnant is now "an *alef-beyz* in name only." They set out immediately to search for the missing letters, encountering *lamed* and *vov*, who together evoke the *lamed-vovniks*, or thirty-six righteous individuals in whose merit the world goes on spinning. They are bereft:

Vov:

I know . . . I hear a great cry
From letters the world over
In cities, villages, forests and fields.
The cry of letters hovering,
Expelled from their parchment-lives [*parmet-lebn*].
They can't find a place for themselves
And they long for their nests, to go back to the word
That was pulverized, crushed, and burned!

Lamed:

The whole language was defiled
Nary a word without a corpse
And everyone waits for a miracle![26]

As the Jewish people have been expelled from their homes and decimated, so have the letters been driven out of their settled existence, the words that were their "nests." "The tiny Jewish letters," notes Shmuel Charney, "are living creatures for Alef Kats. *Alef, beys, giml, lamed* and *vov, nun* and *samekh* are the heroes and play roles in this dramatic work. . . . The tragic drama of the Jewish letters becomes an allusion for Kats to the tragedy of the Jewish people, who are the people of writing, the people of the letter."[27] The four reunited letters cross paths with the fiery lion who has wrought the destruction by gorging on—burning—books. His terrifying monologue is a portrait of rapacity, complete with the identification of the letter *yud* with the person *yid*. He roars out his hunger for a seed kernel (*yoderl*) to chew on, a *yidele* to digest. Eventually the conflagration expires, appropriately enough as they run into *nun* and *samekh*, who spell *nes*, or miracle. A heavenly voice joins the six letters' colloquy, absolving them of guilt. Soon all the letters are reunited, but there are no scribes, authors, or speakers to give them life. At last, the prophet Elijah appears with a boy and begins teaching him to recite the alphabet. The letters rejoice at the new life they will enjoy through the surviving child.[28]

In reading Kats's drama alongside sunnier works that also use the motif of the missing letter, it becomes clear that the alphabet can represent not only the dolors of displaced persons but also a general communitarian ideal of mutual accountability. The letters inscribe a model of *di kinder fun yisroel*, the Jewish collectivity, wherein one lost or silenced member jeopardizes the well-being and functionality of the whole and constitutes a crisis on which all possible resources must immediately be brought to bear. This holds true whether the conflict results from a hasty judgment being imposed on the "big, bad *beyz*" that YIVO's founding linguist, Max Weinreich, devised to tickle the fancy of his seven-year-old son, Gabi, or a letter gone missing, which supplies a ready-made quest plot.[29] In a restrictive sense, all twenty-two letters are bound together and mutually interdependent to form words and convey meaning, but in a far broader sense, as for Kats, all Hebrew-Yiddish letters everywhere are bound to the fate of the Jewish people.

AFTERWORD

HASIDIC HERRING AND SWEDISH FISH: WHERE YIDDISH CHILDREN'S LITERATURE LIVES TODAY

WHERE DOES Yiddish children's literature live today? It thrives, as does the Yiddish language, in two distinct milieux. One is the secularist circles that are the most direct heir to the educational and artistic project documented in this book. Although New York, Melbourne, Buenos Aires, Mexico City, and Tel Aviv might be considered the contemporary capitals of secular Yiddishism, a great deal of publishing activity—especially for young readers—has shifted to Sweden, where Yiddish was designated an official minority language in 1999 and receives government financial support. Swedish public radio and television produce Yiddish-language content for adults and children, and the publishing house Olniansky Tekst, founded in 2010, focuses on stories for young readers. Their offerings include popular works rendered *into* Yiddish, most notably Arun Viswanath's ingenious translation of *Harry Potter and the Philosopher's Stone*, a sold-out blockbuster in relative terms.

The Olniansky catalogue is available on the firm's website and in a virtual storefront on the merchant website Etsy, known for items artistic and artisanal. The married team who founded the enterprise curate a selection of elegantly produced picturebooks and storybooks by contemporary Yiddish authors, as well as reissues of works by classic writers like Kadya Molodowsky. A few of the titles have specific reference to Swedish Jewry, such as *Der Lunder vunder* (*The Wonder from Lund*), while others might have just as easily been published anywhere. All in all, the small scope of the operation reflects the fact that among non-Hasidic speakers and readers, Yiddish functions more as a postvernacular cultural treasure than as an everyday language. The allocation of shared resources, most of which came through the tax dollars of non-Jewish Swedes, represents a broad social consensus in Sweden that Yiddish and a few other minority languages bound up in the country's history are worth preserving.

Hasidic Yiddish is a whole different kettle of herring. Due to the cultural valorization of Yiddish, combined with high birthrates, Hasidic communities constitute an organically thriving market for Yiddish children's merchandise. It is telling that the most dominant companies produce a combination of books, music, toys, and games: empires of interrelated *haymish* (familiar), didactic, mutually reinforcing content.[1] Thanks to vagaries of manufacture and distribution that extend far beyond the scope of my research—but which must surely include factories in Asia and global supply chains, all undergirded by the internet—the available materials for worldmaking now include not only words and music, but also board and card games, plastic action figures (Mitzvah Kinder Mentchees competing with Kindervelt Mentchies), an electronic toy violin preprogrammed with klezmer tunes, and Resticks Reusable Stickers that situate a child's implied avatar in familiar settings that include Shopping (for groceries, toys, shoes, and clothing), Community Chesed (first responders, including the Hatzolah ambulance corps), Mazel Tov (new baby, *upshern* or first haircut, wedding, and birthday), and Dollhouse (kitchen, living room, kids' room, backyard). The backyard, to judge by its proportions and greenery, is not in Brooklyn. The idealized aesthetics of the injection-molded Hasidic family and the settings to which it sticks impart a new meaning to "cultural plasticity."[2]

It is difficult not to notice the sharp gender binary that bisects the visual, aural, and rhetorical world that is being reflected in and perpetually remade by these products. Lechaim Productions offers pink-and-pearl-bedecked Shabbos Mommy and blue Shabbos Tatty sets. The former includes snood, apron, tray, two candles, charity box, and plastic coins to uphold the custom of giving charity when lighting Sabbath and holiday candles. The corresponding set for boys includes kiddush cup, serrated (wooden) knife, two challah loaves, and a cloth cover. Mommies light candles, and tatties preside over the mealtime rituals. In countless Hasidic children's books, girls help their mothers prepare food and clean for Shabbos, while boys and their fathers enter the resplendent household after davening in shul (praying in synagogue). In her study of gender and Hasidic children's literature, Asya Vaisman Schulman notes that while the Divine Father is strongly present, flesh-and-blood fathers are mostly absent.[3] The addressee of these stories is still reading in the orbit of the mother; to gravitate toward the symbolic and actual world of the father is to put down *bikhelekh* (storybooks) and pick up *seforim* (holy books).[4]

A significant disjuncture between Hasidic children's literature and the secular work of a century ago is that contemporary stories and toys aimed at girls seek to hold them closer than ever to the domestic realm. Like the Warsovian original, a contemporary Olke might also enjoy a cozy domesticity for herself under a blue, or now more likely a pink, *parasolke*, but the buttons she is asked to sew might not rebel if they were situated in Hasidic Williamsburg. Reusable stickers seem to occupy an outsize place in the Hasidic toy pantheon, perhaps because of their utility in keeping children quietly occupied on long Shabbos afternoons. In addition to the implicitly gendered Resticks sets from Kinder Shpiel catalogued above, Lechaim Productions ("a leading provider of kosher entertainment and education for the heimishe community and beyond since 1982") explicitly tags "The Babysitting Center" as "Girl," while the "Boy" designation is attached to the more adventuresome "A Tug Tzim Gedenken" (A Day to Remember).[5] Even if only notionally, boys enjoy access to the open road.

It is also notable that "The Babysitting Center" is in English, while the equivalent boys' toy is named in Yiddish. Ayala Fader observes that in most Hasidic communities (with Satmar as the exception), girls' grasp of Yiddish is more tenuous than their brothers' because no dedicated Yiddish-speaking schools existed for girls from the postwar migration to the United States until the 1980s. The generation of girls who attended public or non-Hasidic Jewish day schools and who consequently struggle to use Yiddish as a vernacular are now grandmothers and great-grandmothers.[6] Economic norms whereby women are breadwinners in many families and often work in sectors beyond the relatively insular community reinforce the need for girls to master English, thus distancing them from Yiddish as they mature. However, the passage from girl to mother often renews a woman's purchase on the Yiddish of the kitchen, the nursery, and (where finances permit) the playroom. Even in communities where girls grow up less fluent in *mame-loshn*, Fader has observed "a trans-Hasidic children's register" used for talking with babies and toddlers and, presumably, for spending time in the company of other women who are doing the same.[7] Reproduction pulls women inexorably back to Yiddish.

The covers of the five-volume Kinder Shpiel encyclopedia series *A velt fun yediyes* (A World of Knowledge) are not dissimilar to those of the *One Million Things* titles that my children loved thumbing through. But whereas my children might come across a picture of a sow nursing her piglets or the telltale curves of a woman's silhouette on a page about human anatomy, Hasidic families choose these books and toys specifically to "guard the eyes" against such compromises. Looking at a pig is not tantamount to eating one, but if you avoid so much as looking at one, you certainly won't come to eat one. "Labeling certain texts as 'clean' or 'kosher' creates a parallel between reading and the

Jewish dietary laws [*kashrus*]," notes Fader. "Both the Jewish dietary laws and the censoring of books are attempts to control what is put into the body and mind."[8] A century and a half ago, secularist Yiddish cultural leaders were equally concerned about the literary diet of children in their ambit, giving rise to the invention of what I've called "Enlightenment kale chips." Hasidic families are less tolerant of modernity but perhaps more tolerant of cake.

Consider the Kinder Shpiel title *Yeshayeles upshern* (*Isaiah's First Haircut*), by Rabbi Berl Sofer (see Figure 7). The preschooler depicted on the book's cover, newly shorn and flanked by an older brother, his father, and his teacher, is about to lick honey off a tablet printed with the *alef-beyz*. A celebratory cake stands at the ready. Contemporary Hasidim have fused the ceremony for a boy's first haircut, at age three, with the initiation rituals described in chapter 4 into one megacelebration of becoming visually legible as a boy with earlocks, yarmulke, and ritual fringes, a boy who studies Torah in the actual company of his teacher and the symbolic company of his father.

But I want to talk about Yeshayele's cake. It is inscribed with two biblical verses, in keeping with instructions detailed in the twelfth-century code Sefer HaRokeah, by Rabbi Elazar of Worms.[9] The Torah initiation ceremony that he describes takes place on the holiday of Shvues and seems to entail collective participation by a given town's little boys. Their exact age is not specified, and the Rokeah's language jumps between plural and singular, although the elements of the rite are clearly designed to evoke the Revelation at Sinai. The boy is covered with a garment lest he see a dog, emblem of impurity, on his way to commence learning. He is brought to the synagogue or the teacher's house and placed on his teacher's lap. A tablet bearing the Hebrew alphabet and a few simple verses is placed before him. One by one, he repeats the letters after his teacher forward and backward; after all, the letters are the tools of worldmaking, to be wielded capably in all directions. He repeats the verses, word for word. Honey is smeared on the tablet for the boy to lick from the letters, cementing the association between sweetness and learning. Then comes the honey cake, incised with these ancient—and puzzling—words from Isaiah, 50.4–5:

> The Lord God gave me a skilled tongue,
> To know how to speak timely words to the weary.
> Morning by morning, [God] rouses,
> Rouses my ear
> To give heed like disciples.

FIGURE 7. A storybook cover shows a small child after his first haircut, on the lap of his teacher and with his father and an older brother standing by. On the table before him is a placard with the Hebrew alphabet next to a jar of honey and a cake incised with biblical verses. Cover. Berl Sofer, *Yeshayeles upshern*, 2008.

The Lord God opened my ears,
And I did not disobey,
I did not run away.

Isaiah has preceded these verses with a trenchant rebuke of the people's heedlessness, and he follows them with a declaration of his resolve to "set [his] face like flint" against all who would flog or insult him. He proclaims his defiance and fortitude under the blasting pressures of serving as God's own mouthpiece. Again, instructs the medieval manual, the teacher reads word by word and the new pupil repeats after him. It's not what I would think to write on a birthday cake, but unlike Elazar of Worms, I have not lost my spouse and children in the Crusades.

There is one more element in the Rokeah's version of the ceremony. The boy is served a peeled, hard-boiled egg, inscribed with the words of Ezekiel 3:3. In the biblical context, the prophet has just been instructed to swallow a scroll, "as [God] said to me, 'Mortal, feed your stomach and fill your belly with this scroll that I give you.' I ate it, and in my mouth, it tasted as sweet as honey." Rabbi Elazar instructs, predictably by now, that the teacher read the verse word by word and the boy repeat it. "And they feed the lad," he concludes, "the cake and the egg because it is good for [the] opening [of] his heart."

Yes, they feed him the sweet cake with its bitter words, and the mildly savory egg with its sweet ones, and he ingests it all. That *the words were as honey* was as true for Kadya Molodowsky and Zina Rabinowitz, Leyb Kvitko and Levin Kipnis, as it was for Ezekiel and Isaiah, for Elazar of Worms and for the legions of little Menachem Mendls flung by their parents' sacred *shlikhus*, or mission, to the four corners of this earth. As in the ceremony itself, there is a scrambling together, a simultaneity and fusion—of *haymish* late-capitalist toy-game-book-music empires with medieval martyrdom and improbable survival, of ancient biblical verses with *upshern* party favors and Instagram-worthy tablescapes, of cartoonish illustrations with prophetic disenchantment, of pride in Jewish distinctiveness with shame at Jewish defenselessness, of an alphabet mastered forward and backward, of salty and sweet, bitter and savory, and, even as I write these words, of participant and observer. Yes, the cake and the egg taken together do indeed open the heart.

Throughout these pages, I have argued that we can better understand the shape of a culture's aspirations by examining critically the materials that it hands to its children. As *farbrente yidishistn*, fiery Yiddishists, did a century ago, we are all still counting on children's literature to bequeath a legacy to new generations, a set of vessels for them to fill and fulfill in new yet recognizable ways that connect past to future. A little boy ensconced in a prayer shawl differs in some important ways from a little girl under the blue *parasolke* that constituted her home and sky both—but they speak equally to an enduring Jewish cultural swaddling, a determination to wrap our children in story before sending them into the larger world. The earliest and most urgent parental prerogative—feed the baby!—shades imperceptibly into nourishing the mind with books. Eat this, not that. Don't read *that*; read *this*: It's *haymish* (in Brooklyn), it's *heymish* (in Manhattan).

The wish for a *shenere un besere velt,* a more beautiful and better world, that animated secular Yiddish children's literature is still alive and well in Boro Park, Williamsburg, and Kiryas Joel. The same wistful longing for wholeness is discernible in the retrojection of an idealized past in which the chain of Yiddish fluency is imagined to have continued unbroken. But the wish is equally alive in Overland Park and Brookline, Mexico City, Toronto and Modiin—all places where the break with Yiddish is undeniable. The Yiddish children's literature of the twentieth century satisfies a hunger the body politic has not been aware of even feeling. The time was right, a century ago, to consciously dismantle internalized Jewish shame and to replace it with a capacious vision of Jewish—and human—dignity. It is a quintessentially human urge to hand our children something more whole, more just, more perfect than what was handed to us. New life perforce demands new hope.

A NOTE ON ORTHOGRAPHY, TRANSLITERATION, AND TRANSLATION

YIDDISH WORDS and phrases have generally been rendered according to the transliteration guidelines of the YIVO Institute for Jewish Research, with deviations to enhance clarity, retain significant regional variations (as in rhyming words), or indicate original source spellings that predate the standardization system. With respect to names, I have defaulted to YIVO unless the author was well known by another spelling (Sholem Asch, Kadya Molodowsky) or by an Anglicized version of their name (such as Joseph Schoor). In keeping with prevailing convention, I refer to Sholem Aleichem in English, while utilizing Sholem Aleykhem for Yiddish sources in the bibliography, and deferring to Sholom Aleichem in the bibliography where other authors have chosen that spelling. Translations are mine unless otherwise noted.

ACKNOWLEDGMENTS

THE LONGER it takes to write a book, the more assistance and encouragement there are to acknowledge, and greater grows the risk of forgetting someone. Please forgive the inevitable oversight. It is exceptionally difficult to teach and write at the same time, which is why I am so grateful to the funders who helped me access the quiet to create this volume: the Workmen's Circle/Dr. Emanuel Patt Visiting Professorship in Eastern European Jewish Studies at the YIVO Institute (2015–16), Emory's Interdisciplinary Faculty Fellowship (2015–17), the Senior Fellowship at the Fox Center for Humanistic Inquiry (2018–19), the NEH Public Scholar Grant (2021–22), Scholar-in-Residence in Jewish Women's and Gender Studies at the Hadassah Brandeis Institute (2022), and the Robert S. Rifkind Senior Fellowship at the Center for Jewish History's Institute for Advanced Research (2024–25). To apply for such funding is to articulate the stakes of one's work anew, and this exercise has gradually expanded my own understanding of the book I was writing and its potential. The Covenant Foundation's Family Education Fellowship has enabled me to offer the fruits of my research on Yiddish children's literature to children and families in real time, an extraordinary gift.

Colleagues in Emory's German Studies department and Tam Institute for Jewish Studies tolerated my absences from teaching and academic leadership during academic and parental leaves. For engaging deeply with my ideas, I am especially grateful to Eric Goldstein, Kate Rosenblatt, Caroline Schaumann, Didem Uca, and Ofra Yeglin. Beyond my home units at Emory, I prize intellectual fellowship with Allison Adams, María Carrión, Kevin Corrigan, Rose Deighton-Mohammed, Andra Gillespie, Elena Glazovna-Corrigan, Falguni Sheth, Ben Reiss, Mandy Suhr-Sytsma, Donna Troka, and Yanna Yannakakis. I gratefully acknowledge the support of Michael Elliott, Carla Freeman, and Barbara Krauthamer during critical periods in the completion of this work.

The staff members with whom I have worked most closely, especially since assuming the directorship of the Tam Institute for Jewish Studies in 2022, include Paul Entis, Brent Buckley, and Malory Mibab, as well as Terez Whatley-White in German Studies. No great academic vision comes to fruition without the partnership of staff.

The confidence to read boldly rests on my access to sources in their original languages. I continue to rely on my teachers Bernard Septimus and María Elena Villalba, as well as Yiddishist friends and teachers Zackary Sholem Berger, Kolya Borodulin, Dovid Braun, Dovid Forman, Daniel Galay, Itzik Gottesman, Jordan Kutzik, Brukhe Lang, Eddy Portnoy, Rukhl Schaechter, Asya Vaisman Schulman, Seb Schulman, Perl Teitelbaum, Arun Viswanath, Meena-Lifshe Viswanath, and Sheva Zucker. Two special teachers, who I hope will read the book inextricably as scholars *and* grandparents, are Ruth Wisse and David Roskies.

Something like the Yiddish *glik*, a combination of joy and luck, is what I feel in relation to the generous and insightful "frolleagues" who have united friendship and collegiality: Eliyana Adler, Alona Bach, Adina Bar-El, Elissa Bemporad, Sarah Bunin Benor, Joel Berkowitz, Tali Berner, Dainy Bernstein, Ayelet Brinn, Matthew Brittingham, Alec Leyzer Burko, Justin Cammy, Marc Caplan, Madeleine Cohen, Yael Darr, Sonia Gollance, Jodi Eichler-Levine, Adam Ferziger, Dovid Fishman, Anna Gonshor, Rachel Beth Gross, Kathryn Hellerstein, Lisa Fishbayn Joffe, Irene Kacandes, Miri Freud-Kandel, Ellen Kellman, Barbara Kirshenblatt-Gimblett, Yuliya Komska, Chana Kronfeld, Mikhail Krutikov, Josh Lambert, Jon Levissohn, Adi Mahalel, Viktoriia Medvied, Miriam Mora, Anne Eakin Moss, Kenneth Moss, David Myers, Hannah Pollin-Galay, Michal Raucher, Lawrence Rosenwald, Claudia Rosenzweig, Rachel Rubinstein, Elisha Russ-Fishbane, Allison Schachter, Devorah Schoenfeld, Naomi Seidman, Sasha Senderovich, Karen Skinazi, Samuel Spinner, Anna Elena Torres, Shayna Weiss, Meyer Weinshel, Beruriah Wiegand, Jennifer Young, Saul Noam Zaritt, Jack Zipes, and Steven Zipperstein.

As this material took shape, I cherished invitations to speak on campus from the following: Deena Aranoff (Graduate Theological Union), Sa'ed Atshan (Swarthmore College), Jeremy Dauber and Agi Legutko (Columbia), Emily Finer (University of St. Andrews), Charlotte Fonrobert (Stanford), David Graizbord (Arizona State University), Rachel Harris (Florida Atlantic University), Jessica Kirzane (University of Chicago), Leslie Morris (University of Minnesota), Ranen Omer-Sherman (University of Louisville), Avinoam Patt (New York University), Anna Shternshis (University of Toronto), and Jennifer Thompson (California State University at Northridge).

Some careful readers of the work leading up to this volume grasped the totality of my project as well as or better than I have. I thank Miriam Anzovin,

Michelle Clark, Joanna Degler (Lisek), Caroline Emig, Eitan Kensky, Veronica Schanoes, Emily Schneider, Sean Sidky, and Laura Watkinson for their perceptive reviews.

I thank Carol Henderson and Ari Sollish for reviewing passages with sensitive content about minoritized groups.

I have taught my way into many of the insights in this book, treasuring opportunities to develop courses at the YIVO Institute (thanks to Alex Weiser and Ben Kaplan) and the Yiddish Book Center (thanks to Aaron Lansky, Susan Bronson, and their staff). Other friends have reinforced the currency of this work beyond the academy, including Michael Alpert, Shane Baker, Rachel Barenbaum, Jordan Hirsch, and Rokhl Kafrissen. The Jewish children's literature community, as convened by Susan Wodiska Kusel and Heidi Rabinowitz, has embraced this research, and I owe special thanks to Marjorie Ingall and Nancy Churnin.

If, as kabbalistic teaching maintains, the world's continued flourishing rests on the righteous actions of thirty-six *lamed-vovnikim*, then surely at least twenty-five of them are librarians and archivists. I am indebted to Amanda Miryem-Khaye Seigel and Lyudmila Sholokhova at the New York Public Library Dorot Division, Stefanie Halpern at YIVO, Haim Gottschalk at the Library of Congress, Michelle Margolis at Columbia University Libraries, David Mazower at the Yiddish Book Center, Vardit Samuels at Harvard Judaica Collection, Zachary Baker at Stanford University Libraries (emeritus), and Katalina Rac and Jenny Vitti at Emory Libraries.

Much of this book was researched during the pandemic, when I relied on research assistants Sophie Edelhart, Ari Greenberg, and Michelle Natanzon. Anita Gallers shared Patt family lore and offered me access to her translation of Yankev Patt's chronicle of his niece Hannah's activism during her confinement in the ghetto. Jake Yankl Krakovsky eventually provided some research and translation assistance too, along with teaching assistance and collaboration on the film *Labzik: Tales of a Clever Pup*; more expansively, however, he embodied what it means to follow one's Yiddish dreams. What a privilege to be part of the first steps on his journey into the Yiddish theater arts!

This is a book about what it means to be simultaneously a mother, a scholar, and a writer. Over a decade ago, Marc Caplan observed, trenchantly, that "children's literature research is women's and gender studies by another name." Over many vicissitudes, not all of them cheerful, this manuscript found especially vigorous support and advocacy from its squadron of godmothers: Mara Benjamin, Ayala Fader, Jessica Kirzane, Leslie Morris, and Anita Norich. I acknowledge with gratitude some special sisterhoods: the JAMs, the alumnae of Sara Fredman's blog *Write Like a Mother*, and my colleagues and students at Yeshivat Maharat.

The journey to publication was aided by Elisheva Urbas, who taught me that not every editor's "pass" is a "rejection-rejection" and lifted my spirits by noting, "Once you know what you want to say, you're pretty good at saying it." I am so grateful to acquiring editor Anne Savarese and copyeditor Kelley Blewster for their attentive reading and gentle editorial hands, as well as to the peer reviewers. Likewise, I acknowledge Sherry Gerstein and the production team, working in tandem with the design and marketing teams. It is a blessing to have had Susan Schulman in my corner and to work with Javier Perez on helping the book find its readers.

I wish that I were sharing the joy of publication with some who are with us no longer. Paula Cohen, the illustrator of *Honey on the Page*, would have delighted in this volume. As the endnotes will show, Naomi Prawer Kadar's pioneering study of Yiddish children's periodicals has been my constant companion; I never got to meet her but feel a kinship through our work. Finally, David Biale was an early supporter of my scholarship, and the conceptualization of "the secular" in chapter 3 owes a discernible debt to him.

So many friends and relatives have buoyed me during this book's long gestation; I particularly thank Wendy Amsellem and Mike Moskowitz (who brought me a copy of *Yeshayele's upshern*), Shoshana Dayanim, Cheryl Haas, Miryam Kabakov, Chavi Eve Karkowsky, Yovanna Madhère, Ashley Marx, Rivka Monheit, Ann Schiff, Dena and Eliyahu Schusterman, Ari Sollish, Zelda Stern, Anne Sullivan, Aaron Udel, Ariel Udel, Lisa Fletcher-Udel, Annie Washburn, and all our friends at Congregation Ramath Orah. Deborah Fernhoff has made my thinking more flexible, and DJ Johnson has helped me become the strongest rabbi he knows.

It is a particular thrill to have children old enough to read and engage with my scholarship. Yitz and Kobi, I hope you will enjoy this book even if you do so in microdoses. This volume is dedicated in large part to my parents, with gratitude for the reader that each of them helped me to become.

Earlier, partial versions of chapter 3 appeared in the following articles: "The Second Soul of the People: Secular Sabbatism in Yiddish Children's Literature," *Jewish Social Studies* (Spring 2016), 78–104; and "The Sabbath Tale and Jewish Cultural Renewal," *Children and Yiddish Literature from Early Modernity to Post-Modernity*, ed. Mikhail Krutikov, Gennady Estraikh, and Kerstin Hoge (Oxford: Legenda, 2016), 20–39. An early extract of chapter 8 appeared as "State and

Family in Radical Yiddish Children's Literature," *Paper Brigade*, Jewish Book Council, 2019, under the sagacious editorship of Becca Kantor. Part of chapter 10 appeared in "Tales of Catholic Popes of Jewish Origins: On Jewish Cultural and Ethnic Plasticity," *Eastern Europe Unmapped: Beyond Contiguities*, ed. Irene Kacandes and Yuliya Komska (New York: Berghahn Press, 2018), 31–52.

Manu, when I started researching this book, you hadn't been born yet. When I started writing it in earnest, you were just learning to read. When it is published, you will be well launched on what I hope is a long lifetime of reading to learn—and also, reading to feel, to connect, and to delight. Adam Zachary, you gave our son the gift of that ability, and so many others. And as you have taken your loving scalpel to this manuscript, I have taken my needle and thread to your cartoon heart. Listen to Maria Taylor, if not to your wife:

And did you know electricity favors us

And did you know I'm not reading into anything

And did you know our love will never die.

NOTES

Preface

1. On the ideological contests enshrined in the very name with which the language is identified, see Saul Noam Zaritt, *A Taytsh Manifesto: Yiddish, Translation, and the Making of Modern Yiddish Culture* (New York: Fordham University Press, 2024).

2. On "historical poetics," see Saidiya Hartman, "Intimate History, Radical Narrative," Black Perspectives, website of the African American Intellectual History Society, May 22, 2020, https://www.aaihs.org/intimate-history-radical-narrative/. On "reading against the grain of prevailing knowledge systems," see Daniela K. Rosner, "Critical Fabulations Beyond Design," Medium, June 26, 2018, https://medium.com/@danielarosner/critical-fabulations-beyond-design-on-being-informed-by-saidiya-hartman-3509bd6e4f43

Introduction

1. Molodowsky, *Mayselekh: "Olke" and "Der taykh"* [Stories: "Olke" and "The River"]. For the English, see Kathryn Hellerstein, *Paper Bridges*, 180–89.

2. See Kondo, "Theoretical Scaffolding," 54.

3. For comparable "combined projects of nation-building and worldmaking," in relation to anticolonial nationalism in the Black Atlantic, see Adom Getachew, *Worldmaking After Empire: The Rise and Fall of Self-Determination* (Princeton, NJ: Princeton University Press, 2019), 11.

4. For a collation of contemporaneous articles bemoaning the fate of Yiddish, see Goldstein, "The Struggle over Yiddish in Postimmigrant America," 151, fn. 4.

5. bSotah 11b.

6. Udel, *Honey on the Page*, 42–43.

7. Udel, *Honey on the Page*, 43.

8. Exodus 15:2.

9. Udel, *Honey on the Page*, 44.

10. See Ball, "Max's Colonial Fantasy," and Kohl, *Should We Burn Babar?*

11. Originally composed as notes for a lecture given in March 1967, the French text was published as "Des Espaces Autres," in the French journal *Architecture-Mouvement-Continuité* in October 1984. English translation: Jay Miskowiec, "Of Other Spaces," *Diacritics* 16, no. 1 (1986): 22–27, 24.

12. See Peter Johnson, "Geographies of Heterotopia," 796–97.

13. Johnson, "Geographies of Heterotopia," 798.

14. Hofman, *Kleyne in der groyser velt.*

15. See Hazard, *Books, Children and Men* (1932; translated to English in 1944).

16. Mills, *Ethics and Children's Literature,* 1–12.

17. See Mickenberg and Vallone, *Oxford Handbook of Children's Literature.*

18. For an introductory overview, see Hintz and Tribunella, *Reading Children's Literature,* 53–54.

19. See Tatar, *Hard Facts of the Grimms' Fairy Tales,* especially chap. 1, "Sex and Violence: The Hard Core of Fairy Tales," 3–38.

20. See the introduction to Zipes, *Original Folk and Fairy Tales of the Brothers Grimm.*

21. See Marcus, *Minders of Make-Believe,* and Myers, "Impeccable Governesses."

22. Byford, *Science of the Child in Late Imperial and Early Soviet Russia,* 11.

23. Fishman, *Rise of Modern Yiddish Culture,* 96.

24. Fishman, *Rise of Modern Yiddish Culture,* 113, and Rubin, "'Like a Necklace of Black Pearls Whose String Has Snapped.'"

25. Max Weinreich, "Der YIVO un di problemen fun undzer tsayt" [YIVO and the Problems of Our Time], *YIVO bleter* Volume 25, Number 1, 1945 (3–18), 13.

26. Jake (Yankl) Krakovsky, director and puppeteer of Theater Emory's May 2020 film production of *Labzik: Tales of a Clever Pup.*

27. Ryan Bradburn was the fabricator for the production.

Chapter One: Reading Beyond Mother's Apron

1. Trunk, *Poyln* (English trans. unless otherwise indicated), 24. Quoted in Parush, *Reading Jewish Women* (henceforth RJW), 136–37.

2. Trunk, *Poyln,* 19.

3. Trunk, *Poyln,* 25; for the original Yiddish, see Trunk, *Poyln: Zikhroynes un bilder,* vol. 2, 173.

4. Trunk, *Poyln,* 18.

5. Trunk, *Poyln,* 27–28; Trunk, *Poyln: Zikhroynes un bilder,* vol. 2, 173.

6. On *mayse-bikhlekh,* see Quint, "'Yiddish Literature for the Masses'?" 65.

7. Trunk, *Poyln,* 26, 27, 28.

8. See Parush, RJW, where she argues that the relegation of women to the educational margins afforded them extraordinary freedom to consume fiction off limits to male elites, who were restricted to a diet of Talmud and Jewish Law.

9. Parush insists that women "absorbed maskilic values" from novels and other belletristic literature, even if they read primarily for escapist pleasure. RJW, 134.

10. On custom books in the context of the Jewish book of this period, see Gries, *The Book in the Jewish World.* Printed in Venice, Amsterdam, and Frankfurt, these custom books ushered in an age of illustration for *haggadot* and *bentshers* (grace after meals), though such adornments were not universally welcomed, given a residual suspicion of the visual arts. See Shlomo Berger, "The Spanish Pagan Woman and Ashkenazi Children Reading Yiddish," 11–12.

11. Shmeruk, "Sefer divre haadon shel Yaakov Frank," 99–100. Shmeruk traces the picture Frank describes to the Prague Haggadah of 1526 but leaves open the possibility that there existed

a *Sefer minhagim*, a book of customs, in which the same illustration appears, of which he was unaware. Also see Berner, "Jewish Children and Domestic Devotion in Early Modern Illustrations" (henceforth JCDD), 67–68, and *Al pi darkam* (henceforth APD), 101.

12. See Bereshit Rabba 1:34.

13. See Berner, JCDD, 68, on rhyming captions. Shmeruk, "Sefer divre haadon," 99, notes that in the Prague 1590 haggadah, the illustration was captioned as follows: "Pharaoh bathes in the blood of poor Jewish children / To heal his leprosy and come to no harm." On the vulnerability of books, see Newton, *To Make the Hands Impure.*

14. A further historical irony: Frank's doctrines and political embroilments resulted in a 1757 disputation decided in favor of the Frankists and resulting in the burning of ten thousand copies of the Talmud throughout Poland. The man was hard on books.

15. Seidman, *A Marriage Made in Heaven* (henceforth MMH), 29–30.

16. Chava Weissler traces this oft-cited phrase to the third chapter of the ethical treatise *Brantshpigl* (The Burning Mirror). See "'For Women and for Men Who Are like Women,'" 9–11.

17. In maskilic schools in Russia in the early nineteenth century, gender division and curricular stratification was the norm, with girls receiving more instruction in Russian language. See Parush, RJW, 89–91.

18. Parush, RJW, 136–37. On the distinction between *lernen* and *leyenen*, see Parush, RJW, 133, where she discusses Shmuel Charney's essay "Yiddish Literature and the Female Reader."

19. See Roskies, *Bridge of Longing*, 60.

20. Weissler, "'For Women and for Men Who Are like Women,'" 12–13, cites *Brantshpigl*'s quotation of a midrash to the effect that mothers accrue merit by preparing their sons for lives of literacy and learning.

21. Seidman, MMH, 29.

22. Parush, RJW, 136–37.

23. See Berner, JCDD, 70.

24. Reading aloud on the Sabbath was not an exclusively female prerogative and was often an entertainment for the whole family, which exposed children to adult religious texts. See Berger, "The Spanish Pagan Woman," 10. For reading on winter nights, see Parush, RJW, 140. The Sabbath reading documented in many primary sources forms an instructive contrast with the "bedtime story," a ritual that prevailed in Victorian sources and continues to predominate in the contemporary Western world as the site of shared, intergenerational encounters with books. See Patricia Crain, "Coda," 171–74.

25. *Ani hakatan* is a playful phrase that refers quite literally here to Scharfstein's tender age but that also carries the rhetorical sense of "little old me."

26. Parush, RJW, 137, citing Scharfstein, *Hayei Hayehudim*, 144.

27. See Berner, APD, esp. 101–2 and 160–61, on the expanding presence of printed matter in the typical Jewish home. See also Berner, JCDD, 66–71.

28. Seidman, MMH, 30, citing Weinreich, *History of the Yiddish Language*, 270–71.

29. See Marcus, *Rituals of Childhood.*

30. Seidman, MMH, 3.

31. Seidman, MMH, 29. See Mishna Bava Metzia 2: 11.

32. Seidman, MMH, 30.

33. Seidman, MMH, 30.

34. See Shmuel Charney, "Yiddish Literature and the Female Reader," 72. Charney published under the name Shmuel Niger. Due to its proximity to the racial slur for "Negro," many scholars now choose to identify him by his given surname, as I do throughout this volume. See Bromberg, "We Need to Talk About Shmuel Charney."

35. On age stratification for the sake of literacy instruction, see Berger, "The Spanish Pagan Woman," 14, and Shmeruk, "Sholem-Aleykhem un di onheybn fun der yidisher literatur far kinder" (henceforth SA).

36. Charney cites Eliyohu Bokher's translation of Psalms. He also cites as an early prototype of this formula the 1534 translation of Job. See Weinreich, *History of the Yiddish Language*, 276, for further examples.

37. Scholars debate whether it is more appropriate to treat the *Mayse-bukh* as a text, albeit an unstable one whose content varied throughout its several printings, or a genre—a style of compendium with broad norms and overlapping content. See Claudia Rosenzweig, "Getlekhe un nisht getlekhe mayses." In his foreword to Starck, *Un beau livre d'histoires*, Jerold C. Frakes calls the *Mayse-bukh* "a microcosm of early Yiddish literature."

38. The *Mayse-bukh* is cited from Baumgarten, *Introduction to Old Yiddish Literature*, 299.

39. Baumgarten, *Introduction to Old Yiddish Literature*, 300.

40. Charney, "Yiddish and the Feminine Reader," 71.

41. See Rosenzweig, "Getlekhe un nisht getlekhe mayses," esp. 221–22.

42. Baumgarten, *Introduction to Old Yiddish Literature*, 299.

43. See Roskies, *Bridge of Longing*, 24–25, for a discussion of Jacob ben Abraham's "sales pitch."

44. See BT Sotah 21b and the literature that has grown up to interpret the passage.

45. Baumgarten, *Introduction to Old Yiddish Literature*, 299.

46. Baumgarten, *Introduction to Old Yiddish Literature*, 300.

47. Dik was probably born in 1807, but he often gave out his birth year as 1814, likely to avoid conscription. On Dik, see chap. 3 of Roskies, *Bridge of Longing*. See also Caplan, *How Strange the Change*, and Eli Rosenblatt's introduction to Dik, "Slavery or Serfdom."

48. The exact chronology of Dik's youth still awaits clarification; see Roskies, "I. M. Dik and the Rise of Yiddish Popular Literature," 125.

49. See Rosenzweig, *Bovo d'Antona*, 19.

50. Many of Dik's stories were imported from European popular fiction traditions; see Roskies, "I. M. Dik and the Rise of Yiddish Popular Literature," esp. 223–32, and Roskies, *Bridge of Longing*, chap. 3. See also Roskies, "Yiddish Popular Literature and the Female Reader," 856.

51. For more on Dik's views on women, see Parush's discussion of *A maskils utopye* in RJW, 147–48, and Roskies, "I. M. Dik and the Rise of Yiddish Popular Literature," 232–33.

52. Parush, RJW, 145. See Feigenzohn, "History of the Romm Press."

53. On Dik's specific financial publishing arrangement, see Roskies, "I. M. Dik and the Rise of Yiddish Popular Literature," 114–15.

54. Cited by Parush, RJW, 144–45; and Roskies, "I. M. Dik and the Rise of Yiddish Popular Literature," 103–4, from Dik, "Foreword" to *Point and Counterpoint* [Mahazeh mul mahazeh] (second page of unnumbered text). I have adapted the translation from both sources.

55. In a footnote to *Di alte libe rostet nikht* [Old love doesn't rust] (Vilna, 1876), 17, cited by Roskies in "I. M. Dik and the Rise of Yiddish Popular Literature," 141.

56. See Roskies, *Bridge of Longing*, 72.

57. See Roskies, "I. M. Dik and the Rise of Yiddish Popular Literature," on the "bourgeois exemplum," 240.

58. See Roskies, "I. M. Dik and the Rise of Yiddish Popular Literature," 104.

59. See Cohen, "No More Little Jews Without Beards," 95.

60. Cited by Cammy, "Judging *The Judgment of Shomer*," 110.

61. Peretz, "Di lezerin," 108.

62. See Cammy, "Judging *The Judgment of Shomer*," as well as the translation in the same volume, "The Judgment of Shomer," 129–85.

63. Cammy, "The Judgment of Shomer," 135.

64. Shmeruk infers from Sholem Aleichem that children were reading Shomer ("Sholem-Aleykhem un di onheybn fun der yidisher literatur far kinder," 42), but Dora Schulner's memoir, "The First Writer I Read and Loved," makes it explicit.

65. Cited by Cammy, "Judging *The Judgment of Shomer*," 110. Originally from Reyzin, "Tsum 25stn yortsayt fun Shomer."

66. See Schulner, "First Writer."

67. For more on Jewish women's literacy at this time, see Parush and Brener, "The Politics of Literacy." For more on Jewish literacy in Kiev and its environs, see Meir, "Jews, Ukrainians, and Russians in Kiev," esp. 484–86.

68. Schulner, "First Writer," 29.

69. Schulner, "First Writer," 29, 30.

70. Mintz and Kellogg, *Domestic Revolutions*, 108.

71. See Parush, RJW, 153–54, and Dauber, "Shomer."

72. R. Brainin, "Vos zolen unzere kinder lezen?"

73. Brainin, "Vos zolen unzere kinder lezen?," 23: 2.

74. Brainin, "Vos zolen unzere kinder lezen?," 23: 2.

75. Brainin, "Vos zolen unzere kinder lezen?," 24: 4. Emphasis added.

76. Cammy translation, "The Judgment of Shomer," 134, 136.

77. See Cammy, "Judging *The Judgment of Shomer*," 114.

78. Schulner, "First Writer," 30.

79. Cammy translation, "The Judgment of Shomer," 183.

80. Brainin, "Vos zolen unzere kinder lezen?," 24: 5.

Chapter Two: What Children Need

1. Chone Shmeruk identifies Yoyl Berish Falkovitsh's introduction to his otherwise forgettable Judaizing adaptation of a German play for adults as the first text to mention Yiddish children's literature. See Shmeruk, SA, 41.

2. Shmeruk, SA, 41.

3. For an insightful analysis of the maskilic "pseudo-children's literature" that was created in Hebrew a century earlier, see Iris Idelson-Shein, "The Beginning of the End: Jews, Children, and Enlightenment Pedagogy," *Jewish Quarterly Review* 106, no. 3, (2016): 383–95.

4. Shmeruk infers that the *nyankes*, nannies, were not Jewish (SA, 41). If his supposition is true, Falkovitsh feared contamination from the doubly dangerous Christian and female influences in a Jewish child's life.

5. Cohen, "No More Little Jews Without Beards," 95–96.

6. See excerpt from Abramovitsh, "Introduction to the Collected Works."

7. On the broad cultural resonance of this metaphor, see Yudkoff, *Tubercular Capital*.

8. Brainin, "Vos zolen unzere kinder lezen?," 23: 1.

9. From its inception in the 1860s, Abramovitsh established "reality" as the lodestar of the modern Jewish fiction. See Miron, *A Traveler Disguised*, chap. 1, "The Commitment to Yiddish." David Roskies assesses the effects of Abramovitsh's realist bent on Sholem Aleichem; see his "Mythologist of the Mundane," 28.

10. Shmeruk, SA, 43.

11. In his introduction to the tales, Spektor explains that they were printed (*gedrukt*) for children; Shmeruk infers from this word choice that they might not originally been *written* with children in mind. I do not share Shmeruk's generally negative assessment of these stories. Shmeruk, SA, 42.

12. Udel, *Honey on the Page*, 59.

13. Shmeruk, SA, 43. For a nuanced exploration of "the Jewish primitive," see Samuel Spinner's *Jewish Primitivism*.

14. Shmeruk, SA, 43.

15. Shmeruk, SA, 42.

16. Cohen, "No More Little Jews Without Beards," 97.

17. For an inventory of Sholem Aleichem's writing for children, see Shmeruk, SA, 46.

18. Cited from Leviant's translation, "Why Darkness Befell Me."

19. Roskies, "Mythologist of the Mundane," 43.

20. See Sholem Aleichem, *Holiday Tales*.

21. Leviant translation, "Why Darkness Befell Me."

22. Leviant translation, "Why Darkness Befell Me."

23. Charney disagrees with this assessment, or he lays the emphasis elsewhere: "What a font of joy, what lightness and brightness, what a liveliness streams and sprays forth from the typical Jewish child's life, as Sholem Aleichem depicts it in his stories!" Charney, "Vegn der idisher kinder literatur," 189.

24. Wall, *The Narrator's Voice*, 2–3.

25. Shmeruk observes that while Sholem Aleichem makes no attempt to forge a youthful narratorial persona, the reader can tell the narrator is an adult speaking to children about his own childhood memories (SA, 46).

26. Shmeruk, SA, 47.

27. Published in Peretz's column, Fun bikher-tish [From the Book Desk], in the newspaper *Haynt*, June 28, 1912, 6. Cited in Cohen, "No More Little Jews in Beards," 97; expanded here. Peretz's Romantic sensibility elevated poetry. Brainin likewise invokes "poetry" as an unalloyed good—even if the poetry is drawn from natural history, while regarding prose, which in fact

dominated early Yiddish children's literature, as questionable. See Brainin, "Vos zolen unzere kinder lezen?" 24: 3–4.

28. Cited in Cohen, "No More Little Jews in Beards," 93.

29. Stearns, "Happy Children," 1; see also Steven Mintz, *Huck's Raft.*

30. Stearns, "Happy Children," 2.

31. See Ginger S. Frost, *Victorian Childhoods* (Westport, CT: Greenwood, 2009); Margot Hillel, "'She Faded and Drooped as a Flower': Constructing the Child in the Child-Rescue Literature of Late Victorian England," in *The Child in British Literature*, ed. A. E. Gavin (London: Palgrave Macmillan, 2012); C. Sutphin, "Victorian Childhood. Reading Beyond the 'Innocent Title': Home Thoughts and Home Scenes," in *Children's Literature*, ed. K. Lesnik-Oberstein (London: Palgrave Macmillan, 2004); and Jennifer Sattaur, *Perceptions of Childhood in the Victorian Fin-de-Siècle* (Newcastle, UK: Cambridge Scholars Publishing, 2011).

32. Stearns, "Happy Children," 6.

33. Rousseau, *Emile*, 79.

34. Wordsworth, "Ode: Intimations of Immortality from Recollections of Early Childhood," line 66, *Poems, in Two Volumes*, 1807.

35. See Charney, "Kinder literatur"; and Charney, "Vegn der idisher kinder-literatur," 188–90.

36. Charney, "Vegn der idisher kinder-literatur," 192.

37. For more on the self-conscious relation of Yiddish to "world literature," see Zaritt, *Jewish American Writing and World Literature.*

38. Paul Hazard, *Books, Children and Men* (1932; translated to English in 1944).

39. O'Sullivan, *Comparative Children's Literature*, 8. For a specific example of childhood decoupled from innocence by the violence of lynching, see Eichler-Levine, *Suffer the Little Children*, chap. 4, "Bound to Violence: Lynching, the Holocaust, and the Limits of Representation," 97–127.

40. Kazdan, "Finf un draysik yor yidishe kinder-literatur," 344.

41. Roskies, *A Bridge of Longing*, 150.

42. Shmeruk, SA, 39.

43. Shmeruk, SA, 49.

44. This tendency is notable in Jewish literatures but not entirely unique. Beverly Lyon Clark, offering a feminist history of the critical study of children's literature in America, cites a 1952 essay that describes the nineteenth century as a time "when majors wrote for minors," and "the line between juvenile and adult literature was all but invisible." See Beverly Lyon Clark, "Kiddie Lit in Academe," *Profession* (1996): 149–57. Commenting on the same time and place, Steven Mintz observes, "Many of the era's greatest authors, including Mark Twain, wrote stories for children" (*Huck's Raft*, 186). Perhaps one distinction to be drawn between the American milieu and the Eastern European Jewish one was that the former met market demand while the latter sought, as a project of cultural nationalism, to create it.

45. Kazdan, "Finf un draysik yor yidishe kinder-literatur," 348.

46. See Cohen, "No More Little Jews in Beards," 100, on the series Far unzere kinder [For Our Children] in southern Russia, for example.

47. Cohen, "No More Little Jews in Beards," 98–99, 100.

48. Cohen, "No More Little Jews in Beards," 102.

49. Kadar, *Raising Secular Jews*, 26–28.

50. See Cohen, "No More Little Jews in Beards," 102, as well as Adina Bar-El, *Bein ha'etsim hayerakrakim*, 79–83.

51. Bar-El, "'Grininke beymelekh,'" 19e (English-language abstract).

52. Cohen, "No More Little Jews in Beards," 102.

53. Cohen, "No More Little Jews in Beards," 99.

54. *Di khevre "mefitsei haskole" un di yudishe kinder-literatur (a program far a farlags-tetikeyt)* [Society for the Promotion of Enlightenment and Jewish/Yiddish children's literature (a program for publishing activity)], held in the National Library of Israel, S38, A 943. See Cohen, "No More Little Jews in Beards," 98–99.

55. Charney, "Vegn der idisher kinder literatur," 191.

56. Charney, "Vegn der idisher kinder literatur," 191.

57. On Moriah, see Uriel Ofek, "Moriyah ve-sofre Odesah," in *Sifrut ha-yeladim ha-'ivrit, 1900–1948* (Tel Aviv: Dvir, 1988) 1: 77–122. On the cultural resonance of textual ingathering, or *kinus*, see Moss, *Jewish Renaissance in the Russian Revolution*, 106–9; see also Rubin, "Like a Necklace of Black Pearls Whose String Has Snapped."

58. Charney, "Vegn der idisher kinder literatur," 191.

59. Charney, "Vegn der idisher kinder literatur," 193.

60. On the Jewish refugee crisis, see Marsha Rozenblit, *Reconstructing a National Identity: The Jews of Habsburg Austria During World War One* (New York: Oxford University Press, 2001), 66; David Rechter, "Galicia in Vienna: Jewish Refugees in the First World War," *Austrian History Yearbook* 28 (1997): 113–30; and Beatrix Hoffmann-Holter, "Abreisendmachung," in *Jüdische Kriegsflüchtlinge in Wien, 1914–1923* (Vienna: Bohlau, 1995). On WWI orphans, see O. Faron, "The Age of War Orphans: Construction and Realities of a Group of State Wards Between Education and Assistance (1917–1935)," *The History of the Family: An International Quarterly* 4, no. 1 (1999): 17–29.

61. On the dissolution of the empires, see Friederike Kind-Kovács, "The Heroes' Children: Rescuing the Great War's Orphans," *Journal of Modern European History* 19, no. 2 (2021): 184. On the pogroms that followed WWI, see Jeffrey Veidlinger, *In the Midst of Civilized Europe: The 1918–1921 Pogroms in Ukraine and the Onset of the Holocaust* (New York: Macmillan, 2021). Overall, the data on hard numbers are piecemeal, as historians usually study one country or region and often treat Jewish refugees and orphans as part of a broader study. See Kind-Kovács, "The Heroes' Children," 187, and Peter Gatrell, "Refugees," 4, in *International Encyclopedia of the First World War* (Berlin: Freie Universität Berlin, 2014).

For more on orphans in Central and Eastern Europe, see Andrea Griffante, *Children, Poverty and Nationalism in Lithuania, 1900–1940* (Cham: Springer International Publishing, 2019); Aldis Purs, "Orphaned Testimonies: The Place of Displaced Children in Independent Latvia, 1918–26," in *Displaced Children in Russia and Eastern Europe, 1915–1953*, ed. N. Baron (Leiden: Brill, 2017), 40–69; Nazan Maksudyan, "A Triangle of Regrets: Training of Ottoman Children in Germany During the First World War," in *Childhood in the Late Ottoman Empire and After*, ed. B. C. Dortna (Leiden: Brill, 2016), 141–72; and U. Üngör, "Orphans, Converts, and Prostitutes: Social Consequences of War and Persecution in the Ottoman Empire, 1914–1923," *War in History* 19, no. 2 (2012): 173–92. On the situation in the USSR, see M. K. Stolee, "Homeless Children in the USSR, 1917–1957," *Soviet Studies* 40, no. 1 (January 1988): 64–83. See also Byford, *Science of the Child in Late Imperial and Early Soviet Russia*, 149–54.

62. See Rozenblit, chap. 3, "Mobilizing the Home Front," in *Reconstructing a National Identity*. Also see Kind-Kovács, "The Heroes' Children," 198.

63. The Great War dramatically increased the number of such institutions, but some communities were already attending to similar needs on a smaller scale. Nathan Cohen documents the establishment in 1909 of a Society for the Welfare of Children (*Gezelshaft far kinder farzorgung*) in Vilna, Lithuania. It ran a school that initially possessed a single bookcase with no books in Yiddish. "No More Little Jews in Beards," 100.

64. "Warfare to welfare" is the formulation of Pierluigi Pironti. See his "Warfare to Welfare: World War I and the Development of Social Legislation in Italy," *Historical Social Research / Historische Sozialforschung* 45, no. 2 (2020): 187–216. For more on the "professionalization of welfare," see Kind-Kovács, "The Heroes' Children,"186.

65. Steven Mintz, *Huck's Raft*, 190.

66. Shmeruk, SA, 45.

67. One critic, writing in 1944, discerned "a positive approach to Yiddish" in later poets that was lacking in earlier ones, which he mostly attributes to the flourishing Yiddish schools. See B. Y. Bialototski, "Di yidishes shul un di yidishe literatur," *Kultur un dertsiyung* [Culture and Education], April 1944, 12–14.

68. On the history of Yiddishist schooling in Poland, see Miriam Eisenstein, *Jewish Schools in Poland, 1919–39: Their Philosophy and Development* (New York: Columbia University Press, 1950). For background on Yiddish textbooks, see Evita Wiecki, "Untervegs: A Journey with the Yiddish Textbook," *European Judaism* 42, no. 2 (2009): 47–61. A helpful resource for a study of such texts is Norman Drachler, *A Bibliography of Jewish Education in the United States* (Detroit: Wayne State University Press, 2017).

69. See Tara Zahra, "Teachers, Orphans, and Social Workers," in *Kidnapped Souls: National Indifference and the Battle for Children in the Bohemian Lands, 1900–1948* (Ithaca, NY: Cornell University Press, 2008), 51.

70. Zahra, "Teachers, Orphans, and Social Workers."

71. Zahra, "Teachers, Orphans, and Social Workers," 56. For further discussion of Maria Montessori's and Friedrich Froebel's respective reformist influences on Jewish education, see Moss, *Jewish Renaissance*, 202–3.

72. Zahra, "Teachers, Orphans, and Social Workers," 58.

73. See Joshua D. Zimmerman, *Poles, Jews, and the Politics of Nationality: The Bund and the Polish Socialist Party in Late Tsarist Russian, 1892–1914* (Madison: University of Wisconsin Press, 2004), 243–48.

74. For a chronicle of the four secular Yiddish-school networks active in New York and their respective affiliated children's periodicals, see Kadar, *Raising Secular Jews*. She also surveys the educational associations and schooling networks of Vilna, Warsaw, and other significant locations in Eastern Europe.

75. On Yiddish communist schooling in the United States, see Dylan Kaufman-Obstler, "Language for a Revolution: Yiddish Schools in the United States and the Making of Jewish Proletarian Culture" (PhD diss., University of Wisconsin, 2021).

76. Kadar, *Raising Secular Jews*, 62–64; Kazdan, "Finf un draysik yor yidishe kinder-literatur," 336.

77. Kazdan, "Finf un draysik yor yidishe kinder-literatur," 365.

78. Kadar, *Raising Secular Jews*, 64.

79. Kazdan, "Finf un draysik yor yidishe kinder-literatur," 336–37.

80. Kazdan, "Finf un draysik yor yidishe kinder-literatur," 341, 366.

81. Kazdan, "Finf un draysik yor yidishe kinder-literatur," 347.

82. Kazdan, "Finf un draysik yor yidishe kinder-literatur," 349.

83. Kazdan, "Finf un draysik yor yidishe kinder-literatur," 48–49.

84. For a nuanced discussion of the *limits* of Jewish cultural nationalism in belletristic publishing for children, see Moss, *Jewish Renaissance*, 201–6. Both the Hebrew and Yiddish camps "inclined decisively away from direct strategies of national subject formation" (205).

85. Zahra, "Teachers, Orphans, and Social Workers," 51.

86. See Katharine Capshaw Smith, *Children's Literature of the Harlem Renaissance* (Bloomington: Indiana University Press, 2004). The comparison with the African American children's literature of the Harlem Renaissance is instructive, including emphases on education and outdoor play. For a direct parallel of Jewish and Black children's literature in English, see Eichler-Levine, *Suffer the Little Children*.

87. Cited in Kazdan, "Finf un draysik yor yidishe kinder-literatur," 348.

88. bHagiga 3b.

89. For an analysis and partial translation of Bialik's 105-line poem, see Alan Mintz, "Sefer Ha'aggadah: Triumph or Tragedy?" in *History and Literature: New Readings of Jewish Texts in Honor of Arnold J. Band*, ed. William Cutter and David C. Jacobson (Brown Judaic Studies, 2020).

Chapter Three: A Sabbath for Socialists

1. Most biographical material on Fichman is available only in Hebrew. See *'Arugot: Kovets le-zikhro shel Ya'akov Fikhman*, various eds., 3 vols. (Tel Aviv: ha-Igud ha-'olami shel Yehude Besarabyah [The International Union of Bessarabian Jewry], 1973, 1976, 1983); Hillel Barzel, "Ya'akov Fiḥman: Lirikah epit," in *Shirat ha-teḥiyah: Omane ha-z'aner* (Tel Aviv: Sifriyat po'alim, 1997), 452–553; Nurit Govrin, ed., *Ya'akov Fikhman: Mivḥar ma'amre bikoret 'al yetsirato* (Tel Aviv: 'Am 'oved, 1971); Getzel Kressel, "Fikhman, Ya'akov," in *Leksikon ha-sifrut ha-'ivrit ba-dorot ha-aḥaronim*, ed. Getzel Kressel (Merḥavyah: Sifriyat po'alim, 1976), 602–8; Zvi Luz, *Shirat Ya'akov Fikhman: Monografyah* (Tel Aviv: Papirus, 1989). In English, see Moss, *Jewish Renaissance in the Russian Revolution*, 177–80, 212–13; and Nurit Govrin, "Fichmann, Ya'akov," trans. David Fachler, *The YIVO Encyclopedia of Jews in Eastern Europe*, accessed November 13, 2024, www.yivoencyclopedia.org/article.aspx/Fichmann_Yaakov.

2. Moss, *Jewish Renaissance in the Russian Revolution*, 77.

3. See Yudl Mark, "Yidishkeyt un veltlekhkeyt in un arum undzere shuln" [Jewishness and Secularism In and Around Our Schools], *Shul pinkes: Aroysgegebn lekoved dem tsyantsiḳsṭn yoyvl, 1926–1946* (Chicago: Sholem Aleykhem Folk Institute, 1948).

4. On the Zionist secularization of ancient texts and traditions and invention of folklore, see Darr, "Inventing Tradition and Folklore" (chap. 5), in *The Nation and the Child*. For a parallel

discussion regarding depictions of a secularized Sabbath, see the section "Inventing the Zionist Sabbath," 76–79.

5. For a rich discussion of the folkloric aesthetic, see Spinner, *Jewish Primitivism*, chap. 1.

6. Udel, *Honey on the Page*, 29.

7. Udel, *Honey on the Page*, 31.

8. Udel, *Honey on the Page*, 33.

9. Knox, "Jewish Secularism and the Sabbath," 70.

10. Safran, *Wandering Soul*, 146.

11. Mark, "Yidishkeyt un veltlekhkeyt in un arum undzere shuln," 14, 24.

12. Biale, *Not in the Heavens*, 2.

13. Abraham Joshua Heschel, *The Sabbath: Its Meaning for Modern Man* (New York: Farrar, Straus, and Giroux, 1951), 10.

14. Chaim Zhitlovsky, "Di natsyonial-poetisher vidergeburt fun der yidisher religye" [The National-Poetic Rebirth of the Jewish Religion], *Gezamelte shriftn* [Collected Works] (New York: Dr. Chaim Zhitlovsky Jubilee Committee, 1912), 4: 221–78.

15. This tendency may be contrasted with postwar Yiddish children's literature published in the Americas, which often represented contemporary children observing the holidays realistically, even in a nontraditional milieu. For an example, see the holiday anthology of Zina Rabinowitz, *Der liber yontef* (New York: Farlag Matones, 1958).

16. Udel, *Honey on the Page*, 31.

17. Fishman, *Rise of Modern Yiddish Culture*, 106.

18. Fishman, *Rise of Modern Yiddish Culture*, 100.

19. See especially Mark, "Yidishkeyt un veltlekhkeyt in un arum undzere shuln," 18–22, and his discussion of banished Jewish content sneaking back in through the window of "literature" (20).

20. See Gottesman, *Defining the Yiddish Nation*, 125, and Spinner, *Jewish Primitivism*, chap. 2, 41–80.

21. Dan Miron, "Folklore and Antifolklore in the Yiddish Fiction of the *Haskala*," in *Studies in Jewish Folklore*, ed. Frank Talmage (Cambridge, MA: Association for Jewish Studies, 1980).

22. See Mark W. Kiel, "Vox Populi, Vox Dei: The Centrality of Peretz in Jewish Folkloristics," *Polin* 7 (1992): 88–120.

23. An-sky was in fact quite influenced by Peretz's 1901 essay "Dos yidishe lebn loyt di yidishe folks-lider" [Jewish Life According to Jewish Folk Songs]. Y. L. Peretz, *Literatur un lebn* (Vilna: B. Kletskin, 1926), 26–48.

24. Kiel, "Vox Populi, Vox Dei," 96.

25. On neo-Hasidism more broadly and its Jewish communal uses, see Krah, "Making Jewishness Meaningful in School and in Hasidism" (chap. 8), in *American Jewry and the Re-Invention of the East European Jewish Past*. On Peretz, see Fishman, *Rise of Modern Yiddish Culture*, 102.

26. On An-Sky's ethnographic project, see Nathaniel Deutsch, *The Jewish Dark Continent: Life and Death in the Russian Pale of Settlement* (Cambridge, MA: Harvard University Press, 2011). For a range of contemporary scholarly treatments, see Gabriella Safran and Steven J. Zipperstein, *The Worlds of S. An-sky: A Russian Jewish Intellectual at the Turn of the Century* (Stanford, CA: Stanford University Press, 2006). The rhetoric of folklore as Oral Torah is not unique to An-sky; see Spinner, *Jewish Primitivism*, 25. On Shmuel Charney's application of the "Oral Torah" motif to the work of Y. L. Peretz, see Kiel, "Vox Populi, Vox Dei," 99. For the *locus classicus*

in An-sky's work, see his seminal 1908 essay, "Evreiskoe narodnoe tvorchestvo" (Jewish Folk Art), *Perezhitoe* 1 (1908): 276, translated into Yiddish by Zalmen Reyzn and published in the final volume of An-sky's collected works; see An-Sky, "Der yidisher folks-gayst un zayn shafung" ("The Yiddish/Jewish folk spirit and its artistry"), in *Gezamlte shriftn* (Vilna: Farlag "An-sk," 1925), 15: 15–28. For a gloss of this essay, see Safran, *Wandering Soul*, 143–47, 187–96.

27. Safran, *Wandering Soul*, 191.

28. Roskies, "Mythologist of the Mundane," 33, 34.

29. Biale, *Not in the Heavens*, 12.

30. Rabbinic literature emphasizes this contrast, aligning the dual positive-negative imperatives of Sabbath observance to the varying terms that appear in the commandment to keep the day as it appears in Exodus (*zakhor*) and Deuteronomy (*shamor*).

31. See Gaster, *Ma'aseh Book*, tale 138, as well as Starck's facsimile edition, *Un beau livre d'histoires*, 312–14.

32. Regarding the medieval motif and its contexts and meanings, see Dauber, *In the Demon's Bedroom*, 109–10, 131–34.

33. Gaster, *Ma'aseh Book*, 1: 319–20 (tale 159).

34. For a discussion of the folkloric aspects of Hasidic literature, see Yassif, *The Hebrew Folktale*, 371–407, and Spinner, *Jewish Primitivism*, 22. See Gedalyah Nigal, *Ha-Sipporet ha-Khasidit: Toldote'iha ve-Nose'iha* [Hasidic Narrative: Its History and Themes] (Jerusalem: Marcus, 1981); and Moshe Raysher, *Sha'arei Yerushalayim* (Jerusalem: Safra, 1967 [orig. 1866]).

35. Dauber, *In the Demon's Bedroom*, 47–48, 108–9, takes great care with the generic distinctions. Pat's version of this story is a folk tale rather than a fable, as its essential purpose is not to explain some aspect of why the world is the way it is.

36. Propp developed his account over several works. In English, see Propp, *Morphology of the Folktale*; Vladimir Propp, *Theory and History of Folklore*, ed. Anatoly Liberman, trans. Ariadna Y. Martin and Richard P. Martin (Minneapolis: University of Minnesota Press, 1984); and Vladimir Propp, *The Russian Folktale*, ed. and trans. Sibelan Forrester (Detroit: Wayne State University Press, 2012).

37. Propp, *Russian Folktale*, 147–224.

38. Propp, *Russian Folktale*, 151. This spatial indeterminacy also recalls Mikhail Bakhtin's description of the Greek romance, wherein the hero moves laterally through an unmarked and unspecified but vast spatial expanse; see Mikhail Bakhtin, *The Dialogic Imagination*, ed. Michael Holquist, trans. Caryl Emerson and Michael Holquist (Austin: University of Texas Press, 1981), 105–7.

39. Propp, *Russian Folktale*, 152.

40. Propp, *Russian Folktale*, 153.

41. Propp, *Russian Folktale*, 159.

42. Nigal, *Leksikon*, 76, 168, 239, 244.

43. S. Y. Abramovitsh, *Tales of Mendele the Book Peddler: Fishke the Lame and Benjamin the Third*, ed. Dan Miron and Ken Frieden, trans. Ted Gorelick and Hillel Halkin (New York: Schocken, 1996), 83.

44. Yassif, *Hebrew Folktale*, 405–6, takes up the significance of the inside/outside dichotomy in the traditional Hasidic tale.

45. Erlich, Rachel (Shoshke), "Vos iz taytsh folkstimlekh?," *Yidishe shprakh* 33, nos. 1–3 (1974): 51–52. See Spinner, *Jewish Primitivism*, n. 41, 187.

46. Mordkhe Schaechter, "Folkish un poshet-folkish," *Yidishe shprakh* 33, nos. 1–3 (1974): 52–54.

47. Mendele Moykher Sforim, "From the Introduction to *Collected Works*," trans. Miriam Udel, *PaknTreger*, Summer 2021, www.yiddishbookcenter.org/language-literature-culture/pakn-treger/2021-pakn-treger-digital-translation-issue/introduction.

48. Udel, *Honey on the Page*, 24.

49. By 1940, the trope of the cloistered (and often pasty-faced) Jewish youth stepping out into the sunshine would be so ubiquitous as to be almost tiresome. See the first chapter of *Motl peysi dem khazns* [Motl, the Cantor's Son], by Sholem Aleichem, and the opening scene in *Grine Felder* [Green Fields], from 1937.

50. Udel, *Honey on the Page*, 33.

51. Udel, *Honey on the Page*, 28.

52. On bisemy, see Hans-Heino Ewers, *Fundamental Concepts of Children's Literature Research: Literary and Sociological Approaches* (London: Routledge, 2009), 45–49.

53. Readers steeped in the Yiddish classical canon might also discern the reflection of Peretz's "Bontshe shvayg" [Bontshe the Silent]—albeit with considerably more tenderness and optimism—as a secular meditation on the Jewish afterlife.

54. Ewers, *Fundamental Concepts*, 45.

55. B. B-Bski (pseudonym of Boris Levinson), "Eynike bamerkungen tsum artikl fun E-R vegn natsionaler ertsiung," *Tsaytfragen* 2 (March 1910): 55–60, 56. Cited in Fishman, *Rise of Modern Yiddish Culture*, 104. On the children of secular Jews envying observant neighbors, see Matthew Brittingham, "'No Heart for Faith': Depicting Freethinkers and Debating Freethought in the American Yiddish Press (1880s–1920s)" (unpublished diss., Emory University, 2023), chap. 2.

56. Moss, *Jewish Renaissance in the Russian Revolution*, 205.

57. Felicity Hughes, "Children's Literature," 557.

58. Recapitulation theory in relation to fairy tales and folk literature was not unique to Yiddish culture. On its relation to German *Märchen*, see Bottigheimer, "Fairy Tales and Folk Tales," 263.

59. Shoshke Fligl-Erlikh, "Medem sanatorye bukh," in *Medem sanatorye bukh* [Medem Sanatorium Book], Khaim Shloyme Kazdan (Tel Aviv: Ha-Menorah, 1971), 376.

60. Yankev Fichman, *Far shul un folk* (Warsaw: A. Gitlin, 1912), 9–10.

61. Shmuel Charney,"Folks-shafung" [Folk Artistry], *Kultur un bildung* (Moscow) (1918): 9. The English is a slightly modified version of Moss's translation of the same passage; Moss, *Jewish Renaissance in the Russian Revolution*, 74.

Chapter Four: Room

1. See Zvi Hirsch Koydnover, *Kav-hayashar* (*Kav-hayosher*) (originally Frankfurt am Main, 1705), 72: 6.

2. See Berner, APD, 128–29, for a discussion of Yosef Yozpe Hahn Neuerlingen, Sefer Yosef Ometz (Frankfurt, 1723), to the effect that the father need not interrupt his study in order to take his son to school.

3. The timing of the kheyder initiation also varied by locale and probably depended on the extent to which the local kheyder provided early-childhood care or commenced with actual

elementary education. Yekhiel Shtern describes the initiation ceremony as taking place at age three in his hometown of Tishevits. See "A Kheyder in Tyszowce (Tishevits)," 156. He describes a second, separate ceremony for the commencement of studying Scripture (158–61).

4. For a symbolic reading of the schoolboy as unblemished, bloodless Eucharistic sacrifice, see Ivan Marcus, *Rituals of Childhood*, 94–101.

5. The precise curricular implications of "Torah and Wisdom" are subject to debate, but the pairing of these terms is quite resonant and stretches back to ancient rabbinic culture. See Midrash Mishle 9: 1. See "A kheyder mayse" [A School Tale], in Zalman Yefroiken and Hyman B. Bass, *Dos lebedike vort: Leyenbukh far dem dritn lernyor* [The Living Word: A Reader for Third-Year Students] (New York: Workmen's Circle, 1954/1959), 241.

6. On corporal punishment, see Shtern, "A Kheyder in Tyszowce (Tishevits)," 169.

7. See Marcus, *Rituals of Childhood*, chap. 2, "The Initiation Rite," 18–34. Tali Berner inventories the early modern sources in APD, 120–22. On illustrated alphabet tablets, see Yitzhak Yudlov, "Luhot alf bet italkiyim," *Kiryat sefer* 62 (1988–89): 930–32.

8. Moses ben Henekh Yerushalmi Altshuler of Prague, *Brantshpigl* (Basel, 1602 [orig. Krakow, 1596]), 178a.

9. The trope of freedom through study dates at least to the geonic period (seventh through ninth centuries), as in Avot deRabbi Natan 2:3.

10. "Naftali the Storyteller, and His Horse, Sus," an ars poetica tale by Bashevis, probes the structure of the boy's craving for literacy. See *Stories for Children*, 170.

11. For accounts of the historical kheyder, see the following: David Kraemer, "Images of Childhood and Adolescence in Talmudic Literature," in *The Jewish Family: Metaphor and Memory*, ed. David Kraemer (New York: Oxford University Press, 1990), 65–80, and in the same volume, Gershon Hundert, "Jewish Children and Childhood in Early Modern East Central Europe," 81–94. Also by Hundert: "Approaches to the History of the Jewish Family in Early Modern Poland-Lithuania," in Cohen and Hyman, *The Jewish Family*, 17–28. In the same volume, see David Biale, "Childhood, Marriage, and the Family in the Eastern European Jewish Enlightenment," 45–61.

12. The kheyder is depicted in several languages beyond Yiddish, for example, Henry Roth's novel *Call It Sleep*.

13. Sokoloff, *Imagining the Child in Modern Jewish Fiction*, 8.

14. Sokoloff, "Discoveries of Reading," 324.

15. On girls who attended kheyder, see Berner, APD, 138; Adler, *In Her Hands*; Manekin, *The Rebellion of the Daughters*.

16. See Shtern, "A Kheyder in Tyszowce (Tishevits)," 170, for an account of education at communal expense in small towns.

17. "Benny's Luck," in Sholem Aleichem, *Holiday Tales*.

18. See Alexander Beider's nomenclatural dictionaries, including *A Dictionary of Jewish Surnames from the Russian Empire* (New Haven, CT: Avotaynu, 1993).

19. "Dos dreydl," Yiddish version (Y), 178.

20. Sholem Aleichem, "Dos dreydl," 179.

21. Lightly adapted from Sholom Aleichem, *Some Laughter, Some Tears*, Leviant trans., 66.

22. Sokoloff, *Imagining the Child*, 10.

23. Sholom Aleichem, *Some Laughter, Some Tears*, Leviant trans., 70.

24. Sholom Aleichem, *Some Laughter, Some Tears*, Leviant trans., 71.

25. Sholom Aleichem, *Some Laughter, Some Tears*, Leviant trans., 75.

26. Sholom Aleichem, *Some Laughter, Some Tears*, Leviant trans., 82.

27. Sholom Aleichem, *Some Laughter, Some Tears*, Yiddish 177; Leviant trans., 69.

28. Sholom Aleichem, *Some Laughter, Some Tears*, Leviant trans., 79–80.

29. For an elaboration of the phrase *caer en cuenta*, see Otis H. Green, *The Literary Mind of Medieval and Renaissance Spain* (Lexington: University Press of Kentucky, 1970), 145–48.

30. Sholom Aleichem, *Some Laughter, Some Tears*, Leviant trans., 78.

31. Udel, *Never Better!*, 37–53.

32. On the nexus of geographical and social mobility through train travel, see Neta Stahl, "Conceptions of Time and History in Modern Hebrew and Yiddish Train Stories," *Comparative Literature* 66, no. 3 (2014): 322–39; Sidra deKoven Ezrahi, *Booking Passage: Exile and Homecoming in the Modern Jewish Imagination* (Los Angeles: University of California Press, 2000), 115; and Udel, *Never Better!*, 37–49.

33. Originally published serially in *Forverts* December 31, 1975, January 2, 1976, January 8, 1976, January 9, 1976, the story was reprinted in *Di goldene keyt* 132 (1991): 26–38. The 1991 version is accompanied by a brief critical essay by Chone Shmeruk, "Yitskhok Bashevises dertseylung 'an erev-khanike in varshe.'"

34. This passage, on p. 28 in *Di goldene keyt*, was not included in the English translation; this is my rendering. The tale appears in English translation by Joseph Singer in *Stories for Children* (henceforth SfC), 53–70. The English was first published in the 1975 collection *Naftali the Storyteller, and His Horse, Sus*. Unless otherwise specified, all citations of this story are from Joseph Singer's translation.

35. See Shmeruk, "Yitskhok Bashevis: Der mayse-dertseyler far kinder." Shmeruk speculates that perhaps not all of the events happened at six (the conversation with his father about science and Torah seems awfully precocious for age six, even for a future Nobelist), 235.

36. I have lightly altered Joseph Singer's rendering, SfC, 56.

37. On Bashevis Singer's life-writing recast as fiction, see David Neal Miller, *Fear of Fiction: Narrative Strategies in the Work of Isaac Bashevis Singer* (Albany: SUNY Press, 2012).

38. To distinguish his writing from that of his already renowned older brother, Israel Joshua Singer, Isaac signed himself with the Yiddish matronymic "Bashevis" (Batsheva's). Yiddish-language and Yiddish-informed scholarship and criticism continue to refer to him as Yitskhok Bashevis, while denominating his authorial presence in English as Isaac Bashevis Singer. Because translation played such a key role in the formation of his global literary persona, and because those translations have received so much scrutiny, it is useful to be able to distinguish between the author who composed and initially expected to be read in Yiddish (Bashevis), and the sometimes quite different and savvy one who oversaw translation of his work into English and Hebrew, and then entrusted his work to translators who would usher it into several additional languages (Singer). See Anita Norich, "Isaac Bashevis Singer in America: The Translation Problem," *Judaism: A Quarterly Journal of Jewish Life and Thought* 44, no. 2 (1995): 208–18; Zaritt, *Jewish American Writing and World Literature*, 99–127; and Ezra Mendelsohn, "The Perils of Translation: Isaac Bashevis Singer in English and Hebrew," in *Studies in Contemporary Jewry: XII: Literary Strategies: Jewish Texts and Contexts*, ed. Ezra Mendelsohn (New York: Studies in Contemporary Jewry, 1997).

39. Some of the details may have been intended as a memorial. The opening paragraphs in each language present information missing in the other. The Yiddish mentions that the cold spell is discussed in the "Yiddish newspaper," which older siblings Esther and Joshua buy each morning (probably against the counsel of their pious parents). Unlike the original, the English translation takes care to mention younger brother Moshe, who died in the Holocaust.

40. Bashevis Singer, SfC, 55.

41. In the memoiristic story "Growing Up," he further explains that his parents dressed him "in rabbinical fashion" to underscore their aspirations for him, Bashevis Singer, SfC, 223.

42. Bashevis Singer, SfC, 56.

43. Bashevis Singer, SfC, 55.

44. *Goldene keyt* version, 29.

45. Bashevis Singer, SfC, 58.

46. Sokoloff, "Discoveries of Reading," 332.

47. Bashevis Singer, SfC, 59–60.

48. On Bashevis's demonology, see Udel, *Never Better!*, 53–65.

49. Francelia Butler, "Interview with Isaac Bashevis Singer," in *Sharing Literature with Children: A Thematic Anthology* (New York: David McKay, 1989), 155–60, esp. 158.

50. Bashevis Singer, SfC, 67. Like two of her brothers, Hinde Esther Kreitman grew up to be a novelist and fiction writer, authoring the fictionalized memoir *Deborah* [Der sheydim tants] and several short stories that voiced her anguish at the inequality of education and expectations between her and her brothers.

51. Bashevis Singer, SfC, Author's Note, page unnumbered.

52. Shmeruk, "Yitskhok Bashevis: Der mayse-dertseyler far kinder," 240.

53. From an interview with students at the University of Connecticut on April 3, 1977: "Isaac Bashevis Singer on Writing for Children," *Annual of the Children's Literature Association* 6 (1977): 9–16, esp. 12–13, 14.

54. Bashevis Singer, "Growing Up," SfC, 217–30, esp. 218.

55. Shmeruk, "Yitskhok Bashevis: Der mayse-dertseyler far kinder," 238, 239.

56. Shmeruk observes that Bashevis had at least two reasons for refusing Rotenberg's offer: "He simply didn't believe in any modern children's literature. And moreover, the secular Yiddish school, which had pushed aside traditional Jewish literary texts, was repugnant to him." Shmeruk, "Yitskhok Bashevis: Der mayse-dertseyler far kinder," 244.

57. See Bashevis Singer, "Are Children the Ultimate Literary Critics?," SfC, 336–37.

58. Under the pseudonym D. Segal, see "Amolike shrayber hobn zikh veyniker tsugepast tsum lezer vi di hayntike" [Writers of Yore Accommodated Themselves to the Reader Less than Today's Writers Do], *Forverts*, March 18, 1949, 2.

59. Shmeruk, "Yitskhok Bashevis: Der mayse-dertseyler far kinder," 244.

60. Shmeruk, "Yitskhok Bashevis: Der mayse-dertseyler far kinder," 245.

61. Shmeruk, "Yitskhok Bashevis: Der mayse-dertseyler far kinder," 246.

62. Yitskhok Varshavsky (a pseudonym), "Idishe bikher farn kind un farn dervaksenem" [Yiddish Books for Children and Adults], *Forverts*, February 10, 1963, 21. As Shmeruk points out in "Yitskhok Bashevis: Der mayse-dertseyler far kinder," Bashevis displays a woeful ignorance in this review of nearly a half-century, transnational corpus of Yiddish children's literature (247). The only Yiddish children's writer he can name is the Argentinian Mashe Shtuker (de) Payuk;

perhaps they met during his 1957 trip to Buenos Aires. Her work is exemplary but hardly the sole or foremost avatar of Yiddish children's literature at that time. As Shmeruk notes, Bashevis didn't build up his skills by consuming modern secular children's literature. His storytelling ability came from reading traditional material and embellishing existing stories (249).

63. Shmeruk, "Yitskhok Bashevis: Der mayse-dertseyler far kinder," 247.

64. In addition to the scholarly studies cited above of Singer's relationship with translation, consider Cynthia Ozick's barbed satirical story, "Envy, or Yiddish in America," in *The Pagan Rabbi and Other Stories* (New York: Knopf, 1971).

65. Allison, *Isaac Bashevis Singer*, 22–28.

66. Butler, "Interview," 158. On the author's personae in interviews, see David Neal Miller, "Isaac Bashevis Singer: The Interview as a Fictional Genre," *Contemporary Literature* 25, no. 2 (Summer 1984): 187–204.

67. Shmeruk, "Yitskhok Bashevis: Der mayse-dertseyler far kinder," 248.

68. For example, Shmeruk, "Yitskhok Bashevis: Der mayse-dertseyler far kinder," 248, 271.

69. "Isaac Bashevis Singer on Writing for Children," 12–13.

70. Bashevis Singer, SfC, 337.

71. On December 10, 1978. The speech is archived at "Isaac Bashevis Singer: Banquet Speech," The Nobel Prize, accessed November 24, 2024, www.nobelprize.org/prizes/literature/1978/singer/speech/.

72. See Shmeruk, "Yitskhok Bashevis: Der mayse-dertseyler far kinder," 237–38.

73. Roskies traces the transformation with respect to the fraught topic of Jewish suspicion and animus toward Christianity. See *Bridge of Longing*, 304–6.

74. Roskies, *Bridge of Longing*, 305–6. Marc Caplan extends this insight, positing that Bashevis viewed American Jewry as intrinsically childlike in comparison to that of Polish Jews, who were adultlike in their collective loss of innocence and more sophisticated knowledge of Jewishness (personal communication, January 20, 2022).

75. Marcus, *Rituals of Childhood*, 15.

76. Herbert Spencer, *Essays on Education and Kindred Subjects* (London: Dent, 1861), 5.

77. On Bashevis's nihilism, see Dan Miron, "Passivity and Narration: The Spell of Isaac Bashevis Singer," *Judaism* 41, no. 1 (1992): 6–17. A later version of this essay appears in Miron's collection *The Image of the Shtetl* (Syracuse, NY: Syracuse University Press, 2000), 335–51.

78. Bashevis Singer, SfC, 63.

79. *Goldene keyt* version, 28; not translated into the English.

80. Bashevis Singer, SfC, 68.

81. Bashevis Singer, SfC, 69.

82. Bashevis Singer, SfC, 69–70.

83. Udel, *Honey on the Page*, 194.

84. Udel, *Honey on the Page*, 194.

Chapter Five: The Storm Within

1. Udel, *Honey on the Page*, 212.

2. Udel, *Honey on the Page*, 213.

3. Heywood, *A History of Childhood*, 3.

4. See Barrie Thorne, "Re-visioning Woman and Social Change: Where Are the Children?" in *The Global History of Childhood Reader*, ed. Heidi Morrison (New York: Routledge, 2013), 24–26.

5. While a century ago, humanism posited an encompassing separation between people and "the natural world," skepticism toward this split has characterized more recent ecocritical approaches. See Neil Evernden, "Beyond Ecology: Self, Place, and the Pathetic Fallacy," *North American Review* 263, no. 4 (Winter 1978): 16–20. More recent ecocritical discourse has continued to critique "dualisms that . . . wrench humanity from nature," in the words of Cheryll Glotfelty in her introduction to *The Ecocriticism Reader: Landmarks in Literary Ecology* (Athens: University of Georgia Press, 1996), xxiv. For a comparable case beyond Yiddish letters, see Kimberley Reynolds, *Left Out: The Forgotten Tradition of Radical Publishing for Children in Britain 1910–1949* (Oxford, UK: Oxford University Press, 2016), chap. 4, "Radical Ruralism."

6. See Ariès, *Centuries of Childhood*.

7. See Adrian Wilson, "The Infancy of the History of Childhood: An Appraisal of Philippe Ariès," *History and Theory* 19, no. 2 (1980): 132–53; and Stearns, *Childhood in World History*, 5.

8. Heywood, *A History of Childhood*, 19–20.

9. Andy Byford discusses extensively the scientism of this time in relation to children. See his *Science of the Child in Late Imperial and Early Soviet Russia* for an analysis of the overlapping disciplines that trained their sights on "the child," including pedagogy and special education, psychometric testing, juridical courts, etc.

10. See the (digitized) Vilna Collections at YIVO (New York City), Box 16, Folder 199 (RG10), 21, for a ledger of staff and faculty.

11. The ledger indicates that Kulbak and Etkin were paid at the same rate for their work teaching but not for their supervisory duties. He was a "class supervisor," while she was a "school supervisor," and his rate of pay for this part of the job greatly exceeded hers.

12. Jordan Finkin, "'Like Fires in Overgrown Forests': Moyshe Kulbak's Contemporary Berlin Poetics," in Estraikh and Krutikov, eds., *Yiddish in Weimar Berlin*, 75.

13. Finkin, "'Like Fires in Overgrown Forests,'" 74. Rachel Seelig further probes the motif of escaping the city for the unspoiled landscape of White Russia in Kulbak's poetry. See "A Yiddish Bard in Berlin: Moyshe Kulbak and the Flourishing of Yiddish Poetry in Exile," *Jewish Quarterly Review* 102, no. 1 (Winter 2012): 19–49.

14. *Toyer* in standard YIVO transcription, but *teyer* in Kulbak's Lithuanian dialect, reproduced here for the sake of the rhyme.

15. Meyshe Kulbak, *Naye lider* [New Poems] (Warsaw: Farlag Kultur-lige, 1922), 7. My translation.

16. See Shmuel Rozhanski's introduction to Kulbak's collected works: "Moyshe Kulbak, der bazinger fun primitiver erdishkeyt un yidishn mitos" [Meyshe Kulbak, the Bard of Earthy Primitivism and Jewish Myth], in Moyshe Kulbak, *Oysgeklibene shrift* [Collected Writings], ed. Shmuel Rozhanski (Buenos Aires: Ateneo Literario en el IWO, 1976).

17. The idea of "granting in fantasy" was popularized by Adele Faber and Elaine Mazlish in their parenting manual *How to Talk So Kids Will Listen and Listen So Kids Will Talk* (New York: Avon, 1982).

18. For more on Kulbak's motivations for the fateful move to Minsk, see Kagan, *Leksikon*, as well as Sasha Senderovich's introduction to Kulbak's comic novel *The Zelmenyaners*, xv, and Senderovich's monograph *How the Soviet Jew Was Made*, chap. 2. See also Madeleine Atkins Cohen's dissertation, "Here and Now: The Modernist Poetics of Do'ikayt" (UC Berkeley, 2016), chap. 3.

19. On Dunets's fate, see Senderovich, *Soviet Jew*, 89–90.

20. Two excellent sources in English survey the ideals and operational realities of Medem. See Jacobs, "The Medem Sanatorium" (chap. 4), in *Bundist Counterculture in Interwar Poland*, 62–81, and Kozłowska, "'In Sunshine and In Joy'?"

21. Jacobs, *Bundist Counterculture*, 12.

22. Jacobs, *Bundist Counterculture*, 69.

23. Jewish hopes of an enduringly pluralistic Poland with room for Jewish cultural autonomy would swiftly come to ruin. See Moss, *An Unchosen People*, esp. the introduction, 1–40.

24. Mendelsohn, *The Jews of East Central Europe Between the World Wars*, 35–36.

25. Concern for hygiene as germ theory became well established was a feature of progressive pedagogy in many locales. In her study of the Soviet kindergarten, Lisa Kirschenbaum notes that descriptions of kindergartens typically mentioned how often children washed. See her *Small Comrades*, 67.

Mir kumen on, the documentary film about Medem made by Alexander Ford, Wanda Wasilewka, and Yankev Pat for fundraising purposes, features a funny sequence about two new arrivals who get into an altercation in the boys' bathroom and end up covered in toothpaste powder. It seems likely that the novelty of the substance heightened the sense of their extravagance in wasting it.

26. *Medem sanatorye bukh* (henceforth MSB), compiled and edited by Kazdan, is a compendium of recollections by former teachers, students, and others involved with the institution. Gilinsky, MSB, 26.

27. Gilinsky, MSB, 21.

28. The strong Bundist affiliation sometimes led to conflict with others on the Yiddish left, including an armed attack on the facility by communists in February 1931. See MSB, 163–72, and Jacobs, *Bundist Counterculture*, 67–68.

29. So as not to flatten Gilinsky into a two-dimensional saint of pedagogy, I mention another anecdote that shows a less gentle side of his temperament. Dispatched by the Bund Central Committee to have flyers printed up in Yiddish, Gilinsky commandeered the Matz Press of Vilna, holding proprietor Fradl Matz at gunpoint until the printing job was done. Her grandson, David G. Roskies, recounts the incident in *Yiddishlands: A Memoir* (Detroit: Wayne State University Press, 2008), 50.

30. Blatman, *For Our Freedom and Yours*, 23.

31. Gilinsky, MSB, 65.

32. Anna Gonshor, unpublished lecture at Montreal Jewish Public Library, c. 2010.

33. Gilinsky, MSB, 26.

34. "The Medem Sanatorium was a true children's republic. The children governed (under the supervision, of course, of the teachers) and led all aspects of sanatorium life," wrote Bina Alterman-Shteynberg, MSB, 260.

35. For a detailed description of these administrative structures, see Kozłowska, "'In Sunshine and in Joy'?" 51, and also *Vi lebt dos kind in medem sanatorye* [How Children Live in Medem Sanatorium], 7–9. This pamphlet was authored by Shloyme Gilinsky, although he is uncredited.

36. Kozłowska, "'In Sunshine and in Joy'?" 51–52. Another *sanatoristke*, Sonie Pludermakher-Vaysbrot, makes a similar point in somewhat loftier language: "The focal point of the work lies in giving the children the possibility to jointly create and to carry together the responsibility for collective harmony through joyfulness and love of life." See her "Umfargeslekhe epizodn" [Unforgettable Episodes], MSB, 230. Cited by Jacobs, *Bundist Counterculture*, 137.

37. Gilinsky, MSB, 27.

38. Kozłowska, "'In Sunshine and in Joy'?" 54, cites *W słońcu i w radości; dziecko w sanatorium im. Medema w Miedzeszynie*, 21.

39. On contrasts between Medem and the orphanage of Janusz Korczak, see Kozłowska, "'In Sunshine and in Joy'?" 52. On Yiddishist summer camps in the United States, see Sandra Fox, *The Jews of Summer*, 125–38.

40. Jacobs, *Bundist Counterculture*, 71.

41. See Gilinsky, MSB, 202, 203.

42. For a comprehensive study of Soviet kindergartens in theory and practice, see Kirschenbaum, *Small Comrades*.

43. For summaries of the library's operations, see Kozłowska, "'In Sunshine and in Joy'?" 53, and *Vi azoy lebt dos kind in Medem sanatorye*, 12.

44. *Vi azoy lebt dos kind*, 12.

45. Shtrigler, MSB, 335–36.

46. Lyuba Kantorovitsh-Gilinsky, MSB, 186–87.

47. Fligl-Erlikh, MSB, 378.

48. Biber, *Vinter in vald* [Winter in the Forest], 53.

49. Biber, *Vinter in vald*, 10.

50. Biber, *Vinter in vald*, 12–13.

51. Biber, *Vinter in vald*, 56, 57.

52. Biber, *Vinter in vald*, 57–58.

53. Children were urged to become observers even as they were scientifically observed. Files, including medical and psychological profiles, were kept for each child. See Kazdan, MSB, 66.

54. Gilinsky, MSB, 30.

55. The nature center kept a diary to record observations on hikes and elsewhere on the premises (*Vi azoy lebt dos kind*, 11), which remained as a permanent record beyond the brief stay of any given cohort.

56. Biber, *Friling in vald* [Spring in the Forest], 3.

57. Professor Anna Gonshor generously shared her notes from an unpublished lecture on Medem, including a rich array of passages from the *Medem sanatorye bukh* and the recruiting booklet *Vi azoy lebt dos kind in Medem sanatorye*. In her lecture, Gonshor draws a useful parallel with the Reggio Emilia approach, which enjoys great currency today, as a response to the psychological harm caused by war.

58. On holistic, experiential learning and democracy education at American Jewish summer camps, see Fox, *The Jews of Summer*, chap. 6, 149–72.

59. See Kirschenbaum, *Small Comrades*, 69.

60. Kirschenbaum, *Small Comrades*, 118.

61. These included a range of Polish and international leaders in progressive pedagogy, as Gonshor chronicles.

62. Gilinsky, MSB, 26.

63. Brumberg, MSB, 306–7.

64. Kozłowska, "'In Sunshine and in Joy'?" 55.

65. Gonshor details how the Kommandant of the Nazi garrison in nearby Falinetz inspected the facility and admired its gardens, music, and cleanliness (unpublished lecture).

66. Kazdan, MSB, 63, cited by Jacobs, *Bundist Counterculture*, 81.

67. Fligl-Erlikh, MSB, 378–79.

68. Biber, *Vinter in vald*, 60.

69. James and Prout, *Constructing and Reconstructing Childhood*, 7, 8.

70. Heywood, *A History of Childhood*, 2. We might think in terms of a long process of decolonizing childhood studies. Children's development was understood to bridge the biological and the social, so that the passage from "savage" to "civilized" that received so much attention in a colonial thought paradigm was paralleled by the passage from childhood to adulthood. "Representatives of pre-rational phases, children of various ages were used to discover the sequential process of the emergent rationality of 'the child'" (Heywood, 11). More recently, see Kristen Cheney, "Decolonizing Childhood Studies: Overcoming Patriarchy and Prejudice in Child-Related Research and Practice," in *Reimagining Childhood Studies*, ed. Spyros Spyrou, Rachel Rosen, and Daniel Thomas Cook (London: Bloomsbury Academic, 2018), 91–105; and Manfred Liebel, *Decolonizing Childhoods: From Exclusion to Dignity* (Bristol, UK: Policy Press, 2020).

71. Moses Kligsberg, review of *Medem sanatorye-bukh*, *Kultur un lebn*, November–December 1971, 9–10.

72. Medem remained in operation until a nearby orphanage was bombed in September 1939. No longer certain they could guarantee the safety of their charges, central Bund leadership shuttered the facility and sent away Gilinsky and other leaders. When Warsaw proved equally unsafe a month later, Medem was reopened under the mostly female leadership of Dr. Anna Broide-Heler, Dr. Helena Kelson, Manie Zigelboym (wife of Artur Zigelboym), Sonie Nowogrodska (wife of Emanuel Nowogrodski), and Roze Aykhner. Aykhner accompanied the remaining staff and 250 children then present when they were deported to Treblinka on August 20 (Kozłowska, "'In Sunshine and in Joy'?") or 22 (Jacobs, *Bundist Counterculture*; Pickhan, *Gegen den Strom*), 1942. See Perl Ellenbogen-Cahan, "Di medem-sanatorie in milkhome-tsayt," MSB, 100–111; Khayim Ellenbogen, "Unter der natsisher okupatsie," MSB, 111–15. See also Jacobs, *Bundist Counterculture*, 141, n. 107, and Kozłowska, "'In Sunshine and in Joy'?" 57–58.

Chapter Six: Without

1. Trunk, *Poyln*, 2: 174.

2. Parush, *Reading Jewish Women* (henceforth RJW), 157.

3. Trunk, *Poyln*, 2: 173, 289.

4. On the gender gap, see Burko, "Saving Yiddish," who speculates that the gap reflected "the relatively low cultural value that secular Jewish parents placed on Jewish education. Boys had to prepare for professional careers, but girls had time for a little *yidishkayt*" (46).

5. On the contrasting visual iconography for boys and girls on the covers of Yiddish children's magazines, see Naomi Prawer Kadar, *Raising Secular Jews*, 34.

6. The boy, by contrast, is a *Bildungsheld*. On the schematic contrast between the picaresque and the Bildungsroman as modes, see Udel, *Never Better!*

7. Mitchell, *The New Girl*, 4.

8. On rape culture in fairy tales, see Susan Brownmiller, *Against Our Will: Men, Women, and Rape* (New York: Bantam, 1976), 343–44.

9. Klapper, *Jewish Girls Coming of Age*, 29.

10. The field of children's literary studies critiques the assumption of innocence; see Charles Sarland, "The Impossibility of Innocence: Ideology, Politics, and Children's Literature," in *Understanding Children's Literature* (London: Routledge, 1999), 39–55.

11. Ariès, *Centuries of Childhood*, 101.

12. Anastasia Ulanowicz, "Philippe Ariès," Representing Childhood (website), accessed December 2, 2024, https://www.representingchildhood.pitt.edu/aries.htm.

13. Mitchell, *The New Girl*, 6. An N-gram search confirms that usage of the word was scarcely attested in the eighteenth century, rose steadily throughout the nineteenth, and declined just as steadily in the twentieth until about 1980. Usage has spiked since 2015, perhaps due to the "girl power" movement of recent years.

14. Mintz, *Huck's Raft*, 195.

15. The locution is especially salient in an analysis like Rachel Manekin's *The Rebellion of the Daughters: Jewish Women Runaways in Habsburg Galicia*, which opens with a chapter called "The Origins of the Daughters' Question."

16. DeLuzio, *Female Adolescence*, 133.

17. See Mary E. Odem, *Delinquent Daughters: Protecting and Policing Adolescent Female Sexuality in the United States, 1885–1920* (Chapel Hill: University of North Carolina Press, 2000); and Margo Horn, *Before It's Too Late: The Child Guidance Movement in the United States, 1922–45* (Philadelphia: Temple University Press, 1989).

18. Alexander, "Wayward Girls in New York," 277.

19. The constant threat of arrest that dogged female adolescents and young women drives the plot of Miriam Karpilove's novel, *Diary of a Lonely Girl*, trans. Jessica Kirzane (Syracuse, NY: Syracuse University Press, 2020).

20. Saidiya Hartman, *Wayward Lives, Beautiful Experiments: Intimate Histories of Social Upheaval* (New York: W. W. Norton, 2019).

21. Although aspects of these different impulses operated simultaneously, it is possible to discern a historical sequence as Mary Linehan does in "Sex, Abortion, and Prostitution in the Lives of Gilded Age Chicago Girls," in *Children and Youth During the Gilded Age and Progressive Era*, ed. James Marten (New York: New York University Press, 2014), 166–86.

22. Smith-Rosenberg, *Disorderly Conduct*, 245.

23. See Elizabeth Cady Stanton, "Shall Women Ride the Bicycle?" in Elizabeth Cady Stanton Papers, Reel 35: 1066–1073, Library of Congress, Washington, DC; and Evan Friss, *The Cycling*

City: Bicycles and Urban America in the 1890s (Chicago: University of Chicago Press, 2015), 161–63, 171–76.

24. See Ole Reinsch, "Flapper Girls: Feminism and Consumer Society in the 1920s," *Gender Forum* 42 (2013): 1–6.

25. African American children's literature of the same period offers an instructive comparison in the rhetoric of uplift. See the work of Katharine Capshaw Smith, Kevin Gaines, and Neal A. Lester.

26. Jane Hunter offers an instructive comparison in her finely etched portrait of girls' self-culture through reading and writing in *How Young Ladies Became Girls: The Victorian Origins of American Girlhood* (New Haven, CT: Yale University Press, 2002). On American Jewish girlhood in broad, multicultural context, see Colleen A. Vasconcellos and Jennifer Helgren, eds., *Girlhood: A Global History* (New Brunswick, NJ: Rutgers University Press, 2010).

27. Parush, RJW, 140.

28. Adler, *In Her Hands*, 94, 78–79, 112.

29. See Naomi Seidman, *Sarah Schenirer and the Bais Yaakov Movement: A Revolution in the Name of Tradition* (Liverpool: Liverpool University Press, 2019); the website of the Bais Yaakov Project, accessed December 2, 2024, https://thebaisyaakovproject.religion.utoronto.ca/; and Manekin, *Rebellion of the Daughters*, chap. 6, 182–235.

30. Klapper, *Jewish Girls Coming of Age*, 59.

31. Adler, *In Her Hands*, 99, 111.

32. Paula Hyman, "East European Jewish Women in an Age of Transition, 1880–1930," in *Jewish Women in Historical Perspective*, ed. Judith R. Baskin (Detroit: Wayne State University Press, 1998), 270–86, 280.

33. Regarding newspapers' "women's pages" with male authorship and the phenomenon of male journalists posing pseudonymously as women in the Yiddish press, see Ayelet Brinn, *A Revolution in Type: Gender and the Making of the American Yiddish Press* (New York: New York University Press, 2023).

34. Hyman, "East European Jewish Women," 281. Also see Kimberlé Crenshaw, *On Intersectionality: Essential Writings* (New York: New Press, 2014).

35. DeLuzio, *Female Adolescence*, 134.

36. To better understand the contingent (and transactional) nature of Ashkenazi Jews' purchase on whiteness in America, see Goldstein, *The Price of Whiteness*.

37. Science still erred on the side of setting the male experience as normative; see DeLuzio, *Female Adolescence*, 156, 135.

38. Mitchell, *The New Girl*, 9.

39. Hunter, *How Young Ladies Became Girls*, 56.

40. Udel, *Honey on the Page*, 269.

41. Udel, *Honey on the Page*, 269.

42. See Aleksandra Jakubczak, "The Issue of Jews' Participation in White Slavery and Prostitution as Reflected in Hebrew Press at the Turn of the 19th and the 20th Centuries," *Kwartalnik Historii Żydów (Jewish History Quarterly)* 262, no. 2 (2017): 183–99; and Yarfitz, *Impure Migration*.

43. Yarfitz, *Impure Migration*, 2–5.

44. Yarfitz, *Impure Migration*, 120. The organization's name, punning on *ezres*, refers not only to "aid" but also to the women's section of the synagogue, typically a balcony. Thus does the

name evoke both the requisite protection of women from unsavory men and the protection of upstanding men from the siren-like sexual temptation that women's public visibility was imagined to pose.

45. Yarfitz, *Impure Migration*, 59.

46. Yarfitz, *Impure Migration*, 123, 120–21.

47. For more on Davidman, see Young, "'A Language Is like a Garden.'"

48. Davidman, *A shprakh iz vi a gortn*, 40.

49. Davidman, *A shprakh iz vi a gortn*, 40–42.

50. Davidman, *A shprakh iz vi a gortn*, 43.

51. On the central importance of "soundness of body as well as mind," see Klapper, *Jewish Girls Coming of Age*, 203.

52. Yiddish children's culture often highlighted solidarity between urban Jewish workers and miners, whether in Appalachia or Poland. At the Medem Sanatorium, the children elected to invite a detachment of (non-Jewish) miners' children to the facility in support of their parents' strike, as documented in the film *Mir kumen on*. See also the final chapter of Ḥaver Paver, *Labzik: Tales of a Clever Pup*.

53. Davidman, *A shprakh iz vi a gortn*, 43.

54. The landmark text that established the concept in the cultural firmament was G. Stanley Hall's *Adolescence: Its Psychology and Its Relation to Physiology, Anthropology, Sociology, Sex, Crime, Religion, and Education* (1904). Although Hall's research methods were heavily reliant on self-reported data and outmoded recapitulation theory, and his findings were tainted by tendencies toward eugenics, racism, and antisemitism, his work was critical in establishing the study of child development. For a balanced treatment of Hall, see DeLuzio, *Female Adolescence*, 147.

55. Klapper, *Jewish Girls Coming of Age*, 26, 28.

56. DeLuzio, *Female Adolescence*, 165.

57. See "Teacher Ousted in '17 Asks Reinstatement: S. D. Schmalhausen Seeks to Clear His Record," *New York Times*, March 7, 1939.

58. Klapper, *Jewish Girls Coming of Age*, 34–35.

59. Rodin, *A modne meydl fun bruklin*.

60. On the ethics of identificatory reading, see Newton, *Narrative Ethics*, 83–86, and "Alienated Majesty: On Reading as Othering," in *Ethics and Literary Practice*, 1–16.

The temporal setting of *An Unusual Girl from Brooklyn* is hard to pin down, but clues point to the turn of the twentieth century. Shprintse climbs onto one of the bridges over the East River; the Brooklyn Bridge was completed in 1883, Williamsburg in 1903, and Manhattan in 1909. The text refers to the "modern city of Brooklyn." Though the boroughs consolidated as New York City in 1898, it might have taken a while for casual references to Brooklyn as a city to change. The first chapter features mechanized fire engines; the Fire Department of New York motorized its fleet of trucks in 1911. The plot entails a seaborne adventure on a sailing ship; the Age of Sail ended conclusively by the 1930s.

61. Shprintse embodies the sense of "belatedness" that Marc Caplan centers in his account of Yiddish modernism. See Caplan, *Yiddish Writers in Weimar Berlin*, 29–40, and *How Strange the Change*, 12, 163. On the cultural significance of electrification, see Alona Bach's as yet untitled PhD diss., forthcoming.

62. Hunter, *How Young Ladies Became Girls*, 38.

63. Udel, *Honey on the Page*, 307.

64. On librarians' hostility to dime novels and other popular fiction at the turn of the twentieth century, see Deborah L. Siegel, "Nancy Drew as New Girl Wonder: Solving It All for the 1930s," in *Nancy Drew and Company: Culture, Gender, and Girls' Series*, ed. Sherrie A. Inness (Bowling Green, OH: Bowling Green State University Popular Press, 1997), 159–82.

65. Klapper, *Jewish Girls Coming of Age*, 206–7.

66. See Klapper, *Jewish Girls Coming of Age*, 216–17, on Boston's Saturday Evening Girls, and Hagit Cohen, "The Demands of Integration—The Challenges of Ethnicization: Jewish Women's Yiddish Reading Circles in North America Between the Two World Wars," *Nashim: A Journal of Jewish Women's Studies and Gender Issues*, no. 16, Women and Books (Fall 2008): 98–129.

67. On reading and the intergenerational bond in immigrant families, see Klapper, *Jewish Girls Coming of Age*, 209–10.

68. Rodin, *A modne meydl fun bruklin*, 28.

69. Rodin, *A modne meydl fun bruklin*, 26.

70. Rodin, *A modne meydl fun bruklin*, 30.

71. Rodin, *A modne meydl fun bruklin*, 39.

72. Hunter, *How Young Ladies Became Girls*, 79.

73. Hunter, *How Young Ladies Became Girls*, 105–6.

74. On the activity of reading as variously virtuous and indolent, see Hunter, *How Young Ladies Became Girls*, 71–72.

75. Rodin, *A modne meydl fun bruklin*, 89, 90.

76. Rodin, *A modne meydl fun bruklin*, 112–13.

77. Rodin, *A modne meydl fun bruklin*, 115.

78. Victorian girls' reading and writing practices were closely entwined. Hunter, in *How Young Ladies Became Girls*, documents cases of maturing girls deciding to destroy their diaries in favor of a "domestic world of self-surrender," one of whom experienced the renunciation as "a kind of funeral over herself" (46); see also 86.

79. Hellerstein, *Paper Bridges*, 189.

80. See Nathan Cohen, "Kadya Molodowsky's Status and Activity in the Jewish Literary Milieu in Warsaw," *Bikoret uparshanut* [Criticism and Interpretation] 40 (2008): 163–74.

Chapter Seven: Questions for *Mame*

1. See Emily Style, "Curriculum as Window and Mirror," *Social Science Record*, Fall 1996; and Rudine Sims Bishop, "Window and Mirrors: Children's Books and Parallel Cultures," in *Proceedings of the 14th Annual Reading Conference*, ed. Margaret Atwell and Adria Klein (San Bernardino: California State University San Bernardino Reading Conference, 1990), 3–12.

2. For a thorough and insightful treatment of Sendak, see Moskowitz, *Wild Visionary*.

3. Maze's son, the literary scholar Irving Massey, notes that his mother often reworked English nursery rhymes into Yiddish; he suspects that this short poem might be one of those reworkings (personal communication, November 17, 2020).

4. See Eliot's review essay "The Natural History of German Life," cited in *Middlemarch*, ed. Gregory Maertz, 193.

5. Keen, "Narrative Empathy," para. 4. See also Meretoja, *Ethics of Storytelling*; and Mikhail Baktin, *Art and Answerability: Early Philosophical Essays*, trans. Michael Holquist and Vadim Liapunov (Austin: University of Texas Press, 1990).

6. Mar and Oatley, "Function of Fiction," 181, 182, 183.

7. Zunshine, "Theory of Mind," 271.

8. Mar and Oatley, "Function of Fiction," 181.

9. Zunshine, "Theory of Mind," 270.

10. Nikolajeva, "'Did You Feel as If You Hated People?'" 95–96.

11. Tsai et al., "Learning What Feelings to Desire," cited in Mar and Oatley, "Function of Fiction," 182.

12. See Hogan, *What Literature Teaches Us About Emotion*, 258, 283.

13. Stephen Jay Gould, *The Structure of Evolutionary Theory* (Cambridge, MA: Harvard University Press, 2002), 130–35.

14. Hogan, *What Literature Teaches Us*, 259.

15. Hogan, *What Literature Teaches Us*, 33.

16. Batson, "The Empathy-Altruism Hypothesis," 41.

17. Nikolajeva, "'Did You Feel as If You Hated People?'" 99.

18. Bottigheimer, "Fairy Tales and Folk Tales," 261.

19. See Rosen, *Workers' Tales*, introduction. His classification scheme distinguishes among traditional story forms or allegorical fairy tales and fables (favored by British socialists), and moral tales. The locus classicus for fairy tale schemata is Propp, *Morphology of the Folktale*.

20. Noyes, "Fairy-Tale Economics," 4–5, 6, 10.

21. Zipes, *When Dreams Came True*, 131, and *Victorian Fairy Tales*, xxvii.

22. Bottigheimer, "Fairy Tales and Folk Tales," 267, 269.

23. Noyes, "Fairy-Tale Economics," 11.

24. Krutikov, *Yiddish Fiction and the Crisis of Modernity, 1905–1914*, 38.

25. Translated in Udel, *Honey on the Page*, as "The Magnate of Jerusalem," 154–59.

26. Udel, *Honey on the Page*, 156.

27. Krutikov, *Yiddish Fiction and the Crisis of Modernity*, 64, 28.

28. David Roskies applies the phrase "full-blown shtetl romance" to Asch. *Against the Apocalypse*, 111.

29. Udel, *Honey on the Page*, 156.

30. Udel, *Honey on the Page*, 157.

31. Moses Maimonides, "Shemonah Perakim" [Eight Chapters], chap. 4: 4. For English translation, see "Shemonah Perakim" in *Ethical Writings of Maimonides*, ed. and trans. R. L. Weiss and C. Butterworth, 68.

32. "Shemonah Perakim," 73.

33. Jonathan Jacobs employs distinction between "externalist" and "internalist" ("Plasticity and Perfection," 444). Naturally, Asch is an internalist in that schema.

34. Udel, *Honey on the Page*, 158, 159.

35. Udel, *Honey on the Page*, 159.

36. Hogan, *What Literature Teaches Us*, 278.

37. Hogan, *What Literature Teaches Us*, 280.

38. Molodowsky describes these events in a serialized autobiography in the journal she edited in New York, 1960–1974. See "Tsurik in bereze," 39. Kathryn Hellerstein cites the passage in her biographical sketch of Molodowsky, *Paper Bridges*, 22.

39. Udel, *Honey on the Page*, 167.

40. For a genealogy of the term *tzedakah*, see Jill Jacobs, *There Shall Be No Needy*, 43.

41. On animals in nineteenth-century Jewish children's literature, see Kogman, "The Emergence of Scientific Literature in Hebrew for Children and Youth in the Nineteenth Century."

42. See *Motl Peysi dem khazns*, part 2, chap. 6, "In nyu york af der strit," and *The Letters of Menakhem-Mendl and Sheyne-Sheyndl* and *Motl, the Cantor's Son*, Hillel Halkin trans., 266.

43. Goldstein, *Price of Whiteness* (henceforth PoW), 52, 149.

44. Goldstein, PoW, 153. See also Adam Zachary Newton, "Af der shvel un in der fremd," *In Geveb*, June 21, 2016, https://ingeveb.org/articles/af-der-shvel-un-in-der-fremd-a-feuilleton-on-yiddish-race-and-the-american-literary-imagination.

45. Kreplyak, "Shvarts un vays," unpublished trans. by Jake (Yankl) Krakovsky, with my own slight alterations.

46. Pearl Street has a darker history than Kreplyak may have known In 1711, New York City established a slave market at the corner of Pearl and Wall Streets. See Kamau Ware, "The Slave Market at Pearl Street and Wall Street," *amNY*, February 8, 2021, www.amny.com/sponsored/the-slave-market-at-pearl-street-and-wall-street/.

47. The depiction of Jimmy as presexual contributes to the portrait of his vulnerability and nonthreatening nature. Kreplyak inverts common imagery of Black men as large in relation to Jewish ones, clearly portraying Jimmy as "objectively" small and as small in relation to the "big white boy" that he will perceive Davey to be when the Jewish boy rushes toward him with intent to harm. As Hogan theorizes, "Perhaps the best way to inspire intergroup empathy is to portray the out-group as nonthreatening and as suffering in ways that could be alleviated by the in-group" (*What Literature Teaches Us*, 277).

48. The Yiddish, somewhat softened by the diminutive, uses an equivocal term that could mean "Negro" or the racist epithet beginning with *n*. The more palatable translation is "little Negro," while I fear the more accurate tonal equivalent may be "n----- boy."

49. Goldstein, PoW, 51.

50. Goldstein, PoW, 75.

51. Kreplyak uses the sympathetic diminutive *shvartsinkn* for "Black boy."

52. See Walsh, *History of Medicine in New York*, 786.

53. Goldstein, PoW, 82.

54. Were she Jewish, she might probe his identity with a discreet word of Yiddish.

55. The phrase "similarity bias" originates with the psychologist M. Hoffman, *Empathy and Moral Development*; Kerry Mallan applies it to the study of children's literature in "Empathy: Narrative Empathy and Children's Literature," 107.

56. See Mary-Catherine Harrison, "An Ethics of Place: On North and South by Elizabeth Gaskell," in *My Victorian Novel: Critical Essays in the Personal Voice*, ed. Annette R. Federico and Jane Tompkins (Columbia: University of Missouri Press, 2020), 176.

57. Keen, "Narrative Empathy," para. 12; Keen, *Empathy and the Novel*, 145, 168; Keen, "Novel Readers and the Empathetic Angel of Our Nature," 23.

58. Keen's research counters analyses such as Martha Nussbaum's more wholesale embrace of literary empathy, articulated, for example, in *Love's Knowledge: Essays on Philosophy and Literature* (New York: Oxford University Press, 1990), and in *Poetic Justice: The Literary Imagination and Public Life* (Boston: Beacon Press, 1995). Keen, *Empathy and the Novel*, chap. 6, "Contesting Empathy," 145–68, esp. 147–48.

59. Mallan, "Empathy," 113.

60. Keen, "Novel Readers and the Empathetic Angel of Our Nature," 24, 29–31.

61. Batson, "The Empathy-Altruism Hypothesis," 50.

62. Keen, "Novel Readers and the Empathetic Angel of Our Nature," 24.

63. Kazdan, in his retrospective article "Thirty-Five Years of Yiddish Children's Literature," observed that Yiddish children's literature was inseparable from the Yiddish school networks; its readers were the students in secular schools (337).

64. Keen, "Novel Readers and the Empathetic Angel of Our Nature," 24.

65. Mar and Oatley, "Function of Fiction," 180.

66. Nikolajeva, "'Did You Feel as If You Hated People?'" 102.

67. On transportation, see Keen, "Novel Readers and the Empathic Angel of Our Nature," 24–25; Mar and Oatley, "Function of Fiction," 174; Green, "Transportation into Narrative Worlds"; and Melanie C. Green and T. C. Brock, "The Role of Transportation in the Persuasiveness of Public Narratives," *Journal of Personality and Social Psychology* 79, no. 5 (2000): 701–21.

68. Keen, "Novel Readers and the Empathetic Angel of Our Nature," 25.

69. Keen, "A Theory of Narrative Empathy," 220.

70. Mar and Oatley, "Function of Fiction," 181.

71. See Edward Bradford Titchener, *Lectures on the Experimental Psychology of the Thought-Processes* (New York: Macmillan, 1909).

Chapter Eight: Who's Your *Tate*?

1. On Kvitko's biography, see Estraikh, "The Kharkiv Yiddish Literary World"; and Betti Kvitko and Miron Petrovskii, *Zhizn' i tvorchestvo L'va Kvitko* [The Life and Work of Lev Kvitko] (Moscow: Detskaia literatura, 1976), 135–36.

2. For a comparison between Kvitko's text and two other Yiddish picturebooks featuring boys on horses (by Mani Leyb and Ber Sarin, respectively), see Shulamith Berger, "Moyshe Levin (Ber Sarin) of Yung-Vilne and His Solo Publishing Venture for Children."

3. Another narrative poem by Kvitko, "A Letter to Voroshilov," features a similar first-person, boyish address to another distinguished Soviet military leader. See Kvitko, "A briv dem khaver Voroshilov" [A Letter to Comrade Voroshilov] in *Di royte armey* [The Red Army], 15–17.

4. Gorsuch, *Youth in Revolutionary Russia*, 19.

5. Morse, *Word Play*, 31; and Gorsuch, *Youth in Revolutionary Russia*, 19, 18.

6. Gorsuch, *Youth in Revolutionary Russia*, 15, 12.

7. See Byford, *Science of the Child in Late Imperial and Early Soviet Russia*, 23, on the revolutionary-era revision of existing disciplines like pedagogy and the creation and dissemination of new research disciplines like pedology.

8. On the delicate balance between the child as icon of the future while depending on adult guidance in the present, see Hannah Proctor, *Psychologies in Revolution: Alexander Luria's "Romantic Science" and Soviet Social History* (Cham: Palgrave Macmillan, 2020), 117–63.

9. Byford, *Science*, 5.

10. Gorsuch, *Youth in Revolutionary Russia*, 49.

11. Gorsuch, *Youth in Revolutionary Russia*, 49.

12. This mass scale included Yiddish culture, a minority in relation to Russia but a huge concentration on the Yiddish cultural landscape. See Maeots, "Jewish Heritage in Russian Children's Literature," 82.

13. Gorsuch, *Youth in Revolutionary Russia*, 1.

14. Byford, *Science*, 30–31.

15. Morse, *Word Play*, 31.

16. See Balina, "'It's Grand to Be an Orphan!'" 107. On "the Soviet direction of taste," see Kelly, "'Thank-You for the Wonderful Book,'" 751.

17. Estraikh, "The Kharkiv Yiddish Literary World," 82–83.

18. Kvitko and three other illustrious members of the Kiev Group returned from Germany to Ukraine in 1925–1926, bent on building up Soviet Yiddish culture. See Estraikh, "The Kharkiv Yiddish Literary World," 75.

19. Maeots, "Jewish Heritage in Russian Children's Literature," 84.

20. Udel, *Honey on the Page*, 219.

21. See Kelly, *Children's World*, 76.

22. Tara Zahra, *Kidnapped Souls: National Indifference and the Battle for Children in the Bohemian Lands, 1900–1948* (Ithaca, NY: Cornell University Press, 2011), 68–69.

23. Balina, "'It's Grand to Be an Orphan!'" 103.

24. Kelly, "'Thank-You for the Wonderful Book,'" 749.

25. See Melvin Konner, *The Jewish Body* (New York: Schocken, 2009); and Ethan Calof, "New Men for a New World: Reconstituted Masculinities in Jewish Russian Literature (1903–1925)" (master's thesis, University of Victoria, 2019).

26. Mikhail Krutikov, "An End to Fairy Tales: The 1930s in the *Mayselekh* of Der Nister and Leyb Kvitko," in Estraikh, Hoge, and Krutikov, eds., *Children and Yiddish Literature from Early Modernity to Post-Modernity*, 114, 115.

27. Kelly, "A Joyful Soviet Childhood," 9. See also Balina, "It's Grand to Be an Orphan!" 100.

28. Kelly, "A Joyful Soviet Childhood," 9, 8, 6.

29. Kelly, "A Joyful Soviet Childhood," 9.

30. Kelly, "'Thank-You for the Wonderful Book,'" 729.

31. Udel, *Honey on the Page*, 265.

32. See Denis Petrina, "'Healthy Body, Healthy Mind': The Visual Propaganda of Personal Care During the Cultural Revolution in the Stalinist State," *Vestnik: The Journal of Russian and Asian Studies*, September 20, 2016, https://geohistory.today/propaganda-health-policy-ussr/. See also Gorsuch, *Youth in Revolutionary Russia*, 2.

33. Balina, "It's Grand to be an Orphan!" 103; and Gorsuch, *Youth in Revolutionary Russia*, 2.

34. See D. D. Miller, Susan Williams and Ronald Williams, "Children's Literature in the Soviet Union," *Language Arts* 53, no. 5 (May 1976): 531–35; see also Petrina, "'Healthy Body, Healthy Mind,'" 2.

35. Balina, "It's Grand to be an Orphan!" 100.

36. Byford, *Science*, 106–11.

37. On the importance accorded to handwashing in preschools and kindergartens, see Kirschenbaum, *Small Comrades*, 65–67.

38. Udel, *Honey on the Page*, 267.

39. Byford, *Science*, 23, 30, 123–24, 147.

40. Andy Byford, "The Imperfect Child in Early Twentieth-Century Russia," *History of Education* 46, no. 5 (2017): 595–617; Byford, *Science*, 117.

41. Byford, *Science*, 185, 152, 133.

42. On Kvitko and Markish's definitive break with other Soviet Yiddishists over events in Palestine, see Estraikh, "The Kharkiv Yiddish Literary World," 81.

43. Estraikh, "The Kharkiv Yiddish Literary World," 83; Krutikov, "An End to Fairy Tales," 111–13.

44. Krutikov, "An End to Fairy Tales," 111–13.

45. Kelly, "Riding the Magic Carpet," 207, 204, 206.

46. On the "glorification and sacralization of Lenin and Stalin" through portraiture, see Lyudmila Sholokhova, "Soviet Propaganda in Illustrated Yiddish Children's Books: From the Collections of the YIVO Library, New York," in Estraikh, Hoge, and Krutikov, eds., *Children and Yiddish Literature*, 180. See also Krutikov, "An End to Fairy Tales," 115–16, for a close reading of Kvitko's 1939 "A viglid" [A Lullaby]. Catriona Kelly discusses the same story-poem in its Russian translation in "Riding the Magic Carpet," 213–16. Samuil Marshak, a Jew who wrote in Russian but was often translated into Yiddish, also wrote a "Lullaby" [*Kolybel'naia*] about a mother reassuring her infant that Stalin was personally watching over him; see Kelly, "Riding the Magic Carpet," 212.

47. Kelly, "Riding the Magic Carpet," 199, 204, 203.

48. See Gorsuch, *Youth in Revolutionary Russia*, chap. 8 and epilogue.

49. Balina, "It's Grand to be an Orphan!" 113.

50. Byford, *Science*, 10. Mistrust of parents and children's direct fealty to leaders of the state reached its dark extreme with the case of Pavlik Morozov, the elementary-aged boy who denounced his father to the authorities and was killed by relatives and subsequently celebrated as a Soviet martyr. For the definitive account, see Kelly, *Comrade Pavlik*.

51. Byford, *Science*, 13–14.

52. Kelly, "Riding the Magic Carpet," 199, 204, 215, 219.

53. See Byford, *Science*, 213–17, 252–53.

54. Kelly, "'Thank-You for the Wonderful Book,'" 753.

55. Kelly, "Riding the Magic Carpet," 204.

56. On filiation and affiliation, see Edward W. Said, *The World, the Text and the Critic* (Cambridge, MA: Harvard University Press, 1983).

57. On "normative" family life in the West, see Elizabeth Thiel, *The Fantasy of Family: Nineteenth-Century Children's Literature and the Myth of the Domestic Ideal* (London: Routledge, 2008).

58. Kazdan, "Finf un draysik yor yidishe kinder-literatur" [Thirty-Five Years of Yiddish Children's Literature], 356.

59. Udel, *Honey on the Page*, 281.

60. On the history of the *Ordn-shuln*, see Kadar, *Raising Secular Jews*, 4.

61. On the history of the IWO, see Robert M. Zecker, *"A Road to Peace and Freedom": The International Workers Order and the Struggle for Economic Justice and Civil Rights, 1930–1954* (Philadelphia: Temple University Press, 2018).

62. Before Stalin, American communists by and large felt an unambiguous connection to the USSR. See Harvey Klehr, John Earl Haynes, and Kyrill M. Anderson, *The Soviet World of American Communism* (New Haven, CT: Yale University Press, 2008). An especially rich and accessible primary source is the journal *Prolet Shul*, digitized at Cornell University, accessed December 4, 2024, https://digital.library.cornell.edu/catalog/ss:21072856.

63. This homonym for the Yiddish word for "where" suggests the translation "wherrre" to bring this low growl into English.

64. Thälmann was held in solitary confinement for eleven years before being executed at Buchenwald. Indeed, the main youth group in East Germany after World War II was known as the Thälmann Pioneers.

65. *Manual of the International Workers Order*, 5, Cornell University Digital Collections, accessed December 4, 2024, https://digital.library.cornell.edu/catalog/ss:19043094.

66. Dorothy Day, "Hunger Marchers in Washington," digitized at Catholic Worker Movement, accessed December 4, 2024, www.catholicworker.org/dorothyday/articles/39.pdf.

67. Description of the film is at "The National Hunger March to Washington, 1932," Connexions, accessed December 4, 2024, https://www.connexions.org/CxLibrary/CX16673.htm.

68. The designation here of Tom Lincoln's home as Springfield appears to be an error. He was described earlier as coming from Pittsburgh.

Chapter Nine: "We May Have Sinned Thereby Against Child Psychology"

1. Werber, *Niseles trer*, 36.

2. Werber, *Niseles trer*, 47.

3. See Michel Werber's self-published memoirs of his father, Abusz: *The Word of Abusz Werber* (North Charleston, SC: CreateSpace, 2017), and of being hidden with a Walloon family, *From Under Her Wings: My Life as Louise's Hidden War Child* (Seattle: Amazon Digital Services, 2019).

4. "Keynems land" [No Man's Land] appears in Shifris's story collection *Foygl kanarik un andere mayses* [Canary Bird and Other Stories]. See also Naomi Prawer Kadar's discussion of Yankev Pat's similarly themed story, "Robinson Crusoe," published in *Kinder tsaytung* in February 1939 (Kadar, *Raising Secular Jews*, 158–59).

5. Shifris, *Foygl kanarik*, 71.

6. Shifris, *Foygl kanarik*, 73.

7. Lawrence L. Langer, *Art from the Ashes: A Holocaust Anthology* (New York: Oxford University Press, 1995).

8. On the Zionist reclamation of the Maccabees in children's literature, see Darr, *The Nation and the Child*, 92. See also Zerubavel, *Recovered Roots*, 19–23, 218–21.

9. For the contrast, see Felix Catovsky's *Kleynvarg* (published privately in Bueno Aires, 1945), and Mates Olitzky, *Freylekhe teg* (New York: Arbeter Ring, 1962).

10. Hasia R. Diner, *We Remember with Reverence and Love*, 139–40.

11. Diane K. Roskies identifies a wide variance across languages and denominations in how American children were taught about the Holocaust; see *Teaching the Holocaust to Children*. For an overview of approaches to real-time Holocaust education in America, see 131–33.

12. Mark, "Changes in the Yiddish School," translated by Jacob Golub in *Jewish Education* 19 no. 1 (1947): 34.

13. Mark, "Di vokh fun troyer un protest" [The Week of Sorrow and Protest]. Mark is likely responding to an incident in January 1943 when fighters in the Warsaw Ghetto fired on German troops during an attempted deportation. Their limited success in delaying the scheduled deportation was seen as a prelude to the longer, more encompassing uprising that would take place in April.

For a contrasting view of the narratability of the Holocaust while it was transpiring, see Felman and Laub, *Testimony*, 84.

14. Mark, "Di vokh fun troyer un protest," 3. Mark consistently underscored the need to "tell everything to our children, even about 'Jewish soap.'" See "Un du zolst dertseyln dayn kind . . ." [And You Shall Tell Your Child . . .], cited in Burko, "Saving Yiddish," 56.

15. On this incident, see Judith Tydor Baumel and Jacob J. Shacter, "The Ninety-Three Bais Yaakov Girls of Cracow: History or Typology?" in *Reverence, Righteousness, and Rahamanut: Essays in Memory of Rabbi Dr. Leo Jung*, ed. Jacob J. Schacter (Lanham, MD: J. Aronson, 1992); Naomi Seidman, "Beautiful Martyrs: The Ninety-Three Bais Yaakov Girls," Academia.edu, accessed January 9, 2025, https://www.academia.edu/13843997.

16. Mark, "Di vokh fun troyer un protest," 3.

17. Mark, "Changes in the Yiddish School," 34. Mark seems to address Jewish educators broadly, beyond the ken of the Yiddish-language schools. I have not located the Yiddish original in the press or other periodicals.

18. Mark, "Vegn propagande far undzere shuln" [Regarding Propaganda for Our Schools], cited by Burko, "Saving Yiddish," 49.

19. See the testimony of gynecologist Aharon Peretz in the Eichmann trial regarding abortions under duress, reproduced in Patricia Heberer, *Children During the Holocaust*, 142–44.

20. Heberer, *Children During the Holocaust*, 120, 323.

21. Roskies, *Voices from the Warsaw Ghetto*, 11.

22. Heberer, *Children During the Holocaust*, 108. See, for example, the poem "The Little Smuggler," by Henryka Łazowert, in Roskies, *Voices from the Warsaw Ghetto*, 173–74. See also Yankev Pat's remembrance of his murdered family, *Khan(e)ke*, especially the chapter titled "Even if They Torture Us, We Will Not Say a Word!" A translation by Anita Gallers is forthcoming.

23. See George Eisen, *Children and Play in the Holocaust: Games Among the Shadows* (Amherst: University of Massachusetts Press, 1988). In 1997, Yad Vashem mounted the exhibition No Child's Play: Children in the Holocaust: Creativity and Play.

24. On teens as part of the resistance, see Heberer, *Children During the Holocaust*, 323, and the chapter of Pat's *Khan(e)ke* titled "A Voice Speaks to Us."

25. Josef Zelkowicz, *In Those Terrible Days: Writings from the Lodz Ghetto*, ed. Michal Unger, trans. Naftali Greenwood (Jerusalem: Yad Vashem, 2002), 63–69, cited in Heberer, *Children During the Holocaust*, 118–20.

26. Emmanuel Ringelblum, "Little Stalingrad Defends Itself, c. April 1943," in *"To Live with Honor and Die with Honor": Selected Documents from the Warsaw Ghetto Underground Archives "O.S." (Oneg Shabbath)*, ed. Joseph Kermish (Jerusalem: Yad Vashem, 1986), 601–3; cited in Heberer, *Children During the Holocaust*, 327.

27. For an overview of the periodical literature portraying events of the Holocaust, see Kadar, *Raising Secular Jews*, chap. 7 (156–76).

28. Shandler, "The Holocaust for Beginners," 110. An important contrasting case is Yankev Glatshteyn's novel *Emil un Karl*, set in Vienna during the early days of the Anschluss and published in 1939.

29. Roskies, *Against the Apocalypse*, 80.

30. Panchrony operates variously. One mode blurs the distinction between past and current events through a sacralized construction of history, while another ascribes multiple dire events to a single date on the calendar, so that all may be mourned and recollected on a specific day (Roskies, *Against the Apocalypse*, 13, 17).

31. See the discussion of the Heilesgeschichte form in Tsvi Novick, *Piyyut and Midrash*. Notably for our discussion, Novick regards the serial narrative form as "an expression of the assumption that the canon is coherent" (97).

32. For a poignant example of secularized forms of Jewish medieval martyrdom motifs, see Chanan Kiel's 1971 poem "The Last of the Ghetto," where "kidesh ha'am" (sanctification of the people) is juxtaposed on equal footing with the classical concept of "kidesh hashem" (sanctification of God's name). Kiel's last surviving ghetto fighter hoists the flag with the Star of David and sings "Ani Ma'amin," the Maimonidean credo of Jewish faith:

> High up on the roof, a hero has clambered
> Wrapped in a blue-and-white flag in the flame
> Thus did he fall, the last man of the ghetto
> To hallow the People alongside God's Name [*In ale farbn*, 18].

Diner discusses the use of this melody in postwar memorialization and how it "erased vast ideological differences," *We Remember*, 82.

33. The most conventional reading views "this" as referring to the immediately preceding mention of God's promise to end the exile. A theologically radical parsing posits that the perpetual fact of persecution has spurred Jewish thriving-despite.

34. Mintz, *Popular Culture and the Shaping of Holocaust Memory in America*, 42.

35. Primo Levi, *Survival in Auschwitz* (New York: Simon and Schuster, 1996), 15.

36. For biographical details on Antonovsky, see, Antonovsky and Sagy, "Aaron Antonovsky, the Scholar and the Man Behind Salutogenesis."

37. Antonovsky, "A Somewhat Personal Odyssey," 76.

38. Antonovsky, *Unraveling the Mystery of Health*, 130.

39. Antonovsky specifies that he intended for "disease" to be pronounced "as in John Donne's 'this dis-easeful world'" (Antonovsky, "A Somewhat Personal Odyssey," 75).

40. Manageability may be relative to circumstances. On how the care of a trusted adult, even in a dire situation, could help a child "manage" adequately, see Antonovsky, "A Somewhat Personal Odyssey," 79.

41. Antonovsky, "A Somewhat Personal Odyssey," 79.

42. Antonovsky, "The Sense of Coherence," 12.

43. van der Hal-van Raalte et al., "Sense of Coherence Moderates Late Effects of Early Childhood Holocaust Exposure," 1362.

44. See Antonovsky, "The Sense of Coherence," 16–18.

45. For a synoptic overview of Antonovsky's SOC model in relation to culture, see Benz et al., "Culture in Salutogenesis."

46. Although ghetto and forest settings predominate in Holocaust literature for children, concentration camps and death camps are not wholly absent. See Kadar, *Raising Secular Jews*, 158–63.

47. Roskies, *Against the Apocalypse*, 43.

48. Roskies, *Against the Apocalypse*, 4.

49. M. A. Suhl has also published books under the name "Yuri Suhl." Glik is best remembered for the "Partisan Song" [*Zog nisht keynmol*], still sung at commemorative events. This volume includes his second-best-known ballad, "Di partizanke" [The Partisan Girl], which immortalizes a 1942 railroad attack by partisans Vitke Kempner and Itzik Matskevitch that immobilized a Nazi weapons transport.

Heller's poem, "Dos yingl fun Pavye" [The Boy from Peacock Street], is a stylized ballad memorializing a boy who becomes a hero. Heller was a Polish communist, spent the war years in Russia, returned to (Soviet) Poland, and eventually emigrated to Israel.

50. Kadar, *Raising Secular Jews*, 170.

51. Kadar, *Raising Secular Jews*, 172.

52. On the synchronicity between human life spans and national time in Jewish literature, see Udel, *Never Better!* 7–8.

53. *Kinder heldn*, 40.

54. *Kinder heldn*, 42–43.

55. On the phenomenon of the pin test, see G. M. Stratton, "The Mnemonic Feat of the 'Shass Pollak,'" *Psychological Review* 24, no. 3 (1917): 244–47.

56. Sholem Aleichem, *Tevye the Dairyman and The Railroad Stories*, trans. Hillel Halkin, 163.

57. Saul Noam Zaritt (@saulnoamz), Twitter post, September 13, 2022.

58. Another instance of the "saving Sholem Aleichem" motif occurs in Itshe Goldberg, "Dos yingle vos hot geratevet Sholem-Aleykhem" [The Boy Who Saved Sholem Aleichem], in *Mayn yidish bukh*, vol. 3, ed. M. Gellman (New York: Jewish People's Fraternal Order, 1945), 113–16. See also Kadar, *Raising Secular Jews*, 171.

59. Kadar, *Raising Secular Jews*, 173.

60. For a real-life correlative, see the chapter in Pat's *Khan(e)ke* titled, "The Secret Library in the Ghetto."

61. The story appears in *Kinder heldn*.

62. A contrasting attitude is displayed Felix Catovsky's story "Bay di partizaner" [Among the Partisans], where a child takes the place of his fallen father among the partisans and prepares to blow up railroad tracks. See Catovsky, *Kleynvarg* (Buenos Aires, 1945), 108–13.

63. In her study of the Bielski partisans and their forest encampment, Nechama Tec, *Defiance* (New York: Oxford University Press, 2009), devotes a chapter to "The Fate of Women," including the frequent occurrence of rape in addition to other violence (215–38).

64. Tec, *Defiance*, 191.

65. Heberer, *Children During the Holocaust*, 333, 334.

66. Kadar, *Raising Secular Jews*, 157.

67. For a brief survey, see Karolina Krysińska and David Lester, "The Contribution of Psychology to the Study of the Holocaust," *Dialogue and Universalism* 16, no. 5/6 (2006): 141–56.

68. Brett T. Litz, Nathan Stein, Eileen Delaney, Leslie Lebowitz, William P. Nash, Caroline Silva, and Shira Maguen, "Moral Injury and Moral Repair in War Veterans: A Preliminary Model and Intervention Strategy," *Clinical Psychology Review* 29 (2009): 695–706, 700. On moral injury more broadly, see Joshua Pederson, *Sin Sick: Moral Injury in War and Literature* (Ithaca, NY: Cornell University Press, 2021).

69. Litz et al., "Moral Injury and Moral Repair," 700.

70. A more complicated if inevitable ethical transaction was instrumentalizing the memory of the Holocaust to underwrite subsequent ideological choices, identities, and investments (such as Zionism, Orthodoxy, civil rights work, etc.). On the phenomenon of "using the Holocaust," see Roskies, *Teaching the Holocaust to Children*, 12–16, 20–21; Diner, *We Remember*, 5, 72; and Shai Rudin, "Language, Poetics, and Ideology in Holocaust Literature for Hebrew-Speaking Children," 158–60, 181–84.

For a fuller theorization of the dual sense of "witnessing," see Kelly Oliver, "Witnessing, Recognition, and Response Ethics," *Philosophy and Rhetoric* 48, no. 4, Special Issue: The Rhetorical Contours of Recognition (2015): 473–93, especially 484–85; and Kelly Oliver, *Witnessing: Beyond Recognition* (Minneapolis: University of Minnesota Press, 2001).

71. Felman and Laub, *Testimony*, 81.

Chapter 10: Should I Be Pope Someday?

1. M. A. Nasiram, *"Vos zoln unzere kinder leyenen?"* [What Should Our Children Read?], 19. A separate periodical with the same name was published in Vilna at roughly the same time.

2. On the Yiddish reading level of American children, see educational theorist Kazdan, "Finf un draysik yor."

3. Nasiram, *"Vos zoln unzere kinder leyenen?"* 20.

4. By 1947, Kazdan tells a story of decline; the peak of Yiddish children's publishing in America was 1925–1930.

5. Dovid Roykhl, "Vegn a farvorlozt gebit" [Regarding a Neglected Domain], *Literarishe bleter*, September 5, 1930, 686–87.

6. On women's literary market power, see Parush, *Reading Jewish Women* (henceforth RJW), chap. 6, and Ayelet Brinn, *A Revolution in Type: Gender and the Making of the American Yiddish Press* (New York: New York University Press, 2023), chaps. 4 and 5. Also see Ian Watt, *Rise of the Novel: Studies in Defoe, Richardson and Fielding* (Los Angeles: University of California Press, 2001).

7. See Shloyme Bastomski, (Vilner) *Shul-fraynd*, November 1937, 99–110, 106.

8. See the discussion of Tashrak's story "Against Your Will, You're a Jew" and the *pintele yid* motif in Matthew H. Brittingham, "'No Heart for Faith': Depicting Freethinkers and Debating Freethought in the American Yiddish Press (1880s–1920s)" (PhD diss., Emory University, 2023), 187–89.

9. Udel, *Honey on the Page*, 82.

10. On internal Jewish Orientalism and romanticizing depictions of Sephardic culture, see John M. Efron, *German Jewry and the Allure of the Sephardic* (Princeton, NJ: Princeton University Press, 2016). For Metzker's romanticized capsule history of Iberian Jewry, see Udel, *Honey on the Page*, 83.

11. Udel, *Honey on the Page*, 95.

12. On Columbus's voyages in relation to Iberian Jewry, including claims of the explorer's own Jewishness (dubious) and Jewish financial backing (well supported), see Jonathan D. Sarna, "Columbus and the Jews," *Commentary* 94, no. 5 (November 1992): 38–41.

13. Udel, *Honey on the Page*, 105.

14. Udel, *Honey on the Page*, 102.

15. On the historical phenomenon of Christians abducting and converting Jewish children, see Joel F. Harrington, "Early Modern Child Abduction in the Name of Religion," in Berner and Underwood, *Childhood, Youth and Religious Minorities in Early Modern Europe*, 257. On adolescent conversion, see Ahuva Liberles, "When They Come of Age: Religious Conversion and Puberty in Fifteenth-Century Ashkenaz" (299–318), in the same volume.

16. On Mark as "arguably the most important figure in Yiddish education in the postwar period," see Burko, "Saving Yiddish," 31.

17. In a similar vein, Mark published lives of the explorer David Hareuveni and the messianic reverse-converso Solomon Molkho, two medieval Jewish figures whose exploits are wreathed in myth and mystery. By contrast, the same author wrote biographies for young readers of historical figures in Jewish intellectual history, including Maimonides, Rashi, and Rabbenu Gershom. See his *Der rambam* (New York: Arbeter Ring, 1947), and *Rabenu Gershom, Rashi, Yehuda Khosid* (New York: Kinder Ring, 1941), as well as Yekhiel Shtern, *Der nosi Hillel* [Hillel, the Sage] (Montreal: Yidishe shul, 1946).

18. Burko, "Saving Yiddish," 39.

19. For a thorough treatment of the textual parallels, see Sherman, *The Jewish Pope*, esp. 26–66 and 71. For a compact yet wide-ranging schematization of the motif's medieval attestations (including Sephardic sources) as well as two twentieth-century revisitations, see David Levine Lerner, "The Enduring Legend of the Jewish Pope," *Judaism* 40, no. 2 (Spring 1991): 148–70.

20. For a brief but trenchant discussion of the novella, see Kadar, *Raising Secular Jews*, 204–5. See also Udel, "The 'Jewish Pope' in the 1940s." Ruth Fisher Goodman published *The Jewish Pope: A Yiddish Tale* (McKinleyville, CA: Fithian Press, 2006); however, I cite from my own unpublished translation.

21. Gaster, *Ma'aseh Book*, vol. 1, tale 188, 410–18. A facsimile of the original Yiddish was annotated and translated into French, and published as a lavish bilingual edition by Starck, *Un beau livre d'histoires*, 518–26. In Starck's numbering, it is tale 187. For a thorough textual reconstruction and thematological analysis, see Bamberger, *Ha'afifior Hayehudi* [The Jewish Pope]. See also the discussion of the Jewish Pope legend in Yassif, *Sippur ha-'am ha-'ivri*, 334ff.

22. Gaster, *Ma'aseh Book*, 412.

23. Gaster, *Ma'aseh Book*, 417.

24. The poem plays on the name Elchanan, breaking it into its constituent words "El hanan nahalato beno'am lehashper" (God bestowed grace upon His Portion [Israel], adorning them

with his favor). I am grateful to Bernard Septimus, who aided in the translation of this difficult line. The *piyyut* is annotated in Daniel Goldschmidt, ed., *Mahzor layamim hanora'im*, vol. 1, *Rosh Hashana* (Jerusalem: Koren/Leo Baeck Institute, 1970), 47–50. See Avraham Grossman, *Hakhme ashkenaz harishonim* (Jerusalem: Magnes, 1981), 86ff. On Elchanan, see 89ff. Grossman mentions the custom of early Ashkenazic liturgical poets to allude to their children in their compositions.

25. Several Hebrew and Sephardic sources require Elchanan's martyrdom for the full expiation of his sin. However, the Yiddish version recorded in the *Mayse bukh* does not. See a discussion of a possible reason for this divergence in Sherman, *The Jewish Pope*, 14.

26. Gaster, *Ma'aseh Book*, 416.

27. See BT Shabbat 68b and BT Shavuot 5a.

28. Sherman, *The Jewish Pope*, 18–19.

29. On the historical events, see Mary Stroll, *The Jewish Pope: Ideology and Politics in the Papal Schism of 1130* (Leiden: Brill, 1987); George L. Williams, *Papal Genealogy: The Families and Descendants of the Popes* (Jefferson, NC: McFarland and Company, 1998), 24; and Joachim Prinz, *Popes from the Ghetto* (New York: Schocken, 1968).

30. See Sherman, *The Jewish Pope*, 18. For an analysis of the racial dimension of Anaclet's election and this papal schism, see Irven M. Resnick, "Race, Anti-Jewish Polemic, Arnulf of Seéz, and the Contested Papal Election of Anaclet II (A.D. 1130)," in *Jews in Medieval Christendom: Slay Them Not*, ed. Kristine T. Utterback and Merrall L. Price (Leiden: Brill, 2013), 45–70. See also Resnick's *Marks of Distinctions: Christian Perceptions of Jews in the High Middle Ages* (Washington, DC: Catholic University of America Press, 2012), 270–85.

31. Lerner, "The Enduring Legend," 164.

32. For the real-life story of an 1858 papal abduction, see David I. Kertzer, *The Kidnapping of Edgardo Mortara* (New York: Knopf, 1997).

33. Shandler, "The Holocaust for Beginners," 118.

34. Shandler, "Beyond the Mother Tongue," 100.

35. Mark, "Yiddishkeyt un veltlekhkeyt," 45. For more of Mark's articulations of *yidishkeyt* in the periodical literature, see Burko, "Saving Yiddish," 34.

36. Burko, "Saving Yiddish," 48–49.

37. Burko, "Saving Yiddish," 17.

38. Mark, "Di shlikhes fun der yidisher shul," cited in Burko, "Saving Yiddish," 18.

39. Burko explores the intellectual synergy and collaborative yet competitive relationship between the two figures, relating that Mark viewed himself vis-à-vis Weinreich as "his Majesty's opposition" ("Saving Yiddish," 5).

40. David Roskies, "The Legend of Max Weinreich," *Tablet Magazine*, January 27, 2023.

41. For a selection of the submitted essays, see Jeffrey Shandler, ed., *Awakening Lives: Autobiographies of Jewish Youth in Poland Before the Holocaust* (New Haven, CT: Yale University Press, 2002). For a poignant graphic novel adaptation of a few especially eloquent entries, see Ken Krimstein, *When I Grow Up: The Lost Autobiographies of Six Yiddish Teenagers* (New York: Bloomsbury, 2021).

42. Burko, "Saving Yiddish," 68.

43. Kadar, *Raising Secular Jews*, 157.

44. Udel, *Honey on the Page*, 117.

45. Udel, *Honey on the Page*, 125.

46. Udel, *Honey on the Page*, 130.

47. Udel, *Honey on the Page*, 138–39.

48. Udel, *Honey on the Page*, 146–47.

49. On the symbolism of trees and their roots in pre-State Palestine, see Zerubavel, "The Forest as a National Icon," 60.

50. While in many frontier cultures, the colonization of wilderness implied deforestation, Zerubavel discusses how for the Zionist settlers, planting trees was a means of reintroducing nature—like the Hebrew nation—into its native landscape ("The Forest," 62).

51. On the Zionist reclamation and celebration of Tu Bishvat, see Shoham, *Israel Celebrates*, chap. 2. On the political and cultural context of afforestation efforts, see 74–83.

52. Zerubavel, "The Forest," 63, 89. On a similar theme, see Zvi Hirsch Gelberg, "Hamisha asar bishvat" [The 15th of Shevat], *Hamagid*, January 30, 1896, 1. For deeper analysis of the analogy, see Celina Mashiach, *Yaldut u-le'ummiyut: Dyoqan yaldut medumyenet be-sifrut ha-yeladim ha-ivrit* [Childhood and Nationalism: Imagined Childhood in Hebrew Children's Literature, 1790–1948] (Tel Aviv: Tcherikover, 2000), 123–40.

53. Shoham, *Israel Celebrates*, 81.

54. Shoham, *Israel Celebrates*, 74.

55. Udel, *Honey on the Page*, 131, 147.

56. Shoham, *Israel Celebrates*, 76, 77–78.

57. See Darr, *The Nation and the Child*, 104. For more on the separate children's residences on kibbutzim, see the documentary film *Children of the Sun*, dir. Ran Tal (Lama Films, 2007).

58. Darr, *The Nation and the Child*, 104, 16.

59. Darr notes that Lea Goldberg's narrative poem "Al hadeshe," with its tender bedtime scene between ants, subverts the kibbutz norm of a separate residence where children slept (*The Nation and the Child*, 65–67).

60. See Darr, *The Nation and the Child*, 12–16, for an insightful discussion of teachers' central role in nation building.

61. See Darr's discussion of Eliezer Smoli's novel *Bnei ha-yoreh* [Children of the First Rain], where schoolchildren are figured as plants that grow in the soil of their homeland (*The Nation and the Child*, 14–16).

62. For a full treatment of the post-Holocaust softening toward Yiddish, see Darr, *The Nation and the Child*, chap. 6, "Making Amends with Yiddish in the Aftermath of the Holocaust," 81–90. Publication: "Ma'ase bemakel" in 1960 in New York by the Board of Jewish Education (Lador Library), 27.

63. Rudin, "Language, Poetics, and Ideology in Holocaust Literature for Hebrew-Speaking Children," 158, 162.

64. See Darr, *The Nation and the Child*, chap. 7, "Calling Children to Arms Through National War Narratives," 91–102.

Conclusion

1. For an introduction to the *silabarios*, see Sarah Zaides, "Learning Ladino—Then and Now," Stroum Center for Jewish Studies, University of Washington, accessed December 8, 2024, https://jewishstudies.washington.edu/sephardic-studies/learning-ladino-ottoman-empire/.

2. Although I encountered the essay in the two volumes of stories, it appears in a more accessible version with an English glossary online. See Kipnis, "Mayn mame-loshn" [My Mother Tongue]. The essay was also published in the anthology by Hirsh Osherovitsh, ed., *Yidish-literatur in medines-yisroel* [Yiddish Literature in the State of Israel] (Tel-Aviv: H. Leyvik Farlag, 1991), 2: 304–9.

3. Seidman, *A Marriage Made in Heaven* (henceforth MMH), 31.

4. *Akdomus* is an Aramaic liturgical poem recited on the holiday of Shvues.

5. Kipnis, "Mayn mame-loshn," 3.

6. Kipnis, "Mayn mame-loshn," 4.

7. Kipnis, "Mayn mame-loshn," 7.

8. Kipnis, "Mayn mame-loshn," 7.

9. See Jeremiah 31:15 and Eicha Rabba 24.

10. Yankev Glatshteyn also figured the Matriarch Rachel as a mournful Mother Yiddish. For a discussion of this motif in his work, see Seidman, MMH, 122.

11. *The Mendele Review* (online), November 30, 1999, https://yiddish.haifa.ac.il/tmr/tmr03/tmr03018.txt.

12. Indelman, *Gut yontef, kinder*, 38.

13. Indelman, *Gut yontef, kinder*, 50.

14. Indelman, *Gut yontef, kinder*, 51.

15. Indelman, *Gut yontef, kinder*, 50.

16. Indelman, *Gut yontef, kinder*, 50.

17. On the ideology of Soviet Yiddish orthography, see David Shneer, *Yiddish and the Creation of Soviet Jewish Culture: 1918–1930* (New York: Cambridge University Press, 2004), 67–70; and Gennady Estraikh, *Soviet Yiddish: Language-Planning and Linguistic Development* (New York: Oxford University Press, 1999), esp. chap. 5, "Soviet Yiddish Orthography," 115–40.

18. Kvitko, *Alefbeys*, 3.

19. Matrosev was an infantryman of nineteen who died heroically in the Second World War by blocking a German machine gun with his body so that his comrades could advance.

20. See Carly Gould and Chyllis E. Scott, "The Reading Pendulum: Phonics, Word Method, and Whole Language," *Data Journal of Literacy Innovation* 3, no. 1 (2018): 4–15. For a brief, accessible history of Anglophone literacy instruction, see Stephen Parker, "A Brief History of Reading Instruction," Parker's website, updated December 23, 2021, www.parkerphonics.com/post/a-brief-history-of-reading-instruction.

21. See David Hochberg, *Di naye shul: An ilusṭrirṭer Alef-beys miṭ a groysn maṭeryal tsum leyenen nokhn Alef-beys* [The New School: An Illustrated Abecedary with Lots of Material for Mastering Alphabetic Literacy] (Ṿilna: B. A. Ḳletsḳin, n.d.).

22. See Deborah Tarant, *Mayn alefbeys: Leyenbukh far onfanger* [My Alphabet: A Textbook for Beginners] (New York: International Workers Order, 1937).

23. Pen name of Moyshe-Avrohom Kats or Abraham Morris Katz.

24. *Gut morgn, alef!* [Good Morning, Alef!] was initially published in *Tsukunft* [Future] in New York (March 1946) and later appeared in a book, *Tsvey shpiln un a mayse: Gut morgn, alef, purim-shpil un yosele* [Two Plays and a Story: Good Morning, Alef, a Purim play, and Yosele] (New York: 1950). See the note in the book's front matter about the publication history of each part and past performances of the plays.

25. Kats, *Gut morgn, alef!* 8.

26. Kats, *Gut morgn, alef!* 15.

27. Shmuel Charney championed Kats's poetry in his literature column. See his review, "A mol iz geven a mayse . . . ," *Der tog* (New York), March 31, 1946, sec. 2, p. 4, and Charney, "Geleyent un geshribn," subheading "Fishke der shtumer," *Der Tog-morgn-zhurnal* (New York), May 17, 1953, sec. 2, p. 4.

28. In a lighter vein, the letters collectively attack protagonist Mikhl after his summer of neglecting them while on summer vacation in Moyshe Shifris's story "The Alphabet Gets Angry" (Udel, *Honey on the Page*, 241–45). And in a yet darker vein, consider Tea Arciszewska's never fully staged play about children and wartime trauma, *Miryeml*, being translated by Sonia Gollance. An excerpt, retrieved January 14, 2025, is available here: www.yiddishbookcenter.org/discover/yiddish-translation/drama/miryeml-excerpt.

29. See Chani Altein, *Af der alefbeyz shifl* (published simultaneously in English as *The Alef-Bais Trip on the Alef-Bais Ship*) (New York: Hechai, 2009).

Afterword

1. On the didactic nature and *haymish* characteristics of Hasidic children's literature, see Ayala Fader, "Literacy, Bilingualism and Gender in a Hasidic Community," *Linguistics and Education* 12, no. 3 (Autumn 2001): 261–83.

2. For more on the material culture of Hasidic and non-Hasidic Orthodox childhood, see Dainy Bernstein, ed., *Artifacts of Orthodox Jewish Childhoods: Personal and Critical Essays* (New York: Ben Yehuda Press, 2022).

3. Asya Vaisman Schulman, "*Heavenly Father*: Portraying the Family in Hasidic Yiddish Children's Literature," in Estraikh et al., *Children and Yiddish Literature: From Early Modernity to Post-Modernity*, 43.

4. See Fader, "Literacy, Bilingualism and Gender," 275–76.

5. See "About Lechaim" on the company website, accessed December 8, 2024, www.lchaimusa.com/pages/about-lchaim.

6. Fader, "Literacy, Bilingualism and Gender," 270.

7. Fader, personal communication, July 6, 2023.

8. Fader, "Literacy, Bilingualism and Gender," 272.

9. Sefer HaRokeah, Hilkhot Shavuot, Siman 296.

SELECTED BIBLIOGRAPHY

For the reader's convenience, I have divided the bibliography between primary and secondary sources, while acknowledging that the line of demarcation between the two is sometimes blurry. This is especially true of Yiddish-language articles that appeared in newspapers and educational periodicals during the first half of the twentieth century or even earlier. Generally, sources directly related to this book's subject matter are included in the bibliography, while more tangentially relevant sources are cited only in the notes.

Primary Literature

Abramovitsh, S. Y. "From the Introduction to the *Collected Works*." Translated by Miriam Udel. *PaknTreger*, Summer 2021. https://www.yiddishbookcenter.org/language-literature-culture/pakn-treger/2021-pakn-treger-digital-translation-issue/introduction.

Asch, Sholem. *Far yugnt: Dertseylungen un bilder* [For Youth: Stories and Pictures]. Warsaw: Farlag Kultur-lige, 1929.

Bashevis Singer, Isaac. *Stories for Children*. New York: Farrar, Straus and Giroux, 1984.

Biber, Yisroel. *Friling in vald* [Spring in the Forest]. Warsaw: Kinderfraynd, 1937.

———. *Vinter in vald* [Winter in the Forest]. Warsaw: Kinderfraynd, 1937.

Brainin, Ruvn. "Vos zolen unzere kinder lezen?" [What Should Our Children Read?]. *Der yud*, 23 and 24 (June 7 and June 14, 1900): 1–2; 3–5 respectively.

Charney, Shmuel (Niger). *Di Yidishe literatur un di lezerin* [Yiddish Literature and the Female Reader]. Vilna: Vilner farlag, 1919.

———. "Kinder literatur" [Children's Literature]. *Di yudishe velt* 9 (1913): 143.

———. "Vegn der idisher kinder literatur." *Shul-almanakh* (1935): 188–95.

———. "Yiddish Literature and the Female Reader." Translated and abridged by Sheva Zucker. In *Women of the Word: Jewish Women and Jewish Writing*, edited by Judith Baskin. Detroit: Wayne State University Press, 1994, 70–90.

Chaver Paver (Gershon Einbinder). *Labzik: Mayselekh vegn klugn hintele Labzik* [Labzik: Tales of a Clever Pup]. New York: International Workers Order, 1935.

———. *Labzik: Tales of a Clever Pup*. Translated by Miriam Udel. Forthcoming from State University of New York Press.

Davidman. Shloyme. *A shprakh iz vi a gortn* [A Language Is like a Garden]. New York: publisher unspecified, 1952.

Dik, Isaac Meir. *Di alte libe rostet nikht*. Vilnius: Romm Press, 1876.

———. "Slavery or Serfdom." Translated by Eli Rosenblatt. *In geveb*, November 17, 2015. https://ingeveb.org/texts-and-translations/slavery-or-serfdom.

Eliot, George. "The Natural History of German Life." *Westminster Review* 66 (July 1856): 28–44.

Fichman, Yankev. *A shabes in vald* [A Sabbath in the Forest]. Warsaw: Kultur-lige, 1924.

Gaster, Moses, ed. and trans. *Ma'aseh Book: Book of Jewish Tales and Legends*. Philadelphia: Jewish Publication Society, 1934.

Heberer, Patricia. *Children During the Holocaust*. Documenting Life and Destruction: Holocaust Sources in Context. Lanham, MD: AltaMira Press in association with the United States Holocaust Memorial Museum, 2011.

Hellerstein, Kathryn. *Paper Bridges: Selected Poems of Kadya Molodowsky*. Detroit: Wayne State University Press, 1999.

Hofman, Kapilowitz Leah. *Kleyne in der groyser velt* [Little Ones in the Big World]. New York: Leben, 1920.

Indelman, Elkhonen. *Gut yontef, kinder* [Happy Holiday, Children]. New York: Jewish Educational Committee Press, 1958.

Kats, Alef. *Fun alef biz sof* [From A to Z]. New York: Farlag Atlantik, 1939.

Kazdan, Khaim Shloyme. "Finf un draysik yor yidishe kinder-literatur" [Thirty-Five Years of Yiddish Children's Literature]. In *Shul pinkes* [School Register], edited by Sh. Berkovich, M. Bronshteyn, Yudl Mark, and I. Chaim Pomerantz. Chicago: Sholem Aleichem Folk Institute, 1948.

———. *Medem sanatorye bukh* [Medem Sanatorium Book]. Tel Aviv: Ha-Menorah, 1971.

Kiel, Chanan. *In ale farbn: lider* [In Every Shade: Poems]. Pittsburgh: privately published, 1971.

Kinder heldn [Child Heroes]. Buenos Aires: Farlag IKUF, 1953.

Kipnis, Levin. "Mayn mame-loshn" [My Mother Tongue]. *Mendele Review* 3, no. 18 (1999): 1–8.

———. *Untern bokserboym*. Tel Aviv: Yisroel bukh, 1993.

———. *Untern faygnboym*. Tel Aviv: Yisroel bukh, 1993.

———. *Untern Teytlboym*. New York: Matones, 1961.

Kulbak, Moyshe. *The Zelmenyaners*. Translated by Hillel Halkin with an introduction by Sasha Senderovich. New Haven, CT: Yale University Press, 2013.

Kvitko, Leyb (Lev). *A tsig mit zibn tsigelekh* [A Nanny Goat with Seven Kids]. Kharkov: Tsentralfarlag, 1928.

———. *Akh, az ikh vel oysvaksn!* [Ah, When I Grow Up!]. Odessa: Kinder farlag, n.d.

———. *Alefbeys* [Alphabet]. Moscow: Melukhe-farlag "Der emes," 1947.

———. *Di royte armey* [The Red Army]. Moscow: Farlag "emes," 1938?.

———. *Vemes iz es meydele?* [Whose Girl Is This?]. Moscow: Melukhe-farlag "Der emes," 1940.

Lit-Man (Simkhe Geltman/Freylekh). *Mayselekh* [Stories]. Warsaw: Kinder-fraynd, 1936.

Maimonides, Moses. "Eight Chapters." In *Ethical Writings of Maimonides*, edited and translated by R. L. Weiss and C. Butterworth. New York: Dover Publications, 1983.

Mark, Yud(e)l. "Changes in the Yiddish School." *Jewish Education* 19, no. 1 (1947): 31–38.

———. *Der yidisher poyps: A geveb fun legende, geshikhte un fantazye* [The Jewish Pope: A Web of Legend, History and Fantasy]. New York: Kinder ring (Educational Committee of the Workmen's Circle), 1947.

———. "Di shlikhes fun der yidisher shul" [The Mission of the Yiddish School]. *Kultur un dertsiung*, May 1954.

———. "Di vokh fun troyer un protest" [The Week of Sorrow and Protest]. *Der pedagogisher buleten*, February 1943, 1–5.

———. *The Jewish Pope: A Yiddish Tale*. Translated by Ruth Fisher Goodman. McKinleyville, CA: Daniel and Daniel, 2006.

———. "Un du zolst dertseyln dayn kind . . ." *Pedagogisher buleten* 12 (December 1942): 1–2

———. "Vegn propagande far undzere shuln." *Pedagogisher buleten* (October 1952): 7–9.

———. "Yidishkeyt un veltlekhkeyt in un arum undzere shuln" [Jewishness and Secularism in and Around Our Schools]. In *Shul pinkes* [School Register], edited by Sh. Berkovich, M. Bronshteyn, Yudl Mark, and I. Chaim Pomerantz. Chicago: Sholem Aleichem Folk Institute, 1948.

Marx, Erik. *Di geshikhte fun der yidisher literatur fun di eltste tsaytn biz der haskole-tkufe* [The History of Yiddish Literature from Its Inception Until the Enlightenment]. Warsaw: Kulturlige, 1928.

Metzker, Isaac. *Don Yitskhok Abravanel, 1437–1509*. New York: Kinder ring, 1941.

Molodowsky, Kadya. *Martsepanes: Mayselekh un lider far kinder un yugnt* [Marzipans: Stories and Poems for Children and Youth]. New York: Educational Committee of the Workmen's Circle and CYCO, 1970.

———. *Mayselekh* [Stories]. Warsaw: Yiddish School Organization, 1931.

———. "Tsurik in bereze (kapitl 41 fun 'mayn elterzeydns yerushe')" [Back to Bereze (Ch. 41 of "My Great-Grandfather's Legacy"]. *Svive* 34 (August 1971): 39.

———. *Yidishe kinder: Mayselekh* [Jewish Children: Stories]. New York: Central Committee of Yiddish Folk Schools of the US and Canada, 1945.

Nasiram, M. A. *"Vos zoln unzere kinder leyenen?"* ["What Should Our Children Read?"]. *Shul un heym* (New York), June 1930, 19.

Oyerbakh, B. *Dos farblondzete Khava'le* [Evie Gets Lost]. (Sometimes listed as *Mirten*.) Warsaw: Farlag mitspe, 1920.

Pat, Yankev. *Der vunderlekher leyb* [The Magic Lion]. Warsaw: Farlag A. Gitlin, 1921.

———. *Khan(e)ke: Di tokhter fun der lererin Sheyne* [Hannah: Daughter of Sheyne the Teacher]. Buenos Aires: Farlag Yidbukh, 1964.

Peretz, Y. L. "Di lezerin." In *Ale verk*, vol. 2, *Dertseylungen, mayselekh, bilder*. New York: CYCO, 1947.

Rabinowitz, Zina. *A mayse mit a shtekele* [The Story of a Stick]. Mexico City: Yiddish School in Mexico, 1958.

———. *Der liber yontef* [The Precious Holidays]. New York: Farlag Matones, 1958.

Reyzin, Avrom. "Tsum 25stn yortsayt fun Shomer." *Forverts* (New York), December 6, 1930; reprinted in Roze Shomer-Batshelis, *Undzer foter shomer*. New York, IKUF 1950, 199–205.

Reyzen, Zalman. *Leḳsiḳon fun der Yidisher liṭeraṭur, prese un filologye*. 4 vols. Vilnius: B. Kletskin, 1926.

Rodin, Dovid (Elye Levin). *A modne meydl fun bruklin*. Tel Aviv: Farlag Y.L. Peretz, 1973.

Rosenzweig, Claudia. *Bovo d'Antona by Elye Bokher: A Yiddish Romance: A Critical Edition with Commentary*. Leiden: Brill, 2015.

Roskies, Diane K., and David G. Roskies, eds. *The Shtetl Book*. New York: Ktav, 1975.

Rousseau, Jean Jacques. *Emile, or On Education*. Edited and translated by Allan Bloom. New York: Basic Books, 1979.

Schulner, Dora. "The First Writer I Read and Loved." Translated by Jessica Kirzane. *Pakn Treger* 80 (Fall 2019): 28–30.

Shifris, Moyshe. *Foygl kanarik un andere mayses* [Canary Bird and Other Stories]. New York: Moyshe Shifris bukh komitet, 1950.

Sholem Aleichem. "Dos dreydl." In *Mayses far Yidishe kinder* [Stories for Jewish Children]. Vol. 9, book 2 of *Ale verk fun Sholem-Aleykhem* [The Complete Works of Sholem Aleichem]. New York: Sholem-Aleykhem folksfond, 1918.

———. *Holiday Tales.* Translated by Aliza Shevrin. Mineola, NY: Dover, 1979.

———. "The Judgment of Shomer." Translated by Justin Cammy. In Cammy et al., *Arguing the Modern Jewish Canon.*

———. *The Letters of Menakhem-Mendl and Sheyne-Sheyndl and, Motl, the Cantor's Son.* Translated by Hillel Halkin. New Haven, CT: Yale University Press, 2002.

———. *Tevye the Dairyman and The Railroad Stories.* Translated by Hillel Halkin. New York: Schocken, 1987.

Sholom Aleichem. *Some Laughter, Some Tears: Tales from the Old World and the New.* Translated by Curt Leviant. New York: Putnam, 1968.

Shomer- Bachelis, Roze. *Undzer foter Shomer* [Our Father, Shomer]. New York: Ikuf, 1950.

Shtern, Yekhiel. "A Kheyder in Tyszowce (Tishevits)." Translated by Shlomo Noble. *YIVO Annual of Jewish Social Science* 5 (1950): 152–71.

Shtuker-Paiuk, Malke. *Gut yontef: Lider, tsenkes, un agodes.* Buenos Aires: privately published by subscription, 1957.

Sofer, Berl. *Yeshayeles upshern* [Yeshayele's First Haircut]. New York: Kinder Shpiel, 2008.

Spektor, Mordkhe. *Kinder.* Vilna: Farlag B. Kletskin, 1912.

Starck, Astrid. *Un beau livre d'histoires: Eyn Shön Mayse Bukh: Fac-Similé De L'editio Princeps De Bâle (1602).* 2 vols. Basel: Schwabe, 2004.

Steinberg, Judah. *Fragen* [Questions]. New York: Max N. Maisel, Idisher farlag far literatur un visnshaft, 1918.

Trunk, Yehiel Yeshaye. *Poyln: My Life Within Jewish Life in Poland, Sketches and Images.* Translated by Anna Clarke. Toronto: University of Toronto Press, 2007.

———. *Poyln: Zikhroynes un bilder.* New York: Medem-Klub, 1944.

Udel, Miriam, ed. and trans. *Honey on the Page: A Treasury of Yiddish Children's Literature.* New York: NYU Press, 2020.

Vi azoy lebt dos kind in medem sanatorye [How Children Live in the Medem Sanatorium]. Attributed to Shloyme Gilinsky. Warsaw: Board of Directors of the Medem Sanatorium, 1932.

Weizmann-Lichtenstein, Haya. *Betzel Koratenu* [In the Shade of Our Roof]. Tel Aviv: Am Oved, 1948.

Werber, Szyfra. *Niseles trer.* Brussels: School and Education Committee for Belgium, 1950.

Secondary Literature

Adler, Eliyana. *In Her Hands: The Education of Jewish Girls in Tsarist Russia.* Detroit: Wayne State University Press, 2011.

Alexander, Ruth M. "Wayward Girls in New York." In *Small Worlds: Children and Adolescents in America, 1850–1950,* edited by Elliott West and Paula Petrik. Lawrence: University Press of Kansas, 1992.

Allison, Alida. *Isaac Bashevis Singer: Children's Stories and Childhood Memoirs.* Woodbridge, CT: Twayne, 1996.

Antonovsky, Aaron. "The Sense of Coherence: An Historical and Future Perspective." In *Stress, Coping and Health in Families: Sense of Coherence and Resiliency,* edited by Hamilton I. McCubbin, Elizabeth A. Thompson, Anne I. Thompson, and Julie E. Fromer. London: SAGE Publications, 1998.

———. "A Somewhat Personal Odyssey in Studying the Stress Process." *Stress Medicine* 6, no. 2 (April/June 1990): 71–80.

———. *Unraveling the Mystery of Health : How People Manage Stress and Stay Well.* San Francisco: Jossey-Bass, 1987.

Antonovsky, Avishai, and Shifra Sagy. "Aaron Antonovsky, the Scholar and the Man Behind Salutogenesis." In *The Handbook of Salutogenesis,* edited by M. B. Mittelmark, S. Sagy, M. Eriksson, et al. New York: Springer, 2017.

Ariès, Philippe. *Centuries of Childhood: A Social History of Family Life.* New York: Knopf, 1962.

Balina, Marina. "Crafting the Self: Narratives of Prerevolutionary Childhood in Soviet Literature." In Balina and Rudova, *Russian Children's Literature and Culture.*

———. "'It's Grand to Be an Orphan!': Crafting Happy Citizens in Soviet Children's Literature in the 1920s." In Balina and Dobrenko, *Petrified Utopia.*

Balina, Marina, and Evgeny Dobrenko, eds. *Petrified Utopia: Happiness Soviet Style.* London: Anthem Press, 2011.

Balina, Marina, and Larissa Rudova, eds. *Russian Children's Literature and Culture.* New York: Routledge, 2008.

Ball, John Clement. "Max's Colonial Fantasy: Rereading Sendak's 'Where the Wild Things Are.'" *Ariel* 28, no. 1 (1997): 167–79.

Bamberger, Joseph. *Ha'afifior hayehudi: Letoldoteha shel 'aggadà mime' habenaym be'ashkenaz* [The Jewish Pope: History of a Medieval Ashkenazic Legend]. Ramat-Gan: Bar-Ilan University Press, 2009.

Bar-El, Adina. *Bein ha'etsim hayerakrakim: Itonei yeladim beYidish uve'Ivrit bePolin, 1918–1939* [Under the Little Green Trees: Yiddish and Hebrew Children's Periodicals in Poland, 1918–1939]. Jerusalem: Sifriyah ha-Tsiyonit-Makhon Dov Sadan, 2006.

———. "'Grininke beymelekh'—hahathala: Letoldotav shel iton yeladim yidi bepolin" [Little Green Trees—The Beginning: Toward a History of a Yiddish Children's Periodical in Poland]. *Qesher* 27 (May 2000): 99–106.

———. "Imma mesaperet vesavta mesaperet od: Hashpa'atan shel nashim al sifrut hayeladim beidish" [Mama Tells Stories and Grandma Tells More: Women's Influence on Yiddish Children's Literature]. *Ketav et leiyun umehkar* 9 (2003): 127–46.

———. "Min hanitsanim harishonim ve'ad haperiha: Sifrut yeladim beYidish bemizrah Eiropa" [From the First Buds to the Blossom: Yiddish Children's Literature in Eastern Europe]. *Moznayim* 81, nos. 3–4 (2008): 66–69.

Batson, C. Daniel. "The Empathy-Altruism Hypothesis: Issues and Implications." In *Empathy: from Bench to Bedside,* edited by Jean Decety. Cambridge, MA: MIT Press, 2014.

Baumgarten, Jean. *Introduction to Old Yiddish Literature.* Oxford, UK: Oxford University Press, 2005.

Benz, Carina, Torill Bull, Maurice Mittelmark, and Lenneke Vaandrager. "Culture in Salutogenesis: the Scholarship of Aaron Antonovsky." *Global Health Promotion* 21, no. 4 (December 2014): 16–23.

Berger, Shlomo. "The Spanish Pagan Woman and Ashkenazi Children Reading Yiddish Circa 1700." In Estraikh et al., *Children and Yiddish Literature: From Early Modernity to Post-Modernity*. Cambridge, UK: Modern Humanities Research Association, 2016.

Berger, Shulamith. "Moyshe Levin (Ber Sarin) of Yung-Vilne and His Solo Publishing Venture for Children." *Judaica Librarianship* 20 (2017): 100–33.

Berner, Tali. *Al pi darkam: Yeladim veyaldut beashkenaz*. Jerusalem: Merkaz Zalman Shazar, 2018.

———. "Jewish Children and Domestic Devotion in Early Modern Illustrations." In Berner and Underwood, *Childhood, Youth and Religious Minorities in Early Modern Europe*.

Berner, Tali, and Lucy Underwood, eds. *Childhood, Youth and Religious Minorities in Early Modern Europe*. Cham: Springer International Publishing, 2021.

Biale, David. *Not in the Heavens: The Tradition of Jewish Secular Thought*. Princeton, NJ: Princeton University Press, 2015.

Blatman, Daniel. *For Our Freedom and Yours: The Jewish Labour Bund in Poland 1939–1949*. Chicago: Vallentine Mitchell, 2003.

Bottigheimer, Ruth B. "Fairy Tales and Folk Tales." In *International Companion Encyclopedia of Children's Literature*, edited by Peter Hunt. New York: Routledge, 2004.

Bromberg, Eli. "We Need to Talk About Shmuel Charney." *In geveb*, October 2, 2019, https://ingeveb.org/articles/we-need-to-talk-about-shmuel-charney.

Burko, Alec Eliezer. "Saving Yiddish: Yiddish Studies and the Language Sciences in America, 1940–1970." PhD diss., Jewish Theological Seminary of America, 2019.

Byford, Andy. *Science of the Child in Late Imperial and Early Soviet Russia*. Oxford, UK: Oxford University Press, 2020.

Cammy, Justin D. "Judging *The Judgment of Shomer*: Jewish Literature Versus Jewish Reading." In Cammy et al., *Arguing the Modern Jewish Canon*.

Cammy, Justin D., Dara Horn, Alyssa Quint, and Rachel Rubinstein, eds. *Arguing the Modern Jewish Canon: Essays on Literature in Honor of Ruth Wisse*, edited by Cambridge, MA: Harvard University Press, 2008.

Caplan, Marc. *How Strange the Change: Language Temporality and Narrative Form in Peripheral Modernisms*. Stanford, CA: Stanford University Press, 2011.

———. *Yiddish Writers in Weimar Berlin: A Fugitive Modernism*. Bloomington, IN: Indiana University Press, 2021.

Cohen, Nathan. "No More Little Jews Without Beards: Insights into Yiddish Children's Literature in Eastern Europe Prior to World War I." *Modern Judaism* 41, no. 1 (2021): 92–109.

Cohen, Steven M., and Paula E. Hyman, eds. *The Jewish Family: Myths and Reality*. New York: Holmes and Meier, 1986.

Crain, Patricia. "Coda. Bedtime Stories." In *Reading Children: Literacy, Property, and the Dilemmas of Childhood in Nineteenth-Century America*. Philadelphia: University of Pennsylvania Press, 2016.

Darr, Yael. *Kanon bekhama kolot: Sifrut hayeladim shel tenuat hapo'alim 1930–1950* [A Canon in Many Voices: Children's Literature of the Labor Movement 1930–1950]. Jerusalem: Yad Yitzhak ben Zvi, 2013.

———. *The Nation and the Child: Nation Building in Hebrew Children's Literature 1930–1970*. Amsterdam: John Benjamins Publishing Company, 2018.

———. *Umisafsal halimudim lukahnu: Hayishuv lenokhah sho'ah velikrat medinah besifrut hayeladim haErets-Yisre'elit, 1939–1948* [Called Away from Our School-Desks: The Yishuv in the Shadow of the Holocaust and in Anticipation of Statehood in the Children's Literature of Eretz Israel]. Jerusalem: Magnes Press, 2006.

Dauber, Jeremy A. *In the Demon's Bedroom: Yiddish Literature and the Early Modern*. New Haven, CT: Yale University Press, 2010.

———. "Shomer." In *YIVO Encyclopedia of Jews in Eastern Europe*. October 15, 2010. https://yivoencyclopedia.org/article.aspx/Shomer.

DeLuzio, Crista. *Female Adolescence in American Scientific Thought, 1830–1930*. Baltimore: Johns Hopkins University Press, 2007.

Diner, Hasia R. *We Remember with Reverence and Love: American Jews and the Myth of Silence After the Holocaust, 1945–1962*. New York: NYU Press, 2009.

Eichler-Levine, Jodi. *Suffer the Little Children: Uses of the Past in Jewish and African American Children's Literature*. New York: NYU Press, 2015.

Eliot, George. *Middlemarch: A Study of Provincial Life*. Edited by Gregory Maertz. Peterborough, ON: Broadview Press, 2004.

Estraikh, Gennady. "The Kharkiv Yiddish Literary World, 1920s–mid–1930s." *East European Jewish Affairs* 32, no. 2 (2002): 70–88.

———. *Transatlantic Russian Jewishness: Ideological Voyages of the Yiddish Daily Forverts in the First Half of the Twentieth Century*. Brookline, MA: Academic Studies Press, 2020.

Estraikh, Gennady, and Mikhail Krutikov, eds. *Yiddish in Weimar Berlin*. Oxford, UK: Oxford Legenda, 2010.

Estraikh, Gennady, Kerstin Hoge, and Mikhail Krutikov, eds. *Children and Yiddish Literature: From Early Modernity to Post-Modernity*. New York: Legenda, 2016.

Faierstein, Morris M. "The *Dibbuk* in the *Mayse Bukh*." *Shofar* 30, no. 1 (2011): 94–103.

Feigenzohn, Shmuel Shraga. "The History of the Romm Press." In *Yahadut Lita*, vol.1, *Yehude Lita meha-me'ah ha-15 'ad 1918*, edited by Natan Goren, Leib Garfunkle, Rafael Hasman, et al. Tel Aviv: Am Ha-Sefer, 1959.

Felman, Shoshana, and Dori Laub. *Testimony: Crises of Witnessing in Literature, Psychoanalysis and History*. New York: Routledge, 1992.

Fishman, David E. *The Rise of Modern Yiddish Culture*. Pittsburgh, PA: University of Pittsburgh Press, 2005.

Foucault, Michel, and Jay Miskowiec. "Of Other Spaces." *Diacritics* 16, no. 1 (1986): 22–27.

Fox, Sandy. *The Jews of Summer: Summer Camp and Jewish Culture in Postwar America*. Redwood City, CA: Stanford University Press, 2023.

Freeze, ChaeRan, Paula Hyman, and Antony Polonsky, eds. *Polin: Studies in Polish Jewry Volume 18: Jewish Women in Eastern Europe*. Liverpool, UK: Liverpool University Press, 2007.

Gabriel, Shira, and Ariana F. Young. "Becoming a Vampire Without Being Bitten: The Narrative Collective-Assimilation Hypothesis." *Psychological Science* 22, no. 8 (2011): 990–94.

Goldstein, Eric L. *The Price of Whiteness*. Princeton, NJ: Princeton University Press, 2006.

———. "The Struggle over Yiddish in Postimmigrant America." In *1929: Mapping the Jewish World*, edited by Hasia R. Diner and Gennady Estraikh. New York: NYU Press, 2013.

Gonshor, Anna Fishman. "Kadye Molodowsky in *Literarishe Bleter* 1925–35: Annotated Bibliography." Master's thesis, McGill University, 1997.

Gorsuch, Anne E. *Youth in Revolutionary Russia: Enthusiasts, Bohemians, Delinquents.* Bloomington: Indiana University Press, 2000.

Gottesman, Itzik. *Defining the Yiddish Nation: The Jewish Folklorists of Poland.* Detroit: Wayne State University Press, 2003.

Green, Melanie C. "Transportation into Narrative Worlds: The Role of Prior Knowledge and Perceived Realism." *Discourse Processes* 38, no. 2 (2004): 247–66.

Gries, Zeev. *The Book in the Jewish World, 1700–1900.* Oxford, UK: Littman Library of Jewish Civilization, 2007.

Grinberg, Marat. *The Soviet Jewish Bookshelf: Jewish Culture and Identity Between the Lines.* Waltham, MA: Brandeis University Press, 2023.

Hammond, Meghan Marie, and Sue J. Kim, eds. *Rethinking Empathy Through Literature.* New York: Routledge, 2014.

Han, S., and S. Shavitt. "Persuasion and Culture: Advertising Appeals in Individualistic and Collectivistic Societies." *Journal of Experimental Social Psychology* 30, no. 4 (1994): 326–50.

Harrison, Mary-Catherine. "An Ethics of Place: On North and South by Elizabeth Gaskell." In *My Victorian Novel: Critical Essays in the Personal Voice*, edited by Annette R. Federico and Jane Tompkins. Columbia: University of Missouri Press, 2020.

———. "Victorian Lessons in Empathy and Difference." *Journal of Victorian Culture* 18, no. 3 (September 1, 2013): 412–15.

Hazard, Paul. *Books, Children and Men* [Les livres, les enfants, et les hommes]. Translated by Marguerite MacKellar Mitchell. Boston: Horn Book, 1944.

Heywood, Colin. *A History of Childhood: Children and Childhood in the West from Medieval to Modern Times.* Malden, MA: Polity, 2001.

Hintz, Carrie. *Children's Literature.* Abingdon, UK: Routledge, 2019.

Hintz, Carrie, and Eric L. Tribunella. *Reading Children's Literature: A Critical Introduction.* Peterborough, ON: Broadview Press, 2019.

Hoffman, Martin L. *Empathy and Moral Development: Implications for Caring and Justice.* Cambridge, UK: Cambridge University Press, 2000.

Hogan, Patrick Colm. *What Literature Teaches Us About Emotion.* Cambridge: Cambridge University Press, 2011.

Hughes, Felicity A. "Children's Literature: Theory and Practice." *ELH* 45, no. 3 (Autumn 1978): 542–61.

Jacobs, Jack. *Bundist Counterculture in Interwar Poland.* Syracuse, NY: Syracuse University Press, 2009.

Jacobs, Jill. *There Shall Be No Needy: Pursuing Social Justice Through Jewish Law and Tradition.* Woodstock, VT: Jewish Lights Publishing, 2009.

Jacobs, Jonathan. "Plasticity and Perfection: Maimonides and Aristotle on Character." *Religious Studies* 33, no. 4 (1997): 443–54.

James, Allison, and Alan Prout. *Constructing and Reconstructing Childhood: Contemporary Issues in the Sociological Study of Childhood.* New York: Routledge, 2015.

Johnson, Peter. "The Geographies of Heterotopia." *Geography Compass* 7, no. 11 (2013): 790–803.

Kadar, Naomi Prawer. *Raising Secular Jews: Yiddish Schools and Their Periodicals for American Children, 1917–1950.* Waltham, MA: Brandeis University Press, 2017.

Kagan, Berl, ed. *Leksikon fun Yidish-shraybers: Mit hesofes un tikunim tsum Leksikon fun der nayer Yidisher literatur, un 5,800 pseydonimen*. New York: American Academy of Jewish Research, 1986.

Karlip, Joshua M. *The Tragedy of a Generation: The Rise and Fall of Jewish Nationalism in Eastern Europe*. Cambridge, MA: Harvard University Press, 2013.

Keen, Suzanne. "Contesting Empathy." In *Empathy and the Novel*.

———. *Empathy and the Novel*. Oxford, UK: Oxford University Press, 2007.

———. "Narrative Empathy." In *The Living Handbook of Narratology* (online), edited by Peter Hühn et al. Revised September 14, 2013. www-archiv.fdm.uni-hamburg.de/lhn/node/42.html.

———. "Novel Readers and the Empathetic Angel of Our Nature." In Hammond and Kim, *Rethinking Empathy Through Literature*.

———. "A Theory of Narrative Empathy." *Narrative* 14, no. 3 (2006): 207–36.

Kelly, Catriona. *Children's World: Growing Up in Russia, 1890–1991*. New Haven, CT: Yale University Press, 2007.

———. *Comrade Pavlik: The Rise and Fall of a Soviet Boy Hero*. London: Granta, 2014.

———. "A Joyful Soviet Childhood: Licensed Happiness for Little Ones." In Balina and Dobrenko, *Petrified Utopia*.

———. "Learning About the Nation: Ethnographic Representations of Children, Representations of Ethnography for Children." In *An Empire of Others: Creating Ethnographic Knowledge in Imperial Russia and the USSR*, edited by Roland Cvetkovski and Alexis Hofmeister. Budapest: Central European University Press, 2014.

———. "Riding the Magic Carpet: Children and Leader Cult in the Stalin Era." In "Russian Children's Literature: Changing Paradigms," ed. Marina Balina and Larissa Rudova, special forum issue, *Slavic and East European Journal* 49, no. 2 (Summer 2005): 199–224.

———. "'Thank-You for the Wonderful Book': Soviet Child Readers and the Management of Children's Reading, 1950–1975." *Kritika: Explorations in Russian and Eurasian History* 6, no. 4 (Fall 2005): 717–53.

Kidd, Kenneth B. *Making American Boys: Boyology and the Feral Tale*. Minneapolis: University of Minnesota Press, 2004.

Kirschenbaum, Lisa. *Small Comrades: Revolutionizing Childhood in Soviet Russia, 1917–1932*. New York: Routledge, 2013.

Kirzane, Jessica. "Teaching Guide for Dik's 'Slavery or Serfdom' (Trans. Rosenblatt)." *In geveb*, October 25, 2016. https://ingeveb.org/pedagogy/teaching-guide-for-diks-slavery-or-serfdom-trans-rosenblatt.

Klapper, Melissa R. *Jewish Girls Coming of Age in America, 1860–1920*. New York: NYU Press, 2005.

Knox, Israel. "Jewish Secularism and the Sabbath." *Judaism* 31, no. 1 (Winter 1982): 70–74.

Kogman, Tal. "The Emergence of Scientific Literature in Hebrew for Children and Youth in the Nineteenth Century: Preliminary Directions for Research." *Jewish Culture and History* 17, no. 3 (2016): 249–63.

———. "Texts for Boys and for Girls: Concepts of Childhood, Gender and Education in German Jewish Society in the Eighteenth and Nineteenth Centuries." *Journal of Jewish Studies* 70, no. 2 (2019): 357–74.

Kohl, Herbert R. *Should We Burn Babar?: Essays on Children's Literature and the Power of Stories*. New York: New Press, 2007.

Kondo, Dorinne. "Theoretical Scaffolding, Formal Architecture." In *Worldmaking: Race, Performance, and the Work of Creativity*. Durham, NC: Duke University Press, 2018.

Kozłowska, Magdalena. "'In Sunshine and in Joy'? The Story of Medem Sanatorium in Miedzeszyn." *East European Politics and Societies and Cultures* 28, no. 1 (February 2014): 49–62.

Krah Markus. *American Jewry and the Re-Invention of the East European Jewish Past*. Berlin: De Gruyter Oldenbourg, 2018.

Krutikov, Mikhail. *Yiddish Fiction and the Crisis of Modernity 1905–1914*. Redwood City, CA: Stanford University Press, 2001.

Litvak, Olga. *Haskalah: The Romantic Movement in Judaism*. New Brunswick, NJ: Rutgers University Press, 2012.

Maeots, Olga. "Jewish Heritage in Russian Children's Literature." *New Review of Children's Literature and Librarianship* 6, no. 1 (2000): 77–89.

Mallan, Kerry. "Empathy: Narrative Empathy and Children's Literature." In *(Re)imagining the World: Children's Literature's Response to Changing Times*, edited by Yan Wu, Kerry Mallan, and Roderick McGillis. Heidelberg: Springer Berlin, 2013.

Manekin, Rachel. *The Rebellion of the Daughters: Jewish Women Runaways in Habsburg Galicia*. Princeton, NJ: Princeton University Press, 2020.

Mar, Raymond A., and Keith Oatley. "The Function of Fiction Is the Abstraction and Simulation of Social Experience." *Perspectives on Psychological Science* 3, no. 3 (May 2008): 173–92.

Marcus, Ivan. *Rituals of Childhood: Jewish Acculturation in Medieval Europe*. New Haven, CT: Yale University Press, 1998.

Marcus, Leonard S. *Minders of Make-Believe: Idealists, Entrepreneurs and the Shaping of American Children's Literature*. Boston: Houghton Mifflin, 2008.

Meir, Natan M. "Jews, Ukrainians, and Russians in Kiev: Intergroup Relations in Late Imperial Associational Life." *Slavic Review* 65, no. 3 (2006): 475–501.

Meitlis, Jakob. *Das Ma'assebuch Seine Entstehung Und Quellengeschichte Zugleich Ein Beitrag Zur Einführung in Die Altjiddische Agada*. Berlin: Buchhandlung Rubin Mas, 1933.

Mendelsohn, Ezra. *The Jews of East Central Europe Between the World Wars*. Bloomington: Indiana University Press, 1983.

Meretoja, Hanna. *The Ethics of Storytelling: Narrative Hermeneutics, History, and the Possible*. New York: Oxford University Press, 2017.

Michels, Tony. *A Fire in Their Hearts: Yiddish Socialists in New York*. Cambridge, MA: Harvard University Press, 2009.

Mickenberg, Julia L., and Lynne Vallone. *The Oxford Handbook of Children's Literature*. Oxford, UK: Oxford University Press, 2011.

Mills, Claudia, ed., *Ethics and Children's Literature*. Ashgate Studies in Childhood, 1700 to the Present. Burlington, VT: Ashgate, 2014.

Mintz, Alan. *Popular Culture and the Shaping of Holocaust Memory in America*. Seattle: University of Washington Press, 2001.

Mintz, Steven. *Huck's Raft: A History of American Childhood*. Cambridge, MA: Belknap Press, 2006.

Mintz, Steven, and Susan Kellogg. *Domestic Revolutions: A Social History of American Family Life*. New York: Simon and Schuster, 1989.

Miron, Dan. *A Traveler Disguised: The Rise of Modern Yiddish Fiction in the Nineteenth Century.* Syracuse, NY: Syracuse University Press, 1996.

Mitchell, Sally. *The New Girl: Girls' Culture in England, 1880–1915.* New York: Columbia University Press, 1995.

Morse, Ainsley. *Word Play: Experimental Poetry and Soviet Children's Literature.* Evanston, IL: Northwestern University Press, 2021.

Moskowitz, Golan Y. *Wild Visionary: Maurice Sendak in Queer Jewish Context.* Palo Alto, CA: Stanford University Press, 2021.

Moss, Kenneth B. *Jewish Renaissance in the Russian Revolution.* Cambridge, MA: Harvard University Press, 2010.

———. *An Unchosen People: Jewish Political Reckoning in Interwar Poland.* Cambridge, MA: Harvard University Press, 2021.

Myers, Mitzi. "Impeccable Governesses, Rational Dames, and Moral Mothers: Mary Wollstonecraft and the Female Tradition in Georgian Children's Books." *Children's Literature* 14 (1986): 31–59.

Newton, Adam Zachary. *Ethics and Literary Practice.* Basel: MDPI, 2020.

———. *To Make the Hands Impure: Art, Ethical Adventure, the Difficult, and the Holy.* New York: Fordham University Press, 2014.

———. *Narrative Ethics: The Intersubjective Claim of Fiction.* Cambridge, MA: Harvard University Press, 1992.

Nikolajeva, Maria. "'Did You Feel as If You Hated People?': Emotional Literacy Through Fiction." *New Review of Children's Literature and Librarianship* 19, no. 2 (2013): 95–107.

Novick, Tzvi. *Piyyut and Midrash: Form, Genre, and History.* Göttingen: Vandenhoeck and Ruprecht, 2018.

Noyes, Dorothy. "Fairy-Tale Economics: Scarcity, Risk, Choice." *Narrative Culture* 2, no. 1 (Spring 2015): 1–26.

O'Sullivan, Emer. *Comparative Children's Literature.* New York: Routledge, 2005.

Parush, Iris. *Reading Jewish Women: Marginality and Modernization in Nineteenth-Century Eastern European Jewish Society.* Waltham, MA: Brandeis University Press, 2004.

Parush, Iris, and Ann Brener. "The Politics of Literacy: Women and Foreign Languages in Jewish Society of 19th-Century Eastern Europe." *Modern Judaism* 15, no. 2 (1995): 183–206.

Pickhan, Gertrud. *"Gegen den Strom": Der Allgemeine Jüdische Arbeiterbund "Bund" in Polen 1918–1939* ["Against the Current": The General Jewish Workers' Bund in Poland 1918–1939]. Stuttgart: Deutsche Verlags-Anstalt, 2001.

Propp, Vladimir. *Morphology of the Folktale.* Bloomington: Indiana University Press, 1958.

Quint, Alyssa. "'Yiddish Literature for the Masses'?: A Reconsideration of Who Read What in Jewish Eastern Europe." *AJS Review* 29, no. 1 (2005): 61–89.

Rosen, Michael. *Workers' Tales: Socialist Fairy Tales, Fables and Allegories from Great Britain.* Princeton, NJ: Princeton University Press, 2018.

Rosenzweig, Claudia. "Getlekhe un nisht getlekhe mayses: The Mayse-Bukh and Its Readership." *Jewish Studies Quarterly* 26, no. 3 (2019): 203–23.

Roskies, David G. *Against the Apocalypse: Responses to Catastrophe in Modern Jewish Culture.* Syracuse, NY: Syracuse University Press, 1999.

———. *A Bridge of Longing.* Cambridge, MA: Harvard University Press, 1995.

———. "I. M. Dik and the Rise of Yiddish Popular Literature." PhD diss., Brandeis University, 1975.

———. *The Jewish Search for a Usable Past*. Bloomington: Indiana University Press, 1999.

———. "Sholem Aleichem: Mythologist of the Mundane." *AJS Review* 13, no. 1–2 (Spring 1988): 27–46.

———. *Voices from the Warsaw Ghetto: Writing Our History*. New Haven, CT: Yale University Press, 2019.

______. "Yiddish Popular Literature and the Female Reader." *Journal of Popular Culture* 10, no. 4 (Spring 1977): 852–58.

Roskies, Diane K. *Teaching the Holocaust to Children: A Review and Bibliography*. New York: Ktav, 1975.

Rubin, Adam. "'Like A Necklace of Black Pearls Whose String Has Snapped': Bialik's 'Aron ha-sefarim' and the Sacralization of Zionism." *Prooftexts* 28, no. 2 (2008): 157–96.

Rudin, Shai. "Language, Poetics, and Ideology in Holocaust Literature for Hebrew-Speaking Children." *Children's Literature* 49 (2021): 157–88.

Safran, Gabriella. *Wandering Soul:* The Dybbuk's *Creator, S. An-sky*. Cambridge, MA: Harvard University Press, 2010.

Scharfstein, Zevi. *Hayei Hayehudim Bemizrah Eropa Badorot Haaharonim* [The Life of Eastern European Jews in Modern Times]. Translated by Saadya Sternberg. Tel-Aviv: Yavne, 1973.

Seidman, Naomi. *A Marriage Made in Heaven : The Sexual Politics of Hebrew and Yiddish*. Berkeley: University of California Press, 1997.

Şenderovich, Sasha. *How the Soviet Jew Was Made*. Cambridge, MA: Harvard University Press, 2022.

Shandler, Jeffrey. "Beyond the Mother Tongue: Learning the Meaning of Yiddish in America." *Jewish Social Studies* 6, no. 3 (2000): 97–123.

———. "The Holocaust for Beginners: Yankev Glatshteyn's *Emil un Karl* and Other Wartime Works for Young American Yiddish Readers." *MELUS: Multi-Ethnic Literature of the U.S.* 37, no. 2 (Summer 2012): 109–30.

Sherman, Joseph. *The Jewish Pope: Myth, Diaspora and Yiddish Literature*. Oxford, UK: Oxford Legenda, 2003.

Shmeruk, Chone. "Hapirsumim be-idish bi-vrit ha-mo'atsot, 1917–1960" [Yiddish Publications in the USSR, 1917–1960]. In *Pirsumim yehudiyim bi'vrit ha-mo' atsot* [Jewish Publications in the USSR], edited by Chone Shmeruk. Jerusalem: Historical Society of Israel, 1961.

———. "Sefer divre haadon shel Yaakov Frank—gilgulin meyidish lepolanit." In *Hakria'ah Lenavi: Mekhkarei historia vesifrut/Khone Shmeruk*, edited by Israel Bartal. Jerusalem: Merkaz Zalman Shazar, 1999.

———. "Shalom Aleichem ve'reshita shel sifrut hayeladim hamodernit beYidish" [Sholem Aleichem and the Beginning of Modern Children's Literature in Yiddish]. In *Ayarot ukrakhim: Perakim beyetsirato shel Shalom Aleichem*, edited by Chone Shmeruk and Chava Turniansky. Jerusalem: Magnes, 2001.

———. "Sholem-Aleykhem un di onheybn fun der yidisher literatur far kinder" [Sholem Aleichem and the Beginnings of Yiddish Children's Literature]. *Goldene keyt* 112 (1984): 39–53.

———. "Yitskhok Bashevis: Der mayse-dertseyler far kinder." *Oksforder Yiddish* 3 (1995): 233–80.

———. "Yitskhok Bashevises dertseylung 'an erev-khanike in varshe." *Goldene keyt* 132 (1991): 38–40.

Shoham, Hizky. *Israel Celebrates: Jewish Holidays and Civic Culture in Israel.* Leiden: Brill, 2017.

Smith-Rosenberg, Carroll. *Disorderly Conduct: Visions of Gender in Victorian America.* New York: Oxford University Press, 1986.

Sokoloff, Naomi B. "Discoveries of Reading: Stories of Childhood by Bialik, Shahar, and Roth." *Hebrew Annual Review* 9 (1985): 321–42.

———. *Imagining the Child in Modern Jewish Fiction.* Baltimore: Johns Hopkins University Press, 1992.

Spinner, Samuel J. *Jewish Primitivism.* Stanford, CA: Stanford University Press, 2021.

Stearns, Peter N. *Childhood in World History,* 4th ed. London: Routledge, 2021.

———. "Happy Children: A Modern Emotional Commitment." *Frontiers in Psychology* 10 (2019): 1–8.

Tatar, Maria. *The Hard Facts of the Grimms' Fairy Tales.* Princeton, NJ: Princeton University Press, 1987.

Tsai, J. L., J. Y. Louie, E. E. Chen, and Y. Uchida. "Learning What Feelings to Desire: Socialization of Ideal Affect Through Children's Storybooks." *Personality and Social Psychology Bulletin* 33, no. 1 (2007): 182.

Udel, Miriam. "The 'Jewish Pope' in the 1940s: On Jewish Cultural and Ethnic Plasticity." In *Eastern Europe Unmapped: Beyond Border and Peripheries,* edited by Irene Kacandes and Yuliya Komska. New York: Berghahn, 2018.

———. *Never Better!: The Modern Jewish Picaresque.* Ann Arbor: University of Michigan Press, 2016.

Ulanowicz, Anastasia. "Philippe Ariès." Representing Childhood, accessed December 2, 2024. www.representingchildhood.pitt.edu/aries.htm.

van der Hal-van Raalte, Elisheva A. M., Marinus H. van IJzendoorn, Marian J. Bakermans-Kranenburg. "Sense of Coherence Moderates Late Effects of Early Childhood Holocaust Exposure." *Journal of Clinical Psychology* 64, no. 12 (December 2008): 1352–67.

Wall, Barbara. *The Narrator's Voice: The Dilemma of Children's Fiction.* New York: Palgrave Macmillan, 1991.

Walsh, James Joseph. *History of Medicine in New York: Three Centuries of Medical Progress,* vol. 3. New York: National Americana Society, 1919.

Weinreich, Max. *History of the Yiddish Language.* New Haven, CT: Yale University Press, 2008.

Weissler, Chava. "'For Women and for Men Who Are like Women': The Construction of Gender in Yiddish Devotional Literature." *Journal of Feminist Studies in Religion* 5, no. 2 (Fall 1989): 7–24.

Weld, Sara Pankenier. *Voiceless Vanguard: The Infantilist Aesthetic of the Russian Avant-Garde.* Edited by Gary Saul Morson. Evanston, IL: Northwestern University Press, 2014.

Wisse, Ruth. *The Modern Jewish Canon: A Journey Through Language and Culture.* Chicago: University of Chicago Press, 2000.

Yarfitz, Mir. *Impure Migration: Jews and Sex Work in Golden Age Argentina.* New Brunswick, NJ: Rutgers University Press, 2019.

Yassif, Eli. *The Hebrew Folktale: History, Genre, Meaning.* Translated by Jacqueline S. Teitelbaum. Bloomington: Indiana University Press, 1999.

———. *Sippur ha-'am ha-'ivri: Toldotav, sugav, umashma'uto* [The Hebrew Folktale: History, Genre, Meaning]. Jerusalem: Mossad Bialik, 1999.

Young, Jennifer. "'A Language Is Like a Garden': Shloyme Davidman and the Yiddish Communist School Movement in the United States." In Estraikh et al., *Children and Yiddish Literature*.

Yudkoff, Sunny. *Tubercular Capital: Illness and the Conditions of Modern Jewish Writing*. Palo Alto, CA; Stanford University Press, 2018.

Zaritt, Saul Noam. *Jewish American Writing and World Literature: Maybe to Millions, Maybe to Nobody*. Oxford, UK: Oxford University Press, 2020.

———. "A *Taytsh* Manifesto: Yiddish, Translation, and the Making of Modern Jewish Culture." *Jewish Social Studies* 26, no. 3 (2021): 186–222.

Zerubavel, Yael. "The Forest as a National Icon: Literature, Politics, and the Archeology of Memory." *Israel Studies* 1, no. 1 (Spring 1996): 60–99.

———. *Recovered Roots: Collective Memory and the Making of Israeli National Tradition*. Chicago: University of Chicago Press, 1995.

Zipes, Jack, ed. *The Original Folk and Fairy Tales of the Brothers Grimm: The Complete First Edition*. Princeton, NJ: Princeton University Press, 2016.

———. *Victorian Fairy Tales: The Revolt of the Fairies and Elves*. New York: Routledge, 1987.

———. *When Dreams Came True: Classical Fairy Tales and Their Tradition*. New York: Routledge, 2007.

Zunshine, Lisa. "Theory of Mind and Experimental Representations of Fictional Consciousness." *Narrative* 11, no. 3 (Oct 2003): 270–91.

INDEX

Note: page numbers in italics refer to figures. Those followed by n refer to notes, with note number.

A NOTE ON THE TYPE

This book has been composed in Arno, an Old-style serif typeface in the classic Venetian tradition, designed by Robert Slimbach at Adobe.